I Will Restore You
In Faith, In Hope, In Love

12-00

Dear Kathy,
dear friend,
I give this book to you
with much love. I pray
it will touch you as it
did me.

God bless
with love,
Irene

I Will Restore You
In Faith, In Hope, In Love

Queenship

PUBLISHING COMPANY

P.O Box 42028 Santa Barbara, CA 93140-2028

(800) 647-9882 • (805) 957-4893 • Fax: (805) 957-1631

Declaration

The decree of the Congregation for the Propagation of the Faith. A.A.S. 58, 1186 (approved by Pope Paul VI on October 14, 1966) states that the **Nihil Obstat** and **Imprimatur** are no longer required on publications that deal with private revelations, provided they contain nothing contrary to faith and morals.

The author wishes to manifest her unconditional submission to the final and official judgement of the Magisterium of the Church.

© 1997 Queenship Publishing

Library of Congress #: 97-65315

Published by:
    Queenship Publishing
    P.O. Box 42028
    Santa Barbara, CA 93140-2028
    (800) 647-9882 • (805) 957-4893 • Fax: (805) 957-1631

Printed in the United States of America

ISBN: 1-882972-93-7

Acknowledgements

My heartfelt gratitude to the Roman Catholic Church, especially the sacramental system that provides The Eucharist and Reconciliation. These are the sacraments of ongoing conversion. My deepest gratitude to the priest who is my spiritual director. Father, you have courageously assisted in the "birthing" of this book. Thank you for engaging in tremendous spiritual warfare to bring it to fruition. My gratitude and love to The United Hearts of Jesus and Mary Prayer Group, my husband, my parents and brothers. My two sons, you are the blessings of my life. Particular gratitude to Marilyn H. for the countless hours you have devoted to the typing of this manuscript from my handwritten journals. May the sacrifice you offer draw many graces upon your family. Special appreciation to Mr. Neal Hughes for the execution and donation of the cover art portraying an image that I was given. May God continue to use the gift of your talent for the glory of His Church and kingdom. Bob and Claire Schaefer at Queenship Publishing, please accept my deepest gratitude for the gift of your ministry which provides spiritual nourishment for a world in great need of it. You are truly instruments of the Holy Spirit and people of deep faith and prayer. May God reward you. I am very grateful that you were the ones He brought to my door, just as He promised. To all who have interceded with prayer, spiritual warfare and sacrifice for this work, may God bless you abundantly and may His Peace be yours always.

Introduction

Our Lord describes this work in the following manner:
I have thus spoken,
Messages of Love, pure and simple,
Teachings of Truth Everlasting,
Prophetic warnings portraying My Mercy,
That My Creation will be reconciled with the One who is Love.
(Message of 11-3-95)

This book contains messages that have been received from 1992 by way of inner locution by a married woman with two children. They are often followed by her response to the message from Our Lord or Our Lady. Also we have included some of her personal journal entries that reveal the journey of her soul.

She is a cradle Catholic with twelve years of basic Catholic education. Following high school, she attended college for a license in Medical Assisting. She worked as a medical assistant for twelve years before becoming a secretary for her husband in their family business. She has been married for twenty-two years. Before her conversion at the age of thirty-five, she lived a worldly life with very little, if any, spirituality or Church activity. Her family, business, social life were those of an upper middle class American woman. The story of her conversion follows this introduction in her own words. As a result of that conversion, she became very involved in parish and diocesan activities. Three years later, at the age of thirty-eight, she began to receive these messages. Because of family considerations and her ongoing work in the Church at this time it has been discerned in prayer that her name not be published, to leave her the privacy and freedom that she needs.

I first met her in 1992 during a European tour that included Lourdes. It was at the Grotto at Lourdes at midnight that she first heard a message given to her in a sequential manner. The message was from Our Lady for "her children." On the return flight, she was *moved* by Our Lord to talk to me. Several days after returning home, she invited me to lunch, showed me the message received at Lourdes and asked my opinion of it. I told her it was an *inner* locution, i.e., words clearly received in the depths of the heart and known by the receiver as not of their doing. (1) All the usual reactions occurred in my own person to this "message": doubt, disbelief, confusion, perplexity, and finally suspended judgment. The limited time I had known this person left me in a quandary. She was a sane, normal, happy, well-adjusted individual whose conversation, demeanor and deportment drew people to her. Nothing about her indicated any imbalance of her person. It is not unusual for priests to have people come in and tell them that "God told me this or that." Ordinarily something in them sets off alarm bells and you politely listen and politely send them on their way. This woman was different and I could not do this with her. I told her she should have a Spiritual Director to share and discern what was taking place in her. She asked if I would do this. Rather blithely I agreed, wholly unaware of the spiritual journey that was beginning.

The books that I had read as a young monk in a monastery over thirty years ago now became textbooks for understanding some of what I was being told and witnessing before my eyes. When we met weekly to pray the rosary together, I would witness her writing the message by hand. Often she wrote several legal-sized pages within a few minutes. Invariably, whether at a prayer meeting or at home, she would write the message that she was receiving quickly, easily, seemingly without having to stop and think about what she was to write. It was evident that she wrote as one receiving words in a manner of one receiving dictation, not as one composing a message. Sometimes the content of the message would be very simple and on other occasions, extremely rich in theological depth. As one who had no formal theological disciplines in her life, I was amazed and touched and surprised at their richness. In contrast to that, her personal journal entries were done with reflection, requiring the usual time for thoughtful composition. She had many concerns about what was happening to her and relayed everything to me in all honesty. St. John of the Cross (2), St. Teresa of Avila (3), St. Catherine of Siena (4), plus standard textbooks (5) concerning the overall development of the life of grace in the soul and the various mystical graces granted to the Saints over the centuries in the Church became a part of my daily reading and meditation (6). Noting the severe temptations to doubt that she had, I permitted her to read the lives of the saints to teach her that these graces are a part of the tradition of the Church.

During the past four years, the volume and content of the locutions, images, and intellectual visions has deeply touched my life. I had been a Catholic Priest for 33 years. Fifteen of those were spent in a Trappist monastery. Three of those years were spent in Rome in post-graduate work where I received a Licentiate in Theology (S.T.L.) from the University of St. Thomas and a Licentiate in the Bible (S.S.L.) from the Pontifical University (Biblicum). Most of my studies were in areas that dealt with our Catholic faith in a very technical and abstract fashion. The intervening years prior to meeting and reading the messages presented to me were of this nature. The personal, intimate approach of Jesus in the messages touched my heart and developed a love relationship with the Father, Jesus, the Word become flesh, The Holy Spirit, and Mary, the spouse of the Holy Spirit, Our Mother, that has continued to grow. Interest in the lives of the mystics in the Church has changed my whole spiritual life. I have come to believe that the tragedy in the Church of today is an almost complete absence of stress on the treasures we possess in our great mystics. I hope and pray that this book will do the same for you, namely, move the knowledge from your head to the heart. God is Love. The heart is where we "know" according to the Bible.

To read, e.g., the beginning of the message attributed to Our Lord, **Beloved of My Sacred Heart, wretched though you are, I shall create in you a thirst for Me that I alone will satisfy. You shall thirst for souls to present to the Most Holy Trinity. It is I Who will create this unquenchable thirst within the depths of your being.** (7-9-93), leads one into prayer and meditation on the "I thirst" of Jesus on the Cross. All the other aspects of a genuine, deeply Catholic, spiritual life are found in the messages. In them we see the call to surrender to Jesus on the Cross, to overcome the fear this arouses, the warnings of times of persecution, trial and purification of souls, and the Church, the plea of the Father, the Son, and Mary, Our Mother, for conversion cannot be read prayerfully without changes in one's spiritual life.

During a week's retreat in a monastery and meditating over some eighty pages of messages, I became convinced that these messages should be made available to the public. As a priest of thirty four years who had read many spiritual books, I could only hope and desire that many would read these messages and use them as a catalyst for prayer. Who is able to look around the world of today and not see the absolute necessity of prayer, of prayer from the heart, on fire with love?

Not uncommon today are the prayer groups in which various individuals claim to be receiving special messages from the Lord. Some of them are of a personal nature and are meant only for the individual or at best for the prayer group itself. Fr. Arintero, O.P., in his book on "Mystical Evolution" (7) distinguishes locutions that are for personal sanctification and locutions combined with a prophetic gift meant to build up the body of Christ, the Church. (8)

Visions and Locutions

Catholic theology has many subject areas, e.g. Dogma (Systematic Theology), Moral, Pastoral, Ecclesiology, Mystical, etc. It is the subject of Mystical Theology (9) that we are concerned with. Here we study the soul's journey to God and, above all, the higher stages of the soul's communion and communication with God culminating in spiritual marriage. From the experience of the Saints and the theology of grace, we find the rules for discerning, evaluating, and understanding such phenomena.

The fact that these things exist has never been questioned in the Bible or in the lives of the great Saints declared Doctors of the Church such as St. John of the Cross and St. Teresa of Avila, and St. Catherine of Siena. The prophetic books of the Old Testament are replete with such introductions to messages and visions. In the Book of Jeremiah, we read over and over again: "The following message came to Jeremiah from the Lord" (11:1), or "The Word of the Lord came to me thus: Before I formed you in the womb I knew you etc.." (1:4-5). In the call of Isaiah he writes, "I heard the voice of the Lord saying, Whom shall I send? Who will go for us?" "Here I am," I said, "send me!" (6:8)

In the New Testament, the baptism and transfiguration of Our Lord are examples of visions accompanied by words. Peter's vision in Acts 10:9ff, Saul's conversion on the road to Damascus and Ananias' vision of the Lord and their dialogue reveal the lived experiences of God's chosen ones. Paul takes for granted the communication of Jesus, The Holy Spirit, and The Father with His people.

The Bible, the revealed Word of God presented to us by the Church, along with Tradition (apostolic) is considered to be "public revelation" and as such, makes up the "deposit of faith" that is to be held by all Catholic Christians. In treating of Revelation in the Catechism of the Catholic Church (10) we read, "in many and various ways God spoke of old to our fathers by the prophets, but in these last days, he has spoken to us by a Son." (Heb. 1:1-2). The text goes on, "Christ, the Son of God made man, is the Father's one, perfect, and unsurpassable Word. In Him he has said everything; there will be no other Word than this One. St. John of the Cross, among others, commented strikingly on Hebrews 1:1-2:

"In giving us His Son, His Only Word (for He possesses no other), He spoke everything to us at once in this sole Word - and He has no more to say - because what He spoke to the prophets in parts, He has now spoken all at once by giving us the All Who is His Son. Any person questioning God or desiring some vision or revelation would be guilty not only of foolish behavior but also of offending Him by not fixing his eyes entirely upon Christ and by living with the desire for some other novelty." (The Ascent of Mt. Carmel, 2,22,3-5) (11)

In the following two paragraphs (66-67) dealing with "no further revelation" we read, "The Christian economy, therefore since it is the new and definitive Covenant, will never pass away; and no new public revelation is to be expected before the glorious manifestation of Our Lord, Jesus Christ." (DV4; cf. 1 Tim. 6:14; Titus 1:13). Yet even if revelation is already complete, it has not been made completely explicit; it remains for Christian faith gradually *to grasp its full significance* over the course of the centuries.

Throughout the ages, there have been so-called "private" revelations some of which have been recognized by the authority of the Church. They do not belong, however, to the deposit of faith. It is not their role to improve or complete Christ's definitive Revelation, but to *help live more fully by it in a certain period of history.* (emphasis mine) Guided by the Magisterium of the Church, the sensus fidelium *knows how to discern and welcome in these revelations whatever constitutes an authentic call of Christ or His Saints to the Church.* (emphasis mine)

Christian faith cannot accept "revelations" that claim to surpass or correct the Revelation of which Christ is the fulfillment, as is the case in certain non-Christian religions and also in certain sects which base themselves on such "revelations."

Possible Dangers

Some clarification is needed here. In receiving locutions or visions, some authors have written that "in order to protect souls from vain curiosity and to keep them humble, these gifts should never be desired and never to be sought, but rather that these lights are to be renounced." (12) However, Fr. Arintero (13) considers this position one of "guilty exaggeration or a dangerous confusion which should be dispelled." He makes an important distinction here that is applicable to all spiritual gifts, namely: "It would be unlawful to desire them, as often happens, when this desire springs from vanity, curiosity, or attachment to such things." (p.306) He then states what I consider the appropriate attitude to these gifts and all others: "But it is never unlawful when they are desired or sought as a means of knowing, loving, and serving God better." (p.306)

Classes of Visions and Locutions

Both of them are of three types. Fr. Arintero (14) sums it up in this way:

"1. Sensible or external, that is, perceptible by sight or hearing;

2. Imaginative, not perceptible by the external senses, but only by the imagination;

3. Purely intellectual, not perceptible by any sense, either external or internal, but received directly in the intelligence, as spiritual concepts, void of every kind of sensible image or symbol."

There is, of course, the underlying concern that the locution or vision is not from God but the product of another source: namely, the person's own self or the person plus the demonic or diabolic. Here we have the experience and teaching of the great mystics to help in this area. To help determine the authenticity of these gifts St. Teresa and St. John of the Cross have written much. Fr. Dubay (15) lists eleven points or signs drawn from St. Teresa's "Interior Castle" regarding locutions. We can sum up these points in this manner:

1. The locution bears a "sense of power and authority" both in itself and in its effects.

2. The message is in accord with the Catholic Faith and Morals and therefore with Scripture. (No private revelation can negate public revelation.)

3. A word from God brings calm and peace.

4. The recipient praises God out of a sense of lowliness and gratitude.

5. The message stays in the memory for a long time. Some are so indelible that they are there after many years.

6. A certitude that messages relating to a future (prophetic) event will take place.

7. Genuine words from a divine source are clear, not confused. There is clarity, not confusion, in them.

8. It comes at unexpected times and places and is frequently contrary to the inner self.

9. Even a word can contain "a world of meaning."

10. If the locution is genuine, the effect in the recipient is one of humility.

11. The word is so powerful in the mind that everything else is blocked out and one "listens."

If the above criteria are present, St. Teresa states that we can be assured the Word is of God. Fr. Dubay (16) lists the different types and characteristics of visions that are seen in the writings of

St. Teresa. She lists the types that we have seen above, in the summation by Fr. Arintero. They are corporeal or seen with the bodily eyes, imaginative or perceived by the imagination alone, and finally the purely intellectual that are devoid of any sense, image, or symbol. St. Teresa claims to have never had a corporeal vision. The imaginative vision has characteristics that separate it from a purely human construct, namely, it is rapid, like the blink of an eye, and vibrantly alive. It is also of such an awesome nature that it frequently leads to an ecstatic state of being. Finally, it is beyond any kind of control by the recipient. One can neither begin it nor end it. To try and see with curiosity is impossible. One sees and experiences only what the Lord wants a person to see or know.

In the intellectual vision, there is no symbol or sign. Knowledge is given to the person that they themselves cannot explain. Fr. Dubay (17) quotes the passage from the life of St. Teresa where she goes to her confessor for some kind of explanation of this intellectual vision. She writes: "He asked me in what form I saw Him. I answered that I didn't see Him. He asked how I knew that it was Christ. I answered that I didn't know how, but that I couldn't help knowing that He was beside me, that I saw and felt Him clearly, that my recollection of soul was greater, and that I was very continuously in the prayer of quiet, that the effects were much different from those I usually experienced, and that it was very clear."

Except for the face of Padre Pio that was seen corporeally, the receiver of the messages in this book has received only intellectual visions and locutions that are imaginative or intellectual or both. Many of the locutions have images accompanying them and others do not.

Before going on to discuss the contents, I would simply like to add for those who read this book that all of the mystics of the Church, as well as the leaders of the Church, approach all private revelation with a great deal of wariness. Is what is received from the Lord and His Saints or not? Ultimately, it is by the fruits that authenticity is revealed. When Jesus was accused of doing all He did from Beelzebub, His response was a very practical one, that if this were so, Satan would be destroying his own kingdom. So, too, with the contents of this book. The writings are all in the mainstream of Catholic spirituality and can only help us to live ever more fully Christ's definitive revelation.

The Messages

From Our Blessed Mother's first message received at Lourdes (8-5-92) to the ongoing ones from Jesus, The Father, and the Saints as this book goes into print, various themes are continually being repeated. By word and at times with striking imagery, they present to us the grave concern of The Father, His Son, Mary, and the Saints concerning the downward path of man today. The personal and social darkness from man's sin and rebellion is constantly being increased through the unleashed fury of the "powers and principalities" whose goal is to destroy in us our inheritance: *union with God forever.*

Mary's first message to her "children" through our locutionist stressed prayer, sacrifice, and surrender from hearts that have opened to her. Peace in one's heart allows her to be heard and discerned as she promised to call upon them many times in the future. Her role was and is to present their hearts to her Beloved Son.

Although the messages come to her at unexpected moments and places (in her car, in the shower, preparing meals, etc.), most of them come at the daily hour of fixed prayer after Mass, or during the Prayer Group meetings, or at the weekly Rosary with the Spiritual Director. Some of the messages follow an interior questioning or prayers uttered for some particular concern. The message of 2-23-93 with the title line, "Darkness Exists Because Men Have Chosen Darkness," came to her following Communion when she prayed "that Jesus cover the earth with His Light and Love to overcome the tremendous darkness I sensed over the world. I wondered why He allows so much darkness to exist in the world today." Interiorly, He responded: **My daughter, darkness exists because men have chosen darkness.**

The message that follows is beautiful in its pathos that man's free will has been abused by many to bring on the darkness of godlessness, intellectualism, materialism, impurity, etc. The words of Jesus that He weeps over man's choices and their rejection of Him, who alone can give them life and love, are followed by the plea that man not choose death over life, accept the suffering that leads to life, drink of the fountain of grace in the sacraments, and accept the mercy of a loving and forgiving God. It is only in the language of the mystics we find words like this: **I weep for them. My Heart breaks for them,** uttered by the Lord. How is one to understand the words that follow from the Lord? **My daughter, soothe Me and dress My Wounds with your sacrifice and love.** These words do not come from an abstract theological discourse, but the impassioned plea of a person, the Lord, whose love is seen in the total vulnerability of the arms outstretched on the Cross and whose only weapon is love.

The individual state of many human beings in their relation with God is strikingly depicted in the message of 7-17-96 during Rosary with her Spiritual Director.

"The first image I saw was a house. The house looked beautiful from the outside. Seemingly then, Jesus took me inside the house. The inside of the house had been pillaged. I observe with Jesus a "nothingness," a profound "emptiness." That was all that was left inside the house. I experienced a "chill" etc. I understood that each human being is his house." Then Jesus spoke: **My creation, the love of the Most Holy Trinity created you for love, for beauty, goodness, and life abundant. But the spirit of the world has ravaged you, leaving behind empty shells, houses that have been gutted.**

The message goes on to say that these pillaged, emptied homes of His own are replaced by trinkets of our own making that were looked upon as true riches. Even they are now gone and all that is left is "emptiness." This emptiness is experienced and fled to no avail. Jesus pleads in the message to take His hand and allow Him to create anew within us a full and beautiful temple where He alone will dwell, fill and call out for each of us our name.

Suffering predicted for the locutionist in the early messages has been borne out over the succeeding months and years. Personal pain from attacks on her spiritual life that all is an illusion, none of this is real; severe temptations that God has abandoned her, worthy only of hell, and that her only recourse was to return to the ways of the world have plagued her the first couple of years. Less frequent at the present time, they are still there during trials in the family.

Many of the messages deal with Our Lord's and Our Lady's suffering over the sin in the world. A process of identification in the spirit in this suffering adds to her sorrow. One is called to grieve with The Lord and Mary, the Mother of us all.

Sin is opposition to the Will of God. As such, Jesus will say in the message of 8-28-96, in the waiting room of a doctor's office, that a person begins to sin by living a life that is not in balance. Later in the message He says, **One human heart that is out of balance touches another human heart and perpetuates that which is within so that the entire world becomes out of balance, one man at a time because one affects the whole. Does not the infection in one part of the body affect the entire body with fever? Indeed, this is the case in the world today. My creation, you are diseased due to selfish sinfulness!** Jesus calls us to endure all suffering in the spirit of faith, hope, and charity. Wrapped around in love, suffering gains grace, merit, and the building up of the Kingdom of God in the world.

The Church

In the Vatican II Document, "Pastoral Constitution on The Church in the Modern World," (Gaudium et Spes) (paragraph 4) we read, "At all times the Church carries the responsibility of reading the signs of the times and of interpreting them in the light of the gospel if it is to carry out its task."

The chaos and confusion in our world of today deeply affects the Church. She understands the world through the gospel and tradition. Today we see her being helped throughout the world by a flood of messages concerning this chaos and flight from God. There are reports that the Vatican cannot keep up with the flood of messages that are considered to be taken seriously. Both warnings and pleadings for conversion of the world and church are present in these messages. The spirit of prophecy is evident around the world in the messages from people who have no contact with each other. This commonality that exists worldwide is a plea from heaven to open one's heart to Divine Love.

In a message from Our Lady titled, "The Church Shall Suffer Great Trials" on 10-17-94, we read, *My children, the Church, the beloved Bride of Christ, and my son shall suffer great trials. Already, my son (the Pope) suffers more than you can ever imagine. Pray unceasingly for The Church and for my Pope, please. If more souls would offer themselves as sacrifices of love, the sufferings of the Church, the Pope, and the world could be lessened.*

In the message of 2-22-94 from Jesus on the Feast of the Chair of Peter, titled "I Will Restore Solidarity to the Chair of Peter," we read, **My children, it is written, "You, (Simon Peter) are rock and upon this rock I shall build My Church and the jaws of death shall not prevail against it."** (Matthew 16:17) **And it is written: The Lord said to Simon Peter, I have prayed that your faith may not fail and you in turn must strengthen your brother.** (Luke 22-32) **My children, pray for My Vicar, My Peter of Today, My Shepherd. My beloved Shepherd of My Church suffers in union with My bleeding Sacred Heart. Oh how he truly understands the wounds inflicted upon My Body by divisions and apostasy of this generation. He loves My Bride as I love her. He suffers much due to the division within My House. My Bride (church), My beloved Bride, is suffering and infected. I will come. I am her physician. I will tend to her Myself and restore her to the purity of her former age. I will make known to all, Peter is the rock and foundation through whom I shepherd My flock. Until that time when I come to revive her, a time ordained by The Father, My Church and My Peter will suffer much. I ask of you, pray for them always.**

In the message of 3-14-94 from Jesus, entitled, "Zeal for My House," we read, **My Bride is bleeding and My Divine Heart bleeds for her. However, do not become discouraged or sad when you see this through the graces I impart to your soul. Hell is indeed storming her. My Word of Old stands today. She will prevail. She will weather the tempest. Her present woundedness will end in Victory.**

From these two brief examples, we see how private revelation encourages and highlights scriptural passages dealing with the persecution and the trials of the Church in every age and especially our own. I would like to comment that the number and urgency present in messages regarding the Church and the world have increased over the past four years. The ongoing messages not included in this book will be placed in Volume 2.

The personal pleading of Jesus and the profound concern seen in the messages for the Church should arouse in all of us a desire for prayer and sacrifice. We truly live in extraordinary times. As the Holy Spirit came down upon Mary, the Apostles and Disciples, praying in the "Upper Room" at Pentecost, so we must pray for a new coming of the Holy Spirit, a New Pentecost upon the Church and the world that we may have a civilization permeated by the Love of the Holy Spirit. May this Holy Spirit take away our stony hearts and replace them with a new heart and a new spirit. I will put My Spirit within you. (cf. Ezk.36:26-27)

In conclusion, I would urge you who read these messages to take them to prayer especially before the Tabernacle and there ask Jesus to send His Holy Spirit into your heart. May He reveal to you all their depths and richness that you may grow in faith, hope, and love. May Mary, Our Mother, assist you with your prayers.

Fr. Ignatius, S.T.L., S.S.L., Spiritual Director
October 1996, Month of the Holy Rosary

The Messenger's Conversion

"What I relate here, above and beyond the external events, belongs to my deepest being, to my innermost experience. I recall these things above all in order to thank the Lord." (Pope John Paul II, "Gift and Mystery")

To attempt to relate a personal testimony of love is to enter into a mystery. Human words rarely do justice to the mystery. Please keep this in mind. My conversion, that is my deep change of heart, my change of direction, began at the age of thirty-five. I had not responded to God's call by way of deliberate "yes" prior to that time in my life. Looking back, I recognize how God allowed me the freedom to "do it my way" yet His Grace protected me in my state of "unawareness" and ultimately guided me to that moment of awakening to His call on my life. Everything that had happened in my life served to be part of my formation for Him, after all. He permitted me to use God given talents to be "in the world" before I responded to His call. Before I was ever aware of it, I was called. "Before I formed you in the womb, I knew you and before you were born, I consecrated you." (Jer 1:4) We are called! It took me a while to realize it. Our Triune God never ceases to attempt to awaken us to that call and He uses people, places and other various ways that are wondrous by way of grace upon grace to awaken us to that change of heart or conversion. Why? Because He loves us! I am a cradle Catholic and was told that from my earliest years. But I did not "know" it until my conversion. It was difficult to believe that God loved me intimately, unconditionally and infinitely more than I could ever comprehend. The thought that anyone, God included, would be the master of my life was unacceptable to me. The God of the universe could not be that "personally" interested in the details of my daily existence. Every decision was mine. That is why He gave us a "free will." Called to be Holy? A Lay Person? I definitely believed in God. He created me, sustained me, and He would judge me at the end of my life on earth according to how I lived. There was always a fear of offending God because I might end up in Hell. Once, my son asked me, "Why do we go to Church on Sundays?" And I replied, "Just in case there really is a heaven or hell, we'll have our bases covered."

Always thinking in terms of human success, I set out on that path. I was not overly ambitious. I wanted a good job and a good husband. Following high-school, I went to a local college and trained to become a medical assistant. I married my high school sweetheart, best friend since 6th grade. I wanted children (we have two), the right house, the right car and freedom. Freedom was important to me and it was associated with money. I wanted money so as to be free from worry, free to travel, free to do whatever I wanted. My husband and I worked very hard and attained all of these by our early thirties. The grace of God had nothing to do with this. God was "up there" and I was "down here." You can see that my way of thinking had nothing to do with a relationship of love. But it caused me to keep the ten commandments. I had a certain confidence that I was living a good life. Certainly God would not be offended by it. My vocation was to be a wife and mother. These are noble callings from God. But somehow I left God out of them. I wanted a "perfect" family but the One who perfects all things was not the center of it. I wanted for nothing in the world and thought myself happy. My heart was so full of the cult of self that I didn't recognize my need for God's personal love. I rarely thought of God. But He never ceased to Love me at every moment. God is patient.

God is Love. (1 John 4:16). I knew this intellectually but I did not know it in my heart. I think the Catholic Catechism explains this best. "The heart is the dwelling place where I am, where I live; according to the Semitic or Biblical expression, the heart is the place 'to which I withdraw.' The heart is our hidden center, beyond the grasp of our reason and of others; only the Spirit of God can fathom the human heart and know it fully. The heart is the place of decision, deeper than our psychic drives. It is the place of truth, where we choose life or death. It is the place of encounter, because as image of God we live in relation; it is the place of covenant." (#2563) But I had not experienced this covenant of Love. How could I decide for a relationship of love without knowing the Lover? How do we know God? Obviously, it is through the great gift of faith. But I must respond to God's Grace that somehow moves that faith through the mind to the heart. I must desire it. I am convinced that Grace is always present. God is always inviting. For myself, I was not paying attention, being very busy about many worldly things.

In the fall of 1989, I met a woman outside the Catholic school that my sons attended who had returned from a pilgrimage to Medjugorje. She was handing out pictures of Our Lady, pointing out the area of Our Lady's Heart which had turned a pinkish-red color at the time of the film's development. Kodak officials could not explain or duplicate it. She informed me that Our Lady had requested prayer groups to form to pray the fifteen decade rosary and asked me if I would like to join her group. I told her I would think about it but had no intention of attending. I have already shared how I was living my life. I did not have a prayer life, nor could I recall how to say the rosary. As far as a relationship with Our Lady, I know that I had one in grade school. I did the May Crowning a couple of times. I also recall on the day President Kennedy was shot, in sixth grade, at recess, I was drawn to the Church to kneel before Our Lady and pray for our country. Catholic school and the faith of my parents did impact me.

When this woman saw that I was not accepting her persistent invitations to the prayer group, she simply handed me a book by Father René Laurentin. This was a book of messages from Our Lady to the children at Medjugorje. I put the book on my nightstand where it remained for 5 months unopened. One day, while making the bed, I was drawn to the book and opened it in the middle. I read one message to Jelena where Our Lady requested the formation of a prayer group with some other instructions about making prayer a priority in life. Suddenly, a powerful Grace came over me. I became faint. This may sound like an exaggeration. But I assure you, it is not. It seemed to me, at that moment, that I would "die" if I did not listen to Our Lady and get into a prayer group. The Holy Spirit "personalized" that message for me. The immaculate Heart of Mary interceded for my spiritual life which was all but dead. At that graced moment, I was granted a "wake up" call to come to "Life." The Spirit and the Bride say, "Come." (Rev. 22:17)

In the beginning of 1990, I joined the rosary prayer group. I re-learned the rosary and observed devout people pray the 15 mysteries of the rosary, from the heart. After the fifteen decades, they would share what God was doing in their lives. Their faith was alive and their relationship was intimate. Our Lady was truly their Mother. I did not readily open myself up to them, being a very private person, raised to believe matters of faith were private. Unknown to them, I would leave the meeting and cry all the way home. This was a mystery to me that would continue for about a year. Later, Jesus taught me that those tears were the breaking down of the hardened layer around my heart and through this I was being made docile to the Holy Spirit. I kept all this to myself except that I shared everything with my husband. The prayer group helped me by their humble but courageous example of living faith and commitment to prayer and service. Most of them are daily communicants who live "True Devotion to Mary" with openness to the Person of the Holy Spirit. They are diverse in age, background, educations, temperament, careers and come from different parishes. It is wondrous to see the way the Holy Spirit knits together people of prayer. I saw how people of prayer are people of deep love because they live a profound relationship with God. They had accepted the call to Love and responded in service of the Groom and his Bride, Mother Church. Our "Upper Room" is the immaculate Heart of Mary. We gather there in intercession and accept all the gifts of the Holy Spirit that flow through Her Heart. Previously, I disliked the repetition of the rosary, but have learned the power of this prayer! The Holy Rosary is a contemplative prayer of the Gospel message when prayed from the heart. Our Lady would not invite us to pray in this manner if it were not extremely important and powerful. It is a vital weapon against Satan. Community is as important as silence and solitude for a deep prayer life. Small faith-sharing prayer groups afford a certain intimacy and support that is necessary for anyone who is serious about their spiritual journey. I believe that is why Our Lady requests the formation of rosary prayer groups in most of her messages to the world today. Our Lady invites us to pray because it is powerful and transforming for us and the world. It saves souls. Please pray the rosary and join or start a prayer group.

During the first year of my conversion I realized something was awakening inside and Grace moved me to receive Holy Communion daily. This has been my soul's nourishment for seven years. Our souls require the Eucharist. If I miss Holy Communion there is a difference in the strength of my soul for the virtues. In that first year, I read my first spiritual book entitled *The Imitation of Christ* and enrolled in a bible study class at the parish. I admit that I would read scripture and it did not seem to penetrate, until a couple of years later when I was baptized in the Holy Spirit.

My life began to gradually change in the way of detachment from people, places and things. Material things and social outings grew less important to me as the spiritual world was opening. The spiritual world was far more rich, always new and wondrous. I prayed as much as possible. I loved spending time with Jesus. I began each day with Holy Mass. I attended to my duties as wife and mother, working part time in our business during school hours. When every one was asleep, I would pray again. Above all, prayer has transformed my life! According to the Catholic Catechism, "a vital and personal relationship with the living and true God is prayer." (#2558)

I simply responded to Our Lady's invitation to pray. Through her and the rosary, I was led immediately into a relationship with Jesus, Our Eucharistic Lord and made myself available to God. I spent time with Him. He looked at me and I looked at Him. In that gaze I was lost and found in His Love. His Sacred and Holy Heart was mine to explore. Love Himself revealed the rich beauty of the interior life. God initiates everything. He directed my journey according to His Divine Will. I did not choose the path that Our Lord chose for my soul. Nor can anybody because in God's Wisdom, the journey is particular for each soul. He taught me that each soul's light represents a facet of His Infinite Divine Love. Slowly, through

Grace and prayer, I began to surrender "my way" for "His way." That change was not easy. I had put on the thinking of the world. If you cannot see it, touch it, prove it, it isn't real. Without a doubt, the spiritual world that I was experiencing was more real, more tangible than anything I could see, feel or prove. Still, sometimes I wanted to take back "control" of my life. It was difficult for me to live in the grace of the present moment. I wanted to know "the plan." Where are you taking me, Lord? The writings in this book present a picture of how Our Lord and Our Lady led my soul. Jesus calls us to fall in love with Him! He reveals His Unspeakable Beauty, His Majesty, His Infinite Goodness. How can one resist Him? He is truly a lover of souls full of gentleness and compassion. I found Him to by my constant companion. He invited me to tell Him everything, to exclude Him from nothing. He cared about every detail of my existence! He wasn't "up there." He was in my deepest center where there are no secrets.

He spoke of union with Him. He led me to the Eternal Father. The reality of the Communion of Saints and the choirs of angels was being revealed. Still, the idea that God was calling me, a married woman with children, living in the 1990's to a serious life of prayer and union, was not easily understood or accepted. Was I imagining all this? About this time, He desired that I have a Roman Catholic Priest for a Spiritual Director.

A friend organized a pilgrimage to Lourdes that included Rue de Bac (The Miraculous Medal), Paray la Monial (The Sacred Heart) and Ars (The Cure). Many people from the prayer group were going. I asked my husband if our family could go. At the last moment my husband ended up staying home with our youngest son and I went with our oldest son. It was on this pilgrimage that I met the priest that would be my spiritual director as of 1992. He is a patient teacher, knowledgeable in Scripture and Theology. More important, his own rich spiritual life has been a tremendous example and I thank God for the graces in his soul. Most of the prayer group has participated in an annual pilgrimage to places that include The Holy Land, Fatima, Rome, Assisi, San Giovanni and Medjugorje. My spiritual life was deeply enriched by these travels. The apparitions of Our Lady at Lourdes and Fatima are such a gift to us. I was deeply touched that God would send the Blessed Virgin Mary to earth to teach us, to help us. What a loving God! What a beautiful Mother! Seeing the incorrupt body of St. Bernadette, how could anyone not be moved? How do you explain this? A human body, preserved over time by the grace of God? What a wonder. These graces enriched my faith.

At Lourdes Grotto, at midnight, I first heard Our Lady speak interiorly. I wrote down her words on a small piece of paper. At first, it was a little startling. But quickly, I was caught up in simply "listening" and was moved to write down the words. I heard and listened at a very deep interior level. There was more than just hearing the message in that her presence seemed very tangible to me. Her disposition was somehow known. She was serious, gentle, loving and very beautiful. She is beyond description.

On the plane ride home from Lourdes, Our Lord requested that I speak to the priest who served as the spiritual guide for the pilgrimage. A few weeks later we met and I showed him the words received in Lourdes. He advised me to get a Spiritual Director. I asked if he would do this and he agreed. He recommended a daily Holy Hour before the tabernacle. He suggested that I withdraw from some of the ministries I was active in to allow more time for silent prayer and solitude. He led me to dispose myself for the grace of contemplative prayer. God, in His Goodness, eventually granted me the gift of contemplative prayer.

I continued to hear interiorly, words from Our Lord and Our Lady, and eventually, from Our Eternal Father and some Saints. In the beginning, I received messages only occasionally and they were more personal but over the five years the messages have increased to almost daily becoming more prophetic. Many spoke of being chosen to suffer for Love of Him, in Charity for souls. His Divine Love had now consumed me. The consolation of the beginning journey eventually gave way to the profound way of the cross but Love and Union are always the center of everything.

I had worked as a medical assistant, and then, in the business world, and neither one of these fields required much in the way of the "abstract." I had never read a theology book, not even a psychology book. By nature, I am a skeptic, a "doubting Thomas." My first reaction to most spiritual things is to not believe. There were many doubts and fear of deception. It was difficult to understand what was happening. Many priests and laity have a negativity toward any private revelations and/or Marian apparitions. But I could not resist what was happening in my soul. It was too beautiful and powerful. There were many fruits as well. This is so private, so sacred, few have come to know what was stirring in my soul.

My Spiritual Director met with me weekly to hear my confession and pray the rosary. He witnessed the receiving of the messages and other graces as well. Because of ongoing temptations of doubt, he suggested I read the lives of the saints to bring peace of soul and to teach me that others, too, have experienced what I was going through. These graces are part of the Catholic tradition. The Holy Spirit created a thirst for reading the lives of the saints and spiritual material. Just as St. Teresa of Avila recommended, I kept a good spiritual book by my side. Normally, I opened the book randomly and read a paragraph or a page and this served as a catalyst to silent prayer. I never seem to retain much of what I read. I am kept in a state of constant readiness to receive, like an empty blackboard waiting to be written upon. I rarely re-read any of the messages. We are all called to live in the grace of the present moment. Reading the lives of the saints helped me to express what was happening to me. They inspire us along the journey which includes the carrying of heavy crosses, suffering, and many battles with the devil by way of temptations and attacks. Reflecting on the life of St. Teresa of Avila, I am deeply inspired by the fact that she was an outstanding businesswoman, foundress and reformer of many Carmelite convents, a mystic, a contemplative open to all the gifts of the Holy Spirit, and a Doctor of the Church. In her example we learn what it is to be "in the world" but not "of the world." While scripture is the revelation of God's Divine Love, the lives of the Saints are examples of living that revelation on earth.

I am convinced that the deepest formation of my soul can only be reached and guided by God Himself. Peace is found in the knowledge that my spiritual director is given light, wisdom and discernment for my soul. In truth, I saw how sometimes I called pride and fear, "discernment." I doubt that there is a saint in heaven who has not been deceived by the enemy of all souls at some time. That is why we must invoke the Holy Spirit for the great gift of discernment of spirits and true self knowledge. I try not to be preoccupied with the labeling of the gifts of my spiritual life, and trust everything to the Roman Catholic Church. She discerns. I am under her Authority and Wisdom. That is a gift and protection for all of us. I didn't always have appreciation for the Church, on the contrary. But, in loving the Groom, He led me to love His Mystical Bride, Holy Mother Church. In all matters of the spiritual life it is most important that the Person of the Holy Spirit be known and given freedom to lead the soul. I did not know the person of the Holy Spirit prior to my conversion. It helped me to read the book entitled *The Great Unknown* by Antonio Royo Marin, O.P. The Person of the Holy Spirit is the teacher who bears witness to Jesus, the Word Made Flesh to the Glory of the Father. He sanctifies us! Every grace that has come to my soul has come through the Heart of Our Lady, Spouse of the Holy Spirit. She leads me to respond with her own words, "Let it be done to me according to your Word." (Luke 1:38)

There are many messages that speak of purification for the world. Everywhere I look, this purification process has begun, in my soul, in my family, in friends, in our country, in the Church and throughout the world. This is God's mercy and love. Purification leads to restoration. When I see all the suffering I can worry or be afraid. However, in relationship with God (prayer) I believe, hope and trust. My time is best spent saying, "I love You, my Lord and my God." Union with God is the goal, the all important everlasting reality. Since God created us for Union, will He not lead us precisely to that Union? Suffering is a mystery that often leads to that Union with God. My pride of self sufficiency was broken down, first by love, and then through suffering for the sake of love.

I simply "let go." In doing so, I permit Him to lead me. Where He leads is Holy! It is where I want to be, forever. The way He leads each soul is very intimate and particular for that soul. It is difficult to reveal the relationship of love that exists in the privacy of my heart. However, in obedience, I offer this as a testimony of Love. If it helps even one soul to "respond," it will be worth the sacrifice.

I leave you with the words of St. Paul, "For this reason, I bow my knees before the Father, from whom every family in heaven and on earth derives its name, that He would grant you, according to the riches of His Glory to be strengthened with power through faith, and that you, being rooted and grounded in love, may be able to comprehend with all the saints what is the breadth and length and height and depth, and to know the love of Christ which surpasses knowledge that you may be filled up with all the fullness of God. Amen (Eph. 4:13)

Dedicated to the Most Holy Trinity through the Heart of Mary.

A soul,
February 2, 1997, The Feast of the Presentation of the Lord.

MESSAGES

6-19-96 Rosary with my Spiritual Directory, My home
Blessing of the Book

Glorious Mysteries.

As soon as Father began the Resurrection decade, I heard and saw the following:

I saw a book in Father's hand. Immediately, an Angel, which I understood to be the Angel of Enduring Love, came and took the book from Father's hands. The Angel, which was magnificent in its power and light, ascended upward through the heavens. In an instant it seemed, the Angel arrived at the throne of the Most Holy Trinity. The Angel presented the book to Our Triune God laying the book on the ground before the throne of the Most Holy Trinity. Many Angels (being of pure light) and Saints (taking their human form) gathered around to observe God blessing the book. The book was transfigured into Light as the Most Holy Trinity poured graces upon it. These are Graces to be given to the reader. I could see graced light fall upon the pages, transfiguring the book into Light rather than a material book. Somehow the Angels and the Saints blessed it also. At the end of the blessing, the Angel of Enduring Love carried the book back to Father's hands. The Angel of Enduring Love is an extra Angel that God The Father granted my soul in 1996 to help me "endure" an extreme suffering, a great trial. This is an Angel from the Choir of Virtues.

Then I heard Jesus say:
O My Creation!
May your Faith be increased!
Then I heard the Holy Spirit say:

May your Hope be increased!
Then I heard The Father say:
May your Love be increased!

O My Creation
You are walking in darkness.
Receive My Light.
I am your Triune God who Lives.
You are My people living like orphans.
Turn from evil. Live in My Light.
I am God. You are not.
Let Love reign again.
Be transfigured and live in Me.
My Covenant is everlasting!
Be Mine. I am Yours.
Who is like unto your Almighty and Eternal God?
Darkness has covered you,
But I shall wash you with Living Water.
Be cleansed that you may be One with The Light.
Open your hardened hearts.
Let My Fire of Divine Love enter you.
Love alone will transfigure My creation.
The darkness shall not overcome you.
You shall overcome the darkness
by the Power of Divine Love.
No longer will I endure your indifference.
The time of decision has arrived.
Do not be afraid. But Choose Me.
I have chosen you to be Mine forever.
Come. I will dry your tears.
No prayer has been in vain.
No sigh of Love goes unnoticed.
Likewise, no sin goes unnoticed.
But My Mercy is unfathomable.
Do not put off your decision.
There is one thing you have that is eternal.
It is your soul.

Reflect, My Creation, and pray.
I, your Triune, Supreme, and Eternal God
am with you. Turn to Me.
I am Love, Divine, and Unconditional.
All that you seek, all that you require,
I AM.
In all ages I AM.

Second Glorious Mystery.

When Father prayed then, "help us know to the Divine Will of the Father", I saw the following:

I saw a powerful lightening storm in the heavens. When the lightening would strike, it lit up the globe of the world which was in total darkness. Lightening bolts would then hit and pierce the darkness to illumine the earth. When bathed in the light, I could see on earth, people gathered together in small groups, praying and reading spiritual books. A type of resurrection was resulting as souls were enriched and brought back to life becoming bathed in The Light and receiving Love. I understood the darkness on earth to be of a spiritual nature. I was amazed at how utterly dark the whole of creation had become. I understood that God's Divine Providence would transfigure the darkness of the world through a variety of signs, miracles, messages, visitations, sufferings. Grace upon Grace will draw us back to the Light. Lord?

Jesus said: **The Graces of this age are a sign of My Mercy revealing and reminding all of creation, I Am A Living God! In every generation, My Covenant stands and I speak to My people in wondrous ways.**

Next, I saw the prologue of John's Gospel. It was all lit up.

Later, I saw our Prayer Group praying the Rosary. This is a sign of their intercession.

As I am writing this, I see a snake trying to crawl on the notebook of writings on my desk, but immediately Our Lady put the rosary over the writings and the snake disappeared.

11-3-95 Feast of St. Martin de Porres - Adoration of the Blessed Sacrament following 8:30AM Mass

The Point of Another Message Book?

In prayer, I asked Jesus: Please help me to understand the point of another Message Book.

I, the Lord and Savior of all, have thus spoken to you, an ordinary soul, that My creation will know that I am the Living God in your midst, that you may turn back from your present course of darkness to walk into the Light of My Love. I have thus spoken messages of Love, pure and simple; teachings of Truth Everlasting; prophetic warnings portraying My Mercy; that My creation will be reconciled with the One who is Love.

I am the Head, you are My Body. My Body is in need of nourishment. Through the poorest of vessels, I pour Myself out in this age as in all ages when My own have gone astray. The messages are a sign of My Mercy in a world that has great need of My Mercy. This work contains teachings which are nourishment for hungry souls. This work reveals My Thirst and My Hunger for souls! I suffered and died that I might draw all souls unto Myself through the Cross of Salvation.

O My Creation, My Love for you is pure, sacrificial, unconditional, Infinite Love. You have not yet understood My Love. In this present age, the true meaning of love has been forgotten.

I plucked you from the world, the poorest of vessels, and caused you to love Me. I revealed My Voice that I might teach you to love. I melted your cold heart with My Divine Fire of Love. I caused you to burn with love. This is a sign of My Love for all souls. You have been instructed by Me that I may pour Myself out through you as a sign of My charity for souls.

I will bless many through this work. Faith is waning in the world. Therefore, many cannot read the signs of the times because they have lost faith in Me and My works. If your heart is the least bit open, My Holy Spirit will enter and convince you that My works in this age are Truth and Wisdom. Yet your

heart must be docile like a child's heart to reap the graces of My works in this age.

Love is the reason for yet another Message Book.

If I must teach My children one by one as I have taught you, in order to divert the (spiritual) death of many, I will do so! If but one soul is diverted from evil, if but one soul is touched by love through this work, then it will have served a great purpose, an eternal purpose.

Let it be known, this work is the sum of many methods of teaching, as I have taught you through daily Holy Mass, through hours of daily prayer where I infuse My knowledge into your soul and in community through the Prayer Group.

Let this be an example to you, My Creation, that I am the Divine Teacher. I will reveal Myself to you if you but turn to Me in prayer. I am calling you to intimacy. Open your heart and listen.

I was then given the following Scriptures and Teachings.

It is written: (Jeremiah 13:15-17)

Give ear, listen humbly,
For the Lord speaks.
Give Glory to the Lord, your God,
Before it grows dark;
Before your feet stumble
On darkening mountains;
Before the light you look for turns to darkness,
Changes into black clouds.
If you do not listen to this in your pride,
I will weep in secret many tears
For the Lord's flock, led away in exile.

Jesus spoke: **In this age I am pouring grace upon grace. All of Heaven is bending to earth to call you back to God. It is your human pride that prevents My Grace from entering your heart. Your heart is hardened by lack of love and you are full of pride. No one is immune to pride. Yet I will give you the grace to** overcome your pride with humility if you but desire this. Do not be afraid to believe in My works of this age. Do not be afraid to believe what the Holy Spirit is trying to teach you now. Be as little children. Open your hearts. Trust.

I am sending My Mother in your midst again and again. I am sending one messenger after another. They are proclaiming the same Gospel message of love and life. They are a sign to you that I am calling you into intimacy. I am revealing Myself to you that you will accept, once and for all, that you are My creation. You are created for Me. You belong to Me that I may be glorified in your holiness, imparting My own Divine Goodness to you. I am revealing My Love to you, in this age, in order to divert you from your present course. When I ascended to the Father, I had instituted the Sacrament of life-giving nourishment, that I remain with you in the humble form of bread and wine, consecrated under the power of the Holy Spirit into My Flesh and Blood. This Sacrament is life for your souls. In this age, you have turned from this life-giving nourishment.

The Holy Spirit descended upon earth that you would have the spirit of love. You have the Spirit that bears witness to the truth of my teachings. In this age you have turned from the Holy Spirit and from My Truth. I established the Church as a Holy House of Prayer on the Rock of Peter. In this age you have turned from the Church; you have turned from Peter. The evil of this present age is such that great light must enter to dispel the darkness. Greater light must illumine the earth through souls that are full of grace. Souls are being illuminated through the mercy of many heavenly graces. The signs simply bear witness that I am the Living God in your midst, that you might persevere in faith and in hope, living the Gospel message of Love and Truth. You have all that is needed to live as a holy people of God, yet you have turned away from Me, Your Lord and Savior who loves you. I hear your cry, "If there is a God, where is He now?" And I say to you, "I am in your midst. Will you stop running in circles and look within your heart?" If I give to you a Eucharistic miracle, an apparition of My Mother, a prophet in your midst, and you cannot bring yourself to believe, then your heart is closed and pride is blocking grace. Then your faith is too small to be counted. In your pride you will be led away in exile. Not because you didn't believe in a sign, miracle, or messenger, but because you fail to believe in the One who sent them. I weep for you because I love you and want you to partake in My Eternal Salvation. I, the Lord your God, have given you all good things. I have provided for you. You must turn and accept My Grace. Then you will have Love and Peace.

It is written: (2 Timothy 3)

But, understand this: There will be terrifying times in the last days. People will be self-centered and lovers of money, proud, haughty, abusive, disobedient to their parents, ungrateful, irreligious, brutal, hating what is good, traitors, reckless, conceited, lovers of pleasure rather than lovers of God, and they make a pretense of religion but deny its power.

Jesus said: **These are the signs of the enemy. Accept My Grace now and know the enemy so that I can empower you to fight the battle against evil. There is a great battle being waged in these days. The powers of good versus the powers of evil. Avail yourself of all My Graces so that, in My Holy Spirit, you can discern the spirits. In the Holy Spirit, the truth will be made evident. If you are not in My Holy Spirit, in My Grace, loving and seeking the truth, you will be deceived by evil. You are living at the end of one age and the beginning of another age. The transition depends upon you. If you are converted to love and if you pray, there will be less suffering. Disasters can be averted through prayer and fasting. You need not fear. If you know Me and love Me, you will trust in My Love and Wisdom. You can know Me and love Me only in prayer. The greatest prayer of all is the Holy Sacrifice of the Mass. Prayer is love exchanged; the Creator and the creature communicating in love. It is simple. Allow Me to love you and return My Love. You have only to be still, gaze upon a Crucifix and know how much I love you. Partake in My Eucharistic Love and you shall be fortified for I am the Bread of Life. Yet only those who have been reconciled can approach the Eucharistic altar. Blessed are** you who avail yourselves of My Sacraments. Grace upon grace is yours. The enemy will tempt you but you shall remain in My Holy Spirit. The Holy Spirit will bear witness in your very soul to the Truth. Then you will not succumb to the enemy and evil will have no power over you.

It is written: (2 Timothy 4)

I charge you in the presence of God and of Christ, Jesus, who will judge the living and the dead, and by His appearing and His Kingly power: proclaim the word; be persistent whether it is convenient or inconvenient; convince, reprimand, encourage through patience and teaching. For the time will come when people will not tolerate sound doctrine but, following their own desires and insatiable curiosity, will accumulate teachers and will stop listening to the truth and will be diverted to myths. But you, be self-possessed in all circumstances, put up with hardship; perform the work of an evangelist; fulfill your ministry.

Jesus said: **My Creation, your ministry is love. This is My commandment: Love the Lord Your God with all your heart, all your soul, all your mind and all your strength. Love one another as yourself. Live the Gospel of Love even if the world persecutes you. Love will prevail. Persevere in the faith and come against the enemy with love, charity, hope, humility, obedience, and truth. Put aside the ways of the world and embrace My way and you shall endure all trials in peace. In My strength you will stand. In My Mercy you shall be saved forever.**

Be consoled, My creation. Persevere in your faith that you will be found worthy to participate in the victory I have won for you. First you must wash yourselves in the Blood of the Lamb. Repent. Be converted. You are living in decisive times. Prepare yourself with prayer and fasting. Be reconciled to Me, your Triune God. Turn from all evil and darkness. Live as a child of God, pure and holy. For this you were created. For this I suffered and died. I am today preparing you for My Kingdom on earth, a Kingdom of Peace and Love. In the era of peace, you will live as one Holy Family of God. I will manifest Myself to all mankind that you will believe. Then will you give

glory to the Lord and Savior of all who mediated all your transgressions and reconciled you to the Most High Father of all.

The Immaculate Heart of Mary Most Holy is in your midst to prepare the way. Through her heart, grace is showered upon earth now. So, too, The Father has ordained many messengers who bear witness to the Living God by means of their poverty (of spirit) being enriched by Divine Grace. In every corner of the world, My Voice resounds. Are you listening? I am using a variety of messengers who are but little children to confound the wisdom of the world. Blessed are the Little ones who proclaim My message in obedience to My Will. They bear the Cross for many. Yet the messenger is but a vessel. Examine the message with the Light and Love of the Holy Spirit. Then it will bear fruit in your heart. The Holy Spirit alone can bear witness to the truth. All My messengers are imperfect, but in their obedience, they are being perfected through grace. Look at the message as a vehicle of grace. It is a catalyst only. The Holy Spirit makes it so and gives it life. Look then to the God who is reaching out to you. Indeed, I speak to you today. My Voice will lead you back to My Traditions, My Foundation set for your salvation, long, long ago. My Word and My Covenant are everlasting. Every prophet of this age who is from Me proclaims the same Gospel message given to the world long ago. Every messenger of this age who is from Me will point you back to My Word. Your salvation has been revealed to you. That you may be found worthy, you must turn from your present course now.

It is written: (1 Cor. 2:10-15)

For the Spirit scrutinizes everything, even the depths of God. Among human beings, who knows what pertains to a person except the spirit of the person that is within? Similarly, no one knows what pertains to God except the Spirit of God. We have not received the spirit of the world but the Spirit that is from God, so that we may understand the things freely given us by God. And we speak about them not with words taught by human wisdom, but with words taught by the Spirit, describing realities in spiritual terms. Now the natural person does not accept what pertains to the Spirit of God, for him it is foolishness, and he cannot understand it, because it is judged spiritually. The spiritual person, however, can judge everything but is not subject to judgment by anyone.

I have thus spoken:
>**Messages of Love, pure and simple,**
>**Teachings of Truth Everlasting,**
>**Prophetic warnings portraying My Mercy,**
>**That My Creation will be reconciled with the One who is Love.**

8-5-92 Lourdes Grotto 11 PM
Focus on Prayer

My dear children,

*Many of you have asked why I have called you here. There is so much I wish to teach you, my dear ones. First, I have called you here to show you how the faith of one poor girl who said "yes" to my Son and I can affect so many hearts. I call you each to the kind of faith Bernadette showed here at the Grotto. I called you here to get you away from your worldly distractions at home so that you may focus on **prayer.***

I called you here so that I may present your hearts to my Beloved Son. I so desire to fill your hearts with my love and joy. You are my children who have opened your hearts and invited me into your lives, and I thank you for this surrender. I need each and everyone of you to consecrate yourselves here and now to a continued commitment to prayer and sacrifice and service.

Be joyful, my dear ones, for you are my chosen, and so close to my heart. I promise to be with you as you walk on your journey to my Beloved Son. Be obedient and persevere in your prayers. I love you with all my heart, little ones. Be joyful and be refreshed for your journey, as I will call on you many times in the future, and you must be peaceful in your hearts in order to discern my callings. May the peace only my Son can provide dwell in your hearts now and always.

Your Loving Mother

P. S. She requests more frequent Reconciliation.

2-23-93 Tabernacle
Darkness Exists Because Men Have Chosen Darkness

Following Communion, I prayed that Jesus cover the earth with His Light and Love to overcome the tremendous darkness I sensed over the world. I wondered why He allows so much darkness to exist in the world today.

Interiorly, He responded:

My daughter,

Darkness exists because men have chosen darkness. The present darkness exists because so many of My children have chosen the path of darkness over My Light and My Love. I will never interfere with man's free will. Man was created with much dignity that he is able to make choices. Many have chosen to reject My Love and Light and Peace in favor of godlessness, intellectualism, rationalization, materialism, selfishness, power and violence, impurity, indifference, negativity. Instead of choosing to love one another, as I have asked, they oppress and crush soul after soul. Evil delights in this. I weep over man's choices. I weep because I am rejected more today than ever. I weep because I suffered and died that men would live My Love on earth and into eternity.

I make available to all My children all the graces necessary to choose the path of love and light. Many refuse My Grace in favor of immediate gratification of the flesh. The most horrendous sins of the flesh are rampant today. Once a person chooses the path of destruction, the soul's desire for peace and love and purity becomes blocked from the graces which lead it to light due to the sin and darkness existing within that person. Be assured, My daughter, that I constantly attempt to aid and call that soul back into the light of My Love. Be assured that every soul does long for the peace only My Love can provide. Pray that your brothers and sisters choose life over death.

Think of this, My daughter. When your child makes the wrong choice and does something that is not right, you punish him, out of love for him, to put him back on the right path and help him choose the right way in the future. I, too, am a loving

parent. All humanity are My children. The present darkness exists because My children have gone astray and chosen darkness. There will be consequences for their actions. Many will suffer. This I will allow out of love for My people. It is not what I choose for them. It is what they have chosen for themselves.

I desire the world to be put back on the right path. I desire all to exist in My Love and Light. I desire My Church to feed My people and lead them to Me. My Church is not accomplishing this today. I desire My Sacraments, Fountains of Grace, to be frequented by all souls, that they have the strength and wisdom to choose My Love and Light. So many ignore the sacraments today. I created My people to be a holy people. In order that this be accomplished, the present darkness must be destroyed. With a heart that weeps, filled with sorrow, I say to you, many will perish, those who have chosen the path of sin. There will be martyrs. Innocent souls will perish in reparation for the horrendous sins of mankind. The souls of the Martyrs will live in glory with Me and My Father.

My daughter, you have tasted of My Mercy and Compassion. The blood I shed was to cover all My people. I welcome back with open arms even the most hideous of sinners who desire to be right with their God. Pray, My daughter, that people will accept My Love and Mercy now! Pray they choose the Light, the Life. It is the desire of My Sacred Heart, the desire of My Father, the desire of the Immaculate Heart of My Mother.

The Holy Spirit covers the earth at this time, constantly drawing hearts back into the light of My Love. Trust, I will triumph over the darkness. After the punishment brought on by humanity themselves, there will be an Era of Peace, just as My Mother foretold in Fatima. Her Immaculate Heart will reign. People will know I exist and love will abound. Of you I ask sacrifice and prayer for the souls who are on the path to destruction. I weep for them. My heart breaks for them. My daughter, soothe Me and dress My Wounds with your sacrifice and love. Peace be yours. I love you, soul.

Jesus of Mercy

6-14-93 Tabernacle
I Will Build a New Jerusalem

After Communion I had prayed one hour silently when I heard interiorly:

My daughter,
I will build a new Jerusalem, for all the earth has become a desert. Only sparse springs of fervent life exist today. My children exist as bones and flesh alone, as if their God had not breathed His Spirit into them at all. Woe to those who have rejected My Spirit!

Child, enter with Me into the Garden of Gethsemane. Stay beside Me, soothe Me with your love. Feel the agony of My rejection, the agony of betrayal, the agony of My loneliness. In your midst I came to show the Infinite Love of the Father, to grant peace and mercy. I lived among you to teach abundant life, goodness and wisdom. Still, man preferred the darkness. My Light did not penetrate the hardness of your hearts, the vanity of your will. Is it any different today? I am pouring upon the earth, rays of My Divine Mercy. The Father has graced the world with visitations of My Mother. In every corner of the world I have raised disciples and given My Words of Love and warning through them. Is anyone awake?

Oh Creation! You violate My Body still! Children who sleep now will never know rest, for eternity they shall be awake in their sufferings of the consequences of rejecting their God. They will suffer the consequences of being dead to the spirit who knocked on their door to give them true life. So mourn with Me. Mourn and weep with Me. Keep watch with Me. Anoint My wounded Body with the oil of your love. Take courage, My little one, I will build a new Jerusalem. I will breathe My Spirit into God-fearing souls and all of creation will give Me glory! My Mother and her Immaculate Heart will crush forever the serpent, deceiver, thief of your inheritance. The Will of the Father shall be accomplished. My Words I give you for love alone. I have inflamed your heart to console My own. Although I am the Almighty One and need no one, I love infinitely and desire to be loved in return.

Jesus

6-18-93 11 PM Feast of Sacred Heart - Arizona
Console My Heart with Your Own

I had fallen asleep and was awakened when I heard:

Come, come, please listen to My Words and write for Me.

Rejoice, creation, for I have opened the floodgates of Divine Love flowing from My Sacred Heart. Oh Creation, if you only realized how Love loves you! Oh My children, the radiant life-giving love of My Sacred Heart overflows, attempting to find recipients of My Love, hearts open to receive all I desire to give them from My Heart. My Sacred Heart is the fountain of grace for you. Receive creation, receive! My heart aches for you to receive all the riches within.

Oh generation so lost! You cry out, "Lord, where are you? Where are you?" Words from your lips, not from your heart. Your will comes before My Will. You cry out, "Lord, save me from my pain and troubles," seeking Me for consolation, not love. I await you in every tabernacle in the world. Seek Me there. I am not hiding My face from you. I love you. Still you do not recognize Me. Wounded is My Heart of Love. Allow My Grace and Mercy to flow from My Heart to your hardened hearts. Receive My Divine Love and you shall be healed. You shall be strengthened to resist the evil serpent who has held you bound to the vanity of your human will. My love will rescue you, creation. My Sacred Heart, in union with the Immaculate Heart of My Mother, will penetrate your being so that your souls begin to live in the truth.

Offer Me reparation for the ingratitude of creation; the Heart of their Redeemer bleeds for them. Console My Heart with your own. Allow our hearts to beat in unison, loving and sacrificing for one another. I will melt away your weakness and

raise you for Myself. The riches of My Heart shall be yours. Pray the fountain of My Sacred Heart not be denied. Oh generation, wallowing in your own misery, My Sacred Heart awaits you, loving you infinitely, never ceasing to be merciful toward you. I shall rejoice when souls return to My Sacred Heart. In abandonment to the love of My Heart, you shall find fulfillment of your souls, for you are My people. I am your God. Let us love one another. My Peace I give you. Allow My Sacred Heart to reign within you. Rest in Me now. Love is with you.

Sacred Heart of Jesus

6-24-93 My office, 12 noon
Freedom

"I led you from the bondage of your slavery, freeing you from the darkness and leading you into the light of My tender Love. It was not for your sake that I acted in you but because of My holy Name. I poured My purifying water upon you, cleansing you from your defilement. I gave you a new heart and put a new spirit within you. I removed your heart of stone and gave you a heart of flesh. I put My Spirit within you and moved you to follow My decrees and keep My Love." (Ezk. 36:22-27) You were called to enjoy freedom not of the flesh but that which makes you a slave to love alone.

Soul, your weakness is astounding! You have enjoyed our intimate friendship, as I, Myself, have nurtured you like an infant at the breast. Yet, you desire to withhold a portion of yourself. Though you are but a grain of sand, I did not withhold Myself from you. I came to you in love, teaching My way. I humbled Myself for you on the cross, in the Eucharist, and to come into your house. Can you, soul, look into My eyes, after the many gazes of love we have shared and withhold from your Savior a portion of yourself? There is nothing but for Me to pity you. Could you profess your love for Me with your lips and withhold a portion of your heart? Fear has entered you. Fear of total surrender, fear of where I will lead you, fear of persecution and rejection, fear of losing all for

Me. Could fear possibly penetrate your soul more deeply than the fire of My Love?

You consider withholding yourself from Him who hung on the cross for you, ransom for your life. I've carried you in My arms, inviting you into My tent, preparing a home for you there. I will not accept a portion only, nothing less than every fiber of your being do I desire. Not that I need, but that I love, not for you but for My people and My Church. You offer your Lord the balm of your love, then hesitate, afraid to continue. You seek rest when My work never ceases. A moment's rest allows the serpent an opportunity to claim another soul. Bring your fears to Me and I shall annihilate them for you. The world shall cause you pain but My Love shall uphold you. Your security is in My arms. (I had to stop writing at this time)

6-24-93 11:30PM My home.

Please do not deny Me freedom in you. From the moment of creation I ordained to use you as My instrument in this era of grace and mercy. You doubt My words to you, yet who could instruct you, leading your soul to love My Sacraments, My Word, My Church, My People, My Mother and My Sacred Heart? Your thoughts alone, without My Spirit of Truth, led you to self-idolatry and worldliness, your folly leading you along the path to perdition. Your doubt now drives the nails into My hands and feet; your fear lacerates My Sacred Heart.

Come, My beloved, come. Eye has not seen, ear has not heard nor has it dawned on the mind what God has prepared for those who love Him. (1 Cor. 2:9) Soul, you fear the wise will condemn you. I solemnly say, "I will destroy the wisdom of the wise and I will demolish the reasoning of the learned." (1 Cor. 1:18) The wisdom of the world will fail. Wisdom herself instructs you. Abandonment, My daughter, abandonment! I shall keep you steadfast until the end. The great and terrible day approaches. Be a vessel of My Light and Love to My assembly - faithful and true to your Savior. Love rejoices in truth, believes all things, hopes all things and endures all things. Faith requires sacrifice, My little one. I shall keep My promises, My

IN FAITH, IN HOPE, IN LOVE

riches shall be yours. Even now I prepare a room for you. For eternity love will abide with you. Rest in My incomprehensible Love. My Peace I give you. Be joyful, for I am with you.
  Jesus of Mercy

Lord, I give you my fear, my doubt, my lack of faith, lack of hope, and lack of love. I beg pardon for my weakness, hesitation, and doubt. By Your grace alone do I stand. Be merciful and have pity on my poor soul. Jesus, never allow me to offend You. I cannot bear it. I prefer any punishment. I exist only to please you, but the pain of loving you this much is sometimes more than I can bear. Breathe Your Spirit of strength in me. Take away my doubt that I may continue. I seek only truth and love. Be glorified, my King. I love You.

7-4-94 My home, 3 PM.
Fill Their Lamps With Oil

I was napping with my Rosary in my hand in my guest room. I heard interiorly: *Listen to your Mother, please.* I said, "Praised be Jesus." She said: *Praised be Jesus, King of Kings, Victim for sinners, Ruler of all. All Honor, Glory and Praise be His!*

My child,
  Now is the time for all my children to fill their lamps with oil for the great and terrible day. The moment of truth, when each soul sees themselves in the Light of God, will come upon this generation very suddenly. Woe to those unprepared and caught off-guard My children who have received the words of warning from my instruments of Light/Love, for those who have been alert and received in their hearts the call to conversion, they shall remain at peace in the midst of chaos. They will continue to receive grace and protection from all of heaven because they believed, repented and took my messages to heart. The Holy Spirit knocked and they responded. "Enter, welcome"! In God's Divine Mercy for this generation, He poured upon all four corners of the earth His Holy Spirit. Graced has this generation been, even in the midst of the

greatest outrages against the United Sacred and Immaculate Hearts. Love has descended from heaven to awaken and instruct souls.

Please children, acknowledge your Creator in humility and repentance. Offer reparation for your rejection, denial of my Son, for your disobedience of His laws and decrees, for your ingratitude for His love, mercy, grace. Those who served well, with complete generosity of heart, sacrificing their human will for Divine Will, shall partake in the banquet being prepared for the faithful remnant!

Little ones, pray, pray, pray unceasingly for the conversion of all souls. Pray and sacrifice for peace and unity among all people. Peace and unity begin in the heart of each child of God. Listen. Stay alert. Oh generation, the hour is late. Reconcile with God and one another now! I am your Mother and truly I am with you to assist you always. You shared a portion of my pain when your heart was pierced, thinking you had lost your son. My heart is continually pierced by souls who have lost my Beloved Son. I weep and plead for all souls to return to their Lord and Savior. Plead with me.

My child, serve my Beloved Son faithfully, for love alone. Assist, please, in the salvation of our family of souls. Be generous, little one. His Grace and Strength shall enable you to carry out His orders. Do whatever He tells you! Offer your will as sacrifice for sins of this generation. Offer all to Him who clothed your nakedness with His Love and Mercy. Walk along the Via Dolorosa in union with my Son and His cross. His blood washes you and He calls you friend. Do not be afraid of death of your flesh. As your flesh is crucified, the pain is temporary, and will give birth to new life in the spirit. Rejoice as my Son prunes and reshapes you, however painful He does so to create the fullness of beauty within your soul. Happy are those invited to the wedding of the Lamb (Rev. 19:9). You belong to Him. You are His instrument. Respond in abandonment, humility and obedience. I love you, little one. Thank Our Lord for allowing me to speak to you. I bless you.

Your Mother

7-9-93 Communion at Convention
Thirst For Me

Beloved of My Sacred Heart, wretched though you are, I shall create in you a thirst for Me. I, alone, will satisfy. You shall thirst for souls to present to the Most Holy Trinity. It is I who will create this unquenchable thirst within the depths of your being. Though you are My weakest seed, by My own hand I will root you in fertile soil and raise you by My Eternal Spring of life-giving waters. You will grow upright and strong. Your branch will bear fruit for your King and His Kingdom. Thirst for Me, little one, and I will give you to drink of My Eternal Will.

Your Jesus

7-15-93 PM My home
Prayer for Union With the Cross

Jesus, Divine Teacher of my soul, how patiently and lovingly You instruct my poor soul. Your Grace is infusing in my soul the desire to be united to Your Passion and Suffering. It is the cross I cannot stop thinking about. You have created within me a fascination and devotion to Your Passion. I find myself praying and thinking constantly about Your Passion, Your Agony. I desire to know everything about every sorrow You suffered for my nothingness.

At retreat, I gazed upon Your Perfection on the Cross and I saw, with the eyes of my soul, my body between You and the wood of the Cross. Suddenly, there was no other place I desired to be but on the Cross with You. I was filled to overflowing with love for Your Agony and Passion. I desired that You impart to my soul the Love that could cause You to suffer such torture for my nothingness. Graced is this moment, when I can write that I desire to unite myself to Your Passion, in whatever degree necessary to move my soul to greater love, understanding and union with You, Beloved God.

The Cross is ultimate love. The Cross unites Creator with creation. Since the desire of my soul is union with my Lord, I will unite myself to the Cross. So I pray, Dear Lord, grant me this desire, which You, Yourself, have planted in my heart, that I understand more clearly and love more dearly Your Passion and Agony. Love of my soul, I offer all to you. This poor soul of mine requires You! Beloved Jesus, Your Grace enables my soul to say I will be Your victim and sacrifice. Fill me with Your charity. Enable me to co-redeem souls. Unite me to the cross. I ask because You graced me to ask. Your holy and perfect Will be accomplished in my soul. I surrender my human will to be crucified, for Your Honor, Your Glory. Your Grace sustains my lowliness.

Prayer: "Mother Mary, united to the Cross in every way, be with me as you were with your Son. Every step of the way, trusting completely in Divine Providence, even in the midst of the agony of the passion, you humbly submitted.

Heavenly Father, I offer You my life, my will, my joy and suffering in this valley of tears in union with the passion of the Son, His precious Blood and Holy Wounds, in reparation for the atrocities of this generation. Father, have mercy on Your children. We are poor and wretched. Our ignorance, indifference, pride and vanity cause us to reject You still. We crucify Your Son again and again. Instead of loving and uniting, we hate and divide. Your Son is the Way, the Truth, and the Life.

Almighty God, convert our hearts, infuse souls with your Light and Truth. Banish the evil which keeps us shackled to sin/darkness. Only Your Love and Mercy can prevent our damnation. Be generous with grace as Jesus was generous even unto death. Rejoice for all the souls He has purchased for You. And allow my soul to suffer and weep for the souls who refuse Your Love and Truth. Oh God, rescue Your people from the present darkness. May Your Good Shepherd come and revive Your Bride, Your Church, and cover the earth with Your Peace. Yes, finally, Your Peace on earth as in heaven. If You are seeking souls to be Your altar, for the good of all, receive my soul as a sacrifice. I place all my trust in Your loving Will. Please grant me the grace of complete submission to Your Divine Will and be glorified for the workings of Your Grace in my soul."

7-16-93 My home, Feast of Mount Carmel
I Come to Combat the Father of All Lies!

My dear children,

I, your Mother, love and cherish each of you in my Immaculate Heart. I come among you to lead you to the truth. I will lead you along the path to holiness, as each is called to be a holy Child of God. Also, I come to combat the father of all lies. Children, so much of your oppression is due to your entanglement with the deceiver who delights in your downfall. Evil delights in your confusion, your fear, denial, blindness to the light and truth. Turn away from his temptations and sin now. The hour is late. There will be much to suffer for you, your families, your country. Too much innocent blood flows in your streets from the hands of evildoers. The cup overflows. Soon the Good Shepherd will come to separate the good and faithful sheep from the evil ones. No longer will good and evil co-exist. No longer will your sins pierce the Sacred Heart of my Beloved Son.

My children, in you the words of the prophet Isaiah come true (Matthew 13:14-15). "Much as you hear, you do not understand; much as you see, you do not perceive. For the heart of His people has grown dull. Their ears hardly hear and their eyes dare not see. If they were to see with their eyes, hear with their ears and understand with their heart, they would turn back and I would heal them. Blessed are your eyes because they see and your ears because they hear." Listen to the Holy Spirit now! Heed my messages. Prepare now by Loving. Love your Lord, God, with all your heart and strength. Have faith, hope, charity toward Him and toward one another. I desire you be counted among the good and faithful sheep. Little ones, do not doubt. Do not continue to reject the love and mercy being offered so generously at this time in history. Do not force God to deal with you according to what is due you. Rather, humble yourselves before your Savior and accept His Mercy now!

As for my faithful little ones, I ask you, please do not fear the Cross. Accept what Divine Providence has ordained for your journey with complete trust and love. Your momentary suffering will gain much for your soul and other souls. Such is the way of the Kingdom of God. Stand firm and persevere. Cling to my Immaculate Heart. Enter the Sacred Heart of Jesus, where He will ignite your heart with His Love and Hope. Be my children of hope! In the days of turmoil, which the Father will allow your country, be hopeful and faithful. My Son and I shall be with you always. Though justice will claim many, I shall hold you and shelter you. For now, I ask you, pray unceasingly. In prayer you will hear the whisperings of the Holy Spirit, giving you His Divine Orders. Prayer is the answer, the key to uniting yourself to the heart of your God. Reconcile in love, hope and charity. Pray, pray, pray. Sacrifice and offer reparation. Humble yourselves now. Thank you for responding to my call. I so love you, precious children. My daughter, listen to the Holy Spirit. Do not be afraid. Follow His inspirations. My Son chose you for Himself. Rejoice and do not hesitate. I love you.

Your Mother

8-13-93 Sea of Galilee
Remain Faithful to My Peter of Today

My children,

You have been told, Oh man, what is good and what Yahweh requires of you: to do justice, to love mercy, to walk humbly with your God. "The godly have vanished from the earth and not one upright man is to be found. All lie in ambush to shed blood, one hunts another with a net. Their hands are skilled at doing evil. The official demands a bribe, the judge judges for a price and the mighty decides as he pleases. Their kindness is like a brier, their justice worse than a thorn hedge. But the time of punishment has come as foretold by your sentries. Now is the time of confusion for mortal man." (Micah 7:2-4)

Yet My Heart is an abyss of mercy for My people. Who among you is awake to claim the rays of mercy I am pouring upon the earth before justice is poured in equal proportion? You, My little ones, must not be lulled into complacency, nor shall you be blind to the storm which is brewing. For like My disciples on the Sea of Galilee, who rode atop the calm water

when suddenly the storm was upon them and the waves tossed them about, the storm shall come upon you suddenly, tossing you about and trying you in many ways. Just as Peter rose above the stormy waves, as long as you remain steadfast in your love and faith in Me alone, you shall not sink. I know My own and My own know Me. In the time of tribulation I shall not abandon My faithful ones. I will envelop them with My Holy Spirit. I shall pour into their soul My Courage, My Strength, My Love. I have called you each by name to be My disciples. Was not Peter but a simple fisherman? I, your Lord and Savior, empowered him to give glory to My Father and build up My Church.

Come to Me in simplicity and honesty. Humble yourselves and offer Me your very life, and I will fill you with true life in God. I will enable you to give glory to the Father. I will use you to rebuild My Church. Even now My Church is tossed about, and the storm gaining momentum so that she will be divided. I ask you to remain faithful to My Peter of today even as your country entices you to turn away from Rome. My faithful ones, in the springtime, together we will rebuild My Church. Pray, children, pray for My Peter and My Church. My heart is an abyss of Love and Mercy and it is yours. Receive it. Let your hearts be transformed into a furnace of love for one another, so that all may be one, just as My Father and the Holy Spirit and I are one!

Jesus of Mercy

8-14-93 Bethlehem Mass
God Does Not Want Lip Service

My little ones,

I bless you and thank you for coming. Just as I gave birth to the infant Jesus, I desire to give you birth. The birth I desire to give you at this very moment is the birth of your spiritual maturity. For in the near future you must not be as infants, rather, securely grounded in your faith, hope and love for your God and your brothers and sisters. Your God does not want lip service. He wants your heart to be His and your will to be united to His Divine Will. Accept your cross with all the love you have within you. Come, my little ones, let your mother hold you, raise you, nurture you. I love you. The peace of my Son be yours. Pray, Pray, Pray.

Your Mother

8-15-93 Jerusalem - Feast of Assumption of Mary
Love One Another Without Distinction

Today I invite you to rejoice in union with me, for God has done great things for each one of you. Let your hearts be filled with gratitude and love for Him. Today, I invite you to live my messages and grow in holiness. It is not enough to go through the motions or profess with your lips your love of God. I remind you, God sees the deepest recesses of your soul and He knows everything in your heart. So pray, little ones, that by the Power of the Holy Spirit, the truth of your soul be revealed to you. Then you must put aside any unforgiveness, petty jealousy, selfishness, fear, negativity, rationalization. Love the Lord with a pure heart. Love one another without distinction. God desires unity, not division. To love one another is to care more for your brother and sister's welfare than your own. Only then can you grow in holiness.

Pray, pray, pray, my children. Pray for peace in the world, your heart, and Jerusalem. Even now heaven is preparing the banquet for the faithful remnant, for you little ones. Please thank God for allowing me to speak to you now and in the many messages I have given the world. I love you, my children. I desire you choose God and Love. I will assist you always. Be obedient to the Will of God. Be alert to the movement of the Holy Spirit within your soul. Be humble always. Be generous with your love, faith, hope and charity. God is with you. Be at peace.

Your Mother

8-16-93 Jerusalem - Way of the Cross
There is Redemptive Value in All Suffering

My dear children,

Today I wish to speak to you about the way of the Cross. As a follower of my Son, your Lord Jesus Christ, there is no other way but the way of the Cross. The love which Jesus calls you to have must be love willing to embrace the cross. Please understand, there is redemptive value in all suffering. The pain and suffering of your human existence is for the good of the family of man and unites your soul to Jesus on the Cross, which is where no greater love has ever been displayed and realized.

My little ones, the degree of your love truly is in the degree you are willing to accept your suffering and embrace the cross. Do so for love alone. There, is the joy of a true disciple of the Lord, your Redeemer. Within the riches of His Sacred Heart is all you need. His Grace shall always be sufficient for you. Receive my blessing and my love. Pray, pray, pray. Thank you for responding to my call to come to the Holy Land. I love you.

Your Mother

8-18-93 8:30 AM Madrid to Fatima
Thank You for Coming to Fatima

I bless you and thank you for coming to Fatima. Just as I came as a loving mother to Lucia, Jacinta, and Francesco, I come to you today in love. Once again I invite you to live a life of Prayer. Your prayer is urgent. The power of prayer is truly beyond your understanding. I need your prayers. In union with my Immaculate Heart, we are preparing the way for the reign of the United Sacred and Immaculate Hearts and the reign of peace. I invite you to be my peacemakers. Let your hearts live in the peace which comes from faith in the God who loves you so much that He sent His only Son to redeem you.

In that faith, please believe in the infinite value of your soul in the eyes of God. When you truly believe you are beloved of the Heart of your Redeemer, then peace will reign in your heart even in the midst of the chaos which surrounds you. Each day you make many little decisions. I invite you to choose always for God and for Love. Please allow Him to be the center of your life. Pray for detachment from all else. My Fatima message predicted many things for you. Some have come to fruition, some are in progress. As a loving mother, I have given your generation many messages and warnings. The message remains: Conversion, Repentance and Sacrifice, Pray, pray, pray, choose God daily. Do not deny the existence of Satan and evil forces prowling the earth at this time in history. Love above all else. I bless you once again. I invite you to unite with my Immaculate Heart for the salvation of all souls. I love you.

    Your Mother

8-20-93 Leaving Fatima
God Is a Jealous God

My dear children,

    I, your mother, love you and bless you. You have followed the footsteps of a journey of love. You have traced the footsteps of your Lord and Savior. I invite you to continue to walk in His footsteps. I invite you to be a disciple of His Love and Truth.

    God is a jealous God. He desires your heart. Be His completely. Do not put anyone or anything before Him please. Children, please do not offend the tender Heart of your Redeemer! He is offended when you do not love as He asks, when you do not trust as He asks, when you do not sacrifice as He asks and when you do not hope in Him as He asks. He offers His Heart to you constantly. How often do you offer Him your whole heart in prayer? He awaits you at each moment. Come to Him. Love Him. Adore Him. Believe and Trust. Accept His Mercy now. Prepare now. Put oil in your lamps now as the great and terrible day of the Lord approaches! Be alert. Evil is clever. Be aware. We are with you always. If you pray, you will find peace. If you love God and one another, you will find joy. When you return home, put on the renewed love and grace of your journey. Let

zeal for God and His house consume you. The Peace of my Son, your Lord Jesus Christ be yours now and forever. I love you.
    Your Mother

8-25-93 My home
Faith Is a Cornerstone of Your Salvation

My child,
    I, your Lord and Savior, will instruct you on "Faith." Please write. Faith is a cornerstone to your salvation. Faith is trust and belief in the fact that God does indeed exist. Faith acknowledges God without having seen Him in the flesh. I say unto you, My beloved, the Spirit of the Living God is truly with you and your faith in Him saves you. Without the gift of Faith a soul cannot partake in the gift of Salvation, for unless a soul proclaims that Jesus Christ is the Son of God, through whom the Father grants all things and through whom all are saved, unless the soul has faith in this truth, the soul will indeed perish.
    I have planted the seed of Faith in every soul. The soul who acknowledges this seed and indeed accepts their Lord and Savior who lives within them, who walks in the light of this Faith, grows in the truth. Like a healthy seedling it flourishes and bears fruit. For some the seed is squelched by the darkness within a soul who refuses to acknowledge the truth and, refusing to accept the gift of Faith, the soul searches for meaning in finite things, the world, the self. The seed is never given the climate to flourish and bear fruit; rather, it is buried deeper and deeper within the soul. Indeed, it is denied life itself. Still, My beloved, I offer My Light and nourishment to this soul. At every moment I love such a soul and I desire the soul to love Me in return. I patiently wait for the soul to accept divine nourishment in order that my seed grow and bear fruit.
    My little one, pray for an increase in Faith, for your generation is truly lacking in faith. Pray especially for those who profess to have faith with their lips and, indeed, when all is

well their faith is sufficient, but when tested by trials or suffering, oh how their faith fails them and fails Me, their Lord and Savior. So quickly they lose their peace, refusing to trust in Divine Providence. They cry out "Lord, do not try me" or "Lord, where are you?" These poor souls want to control their lives and, due to lack of faith, they are afraid and will not abandon themselves into the arms of a loving and merciful Father, refusing to allow God to be Lord of their life.

Oh generation of little Faith, stop offending the Father! Grow in your faith, hope, and love. He has offered you abundant life by offering you His only Son. Stop offending Him by not acknowledging Him in faith as God of all, Who is, Who was and always will be. My beloved little one, I solemnly say unto you there are few men of Faith today. Many walk in faithless darkness, and still many more profess to have faith, but indeed their faith is very weak and will not stand the test.

Oh My little one, for so long a time, you denied Me by your complete lack of Faith. You believed you controlled your destiny. Through the intercession of your loving Mother, who indeed led you by the hand, teaching you to pray, your soul resisted darkness and turned toward the light, accepted the truth and grew in faith and love. Now you have life abundant and indeed, you, My precious one, enjoy My Peace in your soul. Now you have true joy in Me. You see, My little one, I, Myself, have taught you there is no peace in trying to control your life. There is no peace in attempting to understand mysteries which no human mind can comprehend. There is only peace in faith which acknowledges God is God of all. There is only peace in abandonment to the holy Will of the Father. In true faith, love and happiness are found. So I ask you once again, indeed, I implore you, My beloved child, pray for an increase in faith, for soon, I, the Son of God, the Son of Man will be among you again to gather all My little ones whose faith is in Me, alone. I, your Lord and Savior, have spoken, instructing you, My little one, and I thank you for writing My words. My peace I give you. My love is yours. United are we forever.

Jesus of Mercy

8-29-93 My home
There Is a Raging Battle in My Soul

My Jesus, how little faith I truly have. Please forgive my lack of faith and hope in You. I have almost sunk into despair. There is a raging battle in my soul. I am beginning to understand that deep inside me, there is a resistance to abandonment, even to faith itself. So often this week I have temptations that my experiences of the spiritual world are illusions. Furthermore, there is a part of me that wants to rebel, a part of me that wants to return to the finite world and enjoy it. There is something deep within my human self which does not want to be brought into conformity with Your ways. Yet there is no harmony of body, mind, spirit until I have abandoned myself into Your loving arms.

God continues to reveal my sins to me. In this purification, in the light of His Truth, I find it difficult to believe God would commune with a soul as wretched as mine. Then He reminds me: "The well do not need a physician; I come to heal the sick." Still, deep within, I am truly afraid of letting Him down. My soul is in turmoil. I simply don't have the capacity to love as He asks. The truth is I am impatient with people, I expect too much of people, I lack understanding, and compassion. To love unconditionally is so difficult for me. I fail my Lord.

In His Mercy and Charity, He says to me:

My child,
I ask that you try to love as I have shown you. Try, My beloved; you will not fail Me. Persevere. All I require is that you be faithful unto Me. Even when you fall you do not fail Me. I allow this to teach you. Yes, My dear child, you are utterly dependent upon Me. My arms alone uphold you. I show you your wretchedness in order that you appreciate My Mercy. I hold before you your sins that you may repent, offer reparation, turn from sinning again and never grow proud. The world had seduced you. Oh how much more powerful is My Love! I have forgiven you; forgive yourself. You cannot love others unconditionally until you love yourself unconditionally, for have I not said to you "I show your sins, not to burden you but to set you

free from sin." I am cleansing you, not to bear down on you, rather to lift you up. Truly I say unto you, My beloved child, I desire to create in you a soul as white as snow. Therefore, when I hold before you your sins, let the tears that flow be tears of joy, for I am accomplishing My mighty work within your soul.

Trust Me, My little one, I prepare you for even higher union with Me, and nothing defiled can enter this union, and therefore I say unto you, you will be purified and purified, tried and purified again until you are radiant white. Then I will embellish you with a white gown and a white veil and you will await the groom. Then the groom shall descend upon you at the precise moment He has ordained for our union. Truly, it is I, your Lord, Jesus Christ, who has spoken thus unto you. Believe, My beloved; it is true.

My prayer: "Oh my God, without Your Grace, Your divine assistance, I will surely falter again. I will walk the path to perdition Lord - my spirit is that rebellious. Dying to myself is a death which must occur constantly because the self does not want to die. Yet it weighs down the spirit which desires to soar upward toward heaven, toward its Creator, its home. Oh Lord, that all the seeds of my rebellious ways would die! What freedom! Oh my Jesus, let the purification continue until the seeds have been put to death and buried never to weigh me down again. Then dear Jesus, my Love, only then will I be ready for the groom and the wedding banquet. Oh Lord, how long the exile? How long will my heart feel so burdened by my own sins, my own willfulness? Rescue me, dear Jesus, rescue me. Sometimes it's more than I can bear, this love I have for You. "

In union with Jeremiah I say to you: "You have seduced me and I let myself be seduced. You have taken me by force and prevailed, so I decided to forget about Him and speak no more in His name. But His word in my heart is like a fire imprisoned in my bones. I force myself to hold it in, but that is impossible!" Lord, I had no idea what was in store for me when You came into my heart and soul and caused me to burn with love for You. You caused me to fall completely in love with You, the power of Your Love being beyond my resistance. I could only sigh "yes." I had no idea of the pain of loving You. Nothing prepared me for the deprivation when You turn your face from me. Nothing prepared me for the detachment that would occur, that only You would satisfy me. Sometimes the pain is too much to bear and I really desire to turn from You in order to lessen the fire in my soul for You. However, I cannot turn away. Like the most powerful magnet, I cling to You. Even when I truly want to run from You, I cannot!

Like Jeremiah, I never asked for this, I never dreamed I'd hear Your words or write or speak them. It seems impossible. Then again, with You all things are indeed possible. So, like Jeremiah I have tried to keep Your words within me, and my heart burns with fire, for it is impossible to hold within me the power of Your Love or Your Words. So indeed I turn to You, cling to You, going forward, trying to be faithful and placing all my trust in You. I wish I could promise I will not doubt or that there is no unbelief in me, but You know there is. My Lord, I pray Your Mercy covers me, a sinner, and I pray for the grace of stronger faith, that my belief grow firmer and my unbelief cease.

You, who probe me, You who see the depths of my soul, see the fire of love that burns inside me for You. You reign in me. I cannot resist You. I await Your words and by Your grace, I will be obedient unto them. Even though I fear what You will require of me, I will to trust you for you have revealed You are all love, all mercy, all good. You will never harm me, rather always protect and shelter me. Most importantly, You have revealed to me a portion of Your incomprehensible Love for me. In your perfect love, I am yours. Whatever You require, I will do. Your words of love sustain me in this exile. I offer you much gratitude for my purifications, for I truly desire to be cleansed of my defilement. Even in the suffering, there is joy in loving You so completely. My God, how great thou art!

9-3-93 Prayer Group Rosary
Three Appearances: Joy, Tears and Triumph

As I began to pray aloud the second Joyful Mystery, the Visitation, I was overcome with the presence of Our Lady, my Mother, standing before me. Her presence permeated my being so intensely and profoundly, I had to make an extreme effort to say the Hail Mary's of the decade. As I prayed each Hail Mary, she became clearer and clearer to me. I could see her with the eyes of my soul more vividly than if I was seeing her with my bodily eyes. Her beauty, purity, gentleness, and motherly love was somehow deeply imparted into my heart, which began to burn with intense love. My soul was filled by her beauty, purity, and love. She was a living being of brilliant radiance, a pure and white light. The outlining of her figure was light of different colors. She was a three dimensional being of light from the waist up only, and she was holding the infant Jesus in her arms. She was radiantly beautiful. She looked to be approximately fifteen years of age. I have never experienced interiorly or exteriorly such pure beauty as she possesses.

I observed Mother Mary gazing adoringly upon her infant Jesus. Jesus was wrapped in white cloth and was a bundle of white and gold light rays. Somehow, infused into my soul was the love of the Mother for her Son and the Son for the Mother. The look exchanged between the Mother and her Son was one of intense and pure love. There are no words which I know to describe the ineffable love between Mother and Son. The adoration in the face of our Blessed Mother caused my heart to physically burn in my chest. Each Hail Mary was a concentrated effort. I desired to stop and take in what I was experiencing. I persevered through the decade, all the while experiencing the sight of Our Lady holding Jesus, while the profound love between Mother and Son was imprinted upon my soul.

My prayer sister continued the rosary praying the third Joyful Mystery, the Nativity. As she prayed, the Blessed Mother stood before her, holding the infant Jesus and then she presented the infant into her arms. There was a complete circle of love between the three of them. As the Joyful Mysteries continued to be prayed, Mother Mary went before each person and presented the infant Jesus to each of them. I observed each person adoring Jesus in their arms while Blessed Mother stood before them overseeing the exchange of love. My soul somehow experienced the love each soul had for Jesus and Mary.

Our Lady then spoke these words of love.

I am your gentle mother. I am holding the baby Jesus in my arms. I give Him unto you. Receive Him. Hold Him in your arms and in your heart. Love Him. Obey Him. Honor Him. Give thanks, for you are holding life. He is Love, all Love. So Pure and all Good is He. I present Him to you this night so that you, my little ones, may behold life and love in my Son, your Lord and Savior.

My little ones, in this present age, truly, so few love my Son as they should. I know you will receive Him, for I can see into your heart. You have prepared a place for Him, a nest, a warm and loving home for Him in your heart. Thank you, my little ones, for your faithfulness, your prayers, your love. Pray always. Pray always. Behold, I give you the infant Jesus to hold in your heart always. I am with you. I am your protection. Grace is poured upon you through me. I so love each one of you. Peace be yours through my Son, Jesus Christ, your Lord and Savior.

I somehow experienced some of Blessed Mother's joy. She was pleased with our prayer. She was joyful to be with us. She was happy because she entrusted her infant Son to us and we each received Him in love and adoration. Such joy, Oh my mother, my Mary! I was the last to hold Baby Jesus in my arms. And then I no longer saw Our Lady. Upon completing Joyful Mysteries, we prayed the Chaplet of Holy Wounds. After two decades of the Chaplet, I saw again, with the eyes of my soul, Our Lady. She was a full figure approximately three feet high, suspended in air about three feet off the ground. She wore all black. Tears rolled down her cheek. She did not speak. My heart broke to see her in all black and crying. By the end of the Chaplet, she disappeared.

We continued the Glorious Mysteries. By the second decade, Our Lady appeared again. Full figure, approximately three feet high, she stood atop the globe of the world. She wore a white gown with a blue Mantle and the Crown of twelve stars. Her lips were curved in a gentle smile. She stood over the head of the serpent and was crushing his head between her foot and the globe.

My heart felt her joy, her peace. And then she left us. She is beyond all description. There is nothing to compare. I tried to convey our heavenly visit to the group. I did not see Our Lady with my bodily eyes. I did not see her in my imagination or as if looking into a picture or television. I see her in the deepest recess of my being. I see her with the eyes of my soul. And it is more real than anything I have ever seen with my bodily eyes. Her beauty and love are engraved upon my soul. Not understanding what I was experiencing and desiring to record it, I looked to St. Teresa of Avila to help me record and understand. Her description of an intellectual vision is exact. "The vision is represented through knowledge given to the soul that is clearer than sunlight, a light without your seeing light, illumines the intellect."

9-14-93
Your Hope Must Enter Me Through the Cross

My Jesus, I adore You. When I look into Your eyes all that I am melts away and all that I need is given me. And in You I disappear. You are everything. The pain in my heart melts into joy because the reality of what You have done for me covers what little I can endure for You. I stand accused by mortals but in You I am received. Forgive my weakness, my Lord and Savior. How quickly I retreat from suffering. You have given so much to me and asked so little in return. How could I not offer You this little cross? You have ordained this cross for me that my own will be broken in order to give birth to Your Divine Will. You have ordained this cross to overcome my pride. I bless you, my Jesus, for working over the ground of my soul. Oh my Divine Lover, I truly wish I were capable of giving You this little cross by my own courage and strength, but I cannot accomplish this without your divine assistance; my imperfection is that great. I heard: **My daughter, do you love Me?** Oh Lord, dear Jesus, You know that I love You. **Do not be afraid. I will never leave you. You are afraid My little one, aren't you?** Yes, Lord, I am afraid of never seeing You or hearing You again. I am afraid of offending You, of hurting You. I am afraid of falling into my old ways. Yes, I am afraid of what You'll require of me. And I am afraid that although I will to suffer if You require, as You have foretold me, my mortal self fears suffering and wants to run from the pain.

My daughter,

Again I say unto you, I will never leave you. Have I not been with you in this trial, even in the silence? Each time you turned to Me in prayer, did I not grant you My Peace? My child, am I not worthy of all your trust? Please do not be afraid of the one who holds you and loves you. Perfect Love casts out all fear. I am in you and you are in Me. Your accusers cannot harm you. My Mother and I have protected you from many demons who surrounded you for many days. They attempt to harm you but I will not allow them to touch you. Do not be afraid. The evil one is furious with you. How he delights when you lose your peace. How he loves to torment you. Oh My child, if you only knew the angels I have sent to surround you. And so My beloved, take up your cross, ever so small, deny your very self, and follow Me. I am with you every step of the way. My Divine Will for you has been spoken through the words of your soul's director. Obey him and you obey Me. I have spoken through him and thus I have shown you the way through him. Trust in him and you trust in Me. Doubt him and you doubt Me. My daughter, give thanks for the work I am accomplishing in your soul. Your weakness attracts Me so that I desire to cover you completely with My strength. Believe, daughter! It is true!

I, your Lord and Savior, send you forward. Spread the truth about the darkness which grips your country, covered in the stains of the blood of the innocents. Your country will suffer one calamity after another. Money and power are the god's of your country now, and in choosing death over life it chooses its own demise. My Mother's work brings light to dispel the darkness of the death factories. Did I not foretell you would sacrifice your very self for the good of many souls? Did you not offer to follow in My footsteps? Your love must enter Me through the Cross, as My Love entered you through the Cross. My daughter, have I not dried your tears tonight? Is there anymore that you need? Please receive My Mother, your Mother.

Mary spoke:

My child,

You need not defend yourself. My Immaculate Heart will defend you. Be obedient. Thank you for sharing my work. You are a partner in my peace plan and in the salvation of souls. Keep much in your heart, as I did. By Faith and Love you come to realize the Divine Providence of your heavenly Father works for the greater good of all. By humility and obedience you will receive a crown of glory in your Father's Kingdom. My child, you cannot begin to imagine what awaits you in your Father's Kingdom, your home. Before the crown of glory, receive the crown of thorns. Bear it for love alone, my little one. His Grace shall be sufficient. When your peace is disturbed - pray. The United Sacred and Immaculate Hearts will be with you and your soul will be flooded with the peace of the Living God. I am the protector of you and my beloved priest. Let us pray the "Lord's Prayer" together, please. Thank you for responding to my call. I love you.

Your Mother

I love you, my Mother. I adore you, dear Jesus and I love You. Be glorified in me and all souls.

9-17-93 My home
Prayer of Silence

My Beloved Jesus, when I am before You in the tabernacle, there is such a silence in my soul, the depth of which I never knew could exist. Before You then, I enter such a profound stillness that I am unaware of my senses, unaware of my breathing, unaware of my heart beating, as if I don't have a body. I'm with You, yet I don't even have a thought or an image - nothing - only stillness and peace. Where do my thoughts go? I want to contemplate You or put myself into a particular gospel scene or perhaps meditate on a word from Scripture, but I am immediately taken to a silent, imageless place, where only peace exists. Lord, humanly speaking, I feel I haven't prayed. Spiritually, I know that I must be praying because of the profound peace and stillness which exists in my soul when I'm there with You in the tabernacle.

I pray, dear Jesus, for the grace to integrate this prayer of silence before the tabernacle into all the areas of my life. I am talkative and excitable, and then I lose my sensitivity to the Holy Spirit within me. As I write this Lord, I'm not sure this should be my prayer. It seems very lofty, something a very virtuous person may attain but it feels beyond me except by a great deal of Your Grace. I am so poor in spirit and so lacking in virtue, there is nothing but for me to enter prayer at Your feet. I am putty in Your hand. I am Yours to mold, shape, bend and use in any way You desire.

Something in my spirit prevents me from aspiring to be holy. I know I cannot be. Yet You call us all to holiness. You alone can accomplish this in my soul. I will be as holy as you desire me to be. Only You can accomplish this in me. I am poor and wretched. I depend on You for everything. I am the clay - You the potter. Whatever You create in me, however small or large, will be beautiful because You create only beauty. I thank You, my Savior, for holding the clay that I am in Your powerful hand and loving my nothingness. How good, compassionate and merciful You are. My Lord, how much You are teaching me. The lesson of breaking my own will for the Divine Will is a painful one, but necessary and good for my soul. Thank you, for ordaining my cross out of pure love. Sacred Heart of Jesus, the fire of Your Love is in me. I love You.

I continue to feel the presence of evil spirits around me. They cause agitation. Evil tempts me to selfishness, vanity or sometimes excessive criticism of myself. Evil tries to keep my soul from contemplating Jesus. If evil can cause even a slight agitation, my soul is unable to be united with my Lord, as attention is drawn to the disturbance within, so that my peace is gone. Then evil has succeeded in diverting my contemplation of God. I rebuke you, prince of darkness. Be gone from me in the name of Jesus of Nazareth! St. Michael, protect me, please!

9-19-93
Doubting Thomas

My beloved daughter,

You are tasting of the divine riches of My Love. My arms enfold you. My Love is as oil poured over you, and you are absorbing the Divine Oil, to the core of your very being. Your soul is saturated by My Divine Love. Oh how My Mercy has covered your wretchedness. You, who are a doubting Thomas, look what I have done for you. I come to you and reveal Myself to you in the way I have come throughout the ages to many chosen souls. For many are the souls needed to build up My battered Body (Church) and to overcome the present darkness. I softened your hardened heart, that I may saturate it with My Divine Love, that you would feel with your heart and think not so much with your head because the intellect resists things spiritual, unseen, and desires to reason and receive concrete evidence. But the softened heart receives much in faith, especially as My Divine Love envelops the heart. And thus prepared, Divine Light enters the soul, and the soul ascends to higher and higher levels, always moving toward divine union with its Creator.

Thus is the journey of a chosen soul. Your soul has been chosen to do the work of the Divine Master. It is My Father who has ordained this, choosing the weakest of vessels to do His work. He has chosen one doubting Thomas to touch many doubting Thomases. I am your Divine Teacher, and much is there for you to learn. You shall be taught in many ways by many teachers. Not only shall I speak to you in this way, where you write, but also I shall teach you by your spiritual director, My priest, chosen to teach you much. And I have placed many teachers in your life, for indeed it is no accident or coincidence that I have placed many chosen souls in your path. All are part of your formation in Me. Oh how abundantly I have graced you, My beloved little one. I have chosen you unto Myself, and indeed I will use you to accomplish My Father's work on earth. There will be much to bear in the years to come. By My Divine Love in your soul you will bear much. Knowing you are so very beloved of My Sacred Heart, there is your joy and your strength. Indeed, it shall come from Me.

The evil one sets out his traps for you. He is clever. He studies you, thus observing your weaknesses. He desires to entrap you. Do not fear. Rather be alert and pray always. My Mother is by your side, and many angels surround you and your loved ones. And My priest, your director, receives much heavenly protection. Continue to come unto Me, to sit at My feet, to listen to My words that I may teach you. Pray always, My daughter, pray always. I am with you in prayer and in all things. Rejoice and be glad, for abundant life I am pouring upon you. Let gratitude fill your heart and joy fill your soul. Receive whatever cross I send to you with love. For it is by the Cross that your soul is prepared for divine union, and it is the way a soul can bear fruit for the Kingdom of God. Each cross I send you has been pressed to My divine lips and given unto you by Love Himself. Receive it, press it to your lips and return it unto Me. Thus you shall grow more and more into the image and likeness of your Creator. My peace I give you. I love you My daughter, I love you.

Jesus

9-21-93
Many Have Decided for Darkness

My dear child,

When the lance pierced My side, water and blood gushed from My Body. There, the fountain of Infinite Mercy flowed onto the earth for all mankind. I exclude no one. I am for everyone. Divine Mercy is offered to one and all. Look at the Cross. What more can I offer mankind? In this present age, look and see how My merciful Father ordains to send mercy upon the earth by sending My Mother to visit her children in many areas of the world, to call all souls to reconcile and return to God, indeed, to offer His Mercy and pardon for ways of sinfulness and godlessness. If only My children would repent and decide for God! Look and see, beloved, how many souls I, Myself, have chosen to instruct toward holiness.

Understand, dear child and let it penetrate your heart that the Father so loved the world that He gave His only Son, that whoever believes in Him may not be lost but may have eternal life. The Father did not send Me to condemn the world. Instead, through Me the world is to be saved. Whoever believes in Me will not be condemned. He who does not believe is already condemned because he has not believed in the name of the only Son of God. This is how the judgment is made. Light has come into the world, and people loved darkness rather than light because their ways were evil. For whoever does wrong hates the light and doesn't come to the light for fear that his deeds will be shown as evil. But whoever lives according to the truth comes into the light so that it can be clearly seen that his works have been in God.

Truly, truly, I say unto you, the Most Holy Trinity and the Blessed Virgin Mary are grieved, so very grieved by mortal man's refusal to accept Divine Love and Mercy. Indeed, many prefer the darkness. Many have decided for darkness. Thus the world grows darker and darker, and there will be much to suffer, for every soul is fully accountable before God.

It is pleasing to Me and to My Mother that you pray for the conversion of sinners and the salvation of souls. This is brought about by the mercy of the Father, the ransom of the Son, the love of the Holy Spirit, through the intercession of the Blessed Mother, in cooperation with the blood of the Martyrs and the sufferings of victim souls, the intercession of the Saints, and the prayers and fasting (sacrifices) of fervent souls. Indeed, My child, there will be more victim souls, more martyrs and more fervent souls raised up in order to overcome the present darkness. The value of your prayers, your sacrifice, is beyond your comprehension. Truly, souls are saved when you cooperate with the Will of the Father in all things, especially suffering and in loving. Even little injustices done to you, even small sacrifices, not only benefit your soul but many souls. Do you see how we are one family, how one affects all? The rays of My Mercy flow abundantly upon this generation, yet few receive because many are busy about the world.

Oh My little one, if only My children realized, in choosing the world, they choose death. Beloved, tell My people of My infinite fountain of Mercy - now - the hour is late. Pray and sacrifice for the salvation of the world. Light up the darkness. Let all who see you, see that you are different because you have accepted My Mercy and you have decided to follow Me into the Light. Be there for many, My daughter. My peace I give you. I love you.

Jesus of Mercy

9-23-93 Tabernacle
America

My dear children,

I am your mother who loves you. Truly, I desire to take you by the hand and lead you to Jesus. My Son is the way to eternal life. He is the only way. My dear little children, I desire for you to know how truly serious is the condition of the world in these days of confusion and deception. How grieved the Father is by this generation's rebellious ways. The cup of Divine Justice is near to overflowing. There will be much to suffer.

Oh America, land of exquisite beauty, land of rich soil and plentiful bounty, land of abundant resources, how graced you have been. God has highly favored you and all the while you are turning your face from Him. You have taken for granted all that He has given you. The rebels are many. In the name of freedom, you sin by killing, hating, oppressing. God, Church, Family, Love and Charity are less and less a part of American life. Money and power are who you serve.

My dear children, pray for your country to return to God now! Reconcile, love and offer reparation! Be a people who serve God first. Please take seriously the warnings God has provided for you. As your loving mother, I wish to ask you, my children whom I have raised up, to be light in the darkness. You are to let your light shine. The world will come to know more and more suffering. Your country will grow darker as rebels lead many astray. Do not fear. I am here to bring hope. Even in the midst of suffering I shall protect you. If you place your hand in mine, then give your heart unto my Immaculate Heart. I will accompany you through the darkness. In the chaos you will have peace in your soul. The peace found only in my Son, your Lord and Savior. Your prayers and fasting for conversions and the salvation of the world are very important. My message is urgent. Do not delay.

Please do not be indifferent to what is happening in your country, your neighborhood, your very own family and your very own heart and soul. Daily there are opportunities to love and serve. The poor and oppressed are all around you, needing the love of Jesus Christ which is in you. Lawlessness is all around you; just look at the innocent babies who are aborted. When I see this, my tears become tears of blood. These babies, who are denied human life, partake in eternal life in the spirit as their heavenly family welcomes them with divine love. But woe to those having anything to do with this denial of life, including those who look the other way so as not to see the truth!

I speak to you, my children, to warn you of the coming of God's justice upon your country. I call you to prayer and sacrifice. I ask you to live the sacramental life. I ask you, put God first and prayer first - make them a priority each day, each hour, each minute. It is critical. Do not be like infants, tossed about in the confusion. For this is how the rebel will tempt you, desiring you to be fearful and weak, focusing on yourself and your needs. I have raised you to maturity in faith that you may uphold one another and intercede for the entire family of man. Be steadfast. Be secure in my maternal protection and motherly love. Listen to the Holy Spirit. He speaks to each of you in your heart. Pray! Pray! Pray! There you will find strength and direction.

Please surrender your will, as I did, unto the Divine Will. Then God may use you in the salvation of all souls. Your Father, who is all Loving and all Merciful, will shower graces to those who open their hearts to receive. Through prayer, fasting, and Eucharist and Reconciliation, you will truly save many souls on the path to perdition. Please assist me. I implore you.

Your Mother

10-3-93 My Home
Feed Me Your Divine Will

My daughter,
 The hour of our union has been ordained by the Father, and His perfect Will shall be accomplished at precisely the moment He has chosen. Until that moment is at hand, trust in the Father, for He Himself is preparing you. He is raising you toward the Divine Union. He Himself desires it. He rejoices in each step you take, each "yes" you give unto the Most Holy Trinity. Your obedience pleases Him. Though you do not comprehend, you obey, and grace moves you to increase in love, faith, and abandonment. Have I not promised My Grace would always be sufficient? Come, come unto Me. Child, I desire to teach you. Child, your food shall be the Divine Will of the Father. Ingest His Will. The Divine Will shall be your sustenance. Ingest it, that you may live it.
 Soul, please pray with Me:
 "Father, feed me Your Divine Will that I may live it always. May Your perfect and holy Will be my nourishment. Thank you, Father, for feeding me life. That I may live your will, I beseech Thee, Almighty Father, to clothe me in wisdom. Embellish me with wisdom that I may walk always in the light and in truth. Abba, I am yours. When your Fatherly eyes gaze upon me, see that I am covered in the precious blood of your only Son. Have mercy on my soul and lead me along the path to salvation. Father, I give you my will. Please feed me Your holy Will. All Glory and Honor be Yours Almighty Father. Amen."
(Prayer was dictated by Jesus)

 Interiorly I was given the vision of a scroll on which the Divine Will for me had been inscribed and I was asked to ingest the scroll of the Divine Will and somehow my soul tasted the sweetness and joy filled me. (Happened very quickly)
 Dear Jesus, the Father's will shall be my bread. May Your Grace sustain me when I have temptations to reject the bread of Divine Will, especially if it tastes bitter sometimes. Help me please, to recall the sweetness I was just given. Oh that I would never hesi-

tate to say "yes" to the Most Holy Trinity. Oh that I would yield always to His Holy Will for love alone, like my Blessed Mother, so humble and pure. Dearest Beautiful Lady, help me please. I love you, united Sacred and Immaculate Hearts.

10-21-93 Tabernacle following communion
Divine Love Bridges the Abyss

My Beloved,

Your sighs of love delight Me. Yes, My little one, your Creator, the One who fashioned you with His own hands, receives your love as a salve that heals the many lacerations of My Heart, lacerations caused by souls who refuse My Love, My Mercy, My Grace. My own creation takes the time for everything else in their lives except time to receive the love and grace I desire to shower upon them. So many souls employ their time on emptiness. My Sacred Heart is a furnace burning and overflowing. If only souls would take the time to receive My Love, they would partake in the feast of Divine Love.

My little one, see how I desire to bestow My riches upon every soul, and see how few are willing to receive. My own creation lacerates My Body constantly. However, when a soul takes the time to receive Me, the soul partakes in the feast of love. How I desire to delight that soul, as I am truly delighted to receive love from My creatures. Though there is an abyss between the sovereignty of the Creator and the poverty of the creature, Divine Love bridges that abyss. My Father gave over His only Son to extend from heaven to earth, through the abyss to His creation. Indeed, My blood flowed to prove that God is Love. When My Love is received in a soul who returns My Love, I am so pleased that I bless more souls, because I am moved to more generosity, more mercy, and justice is delayed. And so it is that the feast of Love we partake in, not only feeds and delights one another, but serves for the good of all souls.

I say unto you My beloved, thank you for allowing grace to lead you to the banquet of love. Few souls allow their Lord to lead them to the feast. So it is that I receive your love deep within My Sacred Heart, causing My Love and Mercy to over-flow onto My creation. Souls who ardently desire Me shall receive Me. Oh how I long to be received into many souls as I have been received by you. There is no favoritism with Me. Too often I am refused entry. I am turned away by indifferent souls. I say unto you, thank you for allowing My entry. Thank you for partaking in the feast of My Love. You are a steward of My Divine Love and grace. I am supping with you. Draw from Me. Know that while I am delighted by your love, while you are delighted by My Love, souls are revived, death averted, justice delayed. This is the fruit of the feast of Love. Continue to partake. The feast is never ending. Many are invited, few partake. My peace I give you.

Jesus of Mercy

11-7-93
Many Messengers, One Word

My dear child,

Do you see how I guide your every step? See how I bring together souls chosen for My Mission, My Harvest? As you share with one another, are not your fears put to rest? See how I have chosen many to rebuild My Church? You shall come to know one another well. Through many trials in the near future you shall uphold one another. Is your faith not greatly increased when you hear how others are hearing My Voice as you are? I teach many as I teach you. I teach the same word today as My Word of old. For there is only one Word, the same always, never ever changing. The Teacher and the Message are the same, though spoken through different vessels. It pleases Me to see My little ones share My gifts, in love and gratitude, and without jealousy. Indeed, I am blessing many as I weave My faithful remnant. Your loving and sharing give glory to your Lord and Savior, for I have taught you that alone you cannot stand, but together, you give glory to the Father, through and in Me, the only Son of God. My Mercy, Love and Peace are yours.

Jesus of Mercy

Do you love Me, My daughter?

Oh my Jesus, with all my strength and capacity to love, I do love You and I adore You. How is it you ask what you already know when You look within me?

Because I too love being told I am loved! In the spirit of dear Francis, live spiritually poor, let charity reign in you and help rebuild My church. My tender hearted Francis will assist you. I love you, little one. Go in My peace.
Jesus

11-9-93 My home 9PM
Spiritual Guidance

My dear daughter,
Please allow Me to teach you regarding spiritual direction. You are having temptations to be independent of your spiritual director. Please understand My child, you are dependent upon Me, your Lord, Jesus Christ only. Yet you are interdependent upon your spiritual director. It is not the man who you depend upon, it is his spiritual guidance. Your reluctance to call upon him is really a matter of your pride, not simply an act of kindness toward him. This is not pleasing to Me. You have been confused in this matter, so now I am showing you the way. My Grace abounds in him and through him for your soul. He has been divinely chosen and guided for the good of your soul. Since he represents Me in the flesh, you are to seek his counsel in all matters of your spiritual life. Complete obedience to him is required of you.
Jesus

11-14-93
The Season of Your Soul

My dear child,

Though there will be many seasons of your soul, the illumination of My Divine Love will exist endlessly, whether you sense the darkness of winter, the liveliness of spring, the heat and dryness of summer, or the coolness of fall. I have provided a lengthy springtime for you. Think of a rosebud in spring. You were the rosebud closed tightly, waiting to bloom, needing the spring showers and sunshine to move you to open up unto a new world, the world of Divine Love. So I came to you and provided My endless fountain of spring water, life-giving water. And My Divine Sunshine penetrated your closed heart. Slowly as the rosebud opens up, you began to bloom. For indeed, the Son Himself had penetrated you. Your fragrance became heavenly instead of worldly. And I blew on you fragrance, allowing others to partake in its newfound loveliness. Love in springtime is so new, so fresh, so delightful. I allowed all your senses to be overcome with the delight of My Divine Love in your soul.

Now, dear one, I shall take you through all the seasons of your soul. You have tasted some of the dryness of summer. Like the roses in your garden, you will thirst for My living water and you may feel scorched by the dryness, but you will not wither completely. You will remain in waiting because you know I will come for you. You shall come to know, all the seasons have their profound beauty even in the pain of what may feel like separation. You must recall always, My Divine Light exists in you even when the clouds cover it completely. Still, I am with you always. Through all the seasons your fragrance will grow more and more heavenly. Unlike the roses in your garden, which die in the darkness and dryness, you will grow into a rose of rare beauty in the darkness and dryness. The senses must be denied for spiritual growth.

The key to persevering through the seasons of your soul is to look within your heart and your soul, in contemplation; there you'll find Me. Do not look for Me without - in the world, or in people, places or things. In the depth of your being I am. Come unto Me there. Enter My Heart in prayer. Trust in Me and persevere through darkness, dryness, temptations, attacks, always anticipating springtime. Go in peace.

Jesus

11-15-93
Seek Me

My dear children,

I am your Lord, your God, and I am Love. Therefore, your journey is to be a journey of love. I am Mercy. Therefore, your journey is to be a journey of mercy. I am justice. Therefore, your journey is to seek justice always. Tonight I invite you into an intimate relationship with your Lord. I know you intimately, for I knew you before I formed you in your mother's womb, and I loved you and I chose you.

Now I invite you to know Me intimately. Now do not seek Me in people, places, or things, or the spirit of the world will surely rob you of who you are in Me. Rather, seek Me in the depths of your own heart, your own soul, for My Peace and My Love are the cornerstones of your soul. Look for Me within, and in contemplation you will find Me loving you. Recall that the language of love is without words. Simply "be" with Me and I will fill you with the certainty of knowing you have found Me and I, you. Here, within, you will taste of the everlasting love I have for you. My peace I give unto you.

Jesus

11-17-93
True Self Knowledge

Dear child,

Do not become discouraged as I reveal to you true self knowledge. When I allow you to see your brokenness, your weaknesses, your sinful tendency, I give you a most valuable gift. When you think you are not progressing in overcoming your sinfulness, you truly are. Please understand that I love you in your brokenness and weaknesses. You get discouraged because you expect perfection; not I. Do you not understand that I am the covering for your sins? The self knowledge I allow you keeps you in Me. For when you look at yourself, you'll see only wretchedness. So then you'll turn to Me and find beauty and perfection. Having taken on the fullness of the human being, I am fully aware of human weakness. It is right that you reject sin and try to overcome your passions.

This is a battle you will always partake of no matter the level of spiritual maturity I choose to take you to. You will always battle to deny your very self. Do not be anxious about this. Be patient with yourself as I am with you. I see the purity of your intentions. You are to love yourself in spite of your sinfulness because I am in you. Do not be discouraged because I heighten your awareness of your sins, as this is a true grace. There is still much of yourself which is to be denied, and this shall be accomplished in My Way, My Time, and by My Grace. I desire you to be at peace with yourself. Do not scrutinize your ways, rather My ways. Do not complicate this process by delving into self. Rather, it shall be made simple by delving into Me. Look not elsewhere, only to Me. My Mother assists you always and, as the Angels attended Me in the Garden of Gethsemane, they attend you. Be at peace, My love.

Jesus

11-19-93 My home 3PM Message for Prayer Group
Every Human Being is My Temple

Little ones,

I am your Lord, your God. Therefore, I ask you, love Me with all your heart, all your soul, all your mind and with all your strength. Above all, people, places and things, I am to be the center of your very existence. In loving Me will flow the grace to love yourselves. Truly, few of My children can love themselves. Few believe I exist in them, yet they are My Temples. Every human being is My Temple called to love, purity, dignity, mercy, charity and hope. Sometimes My Temples become defiled by allowing the rebel, the deceiver, to enter in some area of their lives. Still, I desire they turn, repent, and come unto their Lord. Not one soul do I wish to lose.

You, who have gathered under the Mantle of My Mother, have, by My Grace, become My Vessels of Love. I have poured My Divine Love and Light into each of your souls. Of you, I ask extraordinary love, supernatural love, made possible by the love I provide for you. Now, do not fear, rather trust, as I say to you that days of trial and tribulation shall come to pass in the near future. These days will require extraordinary love from each one of you. Do not become discouraged or worried about your own spiritual state or the state of your family members. Rather, invest in love and prayer and focus on your Lord. I am merciful toward My own. I will see within. Your intentions are pure and good. Because you have loved, prayed and been merciful, I shall deal mercifully with your families.

The call to extraordinary love is urgent. I ask you to extend love beyond Me, yourselves, and your families to My very poor and needy people. As vessels of My Love and Light, it is you who shall be the catalyst of love to the darkness and poverty of the world. The days ahead will be challenging. Do not focus on the hardship; rather, see them as an opportunity to love and serve your Lord and God. Though the days of hardship seem long, they are nothing to your days in the Glory of your God. Take heart and courage in Me. I shall never abandon you, My little ones. My Love. My Peace.

Jesus

11-21-93 Feast of Christ the King
King of Kings

My child,

I am King of all Kings, Lord of all. My Father has glorified Me as I have glorified Him. I have taken My seat at the right hand of the Father. Together with the Holy Spirit, We reign in His Kingdom in Heaven. As the Father so loves His creation, He desires to welcome all souls into His heavenly Kingdom as children of the King. Such is the inheritance laid before all creation. However, His creatures have rejected their inheritance by rebelling against the King. Indeed, they proclaim themselves king, thus the refusal to serve the true King. The loyal and loving servants who will partake in their inheritance are few, much to the regret of all heaven.

My child, what would you have your Lord do to procure the heavenly inheritance for all His people, which has not already been done? What greater sacrifice than the King laying down His life? What greater sacrifice than the King becoming the Servant of all. Still, man desires to rule as lord of himself and master of his earthly life, which he lives as if it is his only life, denying it is prelude only, to an eternal life in God. Is it so difficult for mankind to comprehend that, when you surrender completely to the Lord and Master of all and choose to serve the King, you partake fully in the royal family, not merely as servant but as a royal priesthood? For when My people humble themselves before their King and say: "I will serve," I shall reply: "I will not call you servant but rather friend." In that friendship, the King will grant all your needs, upholding you in all areas of your earthly life until welcoming you into His heavenly court for all eternity. Man's rebellion and arrogance leads to the emptiness of false happiness on earth and robs the soul of true happiness in heaven. Through pride and impatience, man forfeits an inheritance beyond any human imagination.

Joy is for those of My children who discover that obedience and humility to the King is the way to the fulfillment of love everlasting. So, as the Father glorified Me, I glorify Him. He ordained I enter you, wretched though you are, in order that you glorify Him. Therefore dear one, humble yourself, obey and surrender all to the King of Kings. Blessed are they who give glory to the King. Their lowliness shall be exalted in the Kingdom of God, where the Most Holy Trinity, Father, Son, and Holy Spirit, reign together with the Most Blessed Virgin Mary, Queen of Heaven and Earth. Go in peace, dear one. My Love.

Jesus

11-27-93 Eve of First Sunday of Advent
The Truth That Entered My Soul - I Am a Sinner

The gospel today tells me to "keep watch" and "wake from sleep." When the Messiah came, few were really expecting him. John 1:11 says, "He came unto His own and His own received him not." Most people of the time were blind to what was most essential in their lives and in the life of the world. Two thousand years later, this is true still. I promised my Beloved this night to prepare for His coming as never before. I've asked Mother Mary to assist me in Advent season that my love grow more fervent, never lukewarm. I asked that she assist me to discipline myself in order to grow in the virtues which reign in her: faith, hope and charity. I will decide for God every minute of every day, rebuking the enemy, his temptations and disciplining myself in order that I not compromise my prayer time. My goal is to make this Advent a most spiritual time to prepare for the coming of my Lord. As the three wise men presented their gift that Holy Night, I shall present my gift to the infant King. I shall present my soul and my will to my Lord. Because He is merciful, the stains of sins which cover my gift will be consumed by the fire He himself ignited, and He shall behold a soul, a poor soul, inflamed with love. Oh Holy Night! Thank you, Father, for the gift of Your Son. You are Love.

There is so much happening in my soul. It's difficult to know what to record. I'll write what I feel I am to share with my director. Perhaps one day my sons will read and understand the most incredible and beautiful journey God has allowed my soul in these days of Mercy for the world. If there is one common thread in my writings, it is the continuous thread of God's unfathomable Mercy poured in abundance into my poor soul. If not for His Mercy, I would not taste of these heavenly graces. More importantly, my soul would still be sick and darkened as a soul enslaved in the world.

Prior to my conversion in 1990, the eyes of my soul were so dulled that my reasoning thought itself to be self-sufficient. As J. Escrivia describes perfectly the darkness in which my soul existed, I will quote him: "Reason thinks itself to be self-sufficient, dispensing with God as unnecessary. Seduced by this temptation, the human intelligence regards itself as the center of the universe, reverting with delight to the words of the serpent in Genesis, 'You shall be like Gods.' And being filled with love of self, turns its back on God's love. Our existence can, in this way surrender itself unconditionally into the hands of the enemy "Pride of Life." Let us not fool ourselves, this is the worst of all evils, the root of every conceivable deviation."

So let it be known that my soul existed in the darkness and sin described above. On the "outside" I was a success. I never stopped the rat race long enough to think about the inside. Though the world seduced me, I definitely believed in God. (Thanks to my parents and twelve years of Catholic school.) He was a distant God who would judge me at my death. I kept the Ten Commandments out of fear, not love. The pride of life distorts the truth and the soul is darkened. I thought myself to be happy. I was enjoying the world. I "had it all." I had a loving family and financial success, which enabled me to do whatever pleased my desires. By age 35 I'd experienced much of the "excitement" and "success" the world could offer.

I do not exaggerate when I say, the excitement and adventure that the finite world offers is nothing compared to the wonders of the spiritual world. From the moment of my conversion, God has taken my soul on the most exciting journey, beyond my imagination. Prior to my conversion, I was in denial of a most important truth. My soul was darkened by the pride of life, which says "You are not a sinner." When God granted me the gift of my conversion, He entered my soul, overcoming me with His Omnipotence and Love. In His Presence, my soul cried out "I am a sinner." The Truth had entered my soul! And by the love He ignited in me, I knew He was not a distant God. In fact, He was the most intimate love I'd ever experienced. My soul found its center, which is God. As God is Love, my soul discovered a world of Divine Love. Only in this Divine Love does my soul find fulfillment. True happiness and true self are found as the soul acknowledges God as Master and Lover and places itself at His service. How liberating is truth! The spiritual world is infinite beauty and love. An eternity is not enough time to thank my God for the gift of my conversion.

Prayer: "Furnace of Love, You ignited my very soul. Now I am aflame with love for You. You dispelled the dullness and darkness of my soul with your brilliant light and truth. Your Love sustains me. Your Blood washes me clean. Your Body is my daily sustenance. Your Word lights my way. Zeal for Your house consumes me. Loving You is my life now. I praise Your Holy Name. Oh my Beloved, place me in the furnace of Your Sacred Heart and never allow the flame of our love to grow cold. My entire being aches and longs for You. You are my home now. How long, Lord? How long before I can live in You completely? Sometimes waiting is unbearable. Amen."

11-29-93 2 PM My spiritual director asked I pray for the Church. **Put My House in Order**

As I began to pray for the Church, I heard interiorly:

Dear child,
Indeed I will come to put My House in order. Renegades have penetrated My House and she is in shambles. My beloved

Bride, My Church, you are to be adorned with truth, not scandal. Heresy penetrates the walls of My house and your unfaithfulness echoes within. Like the groom who gazes into the eyes of his bride and finds infidelity within, My Sacred Heart bleeds profusely for you. The groom will revive his bride! The cornerstone remains unchanged. The renegades will be banished. Woe to those who have led my sheep astray, offering falsehood disguised as new light and modernism.

There is one truth, the same forever. My Word is word for all ages. My Vicar, My Peter of today, walks in light and grace of the truth. He leads My bride on the right path. Walk in union with him and you shall remain in union with the Father, Son and Holy Spirit. My Mother stands beside him always, loving, guiding and protecting. The falsehood of the renegades will cause division in My house. Justice shall overcome anyone sowing division. My Mercy will cover the innocent victims. My Heart bleeds as the apostasy has begun. Pray for My Bride, dear one. Indeed, I shall revive her to the fullness of her radiance, as she remains in Me and I in her.

As I asked My beloved Francis, I ask you, dear one, rebuild My Church? Will you be My hands, My feet, My mouthpiece? Will you allow Me to use you to revive My Bride? Will you love her as I love her? The seeds of division have been sown. Be alert, awake. Weep with Me. But do not despair. She and I will be triumphant! My love. My peace.

Jesus

12-1-93
Consecration on the Feast of the Immaculate Conception

Dear Child,

Please write for my little ones who make their consecration to me on the Feast of my Immaculate Conception. Thank you, dear ones, for deciding to allow your Mother to lead you to your Savior, my son, Jesus. As He glorifies the Father, He and I will lead you to glorify the Father. My beloved Spouse, the Holy Spirit, will fill your soul, enabling you to accomplish the Will of the Father, just as He descended upon my soul, leading me by love and grace to give God my "fiat."

While each one of you has a distinct journey toward your sanctification, I will lead you along the path of that journey, teaching humility and obedience in order that you increase in the virtues of Faith, Hope, and Charity. As you dedicate to my Immaculate Heart all your works and goods, spiritual and temporal, I will cherish all that you give me, as a loving mother cherishes the simplest gift given from her child with the greatest of love. I will gather all that you dedicate to me for the good of all souls toward the salvation of the world, for such is the Will of the Father. Today we are bonded by the infinite love of the Holy Spirit. Let us give thanks and rejoice, for the Mighty One has done great things for us, and holy is His name forever. As I was chosen, so you have been chosen.

My children, the journey to the glorious union with your God is truly a journey of love and faith. The ultimate measure of love being the cross, please accept whatever cross God sees fit to have you carry. Do not fear the cross. In your crosses or your joys, you are never alone. Nor are you tried beyond your capacity to bear. Your earthly journey, with its tribulation and pain, is but a flicker of time. Even on earth you can foretaste of the heavenly banquet awaiting you when you allow your soul to soar to the heights of love in prayer and contemplation. And in the service of your Lord and Savior through your brothers and sisters, you look into the eyes of God as He exists in every soul. As your Mother who loves you, I will assist you in all your needs.

As the Holy Spirit has ignited the flame of His love and renewal from the four corners of the earth in order to usher in the season of peace on earth, let us go forward as His peacemakers in a world searching for the peace which only my Son, Jesus Christ, can provide. Blessed are the peacemakers for they shall be called the children of God. In all things strive for peace, spiritual peace. Above all, have faith and love. Your spiritual life is not an illusion! Every day your mortal body grows closer to returning to dust and every day your spiritual body, your soul, grows closer to its home eternal, our Creator, our Lord, our Triune God. Glory to God forever. Even now He prepares a place for you at His heavenly banquet. Thank you for responding to my call. In my heart you live. I

love you. Pray, pray, pray above all. That is the key!
Mary, your Mother, the Immaculate Conception
    My Maternal blessing will be given to each on their day of
consecration.

12-2-93
Advent: What Will You Present Your Newborn King?

Dear Child,
    Please write for my little ones. I am your Mother who is with
you. I come to bless you during Advent, a season of preparation, a
season of anticipation, a season of love and joy. Think of the joy
and wonder which overcame me as God overshadowed my lowly
being with the power of His Holy Spirit, and ordained His Son to
enter my womb. Think of the Son, the Word made flesh, who bowed
in humility and obedience to the Father, taking on our human form
in all its fullness, while retaining the fullness of His divinity as the
Second Person of the Most Holy Trinity. The human mind and heart
cannot comprehend the love which extended from heaven to earth
through my womb. While it is not necessary (nor possible) that you
comprehend this infinite Divine Love, it is necessary for the life of
your soul, to respond to God's love in order to thrive in it! Oh
creatures of earth, all souls created by Him, is it too much to ask
that you prepare a fitting home in your soul for the infant King?
    As God the Father and God the Holy Spirit birthed the Son in
me, their servant, on that holy night, God desires to birth His son
Jesus in your soul by the power of the Holy Spirit, who is Divine
Love. If you allow the Son to be birthed in you, you will grow in the
image and likeness of Him who is in you. The love your soul hun-
gers and thirsts for will grow in you. Your soul, finding its fulfill-
ment, will soar to spiritual heights beyond your human imagina-
tion, for the spirit is not bound by the limitations of the finite world.
Your earthly pilgrimage, with its burdens, will become a walk of
faith which enables you to endure all things in peace and love be-
cause the One who is in you makes all things bearable by His Grace.
This I learned at the foot of the cross.

Let your journey of the spirit begin anew this season. Let the birth of Jesus, Redeemer of all mankind, take place in your very soul this holy Christmas night. Take the time now to prepare a fitting home for the King by praying always, rebuking the spirit of the world, frequenting the sacraments, especially Reconciliation and Eucharist. Turn your eyes toward the heavens, your home eternal. Appreciate, my dear ones, appreciate Who came down from the heavens, through a lowly handmaiden, to you, for love of you. Prepare. Anticipate. Make ready to share with me the joy of the Most Holy Night in Bethlehem. Make haste to prepare. He is coming! What will you present your newborn King? He desires your very heart! My blessings of love and peace to you! Glory to God eternally!

Mary, your Mother.

12-5-93 Midnight
Messages are Like Kindling to Start a Fire

My dear daughter,

I, who am your Mother, bless you with a blessing from my Immaculate Heart on this, the day of your birth. I come in the name of the Father, the Son and the Holy Spirit. Listen with your heart as I assist you toward a fuller understanding of graces which God has ordained for your soul.

*1.) A plea from Heaven: **Return to God**.*

God the Father has permitted my visitations around the world in order to awaken His creation to the reality of His Divine Love, Divine Mercy and Divine Justice. Such is His Divine Providence for His people, whom He loves beyond the scope of human understanding. I come to tell the world, "God Exists!" He loves you intimately and personally with His endless Divine Love. He offers His Mercy, which flows from His Sacred Heart like a fountain overflowing and covering the earth. Also, I come to warn. Divine Justice will cover the four corners of the earth to the degree that mankind accept or refuse God's Mercy and to the degree of the conversion of mankind. Toward the conversion of souls, God has allowed many apparitions and messages through various messengers around the world.

God's providential Love and His merciful Grace have always provided forewarnings of important manifestations of God to His creation. Therefore, on the day of reckoning, it cannot be said that God did not warn His people. While many hear the callings and the warnings, few respond with more than momentary changes of the heart. Still, heaven rejoices for the few who do heed the call and persevere in faith.

Many, in their pride and greed, refuse to believe that God's Love is infinitely personal for each soul, and that He would bend from Heaven down to the earth again and again to call the sinner home to His Sacred Heart of Love. Are not all things possible with God? How grieved the One who extends His Love, only to be turned away. How grieved the heart of the Redeemer by the shepherds, our priests, who harden their hearts to the possibility of heavenly visitations and messages. They hide in the pretense of protecting Mother Church, which we would have them do, but in reality they protect themselves, their pride, and the scrutiny of others whose opinions are more important to them than the Will of the Father, who knocks on the door of their hearts, offering grace through the visitations and messages. Blessed are the shepherds, our priests, who have themselves believed again and again, accepting the grace of the messages and visitations because they lead the flock with the fervent flame of Divine Love radiating from them, and their sheep know the flame is within them. Pray, child, pray for the shepherds. Love them as we love them.

Long pause. (Titles from Mary)

2.) His Grace in your Soul

Dear Child,

When God chooses to grace a soul as He has graced your soul, it is for the honor and glory of the Father as well as for the building up of the mystical Body of Christ. Your soul is penetrated by Divine Love profoundly, becoming a furnace of His Love. So intense does He create the fire in your soul that the flames radiate outward to other souls. Your soul becomes so filled with the confidence that it is loved by and filled with its Creator that your soul can soar to heights beyond your comprehension. God imparts to your soul such deep realization of its nothingness (truth) that, in acknowledging its lowliness, constantly and by grace, it is capable of yielding more and more of itself to the Holy Spirit, whose flame of love burns stronger and brighter, increasing and increasing because the spirit has no boundaries. The soul becomes His vessel, yielded to its Creator and Lover. The converted soul is prepared to be used by God to accomplish His Divine Will because the Will of the Father becomes the desire of the soul who aims to please His love within.

One of the ways the Father has led your soul into surrender has been the writing of the words heard interiorly, spoken by my Son or myself, your Mother. The words you hear interiorly are placed from the Sacred Heart or Immaculate Heart into your heart. Your soul is being enkindled by the very placement of the words within. The power of the Holy Spirit acts in you to write, and the same Holy Spirit acts upon the reader of the written words. It is the Holy Spirit who gives life to the written words. He penetrates hearts, personalizing the message for the soul of the reader. The soul of the reader of my messages is acted upon by God Himself. The vessel through whom the writing is accomplished disappears as an instrument only. The messages received by you are simple statements of God's personal Love and Mercy for creation, all of which has been given generation unto generation in Sacred Scripture, which is complete in and of itself. Therefore, there can be no additions or alterations.

In the beginning, we dictated messages to penetrate your own heart toward a personal and intimate love of God, leading you to conversion of your own. Love has led you to surrender. We will continue to instruct you toward growth in Love, Faith, Hope, Charity, through obedience and humility. However, if you allow, we desire to instruct other souls toward conversion by the continuation of the writing of our words of love and instruction through you. The messages themselves are like kindling to start the fire, but rather quickly they are consumed by the fire itself. The Holy

Spirit strengthens the soul to journey in faith and love, facilitated by a desire for Prayer, the Eucharist, and Reconciliation. The soul is propelled forward, into the community of the faithful, where it is enabled to carry out acts of love for the good of all souls and for the glorification of God. However small, the messages do serve a divine purpose.

Until a time well known to the Father, please remain in silence of the graces you are receiving. Continue to share everything with your spiritual director. Occasionally, you will be led by the Holy Spirit to share a message with your Prayer Group. This is possible because the Holy Spirit has gone before you to prepare their hearts to receive our written words as their personal messages of love. Upon receiving the messages I will occasionally provide for them, they too are bound by obedience to silence. Here is the reason I wish for you to explain to them and to your Spiritual Director. As the Holy Spirit preceded the messages to prepare their hearts to receive the messages as personal for them and to accept them as true, so the Holy Spirit goes before you to prepare the hearts of more people to receive the messages written through you. Always wait patiently on the Lord, whose timing is perfect. He will reveal to you and to your spiritual director the time and the method of spreading the messages. Trust - the foundation is being laid. You and your spiritual director have been presented with many situations which we have ordained in order to show you the way to proceed. For now, silence is your protection. At the appointed time for your messages to come to light, there will be souls ready to receive in faith, as well as hardened hearts who will not believe. There will be persecution for all who bear witness to my Son carrying the Cross.

Believe, dear one, the conversion of even one soul is so great a gift to present to your Lord and Savior. At the appointed time, you will present these messages to the authority of the Church. Do not be anxious, little one, the Holy Spirit will guide you lovingly and gently. As your spiritual director represents the Church, the process of submitting to the church has already begun. In this season of Advent, I simply ask you continue to respond to the intimate love of my Son, Jesus, in your soul. He chose you unto Himself. Go forward, bear witness to Divine Love, Divine Mercy and Divine

Justice. Mirror the light within you who is your rock, your strong-hold. Recall the joy of watching your children take their first steps walking. I too rejoice as you take step by step with me by your side, toward your Triune God, who awaits the fullness of your union for an eternity of love. My Maternal Love, dear child. Peace and joy.
Your Mother

12-12-93
What Causes You To Weep?

In contemplation I asked Jesus - "What causes you to weep?" I heard:

I weep over man's refusal to love. The world refuses to love their God and one another. The greatest sin is that which destroys or prevents love. The world is wallowing in this sin. My Sacred Heart is an abyss of love and it overflows upon the earth. Still I am refused and turned away. I weep because I love My creation. I agonize over the loss of even one soul. And in this present age, there are so many who decide against God. I weep for these souls because in choosing a partnership with the beast, they choose an eternity of suffering the agony of separation from their God. Completely lost, they become like the beast himself. Would you not weep if one of your children chose the way of eternal darkness? A long pause - Here I felt our Lord's pain and sadness. **My child, pray unceasingly for the souls on the path to perdition.**

12-12-93 1 AM Feast of Our Lady of Guadalupe
Juan Diego

My dear child,
On this, the anniversary of my visitation to Juan Diego in Tepeyac, I come to bless you and to say to you, as I said long ago to Juan Diego, "Let nothing alter the countenance of your heart!" I am your Mother. I am close to you. What more do you need?

Through trials and tribulations, through temptations and obstacles, persevere with your heart steadfast in love, for you possess God because you have allowed Him to possess you. In giving Him possession of your very heart, you have gained everything. For it is in surrendering one's heart that one's soul gains life itself. Thereby, the riches of the spiritual life and Divine Love are given in abundance. When a soul has allowed God to take possession of it, in other words, the soul has decided for God; it possesses indescribable joy. No matter the obstacles or hardships present, the surrendered soul experiences Joy. Possessing God is Joy. Loving God in response to His Love is Joy. Joy is union with God. Agony is separation from God.

The simple Juan Diego did not understand my visitation nor my request. Though he was perplexed, he obeyed because he loved. The radiance which overcame him was truly Divine Love and Light radiating through my Immaculate Heart into his heart. Pure love caused this humble and simple vessel to obey. Thereby, the Will of the Father was accomplished. We ask nothing more of any soul. God's ways are simple. Man's pride complicates them. That is why my Son has said, "Unless you become like little children, you cannot enter the Kingdom of God." Children are pure and simple. They are trusting, therefore, blindly obedient. They are totally dependent, therefore humble, because one who acknowledges his dependence upon God cannot get puffed up with himself.

It is through childlike simplicity that Joy can be present always, once you have entered into a surrendered love relationship with your Lord. An interior simplicity will lead to an exterior simplicity. Simplicity of heart is to have need of God alone. God is everything to the soul. No matter your earthly circumstance, your soul can possess the Joy of God if you have surrendered to His infinite Love of you. In accepting His Divine Love, you accept His precepts, because they flow from His Love and are in accordance with His Love.

Think of St. Joseph and I on that Holy Night in the stable at Bethlehem. Herein is an example of the joy of simplicity and surrender to Divine Love. The time of His birth had come. I knew within me was the infant King. Though I had hoped for a fitting room to birth my Son, my joy could not be diminished as we settled, in the cold of the night, in a stable. Even as I lay His perfect infant Body on a bed of straw I knew indescribable joy. His love possessed me; what more did I require? Circumstances and hardships should not alter your joy because your joy is the fruit of Divine Love, which you possess in full in any circumstance or hardship. Indeed, His Grace will most likely be more abundant in the face of hardship. Therefore, let nothing alter the countenance of your heart in the days to come. I am with you.

My child, I love you. Thank you for writing though you are tired. There are many demands on your time and I thank you for making our time together a priority in your life. There is one who will refresh you. He awaits you. Be with Him. My blessing of Joy. My love. Pray always.

Your Mother

12-21-93 My Home 11:30 PM
Holy Families

My child,

As long as my children refuse to love, poverty will exist. As love diminishes in the world, poverty will increase as well as the woundedness of the human condition. As long as the structure of the family continues to break down, there will be fewer and fewer children reared in the way of God's Love and in the knowledge of He who created them. It is the responsibility of the mother and father to teach their children of God and His ways. This requires sacrificial and unconditional love. Also required is time spent together as a family.

Satan's plot against the family unit is strong because he realizes the value and strength of the family toward the goodness of a society, and he desires to destroy it. In many ways, he has succeeded to do just that, thereby destroying the very structure and means God ordained for Divine Love to enter, grow, and to be passed on, generation unto generation. This is the very battle I come to combat; the demise of the family. I plead before the Father on behalf of all families. I will not allow Satan to continue to break down the family. Therefore, I implore families to pray together and to stay together no matter the sacrifice.

The family is the center of my Immaculate Heart. Also, I desire to be the center of every family so that I may lead them to my Son, Jesus Christ. It is within the family that the knowledge of God is best born through teaching and example. Within families the seeds of Divine Love and Faith are planted. Each member is nourishment for growth, through the interaction of love and sacrifice within. Especially in America, too many families choose to exchange time together (where love is imparted toward one another) for the attainment of material goods. Many wives and husbands do not welcome children due to a lack of sacrificial love, selfishness. Those who do have children often spend much time and effort trying to provide for the success of the child, by worldly standards. Little time and energy is spent simply being in each other's presence, loving and teaching about Jesus, His life, His ways. This above all provides for the good of a child. Within the family environment a soul is given the ability to perceive himself lovable. When parents teach the knowledge of God and His laws, in addition to their example of loving and sacrificing for one another, the entire family grows in faith and confidence in God's Love. He Himself permeates the family; therein souls are grounded in love. Also, a receptivity to God's Grace throughout a lifetime can be born.

As mother of all families I implore you, pray together. I advise you, set aside time together and I ask this be a priority. Whatever sacrifice this requires, so be it. God will bless the family beyond measure. I promise the vitality of the love in the family will flourish if committed to prayer in unity. If one or two resist, be patient and kind. Gather anyway and pray for a change of heart for the one resisting. Even one decade of the Rosary can accomplish much growth in prayer, love, and unity. In this season of Advent, look to the example of my Son, Jesus Christ, who chose to come to the world as a member of a family. Thereby His Presence created a Holy Family. The Father desires all families be holy. It is the Presence of Jesus which accomplishes holiness. The power of holy families of prayer can change the complexion of the earth from unloving to loving.

My children, take my words to heart. I come as the Father allows so that I may guide you to Him. Thank you for responding to my call. Change is difficult, but if you allow, I will assist you. You have only to make a small effort and I will be there to enable the change leading to growth in love - holiness. My maternal blessing. I love you.

Your Mother

12-24-93 Christmas Eve 3 PM
Partake in My Suffering for Love Alone

For two days, I had experienced interiorly, Jesus' suffering of rejection - His Love spurned by many. I was feeling so burdened I could scarcely function. Due to physical illness, I was unable to attend 8:30AM mass for two days in a row. I was suffering spiritually from the deprivation of the Eucharist. My first reaction to the intense interior suffering was to be upset with God for His "timing." I willed to partake in His sufferings because I love Him beyond words, yet I was frustrated that I could not rise above the interior suffering enough to put on an exterior composure to provide a joyful Christmas for my family. My heart being heavily burdened, feeling almost crushed by the weight of His pain, I called my Spiritual Director to ask for prayer. He offered to bring over the Eucharist. After Confession and Holy Communion, I wept in thanksgiving of the Eucharist and Father's blessing. My soul was filled with Him.

Jesus spoke.

x**There are so few generous souls on earth who are willing to partake in My sufferings for love alone. Please allow Me to rest in you, thereby allowing your soul to partake in a portion of My own sufferings, as the Father's Will permits. Bear in union with Me the mutilation of My Body caused daily by the continual rejection of My Love. Deny your self comfort in order to bear My discomfort. Be My altar. I will form you to bear for Me My sufferings, and increase in you the capacity to offer My Heart sacrificial love. The balm of your love made fragrant by what you bear for Me will rise from you, My altar, like incense to the Father.**

Love is a state of union, unity of heart. My Sacred Heart of Love chooses, for Myself, to embrace your sinner's heart. Our state of union is to be one in which you will experience the sufferings and joys contained within My Heart. Is not unity of heart a molding of two hearts into one heart of love? Willingly accept all within My Heart in order to facilitate our union. As My Heart aches, so shall yours, your heart no longer yearning because it is fulfilled in My Heart. Therefore, your joy consists in this: you are chosen to abide in My Love. Being consumed in My Heart, you experience what I experience in My Heart. If the world shall cause Me sorrow, you shall feel My sorrow. This is sacrificial love and I desire this from you. My altar, put aside your timing for My timing. You will not know the hour I ask you to bear My suffering nor the hour I allow you experience My Joy. Soul, let Thy Master be Thy Master! Bend in humility and docility. Your intention is to yield. Yet in reality there is resistance still. I will purify you thus you will ascend until there remains no resistance, only yielding, for I have chosen to liberate you from yourself in order to claim you as completely Mine.

Contemplate the Father's Love, the Joy of Christmas. The joy of Christmas is this: the Father so loved the world that He gave His only begotten Son. The Word became flesh to teach the way of love and peace, making possible the salvation of souls. I walked the earth to glorify My Father. This Holy Night, contemplate My Beloved Father, Creator and giver of life. Moved by incomprehensible love of His creation, He sends His only Son. Fully divine and fully human, by the power of the Holy Spirit, I entered the womb of the most pure Virgin Mary. I entered the world a poor infant. My Mother presented Me to the world, in fulfillment of the Father's Will. I was sent to show the way to eternal life, the truth, the absolute truth, and to bring True Life through love and peace to mankind on earth. As a propitiation for sins I am the salvation of the world.

Man imagined a different king and a different kingdom. Few recognized the true King and the Kingdom of the poor and humble, born not of earthly nobility, rather poverty so as to be the Light and Hope of all creation. Only those who humbled themselves and those obedient to the grace of the Holy

Spirit would recognize the Messiah who would fulfill the Scriptures. My people prayed, Messiah, come! Yet even those I lived among would ask, "Are you the One, our Messiah? Even as I revealed Myself the Son of God, I was rejected. Man could not comprehend a King such as I. I am the Light shining in the darkness age after age, and still darkness remains.

In accordance with the Father's Will, today My Mother presents her Son again. Still, the world does not comprehend who is being presented to them. I am not recognized. Indeed, I am rejected again. Until such time as man humbles himself, lowering His own Voice, acknowledging My Name as Son of God and Savior, darkness will cloud the earth and its falsehood will claim many souls. You have witnessed an era of Mercy ordained by the Father. So loving His creation, He sent the power of the Holy Spirit upon the earth. In this present age, the Holy Spirit is being rejected. This grieves My Father beyond all else. This will be the downfall of many. Woe to the souls who reject the Holy Spirit of God! Blessed are they who embrace the Holy Spirit, drinking Him in; He will permeate them.

In this era of Mercy, the Father has allowed visitation of the Blessed Mother to help gather creation under her mantle of love and peace. She, too, is rejected by many. Also rejected, My prophets of today. In union with Mary, My prophets proclaim: awaken - convert - repent - pray - sacrifice - live truth - love. For the most part the messages are scrutinized, not lived, and the messengers are persecuted. Therefore, My Father, who is Incomprehensible and Infinite Love, is made to suffer rejection of His Love through the person of His Son, through the person of His Holy Spirit, through the person of the Blessed Virgin Mary, and through the person of His prophets of today.

As My Father is made to endure again rejection of His Love, I am in agony, My wounds torn wide open. I am grieved beyond human comprehension as the pride and arrogance of humanity rejects the Father's attempts to reconcile His creation in the power of love and in the spirit of the absolute truth. The pain the Father endures at this time in history is indescribable in human terms. Your being would die from this much pain! Therefore, more souls who have love will be allowed a portion of our suffering, brought on by man himself, to alleviate our pain, and as a love offering to the Father. The Father's Justice will flow upon earth, not that He willed but that man chose justice over mercy.

The days of extraordinary graces of Mercy are numbered. Close at hand is an increase in hardships for many. Close at hand are signs and wonders which will cause men to bend their knees and turn their eyes toward heaven to cry out "Abba, Abba." I will come again to shine the fullness of My Light into every soul on earth. For a moment in time, My Truth will prevail in every soul in the world. As this comes to pass, souls will be revived, and some souls will not survive My illumination. I will come to revive My Bride, My beloved Church. I will come to usher in the era of sanctification and peace, where the United Sacred and Immaculate Heart will reign as the Holy Spirit permeates creation!

All that is, My Father has given to Me that I may glorify Him, as He and I are one. I will gather all that is, to present to Him His creation, reconciled to the truth and reconciled to the fullness of His love. In due season, He will be glorified by all creation. In the era of peace, sanctified souls will accept His Love and reject only that which does not flow from His Love.

Soul, thank you for allowing Me to rest in you. Thank you for sharing My pain. Two hearts united in love will weep in union with one another. Such is the relationship of pure love. The joy of suffering with Me is knowing you accomplish the Will of the Father in allowing whatever He asks to be accomplished in you and through you for the good of all. Your love consoles Me. Dear, dear one, I love you. I bless you. Peace.

Jesus

12-28-93 My home - Rosary with my Spiritual Director
The Maternal Heart Pierced

At the Third Joyful Mystery: The Nativity
Father was leading the meditation when a sudden jolt of physical pain shot through the front of my heart and out through my

back and seemed to "pin" me to the chair I was sitting in. The physical pain was very sharp and it intensified at certain points in the rosary, but most especially when I prayed for God's mercy upon sinners in the Fatima prayer of "Oh My Jesus, forgive us our sin and lead all souls to heaven especially those most in need of Thy Mercy."

By the end of the Rosary, I still had the pain but in a subdued intensity. My first reaction to the pain surprised me. I immediately thought, "This is a gift from God."

After awhile, Our Lady spoke: *My daughter, share with me my sorrow in reparation for the atrocious sin of abortion. My Maternal Heart is pierced as the sword of death kills innocent little ones. Thank you for offering yourself as a sacrifice for souls. From time to time you shall share in the pain and sufferings of my sorrowful heart. I bless you and I am with you always. I love you.*

Your Mother

12-29-93
Power of the Rosary

My beloved,

Blessed be the Holy Name of God. Time is of the essence, my little ones. I ask you to live my messages as never before, especially my message of prayer and sacrifice. Pray always. In all that you do, all that you think, let me and my Son be present to you. Continue to pray my Rosary. You will never comprehend the power of the Rosary. I am with you each and every time you pray my Rosary. The world situation is so very critical. My Immaculate Heart longs to embrace the entire world in order to present it to the Father. I have embraced you, my little ones, and you are indeed living within my Immaculate Heart. In union with my heart, let the rays of my Son's grace flow from you onto other souls. By this means, more graces can be spread upon the earth and by this means we work in union for the salvation of all souls.

By remaining faithful to prayer, you will remain faithful to your calling. God's grace will enable you to accomplish much for the Kingdom. The Holy Spirit has overshadowed your souls, thereby sanctifying your soul. This is for the greater glory of your Father in heaven. Know that I bless you this day and always. Live within my Immaculate Heart so that I may dispose your hearts for the work at hand in this era of Mercy. Be at peace in the confidence of my maternal love. I bless you. My joy.

Your Mother, Mary

12-28-93 Continued

At the Third Joyful Mystery, I saw the Immaculate Heart of Mary. A Sword had pierced her heart. Then I saw another sword penetrating her heart. Within her heart were her priests. Rays of grace radiated from her heart down to the earth. I saw the globe of the earth. I asked Our Lady to explain what I saw during our rosary today. This is what she taught me.

My Immaculate Heart represents the core and center of my being. It is the resting place of the Holy Spirit of God and a reservoir of His virtues and graces. It is crowned by the theological virtues of Faith, Hope, and Charity. My heart was originally pierced by the crucifixion of my beloved Son, Jesus; thus I revealed to you my pierced heart. Next shown within my heart were my beloved priests. These priests represent those whom I have embraced and pressed into my heart, as they have received my heart and my maternal love. I can assist them to be faithful to the truth.

Next shown was my heart pierced anew by a sword. This represents priests who have grieved my heart by refusing my maternal love and protection. In addition, this represents those not faithful to the absolute truth. Next shown, rays of grace which flow from God through my heart which I distribute through my faithful and beloved priests for the entire world. The rays of different color represent the different graces and gifts of the Holy Spirit being offered to the world in this, the era of Divine Mercy. My heart, overflowing with maternal love, imparts to your spiritual life continual God-given graces in order to sanctify your soul. I am the Mediatrix of Grace. I bless you.

Your Mother

1-1-94 Epiphany Feast
My Pain and My Joy

I awoke with a severe headache, full migraine. The pain is extreme and seemingly increasing in intensity as the day progressed. Pain incapacitated me so as to cause me to remain in bed with ice packs on my head. I took medication but there was no relief. Ice packs helped a little. While in bed, alone in my room, I experienced severe physical pain. I began to offer the pain to Jesus. I began to experience in my soul the most profound joy! I experienced interiorly, Jesus holding me in His strong arms, gently caressing my head. I was enveloped in His tender love. My thought was this: In the midst of the most excruciating pain, how can I experience this much joy? He elevated my soul to an incredible state of joy, unlike I have ever experienced. I kept offering myself to Him saying, "This is my prayer - my pain and my joy - have Mercy upon the world." The tenderness of His heart became mine. My joy was complete in the midst of extreme physical pain. In pain and silence, My Beloved Jesus unites Himself to me and I to Him. My God, be glorified.

1-1-94 Praying, evening, my home
Silence and Recollection

I am very aware of the Divine Indwelling in my soul. It is as if, minute by minute, the presence of my Lord in my soul is being made known to me. Because of this, I tend to stay in a more recollected state interiorly. At times I experience dryness, yet even in the dryness there is a profound realization of Jesus in me, though He is silent and hiding, so to speak. His presence illuminates my soul so thoroughly so as to keep it in an every-ready state of receiving whatever He desires to impart to my soul. He may impart silence, deprivation, His words spoken within, or consolation, whatever. The point is, He dwells in me to love, to guide, to teach. In order to be attentive to His gentle movement within, I desire more silence and recollection.

My behavior is made quiet as He possesses more of me. He moves me to carry myself as He carries Himself in me, that is, quietly, peacefully, reflectively, lovingly. The result of this profound awareness of my Lord in me is that I keep myself in check, becoming extremely aware of every thought, action, intention, asking, "Are they drawing me closer to my Lord or do they draw away from my Lord?" Many are the temptations and thoughts which I must quickly arrest in order to remain in a state of being acceptable to the one I feel permeating my soul with His Spirit. Absolutely necessary to this is the Eucharist! The Eucharist is sustenance for my soul. The Eucharist increases the capacity of my soul to bear suffering and/or joy according to the Will of my God within.

Sometimes the beauty of the movements of the Divine One in my soul overwhelms me. The sublime and lofty movements of God are beyond human comprehension and/or description. I am ever more grateful for the infinite goodness and generosity of God, who condescends to enter my soul, takes residency within, communing in such an intimate and personal manner. He is my delight and He desires I be His in totality. My soul ardently desires to please Him and fears constantly I will offend Him. Though I do not understand all that takes place within my soul, I praise and thank my God for the sublime favors He has bestowed upon me. I pray for the grace to remain forever His with the willingness to receive all that He desires to give. My Jesus, I love You endlessly.

1-3-94 Tabernacle
Consequences

My beloved, please write for My little ones. My compassion is such that it is important to point out to My creation that much of their suffering is the consequence of their refusal to love God and one another. Salvation lies in the name of Jesus Christ who is Love. The future holds much suffering for mankind. Let it be known that it is man who is destroying the essence of the beauty God desired to be part of their earthly pilgrimage as prelude to the glory of Eternal Life with and in

God. Already man has begun to suffer the consequences of their choices. Many souls suffer lack of love. Many souls run in circles searching for some deeper meaning to their existence. Within each soul exists a desire for the true meaning of life. I am the true meaning of man's existence. I am Life!

The spirit of darkness has spread such confusion and falsehood that many souls are exploring the path leading to perdition. So many blame God. However, I did not destine the world for darkness. I am not to blame. My people are reluctant to take responsibility for their choices. Here is the downfall of many. They fail to follow their conscience toward correct choices and they fail to come and to pray before their Lord to ask My blessing and grace to choose the way to True Life in every instance of their journey. Given unto each soul is the gift of Free Will. Herein lies the opportunity for the soul to choose life or death. Let it be known, the Heart of the Redeemer distributes grace at every moment toward souls. At every opportunity My Grace is available to aid in the choice of life over death. Yet, I will not interfere with a soul's free will.

I will rescue My creation from the forces of darkness. However, My creation shall be allowed to see the consequences of a world choosing falsehood over truth, as man is negligent in distinguishing the spirit of truth from the spirit of deception. I will reveal to every soul how often their choices were based on the delusion of goodness, when indeed, their self-interest and immediate gratification was the basis of their choice. I will permit creation to experience the pain of a world turned away from God and love. It will appear to those who have neglected their spiritual life that I have withdrawn from the world for awhile. In reality, they will witness the consequence of their withdrawal from God. Those walking in My Love know the truth. I will never abandon My creation; all things are permitted to work for the good of all and for the greater Glory of God. In due season, man will look to the heavens with softened hearts. Then I will pour forth into their ripened hearts the fullness of My Love. From that time forward, souls will exist in the intimate relationship of love which I desire for all, leading to union of creation with Creator. In heaven, the Angels and the

Saints sing praises of honor and thanksgiving to their Triune God. I will place this melody of love in the prepared hearts of My creation on earth. In order that this come to pass, I will permit creation to experience the consequences of their unloving state of being for a period of time.

(Here, feeling a little afraid for the future of the world, as Jesus' tone is grave, I begged His mercy for the world. Also, I asked for scripture confirmation. Immediately I heard 1Cor. 1:19. As I'd forgotten my bible, I drove home to read the passage.) New Jerusalem Bible, 1Cor. 1:19 As Scripture says: "I am going to destroy the wisdom of the wise and bring to nothing the understanding of any who understand." Where are the philosophers? Where are the experts? And where are the debaters of this age? Do you not see how God has shown up human wisdom as folly? Since in the wisdom of God the world was unable to recognize God through wisdom, it was God's own pleasure to save believers through the folly of the gospel. While the Jews demand miracles and the Greeks look for wisdom, we are preaching a Crucified Christ: to the Jews an obstacle they cannot get over, to the gentiles foolishness, but to those who have been called, whether they are Jew or Greek, a Christ who is both the Power of God and the Wisdom of God. God's folly is wiser than human wisdom and God's weakness is stronger than human strength. Consider, brothers, how you were called, not many of you are wise by human standard, not many influential, not many from noble families. No, God chose those who by human standards are fools to shame the wise. He chose those who by human standards are weak to shame the strong. Those who by human standards are common and contemptible, indeed, those who count for nothing - to reduce to nothing all those that do count for something so that no human being might feel boastful before God. It is by Him you exist in Christ Jesus, who for us was made wisdom from God, and saving justice and holiness and redemption. As Scripture says: "If anyone wants to boast, let him boast of the Lord!"

**This is all I wish to say for now. I continue to offer My Sacred Heart as shelter for those who seek Me. My Peace. My Love.
Jesus**

1-3-94
Do Not Become Overwhelmed

My daughter,

Do not become overwhelmed. You are in the shelter of My Heart. My Grace leads you. I ask you, take one day at a time. Live in the present only. Focus on only Me. Do not worry. Do not run ahead of Me. Evil is trying to confuse you. Look straight ahead to Me, your home. Do not look to the left or to the right. Much is presented to you because I will to accomplish much through you and in you. Do not be afraid. Place all your trust in Me. My Spirit is breathing His life and love in you. What more is required? In addition, My Mother stands by your side tending to you. Again, I say: Do not become overwhelmed. Take one day at a time. Continue in Me. Praying always to Me. Let My Peace overcome you. My beloved one, My altar, My little one unite yourself to the One who loves you. I rest in you and ask you to rest in Me. Cast out temptations of fear and doubt. All things are possible in Me. Please allow Me freedom in you. And I will allow you to partake in Me to the full. I am yours. Be Mine completely. Go now in My Love. I am with you always.

Your Jesus

1-6-94 Tabernacle
His Nature Is All Yes!

I heard interiorly (the Holy Spirit) 2Cor. 1:19: "The Son of God, Jesus Christ, who was proclaimed to you by Us, that is Me and Silvanus and Timothy, was never Yes and No; His nature is all Yes. For in Him is found the Yes to all God's promises and therefore it is through Him that We answer 'Amen' to give praise to God. It is God who gives us, with you, a sure place in Christ and has both anointed us and marked us with his seal, giving us a pledge of the Spirit in our hearts."

1-6-94 Midnight My home

My Child,

As the Scripture states, the nature of my Son, Jesus Christ, was always a definite "yes" to the Will of the Father through the power of the Holy Spirit. As one united to my Son Jesus, who imparts himself to your soul through the power of the Holy Spirit, you too, are called to a definite "yes" to the Will of the Father.

Offered to you, as well as many other souls in this present age, are many extraordinary graces. As my Son presents grace to you, please offer Him your definite "yes." There is less grace when a soul hesitates. The reason being, hesitation is due to the human nature of man desiring to assess what the offering of himself in a particular grace is going to cost him in human terms. Herein demonstrates a lack of faith, hope, charity and especially love of God.

My little one, my Son, Jesus, requests your being in totality for Himself. Please do not hesitate to allow Him freedom in your soul. Child, true love does not assess the cost. Love does not hesitate or fear. Love does not say "yes" one moment and "no" the next. Love abandons and trustfully endures, caring more for the Lover (Jesus) than for self. Love surrenders with joy and total selflessness. As the Heart of the Redeemer invites your participation in sacrifices of love in accordance with the Will of the Father, trust the Holy Spirit will enable your "yes" as He enabled my "fiat." Allow Him to reign in you so as not to allow your human reasoning to push aside the grace and the inspirations of the Holy Spirit. By the power of the Holy Spirit you are enabled to offer to God yourself in totality!

The Most Holy One within you offers you a sublime grace of union in His suffering and His joy. He invites you into this grace and awaits your definite yes in response. As God's creatures, we have free will. As your Mother, I share with you, that even at the foot of the cross of the most bitter passion of my Son, I did not regret the gift of my will in exchange for the Divine Will. Your will is His gift to you. For love of Him, return this gift to Him by allowing the Divine Will to reign over your human will. You will not regret it.

My little one, remember this always, please. It is your human nature which says yes, no, maybe, on again, off again. The Divine

Nature of my Son and the Holy Spirit of God will consistently say yes to the Divine Will of the Father. Strive to allow the Divine Spirit of God to lead you to total abandonment, overcoming the inconsistency of mediocrity. My Son is Love. What is there to fear? Please read the words of my Son, Jesus, to the disciples and to you in Luke 9:22. "The Son of man must suffer many things and be rejected by the elders and chief priests and scribes and be killed and be raised up on the third day. If anyone wishes to come after me, let him deny himself and take up his Cross and follow Me. For whoever wishes to save his life shall lose it, but whoever loses his life for My sake, he is the one who will save it." *Ponder these words in your heart. I place you in my Immaculate Heart of love to shelter and guide you toward your eternal God. My love.*

Your Mother

1-9-94 Feast Baptism of the Lord
For My Beloved Priests

I bless you, My sons. I am truly with you in these tumultuous times. To counter the rampant evil in the world today I am offering an outpouring of My Holy Spirit in greater proportion. I pour My Grace upon you to assist you in being Good Shepherds of My people.

Dispose your heart for this grace by praying always. Prayer is the key to participation in the divine relationship of love, as well as knowledge of the Divine Will for your soul. Neglect prayer and the fulfillment of your vocation as priests will be severely compromised. To compromise your vocation of priesthood is to cause the wounds of My Body to open widely and bleed profusely. My Church, My mystical Body has been infiltrated by a spirit of dissension and deception because many of My beloved priests have compromised the truth. The very heart of My Church is the Holy Spirit. The power and authority of the Holy Spirit overcomes, even in a whisper, the spirit of falsehood. I will restore My battered Bride to the radiant purity of long ago when truth adorned her through and through.

As for you, My dear sons, vital to your spiritual life is the Sacrament of Reconciliation. Too few priests take advantage of the graces I pour out in the confessional. In the world and in your parishes this is a sacrament which needs more emphasis for souls in all walks of life, including religious life. My Sacred Heart is offended as many priests rationalize away their offenses. This is not truth. Come unto Me in truth. Humble yourself and acknowledge your offenses so as to allow Me, your Lord and Savior, to purify you, creating a clean heart and making you righteous in Me. Come, I am merciful. I await you. I remind you, do not underestimate the power of the Rosary as well as the intercession of My Mother. They will lead you to holiness, as I have called you to the holiness of My Apostles, Saints, and Martyrs.

My Sons, embrace My Holy Spirit and His gifts, so that you may be found pleasing in the eyes of your God. Do not stifle the gifts of the Spirit given to the community to stir up the souls of many as they are led to increase in faith, hope and love. Lead My people in My Name by the power of the Holy Spirit who dwells within your very soul. Be patient and loving as I am. As My people approach you, they approach the One in you. If you allow Me to reign in you, they will increase in faith and love. Many of My sheep are wandering, lost and weak. The Good Shepherd seeks these very sheep. I long to provide for all their needs. Through you, My dear sons, I accomplish this. Keep your own house in order so as to be prepared for the harvesting of souls. Make straight your ways so the way of the Lord is made straight. These times are critical as the foundation is laid for the prophecies of My Mother at Fatima. Prepare. The era of Peace will arrive after the purification of souls.

My beloved sons, some spend countless hours in administration, some in ministry and some in recreation, compromising private prayer time. Yet, the Son of God has always taught the importance of retiring to your room, in private, bending your knees and lifting your heart unto the Father in prayer. As the world situation is grave, I, your Lord and Savior, request you commit to an increase in your prayer life. You will not regret this sacrifice as I bestow My Graces unto you. The vocation of priesthood is so vital to the peace plan for the world. I will strengthen and enlighten you through Prayer and the Sacraments. Many of you have abandoned the devotion to Me in the Blessed Sacrament. If it is possible, I ask you come to Me in the Blessed Sacrament daily. Many are the graces bestowed on souls before My Blessed Sacrament.

At this point in the message, my own fear distracted me. I felt harassed by a spirit of confusion and doubt. Evil mocked me. He mimicked the words of Our Lord in a ridiculing manner. He somehow impressed upon my spirit that no priest in the world would accept a message through me. On the basis of my unworthiness to address priests, my own thinking seemed to agree with the evil one. Realizing I was in a state of confusion and not comfortable with my state of being at all, I put down the pen. I laid by head on my desk. I began to pray to Jesus from my heart. Truth is, I tried to convince Him he had chosen the wrong person for this work. He was silent though He heard me. I quickly went to bed leaving the message unfinished, as Jesus was now silent. Next morning I was in much turmoil. Strong urge to tear up the unfinished message. Strong presence of evil spirits around me causing my soul agitation. Midmorning, I phoned Father requesting prayer. Still, throughout the day, I had to constantly battle to keep my peace. Later that day He would finish the message after the following.

1-10-94 My home, 11 PM

It is I, Jesus. Be at peace. Rebuke the spirit of confusion and deception. Indeed he mocks you. He delights in causing you to lose your peace.

My child, I have not asked too much of you in asking you to record My words. You are simply the vessel. I desire most your heart and your absolute love and faithfulness. It is for you to simply write My words. I have chosen a holy man in Father for all discernment. Do not concern yourself with the

future. Do not attempt to foresee my plan or what I aim to do with these messages. My plan will unfold before you and I will instruct you each step of the way, enlightening Father as to My Will. It is for you to be obedient only. You are Mine. I will lead you as I please, when I please and use you according to the Will of the Father. Even as I formed you in secret you were chosen. From time to time, I will speak to My priests in a message. This is My Mercy! It is not for you to worry who will accept or reject this work. Part of your mission involves praying for My priests. Daily, pray specifically for priests.

My child, I allow temptation to teach you discernment of spirits. I was not offended as you put aside the message. I allowed this for your learning. You were responding to the agitation as you realized your state of being was too disturbed to continue. Rebuke the evil one in My Holy Name. The strength of the one who is in you causes evil to flee as you command! Cling to Me and My Spirit of Peace will envelop you. I will complete the message now. I love you. Jesus

For My Priests continued: As My priests, you are called to detachment from the world in a profound sense. Do not harbor attachment to persons, places, or things of the world. In Me, through Me and with Me is your fulfillment. I alone will provide for your every need as you come unto Me in prayer, persevering toward union with My Sacred Heart of Love, through trials and temptations. Uphold one another. My Grace is yours for the asking. I desire your heart in totality as I give unto you My heart and all the riches within. There is a place of honor reserved for you in My Father's house. Attain your inheritance through love, humility, obedience and faithfulness to the truth. You have not sacrificed in vain. Great will be your reward. Your joy will be complete as My Father, one day shows you the souls you have led to Him. Take heart. Though there is much work and few laborers, I will multiply your strength and efforts so your harvest will be great. I am with you even unto the end of time. I love you, My priests, even as I loved My Apostles of old. My Peace. My Joy.

Jesus

1-10-94 Rosary with Father at my home
The Scourging

The pain across my shoulders and neck became intense during most of the Rosary. This pain has been with me for two days. It feels as if a cross, or at least something very heavy, is placed upon my back and shoulders. My skin is hot and painful to the touch. Inside the pain is also heated, the muscles tense. The pain is intense and distracting in every way. It is intermittent, usually only occurring when I am not needed in my family duties, usually when I am alone. I did not want to presume it was coming from God because I understand to be "chosen" to suffer for souls is a big grace. Still, I desired to know if it was a grace from God, because if it was not, I did not want to suffer it. It is very painful. I took medicine to try to alleviate the pain but did not receive relief.

Following the Rosary, I asked Our Lady saying, "My Mother, what is happening to me? Help me to understand, please." I asked this of her for another reason as well. During the second decade of the rosary, I had the sense of being transformed into Jesus at the scourging. I have experienced Jesus being scourged, as if I were present in the crowd. I also experienced Jesus being scourged by me; this was in Lake Tiberias when Jesus desired to grant me this purification as a teaching. This was excruciating! Presently, I experienced my being scourged; I took Jesus' place now. Now I saw myself taking the blows of the whip. The whip was hurled across my shoulders and upper back and I felt physical heat in this area. Here my skin feels raw. It is much less painful to take Jesus' place, even with the physical suffering, than to observe Jesus being scourged. I understood this is because Jesus is the innocent lamb. I am guilty.

Our Lady spoke: *My daughter,*

God has ordained to make you His loving sacrifice. He has accepted your offering. For the good of souls He receives your suffering and in this you are made one. Holy is your union. My child, God loves all souls as He loves you. Jesus is gathering souls for the Father. He has chosen many souls such as you and such as Father to transfigure into His own reflection of love. Sacrifice is part of love. What greater love exists than to lay down one's life for another? Child, the transformation of your soul is underway so that charity can reign in you.

Daughter, Divine Love saturates a soul as the rain saturates the soil. He fills to overflowing so that love spills onto other souls. This is the divine plan ordained by the Father, made possible by the Son through His holy Blood, and carried out through the Holy Spirit. Your offering is made possible through grace. In prayer, my Son will pour His Peace upon you that you may grow in charity. My Son transfigures a soul into a most beautiful creation. The Cross is the foremost portion because union is facilitated by the cross. Jesus foretold He would create in you a symbol of living charity, and by the Cross this shall come to pass. For this you have been chosen. For this you live. I am with you always to assist you in your "fiat" of love. I bless you this day. I bless my beloved son, leaving the sign of the Cross on your forehead and imparting the grace to surrender unto the Divine Will of the Most Holy Trinity. Sacrifice, pray. It is vital to my peace plan. I love you, daughter. I love you, son. Peace of my Son, Jesus, be yours.

Your Mother

1-14-94 Prayer Group
Your Faith Will Be Tested

Following fifteen decade Rosary, Our Lady asked me to write for the group. The message came so quickly I could hardly keep up the pace of my writing and in a few minutes three legal pages had been written. Her disposition was so gentle and loving. Still there was an urgency to her message as if she is trying to teach us very much, desiring to penetrate our hearts, consoling us as if there is little time left for such special graces.

My Precious Little Ones,
I bless you this night and I thank you for gathering in my honor to pray the Rosary for the greater glory of our Lord, my Son, Jesus Christ. Please never underestimate the power of the Rosary. Even into eternity you will not comprehend the grace which flows from

this prayer. I ask this night that you begin to realize that you have indeed been blessed with so very many graces. I have held each one of you as a mother holds her precious baby to her breast to feed the life giving milk of love. In the future, you may not be allowed to feel the graces you have received in this era of Mercy. Indeed your faith shall be tested. Perhaps you will be tempted, as your soul feels darkness instead of consolation, to think, perhaps you have been orphaned. Truly, I say to you, my Son and I will never abandon you. Let your faith be strengthened in these days of Divine Mercy and Grace. Receive the grace which heaven showers in abundance now.

In the future there will be darkness, sufferings, and temptations which will test your faith, your hope and your love. My Son and I knocked and you allowed us to enter the depths of your being; therefore, you walk in truth and your faith will not grow weak. Many others around you will feel my Son and I have abandoned them. This will never be the case. Your faith will gain for you your reward of eternal happiness and love. Let He who is in you be your Strength and your Light, as you may grow weary and doubtful as you see the world progress in darkness. Please do not blame your God for the sufferings you witness around you. It is man who forsakes God and refuses to love. Therefore, the world suffers the consequences of sin. I have begged the Father on behalf of the entire world. Still, in spite of much grace, many refuse to accept all that is offered in this time of Mercy.

My little ones, remember all that you have received at my breast. You must grow into maturity by eating the true solid food of the soul, which is to walk in faith, indeed, even in darkness. I am by your side, always leading toward the eternal Light of Love, my Son, Our Lord and Savior. Never lose hope. Take courage, which the Holy Spirit will impart to you. Walk in faith to your home eternal, our Father's Kingdom. I await to embrace you in the Kingdom. Indeed, even now, this night I have embraced your soul with my Maternal love and grace. I love you. Peace.

Your Mother

1-18-94 My Home 11 AM
Patiently Proceed in Your Vocation of Motherhood

Following Mass I came home to pray my Rosary before my Fatima statue. I began to pray. I was preoccupied with a situation regarding my children. I had really lost my temper with them yesterday. Realizing I was wrong to lose my temper, I apologized. Still, I was left frustrated because I find myself having to constantly correct them and often feel they are not listening as they should. I desire our family to live in peace but often I am challenged and only get results by raising my voice. I do not enjoy doing this all the time, I am frustrated. There is so much to raising children properly. Often I feel I am falling short of good parenting. Our Lady saw this within my heart and she dictated the following message and left me in much peace.

My dear child,

Be patient and loving with your children, as I am patient and loving with my children, who are all the people of the world. I see in your heart your frustration of having to repeatedly correct and teach the same lessons again and again. I see in your heart your lack of understanding as to why they do not progress as you desire them to progress. You teach and correct. Still, they disobey, as they are sometimes obstinate and desire their own way of behaving.

My daughter, turn to me always as you proceed in your vocation you have as mother. Proceed with much patience and much love so as not to cause your children to lose heart. Allow me to lead you to growth in the virtues of my Immaculate Heart. For love of your children you desire their growth in goodness and wisdom and strength (to avoid temptations) *through discipline and love. You lead by example through a process of growth in patience, joy and love. They become confused when you become impatient because they have witnessed their mother praying much. Therefore, it is important for you to be patient with them. Expect to repeat over and over the same lessons and do this with much tenderness. I have shown you the way by my example.*

Have I not given messages to the entire world regarding Conversion, Fasting, Reparation, and Prayer? Indeed, I have repeated my words of love, desiring to guide my children to holiness. How many have truly converted and live my messages? Few, I tell you, few have embraced my maternal guidance. Yet, I await patiently and lovingly the hearts of all my little ones.

My child, I beg unceasingly before the throne of our Triune God. However, unless more souls cooperate with His Divine Mercy graces, unless more souls offer themselves as sacrifices in reparation of mankind's sins, unless more souls arm themselves with Eucharist, Prayer, and the Rosary, many are the souls who will perish in the near future. This pierces my heart and causes my tears to turn to blood over so many lost souls.

Child, assist me in pleading before the Father, please. Continue to offer yourself as sacrifice in reparation for sins, for you know not the souls averted from hell because of your offering through the Mercy of my Son. Proceed in your vocation of motherhood as I proceed with my motherhood of the world. Patiently teach. Shower your love on them. Take joy in each little step they take. Correct with consistency, yet allow them to know your love of them is unconditional. It is necessary to repeat yourself even as I have repeated myself. When finally you see them progress, rejoice even as I rejoice, each time my little ones allow my teaching and my example to penetrate their hearts.

Motherhood is a high calling from God. The raising of children in the ways of God requires much love, patience, perseverance, courage, wisdom, hope and joy. Thank God for your children and for motherhood. Pray always, dear one, pray for guidance and grace as necessary to be found pleasing before God in the fulfillment of your vocation of mother and wife. I bless you. Peace. I love you. I bless your family.

Your Mother

1-21-94 12:30 PM
Come With Me Into My Agony

Following one business meeting, I drove to another office for another ministry meeting. I heard interiorly moaning and groaning as a person in agony would sound. My first thought was Jesus.

So I said "Jesus?" and heard interiorly "I am with you." Then I heard more groaning. A wave of grace poured over me like a wave overcomes you from head to toe. To be honest, my first thought was, "Oh no, please don't take me through this." Immediately, grace overcame me and I changed and thought - "If you desire, I will go through this. Please allow me to drive home." I was shaking interiorly at the sound of His pain inside of me. So clearly could I hear Him in agony, my first instinct was to cover my exterior ears so as to block out what I was hearing inside of me. I was hearing deep groaning and labored breathing. Only by His Grace could I surrender. Once home, I sat before my altar and Our Lady (statue) and two or three more waves of grace came over me as I could hear Jesus moaning in agony. I began to shake interiorly and exteriorly. I cried. All I desired was to somehow alleviate His pain. After approximately ten minutes of this, a movement of grace caused me to begin to write as Jesus and I conversed. I wrote each word. He spoke very slowly allowing His every word to penetrate me. It was clear to me I was not in my normal state of being as I was completely absorbed in Him. My state of being was somehow elevated by grace in order to accomplish His Will. Our conversation began. Jesus?

I am with you. Do not doubt. Come with Me into My agony. Feel My pain.

Lord, inside I hear You groan in agony. I am shaking inside. I feel Your pain. Lord, please stay with me through this. Please. (Here, I could hear Him groaning. I could scarcely take it in.)

My altar, we are together. (Long pause. I cried. All I desired was to alleviate His pain.) **Soul, your generation causes Me agony. How is it My people cannot recognize Me? I am not dead! I am your Living God. Your generation is so closed to Me.**

I'm sorry, Jesus. I myself rejected You most of my life. But you had pity on me, Jesus; have pity on us. We are truly blind. You are all around us but we cannot see. Even I doubt often. (I who have received abundant grace.) Oh Lord, if not for Your Mercy, death would await us all!

Yes, Soul, you have stated truth. How much longer would you have Me wait? Indeed, I am like a beggar knocking on the hearts of My people. So few let Me in. Your generation is filled with pride, greed, arrogance, which are the catalyst for your hatred and godlessness. Who among you dares to love? Indeed, when I come, will there be any faith left in the world at all?

Jesus, have mercy on us. Lord, what can I do?

Continue to ease My pain by your love. Share My agony.

Lord, by Your Grace, I will.

There are signs all around My people. Who will dare to recognize Me? Soul, I allowed your soul to experience just a portion of My rejection. You shook. You cried. You desired to console Me. My dear one, thank you for this. There is no secret here. I love all My people! Love alone caused Me to endure the most bitter passion. I have purchased My people with every drop of My Blood. I handed over My mutilated Body as ransom to cover your sins. Yet, I am locked outside your houses (souls). **If My people would but open the door I would enter their house. I would sup with them and teach them the way. The door to your houses cannot be opened except by humility. So it is that only the truly humble shall receive their Lord and His riches.**

Jesus, Your ways are so contrary to the ways of the world. Have pity on us as we protect ourselves by wrapping ourselves in pride because we experience such lack of love. Few can even perceive themselves lovable. We make ourselves little gods because our human weakness looks for something tangible to hold on to. The spiritual world requires faith in intangible realities. I beg of you, Oh Living God, come and make yourself known to all as you have done for me.

I will reveal Myself to all in an undeniable way in the near future. Many will suffer unto Me then. And some will continue to deny Me and suffer unto the valley of darkness and death. My children lack love because they do not come to their God, who is Love. Some come only when they have need of Me. Truly I say to you, few know anything of Divine Love because they exist in the falsehood of self-sufficiency. No one can do anything except by My Grace. My Breath keeps the universe in existence! My Omnipotence is utterly incomprehensible to man! Still, man is puffed up with himself as if I, their God, do not exist! The poor, the meek, the simple and the humble know Me. I bless them. My Mercy will cover them. Woe to the arrogant man walking the way of power and greed, oppressing the goodness, for he will become the snake that he is. Indeed the brotherhood of snakes will welcome him. And so too the murderers will be handed over. And many will say, "But, I did not murder!" And I will show them how indeed, they murdered in thought and by their tongue. For the sword of the tongue kills! The conversations of many sicken Me! Your gossip and judgments cause Me to cry out in agony! Are any among you capable of mercy, forgiveness and love?

My Jesus, have mercy on us. We know not what we do!

That is truth! My precepts are in My written Word. Who among you lives them? I invite all. A remnant accept. Oh My beloved creation, I cry out to you - Come, come to Me. My arms will welcome you. My Heart will teach of true love. I will absorb all your pain into My own Heart so as to free you of your burdens. I will teach you to love yourselves because I have loved you, and you are infinitely valuable and precious to My Sacred Heart, which burns with love for you. You will not find my precepts burdensome. You will find them liberating, for even now you are chained like dogs to a post because evil has convinced you that you are not lovable, and that I am a God of wrath, who waits to punish you, if indeed you believe I exist at all! No, My children. Do not settle for this! Mine is the straight and narrow path but it is filled with love and joy and leads to eternal life!

Come, follow Me. I am Love! Put down your armament, which prevents Me from entering your house. I am your Living and True God. Here and now I am present to you. Awaken, Oh blind generation, awaken and let Me in! My signs are all around you. Open your eyes. Decide for Me, your Living God. I am the One you hold onto. I am Love! Tell My people that Divine Justice is indeed merciful and loving. Even the purification of the world at hand is My Mercy, as it serves to prepare the way for peace in the world, which can only exist by separation of the sheep from the goats. This is all I wish to say to My children. Soul, May I rest in you?

My God and My Lord, I will never refuse You for I love You boundlessly. (long silence) Jesus?

I am with you.

Do you see my heart beating so quickly?

Yes, I see your heart.

Jesus, it beats for You alone. It longs to come to You. How long the exile? I am having difficulty, Lord.

I long for you to come home yet the Will of the Father ordains you to be My hands, My feet, My mouthpiece. Please allow Me this.

Jesus, I will that my will be one with the Father's. My love for You only grows deeper and deeper. You occupy me and I am utterly forgetful of many of my duties because I cannot help but contemplate You in everyone, everything and at every moment! Your Majesty overcomes me even when You hide yourself from me. I know You are deep inside me always. I love You with all my capacity to love. Yet, sometimes the longing is unbearable.

I will always dry your tears. You are alive in the radiance of My Sacred Heart and united are we already. Be faithful to your calling until the time when I, Myself, will come for you. Thus our union will be complete. Though you are wretched, your love is pure and sincere. Therefore I rest in you. My Peace. My Love always.

Jesus

1-26-94 10 PM My Home
Simplicity and Naturalness

I was paying my bills at my desk. I looked up at a picture of Our Lady on my desk. She began to speak interiorly.

My Dear Child,

I bless you with my maternal blessing of love and peace. Please write for my children. I desire souls to walk in simplicity and naturalness. Many of my little ones complicate their journey because they believe the precepts of my Son are complicated. This is not truth. My Son loves simplicity and naturalness. His ways are simple. He is Love, unconditional Love. As He loves His creation infinitely, He desires love in return. There is a natural tendency toward loving God in every soul. However, the spirit of the world twists this around through falsehoods of many kind. There is a natural inclination toward God from the beginning. (Romans 1:19 "Because that which is known about God is evident within them: for God made it evident to them.") A soul yearns for its Creator.

Also, a soul has a natural, God-given tendency to know good from evil. It is written on the soul of every man by God Himself. God provides all that is required for a soul to attain his goal, which is union with God. The soul need only be a child in the arms of a loving and merciful Father. The embrace of God sustains the soul. To be simple like a child requires humility and trust, as well as abandonment. If a soul presents as a child to a loving Father, the Father will raise the soul unto Himself, step by step. Hand in hand the soul will grow in virtue and holiness toward union. The jour-

ney is one of Joy because the soul is wrapped in a divine blanket of love. The security of Divine Love causes growth of faith and hope in the soul. As the soul senses himself profoundly loved by God, it is natural to return that love. In the process the capacity for love is increased. The soul overflows with love for God and himself, as a child of God, for family and community. The world becomes his family because he sees all souls destined to live in eternity with God. My children, this is not a complicated or unnatural process. On the contrary, it is completely natural for the soul. It is simple if the soul will be simple. Evil would have you believe it is difficult and unnatural. This is because he is the father of all lies. Trust, my little ones. The Father does not require greatness, only that you love to your full capacity. Love God first, above all else. Love yourself as His child, destined for an eternity of union with Him. Love one another as yourself. See all humanity as your family destined to live forever in love with God, Creator and Lord of all.

If you pray with simplicity, it will be revealed to you in a natural and simple way. God is not impressed by words, deeds, talents or any creature. Only love matters. All you need say is simply (with all your heart) "My God, please help me to know you." He will answer your prayer. He will reveal Himself as your intimate friend. Indeed, He is your Divine Lover. Having probed you, there are no secrets which He does not know in you. He is merciful and unconditional in His Love. He awaits you. If you allow, His Majesty will teach you of Himself. As He is Love then you will know love. Then your life on earth will be filled with awe and wonder of Divine Love, fulfilling your every requirement (spiritual); your joy will be complete. External forces will not cause you anxiety, because interiorly you will possess a profound sense of who you are in Christ. Herein you exist in peace interiorly. Only God provides peace of soul. The formation of an intimate relationship with my Son, Jesus, is a natural one when seen through the simplicity of a child.

Oh my little ones, be still and know God exists. He is calling you to intimacy now! Please allow yourself the "quiet" to hear His Voice calling you. If you allow, I will assist you every step of the way. Please pray, little ones. Pray, pray, pray. I love you.

Your Mother

Pray for the souls walking the path to perdition. (See Romans 1:21 "For even though they knew God, they did not honor Him as God, or give thanks but they became futile in their speculations and their foolish heart was darkened. Professing to be wise they became fools and exchanged the glory of the incorruptible God for an image in the form of corruptible man.")

1-27-94 9:45 AM Tabernacle following 8:30 mass
There Will Be Natural Disasters

I was alone in the church in prayer before the tabernacle. At 9:30 AM an earthquake occurred. I prayed "Jesus, have mercy on us, please." He said: **Do not fear for I am with you.** (long pause) I was thinking how fortunate for me to be right before the Tabernacle in an earthquake. He began to speak: **My power will be revealed.** (long pause) **Perhaps My people will think of Me?** Pause **Soul, it is as if My creation is walking in a dry desert, wandering aimlessly. You walk in circles searching for water for your parched souls. I am the fountain gushing up from the earth in the middle of the desert. I am the end of your searching and the beginning of your life. You, My people, are walking in blindness. You cannot see what is truly before your very eyes. I am showering you from My Eternal Fountain of Grace and you complain of thirst. The Holy Spirit attempts to enter you to bear witness to the Father and I in your very midst. The Holy Spirit is gentle and orderly. He enters when you invite, knock, seek. He will lift the veil from your eyes so that you may see truth. To all who have received My Holy Spirit, be My Light for those wandering in darkness.**

There will be natural disasters. I will allow this. You are called, as My disciples, to look beyond the hardship to the blessing of people helping one another. There will be a unification of people. Look beyond the physical sufferings which will result and see the spiritual healings which will occur. This is the far greater healing! There is nothing to fear, for in losing much, much will be gained. There is no preparation except prayer. Faith and prayer will allow you interior peace in the midst of

LOVE

 master. My children, trust Divine Providence. He (the Merciful, Loving and Just. Do not worry! Live each was the first moment you loved Me and the last day you had to show Me how much you love me. Then you will not be caught off guard.

Consider in your heart the words of St. Paul. (Romans 8:28-39) "And we know that God causes all things to work together for good to those who love God, to those who are called according to His purpose. For whom He foreknew, He also predestined to become conformed to the image of His Son, that He might be the first born among brethren, and whom He predestined, these He called, and whom He called, these He justified and whom He justified, these He also glorified. What then shall we say to these things? If God is for us, who is against us? He who did not spare His own Son, but delivered Him up for us all, how will He not also with Him, freely give us all things? Who shall separate us from the love of Christ? Shall tribulation or distress, or persecution or famine, or nakedness, or peril or sword? Just as it is written 'For Thy sake we are being put to death all day long; we were considered as sheep to be slaughtered.' But in all these things we overwhelmingly conquer through Him who loved us. For I am convinced that neither death, nor life, nor angels, nor principalities, nor present, nor things to come, nor powers, nor height, nor depth, nor any other created thing shall be able to separate us from the love of God, which is in Christ Jesus, our Lord!" Thank you, dear one, for spending time with Me in My Tabernacle. Go in peace. I love you.

Jesus

1-30-94 AM My Home
Unite Yourselves to My Passion

While in the bathroom I heard Our Lord interiorly: **My Child, in preparation for Lent, I desire you and Father pray the Sorrowful Mysteries of the Holy Rosary when you pray together. I implore you and Father to unite yourselves to My Passion this**

Lenten season. **Walk with Me the Way of the Cross toward union. Pluck a thorn from My Crown daily by offering a sacrifice of love which requires denying yourself at least one pleasure daily.** (At this point I had to go. Jesus said he'd finish later)

1-30-94 PM In prayer, my home, Jesus began again.

My child, though you have received much by My Grace, there is much more. I have not chosen you for mediocrity. My chosen souls are chosen for perfection in holiness, which will transform the face of the earth in due season. Uniting yourself to My Way of the Cross not only alleviates My pain but also sanctifies your soul. By My Grace you have taken steps to procure your relationship with Me. Your love is fervent through faithfulness to prayer. Still, there are many imperfections which must be rooted out in you. You are ascending the mountain but you are far from the top, where perfection (sanctity) of a soul unites to the perfection of the Creator. In you are inclinations toward comfort. What I would ask of you is an ardent desire to suffer for souls. I desire to elevate your soul to complete self-forgetfulness. Your appetite for pleasure of earthly food must be reduced to facilitate your spiritual intake of heavenly food. I truly ask of you - sacrifice! Discipline your flesh!

The season of Lent is of vital importance to the world situation and to your own soul. I ask you and Father to sacrifice for Me daily. My Heart desires reparation. Offer reparation for offenses against the perfect Love of My Father. Bind My Wounds for love of Me. Alleviate My pain. A generation of hardened hearts causes My Wounds to open and bleed profusely. Ascend to Me upon the wing of the Holy Spirit. Come. Come.

My beloved, faithfulness to prayer will lead you to new heights within My Heart. Allow My Grace to lead you along the next step to true sacrificial love. My Heart is a furnace of love. Draw close to the fire. The fire will consume only imperfections, as it enkindles your own heart and will to be united to the Divine Heart and Will. Your imperfections are as a veil between you and I. Allow Me to lift the veil. When you give Me your heart so completely that I consume it into My Heart, then

in turn, I must give you My Heart. Sacrifice yourself in order to receive the Heart of your Redeemer in totality. My Heart aches to be received. Did I not reveal My Love through the Cross? Deny yourself, pick up the Cross and reveal your love of Me through the Cross. This season of Lent, walk with Me down the Via Dolorosa. Our love will soothe one another. Come with Me. Child, I will teach you of love and joy beyond understanding. Enter Jerusalem with Me in the hour of man's darkness and God's Light. Truly I say to you, much of creation is in darkness again. The Light of the Resurrection will again illuminate the world so the darkness cannot exist.

My dear child and My dear priest, I thank you for your obedience. I have chosen you to fortify My mystical Body. My Holy Spirit will illuminate your pathway. Trust in Me completely. Pray always. Share everything with Me, as we are intimate friends. You are beloved of My Heart. Be at peace. My Love.
Jesus

2-2-94 Feast of the Presentation 9:30AM Tabernacle following Mass.
Humility Is Truth

My Dear Child,

On this Feast of the Presentation of the Infant Jesus in the Temple, I implore you to contemplate two virtues which are essential to holiness and the keys to the Heart of your Savior. The virtues which I give you example of in presenting my infant Son according to the law are humility and obedience. Contemplate humility. Walk in obedience. Then contemplate humility again. Humility and obedience are interwoven, one flowing from the other. To possess these is to possess the heart of your Mother, who possesses the Heart of her Son.

Humility and obedience will set you free from the snares of the devil. If you possess these, you possess protection which evil cannot penetrate. He may tempt but cannot penetrate. Humility is truth. If you are grounded in humility you are grounded in truth. Truth is this: My Son is God and you are but dust of the earth. You are dependent creatures and all that is, is gift, pure gift. Though you are dust, through His unfathomable Love, He takes residency in you through the person of the Holy Spirit. He who is in you destines you for union. His Blood purchased eternal life for you, though you are His lowly creature. Who can fathom such love?

Today, allow your heart to see my infant Son as the joy and treasure of my Maternal heart. Allow the purity, joy, and perfection of my infant Son to enkindle in your own heart a desire for perfection in holiness through obedience and humility. How infinitely deep the ways of the Lord. When you believe you have loved to your capacity, He increases in you and your capacity to love Him only grows deeper. How shallow the ways of the world. How fleeting the joy of the world. God offers you eternal joy beyond your understanding.

This day I grant you my blessing as I present to you my infant Son. Caress Him in your love. Allow the wisdom of the Holy Spirit to permeate you. As Simeon knew he had seen his God, so too shall you know this. Turn to me often. I am present always to assist you in your journey. My Maternal love and heart is yours.
Mary, your Mother

2-10-94 My Home.
Proceed in Silence

A prayer sister and I were sharing Our Lord's work in our soul. She was seeking advice and I was eager to give it. After hanging up the phone, I began to meditate, looking at the face of Our Lady (a picture). I seemed to be lost in her beauty and peace. Then she spoke: *Please read James 3 child.* (Her voice was such that I knew I was to do this immediately. I quickly read James 3 on the power of the tongue and true wisdom.) Our Lady spoke again.

My dear child,
You know not the workings of God in another soul. I desire you proceed in silence. When people present to you with the workings of God in their soul, simply listen and encourage them to trust in God and themselves. Do not assume to know what God is doing within another soul. Do not be curious about their journey and speak

little of your journey. Wait upon the guidance of the Holy Spirit within you. God is indeed working many wonders of grace in the souls of many who are close to you. If there is speaking to be done, let it be praise and thanksgiving of what God is doing in the souls of many. Be at peace. I will not stand by and watch my little ones falter. I will assist them. Trust in God and His Grace. By the power of the Holy Spirit, He forms and fashions many into the image and likeness of Himself. Give Honor, Glory and Praise always! Pray, my child, pray always. Keep much in the deep recesses of your heart.

My child, there is so much I keep in my heart, reserving it for God alone. Follow my example. I am near you now and always. I am near all my children as the Father has allowed this grace time of visitation. Rest assured, my child, my Son has walked the path before you. Your journey is in His footsteps. He has prepared the way for you. Place yourself in His footprints. Follow Him. As I accompanied my Son in union of my will and my heart, I will accompany you. Praised be to God Almighty for what He has done for you, dear child. And praised be His Holy Name for what He is doing in many souls as His Mercy rescues many from the valley of darkness. I bless you. I am your Mother, dear child. I love you.

Mary

2-2-94 Rosary with my Spiritual Director
Offended by Sins Against Purity

Fourth Joyful Mystery: The eyes of my soul saw Our Lady as a being of white light, translucent in the form of Our Lady of the Miraculous Medal. The Holy Spirit in the form of the Dove was above Her. All the rays of light came from the Holy Spirit filtering directly through Our Lady. From her entire being rays of grace (white light) flowed from her onto us. She simply watched Father and I pray. Then I heard her say: *Help me please, my son and my daughter.* Pause. *Help me gather my children, please.* The image was gone by end of Fourth Joyful Mystery.

At the Fifth Joyful Mystery (during the last two Hail Mary's) she said: *Pray this week, the Rosary for purity. My Immaculate Heart is greatly offended by sins against purity. I love you.*

Your Mother

2-7-94 My Home, 5 PM
Souls Are in Need of Mercy

Cooking dinner, I heard Our Lord dictating a message on Divine Mercy.

My dear children,
This night I wish to penetrate your heart with My Love and My Mercy. Know, My little ones, My Heart is an abyss of love for each of you. From My ardent Love of you flows a river of Mercy. Your sins offend Me. Still, if you turn to Me in acknowledgement of your sins, I will cover you with My blanket of Mercy. I will whisper to you - "You are forgiven. Begin again in Me." Each must stand alone before God in His judgment of you. Your thoughts, words, actions, intentions are accountable before the Most Just Judge. As My Justice would deal your due, would you not ardently seek My Mercy? I have said "Blessed are the merciful for they shall receive mercy." If you desire I embrace you in My Love and Mercy (and this is indeed the desire of My Merciful Heart), then I would ask that you be merciful to all My children, beginning with yourself. Mercy is an extension of love, which should flow naturally onto all souls, as all souls are in need of mercy.

The Father of Mercy has ordained this period of time for an outpouring of grace, the grace of My Love and Mercy. Truly I knock on the door of man's heart, offering My Heart of Love and Mercy to each one. Many are preoccupied with the ways of the world, so they do not hear my knocking. This is their folly. For the world will pass away, and in the end, all that will defend you is My Mercy. This night I invite you to come to the Fount of Mercy and drink your fill. Repent and walk in My forgiveness. Acknowledge your errors and place them in My Holy Wounds. I have already absorbed them within My Body. Emerge pure (cleansed) and resolve to walk in the purity of My Love and Mercy.

If then, I have been merciful toward you, are you not called to be merciful to one another, including yourself? Indeed you are to be merciful to all without distinction. You are witnessing an outpouring of My Grace of Love and Mercy upon a world filled with darkness. Be prudent, My children, fill your lamp with oil now. The day of the Father's Justice will come when you least expect. Fear not; rather, trust. The Father's Justice is merciful as His purification makes way for the reign of peace on earth. Receive My Love and Mercy so that peace may reign in your soul. I love you. I bless you.

Your merciful Jesus

2-17-94 8 PM
Follow Me to Calvary

While driving and praying the Sorrowful Mysteries, I began to cry. I prayed to Jesus saying, "Dear Lord, my God, help me please. I am having many doubts. I do not want to hurt people or Father or my own soul. I want no part of falsehood - only truth." Jesus spoke: ***Soul, you are concerned about not hurting others. Are you concerned about not hurting Me? Has it occurred to to you that your doubts inflict pain upon the One who loves you beyond your comprehension?** (Here I arrived at the place I was driving and Jesus said He'd continue later.)

12 Midnight - My home He continued:

My dear *Soul,
How grieved My Heart when you doubt Me. Have I not revealed Myself as your Living God? I am the love that exists in your soul. I am the Peace that exists in your soul. I am the Mercy which saved your soul. I am the intense flame of Love which you feel burning inside of you. Who can touch you as intimately as I touch you? Can the mortal man whom you see touch you as the One you cannot see? My beloved *Soul, your lack of faith in Me wounds My Heart and My Body. Please do not offer the bridegroom the wedding cup filled with your

---

* An asterisk before the word "Soul" indicates a substitution for the messenger's name.

doubts and fears. Come unto Me with cup overflowing with love, which trusts and casts out fear. Fill the cup of your offering to Your Beloved with the sweetness of faith, hope, and charity. Hold the cup to My lips and let Me drink of your offering to Me. Sacrifice yourself for Me. In turn, I will hold to your lips the cup of My divine riches, and you will taste and drink of the sweetness of My Divine Love.

Come, beloved, come unto Me. I am the God of Abraham, Isaac and Jacob, the God of Moses and Elijah, the God of all the ages and all the prophets. The God of all creation, the Living True God, your God. Come to Me. This day I revealed to you the place where I await you. Follow Me to Calvary, where My arms are stretched out on a Cross for love of you. I await you. Come to the foot of the Cross, allowing your love of Me to cause you to remove the nails from My hands and feet so that we may embrace one another. Will you do this for Me, *Soul?

Only by Your Grace My Lord. Only by Your Grace. Loving you, My Jesus, is at once the most beautiful and the most painful experience of my life. Sometimes loving you seems so clear and other times it seems so unclear. Forgive me my lack of faith. I do not deserve your loving attention. My Savior, I beg of you, increase my faith. How do I grow in faith? How do I progress when it seems to me I am going backwards?

*Soul, My Grace will lead you to progress as I desire for you to progress. As for faith, read My Word; it is My love letter to you. Listen to Father who leads you according to My Will. Do not push aside My Grace for the distractions of the world. You will increase in faith by walking in faith. Trust, when you think I am far from you - I am the closest. Increase in your love of Me and decrease in your selfishness and you will grow in faith of the One you love. What are you afraid of, My beloved?

I am afraid of failing You.

Perhaps it is yourself you fear you'll fail?

To some degree, yes, I suppose I do not want to fail either you, myself, or anyone. Is that wrong, my Lord?

Fear is not of Me. Fear of failure is a human emotion which will prevent true love, human and divine. The heart paralyzed by fear will not permit Divine Love to enter. Fear of failure will choke your soul from ascending to the divine union your soul is destined and created for. To fail is human. Certainly all humans fail. To fear is a trap which will bind your spirit, preventing maturity in the spiritual life. Fear and doubt are seeds of temptation sown deviously by the evil one.

*Soul, discern the spirits. The evil one is toying with you in a more subtle way as he plants his seeds of fear and doubt in you. For love of Me you often walk in faith without fear and with courage. Can you not recognize the spirit of deception when he sets his traps for you? Immediately, throw out these temptations. Come to Me immediately. I will be your strength, your wisdom, your everything! Talk to Me constantly. I am always listening for you, awaiting you. Sometimes you cause Me to wait a long while for you. Share with Me everything and you will be less susceptible to the temptations of the liar and thief of your peace. I am your shelter, *Soul. Hide in Me and be secure in Me. I will never abandon you!

My Love does not depend on your progress or success, your effort or your sacrifice, your holiness or lack thereof. It does not change when you fall or give in to temptation. It is My unconditional gift to you because I love you just the way you are! You need not accomplish anything for Me. What I have asked of you is that you would allow Me to accomplish My Father's Will in and through you. Simply allow My Grace to flow through you and you will gather for Me many souls. Cause Me to be loved by souls by loving Me with all your heart, strength, soul. My infinite Love in you will be the catalyst for many conversions.

Trust Me, dear *Soul. One day I will take you by the hand and show to you the souls you gathered for Me. You have already borne fruit for Me. Thank you. Go and bear more fruit for Me. Take My Peace and let it penetrate your entire being. My Love is all you require and it is freely given in infinite gen-

erosity. Drink of Me to your fill. Now rest in Me, My beloved flower. Believe. I love you.

Jesus

2-22-94 Feast, Chair of Peter - My Home, 10 PM
I Will Restore Solidarity to the Chair of Peter

My children,

It is written: "You (Simon Peter) are rock and on this rock I shall build My Church and the jaws of death will not prevail against it." And it is written: "The Lord said to Simon Peter, I have prayed that your faith may not fail and you in turn must strengthen your brother." (Lk 22-32)

My children, pray for My Vicar, My Peter of today. My shepherd, My beloved shepherd of My Church, suffers in union with My bleeding, Sacred Heart. Oh how he truly understands the wounds inflicted upon My Body by divisions and apostasy of this generation. He loves My Bride as I love her. He weeps for her and prays unceasingly for her, laboring always for love of her and for love of Me. He suffers much due to the division within My house. He is well aware of the elders and priests in My house who compromise the absolute truth in favor of a relative truth, preaching a gospel of their own.

Here, there was a long pause and I entered deep contemplation. My heart began to pound through my chest as I interiorly saw Jesus, His body, one big open bleeding wound. I found myself searching His Body for one area that was not wounded and I could not find even one small area that was not bleeding. Then He spoke again. **In the history of mortal man, never has there been a generation of people so blind and deaf to their God. If anyone has ears let him hear My messages and repent now!**

My Bride (Church), My beloved Bride, is suffering and infected. There is within her body infections like huge boils, which fester and fester until the doctor comes to lance the boil and expel the pus, washing the wound and healing the body. I will come. I am her physician. I will tend to her Myself and restore

her to the purity of her former age. I will restore solidarity to the Chair of Peter. I will make known to all, Peter is the rock and foundation through whom I shepherd My flock. Until that time when I come to revive her, a time ordained by the Father, My Church and My Peter will suffer much. I ask of you, pray for them always.

My Vicar is surrounded by few who comfort him. His greatest comfort is within the shelter of the Immaculate Heart of My holy Mother. She guides, consoles and tends to him with her tender Maternal love. Oh how she loves her son. The favor of the Most Holy Trinity and the Immaculate Heart rests upon him. Blessed is he because he disposes his heart to the workings of the Holy Spirit through the Immaculate Heart of Mary. To all souls, I say, he is your example. Follow him and you follow Me. He is in union with his God, your God, the Alpha and the Omega, neverchanging.

My children, enter the depths of My Sacred Heart, where I can reveal to you the ineffable love I have for My Church and My Peter. Allow Me to impart to you My love so that you will love them for love of Me. Oh lost and wounded generation, if only you would believe My Words. My Words of old and My Words of today are the same. I am shouting to you, as daily the number of souls lost to the abyss of death are many. The stakes are high, My little ones. Eternal death or eternal life? You must decide either for God or against God. Please choose love. Love the Father, God and Creator. Love one another. Come to Me, your Jesus of Mercy. I will show you the way, teach you the truth and give you True Life in Me. Your soul I will satisfy, and joy will be yours.

Truly I say to you, decide now. Repent now. Pray now. Time will be soon that I am among you again to separate the sheep from the goats. There will be much to suffer in the days to come. Those for Me and those against Me will suffer together. However, those for Me will receive the grace to remain in Me. I will walk them through the purification. As for those against Me, there is nothing for Me to do for them except to weep and mourn. Eternally, I will mourn the souls who choose solidarity with Satan.

My dear children, you belong to Me. Give unto Me what is Mine. Come unto Me now! Do not hesitate. I am Love. I will receive you. I will forgive you. All who have ears, let My words penetrate you. This is all for now. (*Soul, pray for My Vicar and tend to My Body.) I love you. My peace I give you. May I rest in you? Your weakness fascinates Me, and I wish all to know of your weakness so that all glory be given unto My Father, who chose you. Be at peace. I will be your strength.

Jesus

I prayed: "My Jesus, it is right you reveal my weakness, my sinfulness, my nothingness for all to see. For this is truth. I desire The Father receive all the glory. Of you I beg only for mercy and love. If I have these I have everything though I deserve nothing. You see, My Savior, my nothingness is covered with Your precious Blood. Your Holy Wounds receive me and hide me so that the Father sees only you and the price you paid for me. Thereby I receive His welcome, even in my nothingness, because I acknowledge I am nothing. I will proclaim my sinfulness to all the world if You require. Before I speak, my lips will profess I am a sinner. How else can I proclaim what You have done for me? No, dear Jesus, I am not afraid to reveal my nothingness. In fact, I would be afraid if I did not reveal my utter dependence upon You. As you are everything, I need be nothing, except in You! I love You."

2:30 AM I looked at my Fatima statue.
Our Lady Dictates a Prayer

Our Lady spoke: *Allow me to teach you a prayer, especially for you.*

"Father, Almighty, I bow before Your Majesty. Receive my nothingness, my weakness, my sin. Occupy my soul with your omnipotence. Allow me to proclaim to others what you have done for my nothingness. All the days of my life may I proclaim my dependence upon You alone. Allow me to lead souls to acknowledge their nothingness, so that You are *glorified through many weak and poor souls who humble themselves for the sake of truth, as they come to you covered in the blood of the most pure and innocent Lamb, your*

Son and my Savior. Empty, empty I shall remain so that I may be for You the poorest vessel, Yours, Almighty Father, whenever and wherever You choose. I proclaim You Master, worthy of all my love. Imperfect as it is, small and weak, it is all I have to give. Take me and do with me as you please. Permit me only this. The gifts you have given me, my life, my heart, my will, be Yours alone that You may be glorified in me, Your nothing. Amen."

2-23-94 Following Rosary with Father
Do Not Focus on Negativity or Chastisement

During Fifth Sorrowful Mystery, I saw interiorly Blessed Mother at foot of the Cross, looking up at Jesus dying on the Cross. St. Francis was present, embracing the Cross while gazing up at Jesus. I was made to understand Francis was there to alleviate the pain of the Cross and be His replacement. Francis aligned himself so closely to Jesus, for love of Jesus, he desired to experience every pain and sorrow that His Beloved experienced in order to understand the love and the joy of the Cross. At the Fifth decade, Mary spoke.

My dear ones,

Be at peace, the peace of my Son, Jesus. I desire that you do not focus on negativity or chastisement. To do so can lead to fear, confusion and distraction, especially in prayer. Be people of faith in God's providence and hope for the future because, this I promise as I foretold in Fatima, in the end, my Immaculate Heart will triumph and God will be glorified. What more must I promise? My call to you is this, (and it is urgent) Pray! Pray! Pray! Prayer can alleviate much suffering and saves souls. While there are some chastisements which man must pass through, there are some which can be lessened or cancelled by the prayers of fervent souls. Trust me, dear ones, there is nothing more important than prayer. I urge you to pray unceasingly. Be ever mindful of the presence of God, who is with you always! Plead His Mercy upon the world, and pray for conversion, conversion, conversion. Focus on your own journey so that you can respond to God's calling, His particular

*mission for you. Thank you for responding to my call. I love you
and bless you.*
Your Mother

2-28-94
Indifference and Complacency

Reference: Luke 16:19-31, Parable of Rich Man and Lazarus.

My dear children,
**Truly, truly I say to you, My Word of old is the same for
today. Never in the history of mortal man has there existed
such indifference, complacency, deafness of ears, and hardness of heart. I am pouring upon the earth the gift of prophecy, as this is an era of Mercy and a time of visitation. Everywhere in the world My Holy Spirit is gracing those whose hearts
are not granite and ears not deaf. I am shouting to you, My
dear ones, wake up! Woe to those who dare not heed My Words
through indifference and complacency. This night, I do not
wish to cause you fear. Those who have received My Light,
those who walk with Me have nothing to fear. To you who have
received My Holy Spirit, I say do not walk among those in
darkness without shining brightly your light and your gifts of
the Holy Spirit that you have received. It is urgent. The fate of
the rich man will come to many who dare remain lukewarm,
complacent and indifferent. I have thus spoken in My Word
and My Word is truth. Let all who have ears, hear and let it
penetrate your heart.**
**I love you, My little ones. In My love of you, I warn you
and guide you. For love of Me, gather one another unto Me.
Your Living God exists and desires an intimate relationship of
love. Lukewarm and indifferent souls reject their Living God.
Therefore, my parable explains, there is an abyss** (in death)
**which cannot be crossed between fervent souls and indifferent
souls. My Spirit of Prophecy is present today in abundance,
even as I spoke through Moses and Abraham and all My Prophets of old. My Words to you are My Love poured out from My**

Heart, thus proclaiming, I am your Living God! For it is written I shall not leave you orphaned. I will send you an advocate. He is with you now. Receive Him!

Happy the souls who slumbered but now awaken because they hear the call of My Holy Spirit. Come. Come all you souls who thirst. Come to the fount of everlasting life. Drink of Me. Be revived. Know your God of Love, Mercy, Joy, and Hope. Allow My riches to permeate you. Prepare now. Receive My warning. The day of reckoning will descend upon you like a thief in the night. This is how you are to prepare. Pray and love. Prayer leads to love and intimacy, which I desire. Intimacy with your God will lead to increase your faith, hope, obedience, and humility. Thus, I will be glorified in you. My blessing. My Love.

Jesus

3-1-94 Tabernacle 9 AM
Your Fill of My Joy

My child, My *Soul,

This day, delight in Me, your Master and your God, as I delight in you. **Open your eyes** (they were closed) **and look around you. You are alone before your God. The church is empty except for you. So it is, I shall give you a gift today, as your faithfulness delights Me. I give to you, your fill of My Joy. As King David danced for Me before the Holy of Holies, be merry and joyful for Me.** (Here my soul felt incredible elation.) **How I love those who come to My Tabernacle, where I enthusiastically await souls. So few come. In faithfulness you come. You sit with Me for love of Me. There is nothing but for Me to take delight in your faithfulness. You are My Joy this day. I see your surprise at My words.** (Here Jesus knew immediately, I was suspicious because His tone was so happy and light in this Lenten season when I expected only the cross and suffering.)

My little soul, your journey is one of hills and valleys, joys and sorrows, the Cross and the Glory. Perhaps tomorrow I will plunge you into the depths of My Passion. You know not what I choose for you. Today I offer you My Joy. I choose to delight you in and through My Joy. I lift from you your burden. There will be time for sorrow, which will pass. I have said there will be fire of purification for humanity. Though it will seem intense and burdensome for a period of time, you (humanity) will pass through it to the other side, where you will experience love and joy which you cannot comprehend now.

My pain (which will be your pain) is the loss of souls who will perish because they decided against Me. Tomorrow I will teach you of this. Today I desire to lift the cares of your heart so that you will dance for Me in joy, as a child, as (King) David. Sing to Me. Delight in Me. All the day, in all you do, let joy and thanksgiving be on your lips and in your heart. You cannot begin to comprehend the paradise that awaits you and all who love Me. My Father's Kingdom is beyond your comprehension. I will lead you to it. Come, My beloved. Be My joy. Allow Me to delight you. I ask nothing more of you this day. My Love.

Jesus

3-4-94 Prayer Group with Father
Our Lady's Embrace

As each one stated their prayer intentions, I saw, with the eyes of my soul, Our Blessed Mother, as a radiant white being of light with a long flowing mantle. Though I see only a suggestion of facial features, her grace and dignity overcome my soul. She is pure, meek, gentle, and Oh, so loving. She stood before each person with a small smile as they prayed, then she leaned over to kiss their forehead in a kiss of such love and tenderness.

She spoke:

My precious ones,

I, who am your mother, bless you. I am with you this night to embrace you as a mother embraces her child. I received your prayer intentions this night as precious jewels to present to the Father. He received them as an offering of your love, as I told Him your intentions are in union with my intentions. Tonight I have pressed your heart into my heart so they can beat in a perfect rhythm and union.

My little ones, do not be sad as you are being taught the way of the Cross. Rather, rejoice, as you are receiving much grace. My Son and I are teaching you the love of the Cross in order to unite you and form you into the image and likeness of your Divine Lover, my Son and your Lord, Jesus. This is what I ask of you. My Son and I search for generous souls, souls willing to unite themselves to the cross for the salvation of the world, souls who beg to carry the Cross of my Son for love of Him alone. We search the world for souls willing to lay down their lives for souls and for love. Who among you can love this much? Who among you will carry the cross for love alone? I have raised you, my little ones. You are, indeed, ready to make such an offering of love. This season, when you remember the price paid for your eternal life, will you kneel before the Cross and ask God to give you the grace to accept the Cross, offering yourself as a libation to my Son? Who among you will soothe His Most Holy Wounds?

You are my Joy, my children. You gather in union with me and you grow in love and faith. Be my children of hope by hoping always for the coming of my Son into the world again. Thus souls will be converted and the reign of my Immaculate Heart can begin. Your prayers are instruments of grace for your own soul and the souls of many. Please pray unceasingly. I thank you for responding to my call even when you are tired or feeling only dryness. The love of my Son is worth your perseverance and sacrifice. Sometimes the journey to divine union is one of much waiting and yearning. Wait for your Beloved in faith, hope, and love. He will come. He will come. Thank Him, my little ones, for allowing me to speak to you this night. Rejoice, for He has provided very generously for each one of you. Trust. You are so very beloved of the United Sacred and Immaculate Hearts. I love you. I bless you.

Your Mother

3-14-94 11:30 PM My House
Zeal for My House

*Soul, Receive My Peace. My peace I give you. In the deepest recesses of your soul I am. Where I am there is peace. Where

I am there is love. I am Love, infinite and unconditional. I am with you. I am your teacher. I have planted in you a burning zeal for My house, My beloved Bride (Church). Behold her with My tenderness. Tend to her. She is in turmoil. Lest you become confused as to the truth in her and through her, I have provided an anchor to the truth in Father. Listen to him and you will learn of My mystical Bride in the truth. Truth is deeply rooted in My priest and he is one of the means of My teaching for your soul.

My Bride is bleeding and My Divine Heart bleeds for her. However, do not become discouraged or sad when you see this through the graces I impart to your soul. Recall My Words. It is written: "You are Peter and upon this rock I will build My Church and the gates of hell shall not overpower it." (Matthew 16:18) Hell is indeed storming her. My Words of old stand today. She will prevail. The truth shall reign in purity and totality. She will weather the tempest. Her present woundedness will end in Victory.

Soul, I will teach you of her that you may serve her. For it is written: "The greatest among you must be the servant of all!" (Luke 22:26) I reveal to you her woundedness that you might heal her. I allow you to view her through the eyes of Divine Love, and with the spiritual vision of My Own Sacred Heart, which burns with love for her. Your hunger and thirst for knowledge and understanding of her, I will quench by My own hand.

Here are the means of My teaching for you. First is prayer. In contemplation I can impart to you more knowledge by the power of the Holy Spirit than many years of study. Secondly, is My Word. Devour it. Thirdly, My messages, which you write. The fourth means is Father, vessel of My Holy Spirit. In the future there will be more formal studies. For now, child, anticipate with spiritual joy the journey which the Father has ordained for you. Once more I say to you, please grant Me complete freedom in you and walk humbly with Me. I will never violate your free will. I will always ask and invite. I desire your heart and soul in totality to be given in complete freedom. Only then can I impart the depths of my riches into your soul. I will instruct you and use you as My vessel at My discretion. Learn to wait patiently for your Beloved. Let us be together always and everywhere. I am Lord and I am with you at every moment, within and without your perceivable knowledge of Me.

Do not follow the example of a generation which moves in and out of Me through inconstancy and rebellion, flirting with Satan and with Me, God of all creation. Thus it is written regarding the lukewarm. "Because you are lukewarm, neither hot nor cold, I will spit you out of My mouth." (Rev. 3:17) Give your God your yes or no. However, do not remain lukewarm. I desire fervent souls. Souls who will allow My furnace of Love to penetrate their heart to ardent and zealous levels. This is all for now, *Soul. You have been gracious for writing My words though you are tired. Rest in Me now. Receive My blessing. Go in My Peace. Your heart is full for Me. This is all I ask of souls. I have received consolation in you. Remain forever in Me. My Love.

Your Jesus

3-16-93 My Home 1 AM
Shine in the Darkness

My child,

My Light I have placed in you. Your preference is to remain among the people of the light. However, you have been given the light to shine in the darkness. I must send you among the darkness in order to dispel the darkness, for it is the children of the darkness who are in need of the light. In My Word, I have taught you. I am the Shepherd who will leave the ninety nine who are with Me, to go after the one lost, who is not with Me, and all of heaven rejoices over the one who was lost and is now found.

Follow My footsteps, My child. Gather the lost. Enter the darkness as a beacon of light. Put aside your fear of rejection. What would it matter that all would reject you if I, your King, accept you? Love risks in complete abandonment, and in risking everything, all is gained. Suffer yourself unto death that you may live in Me. (My will must be willingly crucified in order to live in Him.) I love you.

Jesus

3-22-94 1:15 PM-3:15 PM, My home
Three Scenes: Love, Life, and Death

In the middle of a busy day, in the midst of a meeting, I was overcome with a sudden physical fatigue. I came home immediately, fighting the fatigue. I tried to accomplish some work only feeling weaker and weaker. Thinking a short nap would take care of this, I lay down on the sofa. I had no other option at this point. However, I did not sleep the sleep of the night. I entered a state of deep contemplation. With the eyes of my soul, I saw and heard many heavenly images and words. In the deepest part of my soul, these were pressed into me. For two hours I experienced God's Grace. I felt Divine Light entering my entire body penetrating the depths of my soul. My heart felt pressed upon by His Heart. I clearly was not in a normal state of being nor in a state of regular sleep, though I truly do not understand the state I was in. I seemed to fade in and out of many heavenly scenes. I cannot recall all that I saw but I can recall some of it. It pains me deeply to try to write or describe what is truly indescribable. As Jesus has asked me, I will record what I can recall with Light of the Holy Spirit. Obedience leads me to write.

The first image I saw in this state of prayer was His Sacred Heart. If I had not been lying down at this point, I would have definitely fallen down from the immense power of His Divine Heart. The Sacred Heart of Jesus is completely aflame with love. Like a red hot fire in a fireplace, the iridescent tissues were radiating both heat and light. They do not flicker as a flame in a fireplace. They are constant. The more I gazed at them the more intensely they burned, the greater the heat I felt. His Heart overcame mine, causing me to feel physically a great pressure upon my own heart, which seemingly dissolved into His. (During this scene, more than others, there were many Angels, which I sensed not only interiorly but also exteriorly, as I remember opening my eyes to see if I could actually see anything exteriorly.)

His Sacred Heart contains everything! All spiritual riches are within. His hands opened to hold His Heart open to me and I heard:

Behold the Heart of Divine Love, who longs to be received and loved in return. Behold the riches within, which are scorned and pushed aside for trinkets worth nothing. Behold love rejected. Oh generation lacking faith, Oh generation lacking love, how My Heart bleeds for you.

Look, soul, look how wide open is My Heart. He who wants to enter may do so now. Humble yourselves, Oh generation of pride, and you may enter My Divine furnace of Love. Then, Oh mortal man, the little flicker, the tiny ember of love and faith which remains buried in your mortal heart will be enkindled and set on fire again. Come, Oh cold generation, and warm yourselves by My fire of Love. Come, Oh faithless generation and I will take you to a place of faith that you might believe again. Come, Oh broken and suffering generation. Heal yourselves in Me and My fire of Love and healing Grace. Come, Oh generation of darkness. Shed your sinfulness and ask My forgiveness. I shall say to you, My Mercy is yours; enter forgiven children. Walk through the darkness into the Light of My Sacred Heart. Behold My Heart, that radiates My Love for you. Soul, behold the Heart of the God of Love, the Son of the Living God. Pray My wretched and little soul that your generation will behold this Heart of Mine. (Jesus continued to show me His rejected Sacred Heart. Tears flowed down my face, for I longed to love His Heart enough to make up for the entire world.)

The next (2nd) scene I can recall was the Angel Gabriel announcing to Mary she would become the Mother of God, His chosen Tabernacle. I saw a petite, young Jewish girl in a cave type room with very little light. I saw a huge Angel of magnificent light with so much power of presence, the petite woman fell immediately to her knees. As the Angel Gabriel spoke to her, announcing her motherhood of the Son of God, she became a being of light with such radiance that I could scarcely perceive her human form within a completely transparent illumination ,within her being as well as surrounding her to the point of actually filling the room with such brilliance of light that it was uncomfortable for the eyes of my soul to look at her due to the radiance. Her gentle voice spoke to me.

Behold, my little ones,

The moment when God's Love became flesh for love of you and love of me. Behold unfathomable condescension, when His Majesty descends from heaven to embrace humanity on earth, taking upon His divinity the lowliness of man's humanity. Behold the moment the Loving and Merciful Father gives up His only Son for love of you. Behold the power of the Holy Spirit entering my soul. Only in the Holy Spirit could I surrender my "fiat" to God's Will for me, and only in the Holy Spirit can you surrender to God's Will for you. Though I did not understand my journey's path, I placed myself in His hands, He who understands everything, He who is Master of all. His Holy Spirit and His grace allowed me to unite my human will securely to His Divine Will. If you allow, I will assist you in surrendering unto His Divine Will in all areas of your journey. Here, take my hand.

The last (3rd) scene that I can recall is the Way of the Cross. From the Garden of Gethsemane to His death on Calvary, I watch Jesus suffer for me. In this scene, I saw myself as well as many faces I recognized; for it is this present generation who is carrying out the Crucifixion. He spoke:

Oh My children, humble yourselves, because I died for you and your sins. From the Cross on Calvary, through the blood which flowed into My eyes, yours were the faces I observed, yours were the sins I absorbed by My agony and death. From the beginning of time I knew you and your sinful ways. I saw what your generation would become, a lost generation. Still I willed to suffer and die for you that you may know My Love and allow Me to save you. In the Garden (Garden of Gethsemane) **I saw your faces as I shook with terror and pain. My agony progresses as My very capillaries burst and I sweat blood for love of you. In My agony in that dark night of man's betrayal, I cried, "Abba, Abba, spare Me this cup - yet not Mine, but Thy Will be done." Here is My example to you in your moments of suffering. Cry out Abba, Abba, yet let His Will be done. Love and have faith in Divine Providence, for by the power of the Holy Spirit, you can bear much for love.**

Scourging:

Mortal man, your generation scourges Me again and again. Like an animal I am tied and My flesh is literally torn apart from My bones. Behold My flesh and blood accumulate at My feet. The whip is in your hands as you scourge Me with your sins of pride, greed, hatred, murder, division. Oh pitiable generation, wallowing in your sickness, behold true love and sacrifice in Me. Are there any among you who know the meaning of sacrifice? Oh generation of self-love, offer reparation now. If any among you expect My Mercy, he must be merciful or all would perish except through My Mercy. You shall live only in My Mercy.

Crown of Thorns:

Above all generations, you have crowned Me with your mockery. Your lips profess I am your King. Your actions profess you are king. You mock Me as if you could fool He who sees everything you do, even in secret. Humble yourselves and give unto Me, My Kingship, My Crown. My Crown of Thorns is My Love for you. Pressed upon My head, excruciating pain burst within as My head throbbed for love of you. My Crown of Glory had to be preceded by My Crown of Thorns. So it shall be for you also.

Carrying the Cross:

Behold what is most disliked and most misunderstood by man - the Cross. Mortal man, the Cross is your mortal existence in that it encompasses love and suffering. Like the two crossing boards which form the Cross, love and suffering are intersecting. Accept both the love and the suffering of the Cross.

Death on the Cross:

Behold, My creation, love incomprehensible. Mortal man, your cries are heard as you say: "Oh distant God, where are you hiding? Men of the flesh cannot understand things of the spirit. Put on My Holy Spirit, become spirtual men and you

will find Me as your most intimate God. I am with you and in you by My Holy Spirit. I am your constant companion. Behold how I wait for you with My arms stretched out upon the Cross for love of you. Come to the foot of My Cross and let us embrace one another. Crucify your very sinful ways, crucify your human will and in dying to your will, you will live in the Divine Will of My Father who is your Father.

Let us pray to the Father now: "All Glory and praise be Yours, Almighty Father. Have pity on me, a sinner. I am sorry for all my offenses against Your Majesty. I beg Your pardon and mercy upon my soul and upon all the souls of the world. Washed by the precious Blood of Your only Son and by His merits only, I beg Your mercy. Your cup of justice is full, yet you withhold Divine Justice for the sake of many souls. I trust in Your Divine Providence. I surrender to Your Divine Will. In reparation for my sins and on behalf of all sinners, I offer myself as Your altar and give to you a living sacrifice of my life, my love, and my will. Abba, kind and gentle Father, with the aid of Your Son and Your Holy Spirit, as well as the Blessed Virgin Mary, teach Your creation to love and to serve, that we may give our glory and enter into Your Kingdom, even on earth, in fulfillment of Your divine plan for us. Amen."

Here, Jesus released me to go and pick up my son from school. Still, in a profound spirit of prayer, I prayed my Rosary out loud in my car as I drove to pick up my son. Only when my son was in the car with me did I seem to return to myself.

Jesus, I am madly in love with You!

3-23-94
Fullness of Life in My Holy Spirit

My children,
I am the Son of the Living God, your Lord and Savior. Again I say to you, I am the Living God. I exist. I am alive today and forever. The gift I desire to impart to you this night is the gift of life. I desire to bring forth from the depths of your heart and

soul a new life, which is alive with the fire of My Holy Spirit. I desire your heart spring forth as a new well, gushing with the waters of true life in Me, through the power of My Holy Spirit. As your Lord and lover of your soul, I see within your heart much oppression and affliction. I desire to liberate you from the oppression and heal you of your afflictions. All things are possible in Me. If you allow Me to penetrate your fears and anxieties, if you allow Me into the deepest recesses of your heart, I will come into those hidden places and I will fill them with life and love, bringing forth in you a new wholeness which is beyond your comprehension.

My children, My Love is what I desire to give you. Will you surrender and permit Me, your Lord, to give unto you a new fullness of life in My Holy Spirit? I offer My very heart to you this night. Who among you will enter this furnace of Divine Love? Inside are all the riches of life in the Spirit of the Living God. Enter and partake to the full.

Pray, My children that man will behold this Heart of Mine. My Heart has so loved My creation and My creation has rejected My Love. Tonight, say yes to this Heart of Mine and allow My furnace of Love to enkindle the embers of your own heart, that you may live with My fire of Divine Love. My peace I give unto you. Behold this day, My Mother. Allow her to be your mother. She will hold your hand and teach you to say "yes" to the Father's Will and guide you into the love of My Sacred Heart. My blessings be upon you this night.

Jesus

3-25-94 Feast of Annunciation
Remember, the Father So Loved the World

My dear children,

My Maternal blessing to you. I who am your Mother bless you, as I am truly with you now and always. I accompany my spouse, the Holy Spirit, as He imparts many graces upon this assembly. I especially bless my beloved priests and ministers for responding to the call of the Holy Spirit with hearts which are open, loving and hopeful. My priests and ministers are the catalyst for many conversions, and they are in need of my Maternal love and guidance. The Holy Spirit will bless them abundantly as they receive His enpowerment and as He enkindles the love in their hearts.

Oh my little ones, I ask of you this day, when you remember the Father who so loved the world He sent His only begotten Son upon the earth for love of you, return His Love. He is worthy of all your love. As the Holy Spirit enabled me to surrender my human will to His Divine Will, He shall do this for you. Only permit Him freedom within your heart and soul. God's love is the most precious of all gifts. Cherish His Love in complete humility. Serve Him with complete generosity. Respond to His call to holiness in complete charity. He who breathes His life in you is holy, holy, holy.

My little ones, do not think holiness is a call to greatness. Truth is holiness is smallness, simplicity, purity. You become holy by doing ordinary things with extraordinary love. Simple vocations foster holiness in a spirit of sacrifice where one must lay his life down for the good of others. Here the human spirit who desires to be exalted overcomes His Will in order that God alone is exalted. True measure of holiness is to be found in the degree to which your human will will die in favor of the Divine Will. Prayer is the means to holiness. Prayer facilitates a soul's ability to surrender his free will in faith for the truth of the gospel.

The Holy Spirit who descended upon me, descends upon you. He announces that you are chosen to fulfill a mission only you can fulfill and He promises the graces to carry out your mission. He awaits your fiat of love. Peace of my Son, Your Lord and Savior be yours.

Your Mother

3-25-94 Feast of Annunciation, At a Conference
My Priests

Prayer over some priests.
Our Lady spoke:

My beloved sons, my priests, listen and let it penetrate your hearts. I who am your Mother, protect you, guide you and love you.

You are tucked in the shelter of my Immaculate Heart. From the beginning of time, you were chosen. From the beginning of time you have been prepared to fulfill a mission through the intercession of my Immaculate Heart. Your very lives have been a living sacrifice of love to the Father.

My sons, the world situation is very grave. I am building an army of souls whose love and sacrifice aid in the salvation of the world. Pray, pray, pray for my priests. Pray their hearts will be open so that they too will be vessels of the truth under the protection and guidance of my Immaculate Heart. There will be trials, persecutions, moments of doubt, even moments when you will not wish to walk the path set before you. In these times, I will be with you to console you and urge you on your way. Many are the graces reserved for you. Draw from me, your Mother, all that you need. My very heart is yours. Trust in my love. I love you, my sons, I love you.

Your Mother

3-26-94 At a Conference
He Who Overcomes

Rev. 3:10 "Because you have kept the word of My perseverance, I also will keep you from the hour of testing, that hour which is about to come upon the whole world, to test those who dwell upon the earth. I am coming quickly: hold fast what you have, in order that no one take your crown. He who overcomes, I will make him a pillar in the Temple of My God, and he will not go out from it anymore; and I will write upon him the name of My God and the name of the City of My God, the New Jerusalem, which comes down out of heaven from My God and My new name. He who has an ear, let him hear what the Spirit says to the churches."

This night, the Spirit of the Living God says to the Church: you are My mystical Body and My Holy Spirit is the very heart of My mystical Body. Having taken upon Myself the fullness of your humanity, I have borne in My Body every form of suffering. I willed to do this for love of you. As the Father did not

spare His only Son the agony of human suffering, He will not spare you suffering, rather He will send His grace upon you through the person of the Holy Spirit that you may bear suffering for the sake of love and for the sake of salvation of souls. The Cross is both love and suffering, intersecting as the wooden boards of the Cross intersect one another. Love can and does bear all. For love of you I have offered Myself as ransom for you. My very Blood and Flesh bears witness to My Love of you. My people, you are My Body. Who among you will heal My Body for love of Me? My Love has already healed you. Believe only and you are healed. From My Cross on Calvary I saw your faces in this moment in time, and in the midst of My agony I experienced the joy of loving you with all My Heart. I ask only this of you: that here and now you would know the infinite depth of My Love for you and that you would walk in the confidence of that love. My Peace.

Jesus

3-28-94 My Home
There Is So Much I Don't Understand

My dear child,

I bless you. I am with you in a most intimate way. Many graces will be given unto you as you continue to say "yes" to my Son and I. The outpouring of grace which you are witnessing provides for souls to fill their lamps with oil. This is the infinite Mercy of the Most Holy Trinity. The days will come when the reservoir of precious oil will be required in order to overcome the tumultuous days, a time of great purification, which must occur in order to make way for the triumph of my Immaculate Heart and the reign of the Most Sacred Heart of my Beloved Son, Jesus. Child, please pray for the priests, bishops, and cardinals. Pray for the Church. Prayers of fervent souls truly alleviates suffering and saves souls on the way to perdition. In this holiest of times (Holy Week), contemplate the agony my Son suffered for the sake of the salvation of the world. Unite yourself to His Passion, offering yourself also, as a living sacrifice.

Dear Lady, my mother. There is so much I do not understand. I'm not sure of His Holy Will for me now. Oh dear Lady, please guide this child of yours.

*Soul, listen only to the voice of my Son. The Holy Spirit will guide you and your spiritual director. Tend to your family. Your vocation is wife and mother. Your calling is to prayer and writing. Your mission unfolds before you as you walk with my Son and I. In prayer you will grow in union with God and know His Will for you. We will guide your footsteps. Wait patiently on the Lord. He goes before you, preparing the way. *Soul, He is worthy of your complete trust. His very Body and Blood are sustenance for your soul, enabling you to bloom as a new spring rose blooms. Facing toward the sun, the petals slowly unfold; one by one they open, each in its perfect timing, creating a flower of beauty, unique in its fragrance and grace, embellishing the earth, giving glory to its Creator. Even in silence, its beauty is appreciated by many as a tangible expression of God's Love for His creation, and its fragrance lingers in the hearts and in the memory of many. The rose rests all winter and all fall in order to show itself in springtime and summer. All God's creations wait on the Lord, for His timing is perfect. Rest in Him. For now He teaches you. In due season, more will be revealed to you. Be at Peace. Pray unceasingly. Seek only His Face, His Voice, and His Will. You are His. My love, dear child.
Your Mother*

4-8-94 Prayer Group
White Rose

My dear children,
I, your Mother, bless you and again I come to gather your intentions and your prayers as beautiful offerings of your love. I will present them this night to the loving and merciful Father. I come also to present each one with a white rose from my heavenly garden. This is to be a symbol to you of my love, as well as a symbol to

you of how beautifully you are blooming. Know that each blooms according to the perfect timing and perfect Will of your Lord. He alone truly knows what your soul requires in order to attain the perfect union you are destined to have in His Kingdom.

This night I assure you of the Infinite Mercy of my Son. Come, drink of the unending Fountain of His Mercy. Drink to your fill. Any soul who approaches the ocean of His Mercy will receive in abundance, and none will be turned away. However, I remind you that to receive His Mercy in your soul is to promise Him that you too will be merciful to all souls.

Dear little ones, the hour grows late. The world situation is very grave. Truly the world as you know it is passing away minute by minute. Therefore, little ones, come to the Fountain of Mercy now. Offer daily sacrifices in reparation for the atrocities which wound the most Sacred Heart of my Beloved Son.

My little ones, I come as your Mother requesting of you more prayer, more sacrifice (fasting)*, more love. Your love is to be unconditional. This kind of love can only be accomplished by much prayer and true attention to the graces offered at each minute. Therefore, my children, remain in a state of recollection and peace so as to hear always the voice of the Beloved. Truly He speaks to you in the silence of your heart. Let your strength and perseverance be in the Eucharist, Reconciliation, Adoration and Rosary. The Rosary has united you and protected you from many temptations which attempt to penetrate your unity and faithfulness. Thank you, my children, for praying the Rosary.*

Rest in the most Sacred Heart of Divine Mercy. I love you.
Your Mother

Interiorly at the Visitation, I saw Our Lady present a white rose to each person in the Prayer Group. She was a being of bright white light, approximately four feet tall, and the heavenly rose was radiating white rays of light up and down the stem with the bud slightly open/blooming. She smiled lovingly upon each one as she handed them the heavenly rose. The details of her face were not clear to me because of the brilliance of the light which emits from her.

4-12-94 Tabernacle
Purity of Intention

Dear child,

Give Honor, Glory and Praise to your Savior who is with you always. *Soul, I have covered you because your intention is pure. Therefore, go forward in this new day. The door is closed on the past. Do not spend time reflecting on what is finished. What you have learned you have learned and take with you. However, a new day has begun and there is much work to be accomplished. Seek only My Face, My Will. If I am with you and in you and you are in Me, then what does it matter how the world perceives you? In fact, because I am with you and in you and you are in Me, you can count on the fact that you will be persecuted, rejected and considered a threat. This is because My ways are so very contrary to man's ways. In a world lacking so much love, man cannot recognize love, even when Love Himself is among them, standing face to face. (i.e. the Pope) How quickly the rejection comes because what is meek, pure, peaceful, humble, obedient and docile is in direct opposition to a prideful generation.

Therefore, even in the Name of God, pride speaks out to accomplish its falsehood and deception. Beware, as much is proclaimed in My Name, but is not of Me. It is not My voice of truth nor My way of love. My way will always be a peaceful invitation to love. Only the humble man can truly accept this invitation. Only a humble man will forego his way for My way. Only a humble man will lay down his will for My Will. What is truly lacking, in the situation which has come to pass, is humility and love. I have covered you with My protection. This is not to say there will not be darts flung at you; rather, darts will not penetrate your heart because I have surrounded you with divine protection. I ask you to love, reconcile and embrace those who persecute and disagree with you by being an instrument of My Peace. I will guide you in this way.

*Soul, you have kept Me waiting upon you because too many words are being spoken. I have not forsaken you. Do not forsake Me. Do not seek from friends that which only your most intimate friend can provide. Please, *Soul, do not doubt the voice within you, which is Me. Trust, it is My voice. Oh My doubting Thomas, believe, believe. I am presenting you a resurrection, a new life. Come, follow Me. I love you.

Jesus

Here, interiorly, I saw myself climbing a mountain. I had reached a little higher level as I was approximately one third the way up the mountain, which was steep and rocky. I appeared like a speck on the mountain. I understood I could not move myself. His Grace alone could cause me to ascend. I understood if I abandoned myself to His Grace, He would take me to the mountain top, where His tent awaited me. In my impatience, I desired to run toward the mountain top only to find myself paralyzed until His Grace allowed me to move. I understood the climb would be at His pace and by His Grace. Along the way would be much waiting, felt absences and longing and times of visitation. At each level of the ascent along the way, I was to keep busy accomplishing the work at hand. All the while my heart would live in a constant state of yearning, seeking and waiting for the sublime moments of visitation. Every day I would die a little to myself until by His Grace I would one day rise in Him and enter His tent forever. Oh day of glorious and eternal union! Jesus, I love You and I am Yours forever.

4-15-94 My Home, 1 AM
Purity

"The truth is there is much beyond our power to control and there is much beyond our right to control."

Ready to go to bed, closing up kitchen, I glanced at the picture of Jesus on my refrigerator. I heard interiorly: **Come, *Soul, come. Let us be together. Please write My words.** Here I hesitated as I looked at my watch, thinking it was very late and worried I would not get up to get my son to school on time. Jesus, of course, knew my thoughts and said: ***Soul, I have removed your fatigue, have I not?** I said: Yes, Lord, I do not feel fatigue now, but in the morning! He said: ***Soul, trust Me. You will not be tired in the morn-**

ing. Come, please write My words. I said: My Lord, forgive my hesitation, please. I will do as you ask.

My child,

My beloved flower, I come to you now to teach you, as I am your Divine Teacher. I come to feed you by My own hand. Here, My beloved, receive the chalice. I offer you the wedding cup filled with My Blood. Drink now that you may be purified by the Groom's blood. You are My altar and My altar must be made pure. From the beginning I chose you to be pure for Me. Though the world defiled you, this of your own volition, My Grace came upon you. From the onset of My visitations to your soul began a process of purification. The Father's Mercy, in union with My Blood, in union with the love of the Holy Spirit and in union with the Blessed Virgin Mary, washes your soul of its defilement. Purification by fire leads to purity. Purity is what I require of you, My altar. Purity of soul, heart, mind, body. Pure love. Pure obedience.

Behold My Mother, who is a crystal clear vessel of purity through whom the Holy Spirit radiates more fully than any other human being. To be pure is to be spotless before God in the Light of His Truth. As My Mother was created in such purity and remained in such purity, no purification was necessary in her. In all other chosen souls, purification is required. Indeed all mankind is stained by original sin, washed away by Baptism. Still, man continually falls into sin, for such is the human tendency. Grace alone enables a soul to renounce sin. Humility enables a soul to acknowledge both its sinfulness and need of God's Grace to overcome.

Dear one, your purification shall continue, intense and in rapid time. I have entered your house to sup with you. All the while My Presence requires I purge you, shape you, test you, challenge you, enlighten you, sometimes uncomfortable, sometimes overwhelming, sometimes outright painful, all the while necessary in order to tighten My embrace of you, all the while preparing you for sublime union with the groom, who joyfully awaits his bride, washed white as snow. The more purified you become, the more crystal clear a vessel of the Holy Spirit you shall become. This for the Honor and Glory of the Father who chose you, for Me and in Me, for the good of many souls, whom you will gather for His Kingdom.

*Soul, as I am purging you, so too, I will use you to purge others. As you sometimes resist My purging, so too others will resist you as an instrument through whom they are purged. This is My Mercy. You are a vessel of My Mercy for others. It is in My Mercy and through My Mercy that purging takes place. In spite of the immediate pain and ultimate death of many imperfections, what emerges is a soul resplendent and pure, humble, and pleasing before God.

All Glory to the Father whose mercy is upon you and upon the world. His Mercy is never ending. All Glory to the Father who allows a soul to die a thousand little deaths in preparation to rise in Him and in union for life eternal. All Glory to the Father whose mercy will never cease for the humble and just man, and whose justice will befall the proud and unjust man. In all your joys and your crosses, My dear one, give Honor, Glory and Praise to the merciful Father.

Come follow Me, *Soul. Shed the thinking of mortal men, for I am offering you true wisdom, given only to simple, pure, and humble souls. Soul, My beloved, I await you always. Draw from Me all your requirements. I am in you and you are Mine. I love you, *Soul, I love you.

Jesus

4-20-94 My home with my spiritual director.
Remnant in the Immaculate Heart

During Rosary, around the Fourth Glorious Mystery, the Assumption, I saw Our Lady with arms outstretched to embrace the entire world (globe). She folded her arms around the world and pressed the world into her Immaculate Heart. The world seemed to dissolve in her heart.

I heard interiorly:

My dear children,

How I long to embrace all my children and press them into my Immaculate Heart. Within I can raise them, prepare them to present them to the Most Holy Father. However, so few will allow me to embrace them. Many are the graces which flow through my Immaculate Heart, yet so few accept them. How my heart grieves for you, my children. How many are truly on the path to perdition. Truly only a remnant are sheltered within my heart. Therefore, the remnant, the few who are with me, are very important to my Peace Plan for the world. The prayers of those within my heart are very important toward the salvation of the entire world.

The darkness of the world drives the lance deep within the Most Sacred Heart of my Son, Jesus. Pray, dear children, pray always. The trials and tribulations which will befall humanity have already begun. Still, there will be more suffering as the days progress through a time of purification. Again I say, the Rosary is a great weapon against the evils of your day. Arm yourself with the Rosary. The string and the beads of the Rosary bind you together in my Maternal protection, guidance and love. My little remnant, how I desire to grant you more grace, and how I shall call upon you to aid my peace plan. Be prepared always to answer the call. I am your Mother who loves you and delights in being with you in prayer and always. Trust. Hope. Do not fear. Pray! Pray! Pray!

Your Mother

4-25-94
Embrace and Address the Wounds of My Church

7 AM, my shower, I heard Jesus interiorly.

*Soul, I shall reveal to you My Church in her woundedness. As I reveal gaping wounds from which she bleeds, do not stand staring in amazement and weeping for her only. Rather, embrace her and dress her wounds. Tend to them as I reveal them to you. Quickly apply the ointment of your love, and bind her wounds with the dressing of your charity. Behold her and es-

teem her in your heart, as she is Mine and I love her as unconditionally as I love you, and with the unending generosity of
Grace which I have given you.

Even as I reveal the depth of her woundedness to you, recall always what has been written and promised to you in My
Word. For it is written: "the gates of hell shall not prevail against
her." And though hell has unleashed its fury upon her, in the
end she will triumph. So it is written and so it shall be. Therefore, go forward, for love of Me, tend to her, faithfully and lovingly. As I have done for you, so too shall you do for her. Do
you love Me, *Soul? Then do this for Me. I am with you always, even unto the end of time. My blessing, My Love.

Jesus

10:30 PM My home

My Lord, Jesus. Upon reading above message, I must admit to
You that my understanding of how I am to help your Church is
very limited. Lord, I am not grounded in your Word, theology, or
Catholic teaching. I will do whatever you ask of me because I remain ever more deeply in love with You. Jesus, you have revealed
yourself ever more tangibly to me. More than ever I spend the time
pining for You alone. This intense love for you sustains me always.
In situations which would have previously consumed my time,
thoughts and energy, I find myself walking through peacefully. I
am grounded in the knowledge and security of knowng I am loved
by You in such a way that words cannot describe, because Your
Love is so ineffable.

My Jesus, You have put me to the test lately. Yet, Your Love
and Your Peace in my soul overrides the human heartache. My God,
daily it seems you increase my capacity to love You and to know
you! My Beloved Jesus, Your powerful fire of Love overcomes me.
Your strength presses upon me, infusing me to bear more and more.
My God and Savior, behold this soul of mine. The fire within burns
with love for You. Receive me and have Your way with me, as this
insignificant soul continually whispers "yes" as You tighten Your
embrace of me. It seems I am drowning in Your love!

*Soul, allow Me to teach you, please. Forsake the thinking of mortal men in favor of My spiritual ways. My Holy Spirit fills your soul. You are My Temple. Those who persecute My Temple persecute me. My Temple will not be destroyed and you are My Temple. Do not be concerned about who will receive you in My Church. Many will not. However, many, chosen by Me and prepared by My Holy Spirit, will receive you. I go before you. The doors will be opened for you in My perfect timing. I am the builder and the designer. You are My instrument only. I will place you in the proper situations in the proper time. I will place My words in your heart and you will speak them as I direct you. You speak of not being grounded. I say to you, if you are in My Love and I am teaching you My way, which is true wisdom, then what more do you require? In Me you possess everything! You speak of enduring more and I say to you that indeed I am preparing you. My beloved one, I am strengthening you and teaching you because the days ahead will be very difficult for My faithful ones. My Mercy moves Me to prepare you and many others now.

My child, many will be sent to you and others chosen, as you have been chosen. You will bless, heal, shelter and teach many as the days of purification for this generation progress. You will be My mouthpiece, My vessel of Love and Mercy. My remnant, desiring to remain faithful to My truth, will find living the Gospel a challenge, as the world wallows in its sinfulness and godlessness for a dark period of time. The Father purifies this generation so that peace and love in Him and through Him shall reign on earth as in heaven. In the days of tribulation, the cenacles which began at My Mother's request, through her visitations and intercession, will be the sanctuary where the true faith will be preserved. Blessed are the children who heard My Mother's plea and took her messages to heart. These prayer cenacles will be under her constant Maternal care and protection.

There are many chosen lay people who will participate in the preservation of the one true faith and gospel. You will come to know many of them. You will assist one another through many difficulties in the future. There are chosen priests who are being prepared now. Pray for the priests. My Holy Spirit is doing a mighty work in many of them. Each must decide to accept or reject the call We (the Trinity) are placing within their heart. Remember, dear one, this is a time of the separation of the sheep from the goats. I have taught you this that you are not scandalized by what you witness before your very eyes.

My little one, I will continue to reveal the present darkness to you that you may intercede by your prayer and sacrifice. This is what I ask of you; love, pray and sacrifice on behalf of all souls. Thirst for souls as I thirst for them. Lay down your life as I laid down my life for souls. My altar, I am your intimate lover and friend. You are Mine. Let zeal for My house consume you. On the day of our union I will immerse you in the ocean of My Love and forevermore you will remain one with Me. Even now I give you a foretaste of these that you may know My promise. My words to you are truth.

*Soul, though I come to you in a most intimate way as friend and lover of your soul, be ever mindful that I am the Master and Creator of heaven and earth. In Me all things are possible. You acknowledge your limited understanding of Me and My ways and this pleases Me. So many claim to know Me and understand My ways. But they do not know Me or My ways at all. They are deceived in their thinking. To the humble and contrite heart seeking to know and love their God, I will reveal Myself. This is all I wish to say for now. Come, My beloved. Let us rest in one another. Receive My peace. I love you. I love you.

Jesus

4-29-94 Prayer Group
The Storm is Truly Escalating

As we began to pray the Joyful Mysteries, I saw interiorly the following scene. There was a huge mountain, on top of which was the tent of the Most Holy Trinity. At various points along the mountainside, I saw the members of our prayer group. Each was at a different point on the way up the mountain. Each lead a large group of people toward their goal, union with the Most Holy Trinity. Each member had to wait upon the helping hand of our Blessed

Mother as she took ahold of our right hand, one group of people at a time, to lead the group to ascend the holy mountain. There was much difficulty in ascending the mountain because there was a terrible storm trying to prevent our ascension. The wind and the rain came against us making it impossible to ascend the mountain except through the powerful intercession of our Blessed Mother. Each member of the group had to battle the storm with all their strength! Our Mother's helping hand lead each to safety along the ascension up the mountain. We all waited and prayed for one another and for all the souls which were being led by us.

I then heard interiorly:

My dear children,

Let your ears hear my words. Take them seriously into your heart. My messages, here and all over the world are very serious. My little ones, the world situation is very grave. Evil forces redouble their attack on souls. War is waged over many souls. Believe as I have taught you. Pray, pray, pray always. Offer sacrifice in reparation of the atrocities wrought upon the Most Holy Trinity. Allow me to guide you always by coming to me in prayer. By this means the Holy Spirit will reveal to you the next step of your journey (spiritual journey).

Each of you will lead many souls to the love of Our Lord and Savior. I will place people in your path. Doors will open and you will find yourselves in situations where I can use you as vessels of God's truth and light. You need not attempt to think of ways to help. Rather be attentive to the very situations we place directly before you. The storm is truly escalating. Many souls are at stake. Be careful, children, to discern the spirits and seek spiritual direction in every important step you take. The evil one is very clever. In his subtleties, he deceives many into a false sense of peace and well being. He leads souls to deviate from the one truth. Remember, my Son, Jesus Christ is the Way, the Truth, and the Life. No one enters the Kingdom of God except through Jesus Christ, my beloved Son.

The Good Shepherd will gather unto Himself His faithful flock. He will lead His flock to the safety and security of His Most Sacred

Heart. This does not mean that you will not experience difficulties and/or persecutions. Remember little ones, any witness to the truth will be persecuted. Even as the most innocent and pure lamb was led to the slaughter, so too, you who are innocent and pure (in intention) *will taste of the rejection and persecution of the cross.*

My Maternal heart, in union with the power of the Omnipotent Holy Trinity will teach you to endure all things in peace. By abundant grace you will learn to love, and love bears all things. Your earthly sufferings will end one day as you are welcomed into the Kingdom of God. Then, your face will behold the face of my Beloved Son, Jesus. All Glory be to the Most Holy Trinity. Be steadfast in your faith. Pray, pray, pray. I love you.

Your Mother

5-4-94 12:45 AM My Home
Great Difficulty Will Befall Your Country

My dear child,

A time of great difficulty will soon befall your country. Many will believe God's curse is upon them. However, it is God's Mercy, which will allow a time of purification. In the suffering, the scales will fall from many eyes. Hardened hearts will be rendered softened. Denial of God's existence will require a great resistance to the truth of the Gospel as manifested in the time of purification. The land of plenty is stained with the blood of innocents. The hearts of many are twisted and dying through a lack of any sense of moral values. Falsehood has infected hearts so they are blind to the truth. The Father's loving hand balances the cup of justice, which is overflowing. The Infinite Love of your Triune God will manifest itself through the Cross, the Cross of suffering, which is Love. I have prayed to the Father on behalf of the world saying, "Father, Holy Father, keep them in Thy name (the name which you have given me) that they may be one with Me even as we are one, that you may be glorified." The salvation of mortal man has always been and shall always be through the wisdom of the Cross.

Therefore, My little one, prepare in this manner. When the hour comes that your Cross is placed upon your being, carry it with the love and dignity befitting a soldier of Christ. Now, tend to your heart. Put all your relationships in order. Ours is the first relationship of love which you must tend to. Prayer facilitates this relationship. Therefore, pray unceasingly. Some difficulty can be mitigated by the prayers of fervent souls. Put into order your heart with the hearts of all your brothers and sisters. Forgive, as forgiveness is in order. Love unconditionally. Live charity and mercy daily in all your actions, your speech, your thoughts. Though you will witness much suffering living through much hardship, I implore you, be strong in your faith. Be faithful to the truth, which I am. Be hopeful and joyful of the passing of the purification. As many souls lose their peace, Satan will thwart you to do the same. I implore you, be an instrument of My Peace to all. Cling to My very Heart of Love. I will provide an endless fountain of Grace for you. This is My promise. As I promise you, so too, I promise My priests and faithful souls. My embrace of you will only grow stronger, though you may not perceive this in your senses. In your will and in your spirit, there will exist a certitude of the indwelling of the Most Holy Trinity in your soul. This grace enables your soul to bear much hardship and bear much fruit.

Soul, do I have your fiat to love and surrender unto the Divine Will? What I ask of you is your unwavering Fiat! The sanctification of countless souls will be the fruit of the trial of your country. Do not be afraid. There is nothing to fear. The tempest will clear a path upon which holy souls will walk in harmony with one another. This pathway will lead to the very heart of their Triune God, who is Love, Mercy, Justice.

Prepare now by living the virtues contained in and taught by the Immaculate Heart of Mary. Through the intercession of her Maternal heart, and all those contained within her heart, much suffering can be alleviated. Take to heart the seriousness of her visitations and her messages. My Peace, My Love, dear one.

Your Jesus

Jesus added:

*Soul, Satan is tempting you to distractions of many kinds. Guard your thoughts. Here is how you pray unceasingly. In all your duties, lift your thoughts and heart to Me. I am to be the center of all you do, say, and think. Ponder Me constantly. Be mindful, you are My Temple. I am with you always. There is no time to spend on thoughts other than prayer. I will never forsake you, My dear soul, My altar. I love you.

Jesus

5-4-94 Tabernacle
Satan Desires Your Demise

My dear children,

Please accept the unconditional Love and Mercy flowing through the person of the Holy Spirit, from my heart and the Heart of your Redeemer, my Son, Jesus. Do you not know that we truly understand your human nature? We know intimately the way of your humanness, experiencing all that you experience in body, mind and spirit. Your nature has tendencies toward weakness, woundedness and sinfulness. We understand your humanness, which tends toward self. Mortal man simply cannot accomplish any good in and of himself. Love is a fruit of the Holy Spirit in your soul. Love is God's Grace. Only God can lead you to rise above your human nature.

You simply run in circles without His Grace in your soul. So many of my children strive toward goodness and only fail, becoming discouraged because they strive alone. They do not avail themselves of all the grace at their very disposal. Is it any wonder that frustration leads to a halt in your journey toward holiness? Who can be holy without living the sacramental life and prayer? Believe me, children, many attempt to respond to the call to holiness without commitment to prayer and the sacraments, and quickly the evil one attacks and discouragement sets in. Indeed you are called to be a holy people. Yet this can only be accomplished by your acceptance of the Grace of God to make you holy.

Salvation of the world is through and in Christ. Yet each soul must work out their salvation in and with other souls. This is love, loving one another as Christ has loved you. Ask, seek, and knock. It shall be given unto you. God desires only your higher good and happiness. Satan desires to rob you of God's Grace. Satan desires your demise and many are the souls headed his way. My little ones, come. Come to your Jesus. Take my hand. I will show you the way. It is simple. You are my children. I am your Mother. I love you. I love you. My blessings and peace.

Your Mother

5-6-94 Tabernacle, Scottsdale
Hearts Are His Garden

I closed my eyes to pray in the Adoration Chapel. Immediately I was given an interior image of my own heart. Jesus began to teach me, revealing my heart as a garden, a vast garden. I first noticed the beautiful white rose bushes covered with glistening dew. Jesus taught me the dew represented His Grace. Each petal bore many drops of dew, glistening radiant dew. The rose represented the beauty which had formed as a result of my acceptance and response to His abundant Grace. Jesus seemed pleased and so was I. He then pointed out the many thorns on each stem of the rose. He taught that each thorn was a necessary and integral part of the formation and beauty of each particular rose. The thorns up and down the stem represented the tears, trials, sacrifices, self-denials which were necessary and caused the rose to bloom. I then noted the soil of my garden to be rich looking and well tended to. Jesus taught, the soil, where my very roots are planted, is rich with His Mercy and Love. He taught me; my roots are faith in Him. They must grow deeper and deeper. He promised to always surround them with the rich soil of His Love and Mercy. This would enable my garden to withstand the many storms which would come upon it. Each storm would challenge me. Some will appear to strip my garden bare. Here, He promised the beauty would remain even in vines which were bare, but back, for a season. Because the roots run deep (faith) and the soil was rich (in love and mercy) the branches would bloom again and again. Each season would produce greater abundance and beauty. He promised there would be growth, even when there appeared to be dormancy.

I next noticed weeds, especially around the most beautiful rose bushes. Jesus taught me, these represented "self." He constantly tended these weeds by plucking them, lest they choke off the beauty of the garden. Here I was permitted to see interiorly my Mother Mary and St. Francis, pulling weeds in the garden and tending the roses. My soul was elated! My thought: Who am I to receive such care, such grace? Immediately Jesus said "**I desire to attend to all hearts, all souls, as I attend to yours**." (Here I felt Jesus' sadness that He is denied this by many souls.) Jesus continued to teach me that Satan enters my garden in the darkness and attempts to fertilize the seeds (weeds) of self. Jesus taught that He will never violate my free will. He is a gentleman and invites tenderly. If I were to choose to ingest Satan's poison (because he disguises it as good tasting), it will cause the weeds to choke the beauty of the garden. The poison would de-flower the garden, God's beautiful handiwork. Here Jesus taught me the importance of standing ever vigilant over my heart, which is His garden, His place of rest and beauty. Jesus taught, He searches all hearts, each child of God. His own Sacred Heart aches at the state/condition of many hearts. Rare are the hearts of beauty and love where He is welcome to rest. Here His teaching ended. I entered a very silent, imageless state of contemplation.

(Oh, that all souls would know of His Love!)

5-8-94 AM My home
Motherhood

Our Lady drew me to her image on my living room desk.

Happy Mother's Day. My dear little one,
I who am your Mother forevermore, bless you. My little one, who can comprehend a Mother's love? Who, but another mother,

can know the love, the bond, the depth of mother and child? In your heart rests the joys and tears of raising your own children. In your heart are the countless moments you spent observing them, teaching them, loving them through the peaks and valleys. The connection is constant, strong and of the heart. Even when physically separated, your heart is secured to theirs. My child, can you imagine that I experience this for each and every one of my children? Even at greater depth, my love is maternally unconditional that I may draw my children to my Son. Much of your time is spent equipping your children for their earthly journey. My intercession, my teaching is to equip my children for their spiritual journey, drawing them into an eternal union with our Triune God.

I implore you continue to teach the little ones to pray. Persevere until prayer becomes an integral part of their nature. Prayer facilitates union with God. Let prayer be their first response to all life's joys and sorrows. Simple prayer from the heart is most pleasing to our Lord and Savior. Teach them to converse with Him as their most intimate friend. Teach them the Rosary is the most powerful prayer after the Eucharistic Prayer (Mass). Through the Rosary I can teach them very much, as they become a part of my Immaculate Heart.

The days ahead will be difficult for all my children. However, Satan is actively pursuing the children, desiring their downfall, desiring ownership of the next generation. He knows his time is very limited. Unite to my Immaculate Heart, that together we may intercede on behalf of all God's children. Protect your little ones from Satan's ways of self-destruction. Let that protection be in and through my Immaculate Heart. Together, my little one, let us plead God's unfathomable mercy upon all souls. Let your Light (which is my Son in your soul) dispel the darkness of this present moment in time. Consecrate yourself, your family, daily to my Immaculate Heart. Pray unceasingly for the family of man. All are my dear, dear little ones, whom I love with my maternal heart. Dear child, I love you.

Your Mother

5-9-94 My home - afternoon
Beg Mercy Upon the World

The rays shone through the shutters of my dining room. I looked directly at the beautiful sun and immediately it began to spin. I was delighted and moved to prayer. The sun's radiance and splendor always reminds me of His Majesty. His Love filled my soul. I spoke to Him as my most intimate and loving companion. "My Lord, Your love fills the depths of the chambers of my heart. Thank you, kind Jesus, for all the grace, all the favors, mostly for Your Divine Love in my soul. I am filled by You and for You. If only my love could compensate for all the souls who do not love You. My God, fill me with Your unlimited love that I may love You to the fullest depths possible. Make my heart an ocean of Your Love that I may return love to You in greater and deeper amounts. I live to love You. My soul longs for You, aching for union. Little else can capture my attention, affection for long. All my thoughts lead to You. Oh my Sacred Heart, hide me in the chambers of Your suffering heart. Wash me with Your precious Blood. Make me pure for You, Prince of Purity. Teach me, form me into Your image and likeness that I may cease to see myself outside of You. My God, how long this earthly exile? Union, sweet and holy union! My life is Yours. Take it! Make me thoroughly yours."

Long pause. Jesus replied with the same words He spoke at communion this morning.

My little one,
Raise your voice to the Father Almighty and plead His Mercy upon the world. This is your prayer now, Mercy! Child, how needy the world. How quickly, like wildfire, Satan traps souls in this era of evil. How cold the heart of mortal man. What is sacred? All is pride. How little reverence, how little dignity remains. How cruel the hearts that oppress, murder, cheat, debase. Evil spreads deception, claiming more souls daily. Poor, poor souls. If only souls could realize their dignity before God.

My little one, each soul is created to live in union with God eternally. What Dignity! I implore your prayers for Mercy upon

the world at this late hour. Pray souls would allow one small ray of My unfathomable Mercy to enter their soul. My Mercy in a soul will lead the soul back to Me, so irresistible is My Mercy once received by a soul. At each communion, beg mercy upon the world, that the Father will shower the world in this time of great need. In My name, be mercy for all souls. Mercy is an extension of My Divine Love, whereby I forgive unconditionally, having borne in My Body all debts. My Mercy is deeper than all the oceans. Immerse humanity in my mercy through prayer and sacrifice. I have taught you, pray always. It is urgent. The world, all souls, are in great need of mercy, especially now, to overcome Satan's final hour!

My little one, your prayer soothes My Wounds. I bless you. My Peace, My Love. Be patient, My child. I Myself will come for you when it is finished. I love you.

Jesus

5-12-94 Tabernacle after 8:30 AM Mass
Padre Pio

The grace at Holy Communion increases daily. Upon returning to my pew I simply say the name "Jesus" and seem to enter a state of union in my soul. The church emptied as usual. I closed my eyes and entered contemplation. In a short time, I saw the face of Padre Pio. I saw him as you would see a person on TV - only three dimensionally, black and white only. He appeared with a big warm smile on his face. I felt peace and joy. I wanted to run to him. His face radiated joy. His expression was that of one who knew the best secret and delighted in it! He simply looked at me. He exuded love. He was more exterior to me than the usual way that I see Jesus or Mary (deep in my soul). I was sure I could open my eyes and behold him there in mid-air, head and shoulders only, halfway between me and the tabernacle. I opened my eyes. He was gone.

Because this was "different," I immediately dismissed it as deception from Satan. I was sure he was toying with me. I decided it was false and to forget it. I said "I love you, Jesus," and entered contemplation, which was imageless and silent, for 45 minutes. By the time I left church I'd forgotten about Padre Pio. I had a busy day (meetings, etc.). Late afternoon I rested on the sofa. There were two books on my table. One I just purchased two days ago and had not opened. Its title is "A City on a Mountain," on Padre Pio. I began to read it. Within a few pages, I came upon black and white pictures of Padre Pio's early years. I began to thumb through the book to see the pictures. I was suprised to find the exact picture of the face of Padre Pio which I had seen in church. I read that Padre Pio desired to be a Capuchin, the most recent of the three branches of Franciscans, because they were founded for the purpose of restoring the literal observance of the rule of St. Francis of Assisi. The mode of life was simplicity, austerity, happiness, and cheerfulness.

My first thought was that I was losing my mind. I told my husband, son, and Father, thinking they would agree with me, but they seemed to believe in what I saw. In church, I began to believe in my heart that perhaps Padre Pio really visited me. I wondered why. I began to understand in my soul. He came to encourage me just by his expression of joy, warmth and welcome. He came to urge me in the way of simplicity, purity, humility, and peace. He is a helper of souls.

5-12-94 3 PM
Padre Pio Again – Die to Yourself

My husband and sons went out of town. I have three days of solitude. Having completed my mass, prayers, and errands, I had most of the day free. I thought about going to the mall, but the peace of my home and the presence of Our Lord and Lady beckoned me to stay home. I thought about addressing the paperwork on my desk; this was only to fulfill my need to feel productive. I was feeling guilty about spending the day alone in prayer. Still, there was a strong call to do just that.

I was sitting at my kitchen table vacillating when I picked up the book on Padre Pio again. I read the chapter on confession. Suddenly a series of imperfections and sins were brought to my mind. It was as if a male voice was whispering in my ear. I was reminded that I am not as "detached" from material things as I think I am. I was reminded of my pride. I was reminded of my vanity in desiring the right clothes, etc. I was reminded of subtle resentments harbored deep in my heart.

I then heard an interior male voice:

"To learn the way of tender hearted Francis is to learn the way of the Master. There exists in the heart of a friend of Francis, the strong desire of death of self, because this alone leads to union with the Beloved. To walk in the footsteps of the Beloved is to be crucified, to taste of Calvary. The daily eating and drinking of His Blood and Body will transform you in Him.

Little one, the overcoming of self is a necessary suffering. It is like the cutting out of cancer. When you believe you have overcome self, you are in trouble. Until the moment of separation of soul and body, you will daily battle to overcome what is your self. Yet this is entirely possible by grace, moment to moment. Do not delude yourself, little one. Do not think in terms of progressing, think in terms of faithfulness to grace. It is not yours to progress to Him. It is His to draw you unto Himself. It is yours to learn of utter dependence and nothingness. It is His to do with your wretched soul as He pleases. This is poverty of the spirit, utter neediness of God. This is the way of truth.

In dear Francis is your example of humility, which is truth. His poverty, his little, humble way, tender and compassionate heart are yours to follow. I am the helper of many souls on earth, especially called to learn the way of my friend, Francis. It is unimportant that you know much of Me. I give glory to the Most Holy Trinity by leading souls to them. Praise the infinite goodness of God who looks with favor upon your soul. The taste of Calvary is bitter-sweet. Taste of it. You will rejoice and give thanks. I will assist you, reminding you of poverty of spirit, and especially in the making of a good confession. I bless you in the name of the Father, the Son and the Holy Spirit." Padre Pio

I suddenly had a strong desire for confession. I prayed if God willed this and if Padre Pio was really helping me, that my Spiritual Director would arrive early enough to hear my confession. Sure enough, Father arrived a half hour early and I went to confession. I was given an extraordinary clarity to see my sins. This made for a very graced confession. From the beginning of my conversion, Jesus has taught me through the writings of many saints, and the saints have always been very tangible to my soul. However, to receive this kind of communication caused me to worry about deception. I will note that while I actually saw Padre Pio's face and heard his words, I felt peace. It is only after the fact that I tend to worry about deception.

As I write these words, I hear Jesus: **I ask of you to write only. You are My instrument only. It is Father's to discern. All discernment is in his hands. Therefore, there is no need to worry. If you are being deceived, Father will tell you. Until such time as he says so, continue to record as he requests. Your soul is in his capable guidance. Obedience to him is your safeguard against deception. Never trust your own inclinations, present all matters of your soul to him. Trust, little one. I speak and work through him. My work in your soul will never be between you and I alone. My work in your soul will always include the guidance of a capable director and teacher. Therefore, banish worry from your heart. It only robs Me of the praises I wish to hear from your heart. Remain in My Peace. I love you.**

Jesus

5-13-94 Rosary Prayer Group 8 PM
Mary's Heart Pierced

I saw interiorly two separate scenes as we prayed the Chaplet of Divine Mercy. First, I saw the exposed Immaculate Heart of Mary, pierced by a huge sword and bleeding. Second, I saw many people wounded on the ground. Each of us at the prayer meeting were sent out to bind the wounds of the people. As a prayer sister began the Glorious Mysteries, I heard Our Lady interiorly.

My little, little ones,

Pierced is my Maternal heart when I see how Satan traps so many of my little ones, robbing many of their Peace, Love, Dignity. He intends to rob as many as possible of their inheritance, which is union with my Son, Jesus Christ. My little ones, I desire for you to know the importance and power of your prayers and sacrifices. Know that your intercessory prayer and sacrifice literally rescues many souls who would otherwise be lost. I so love all my children! The tears I shed fall upon the earth to help melt the hearts which are cold and hardened due to lack of love.

Therefore, dear ones, again I ask you to be vessels of life-giving love. Allow my Spouse, the Holy Spirit of God, to fill you, mold you, teach you, and go forth according to His inspirations in your soul. Be ever vigilant over your heart, discerning always the spirits. Draw from my Son everything your soul requires. Fear not, my little ones, as you witness the separation which is taking place as the sheep and the goats are separated. This is the Hour of Decision. If a person is not with my Son, he is against Him. Each soul must decide. Pray that souls will decide for God. I bless you, my dear children. Remain in my heart, pierced by the sins of my children. Pray, pray, pray. Thank you for responding to my call. I love you.

Your Mother

5-15-94 3 PM
Ascension – Above all is Love

My child,

All Honor and Glory be to the Father, most High. When it was finished, when I had glorified Him, He drew unto Himself My Body and Soul to sit at His right hand in Paradise. Oh glorious day for the Most Holy Trinity. Oh glorious day for mankind. Having completed the work of salvation in My Body according to the Will of the Father, I ascended unto Him. In doing so, the message of the Gospel was to be spread by My disciples. That man not be orphaned, the Third Person of the Holy Trinity would descend upon earth and remain forever. All souls will experience an ascension to the Father. Souls will stand before the Most High Judge of souls. From the throne of the Most High shines the Light of Divine Truth. Herein the soul will enter either the gates of paradise, the gates of purification, or the gates of eternal fire, each according to their love or lack of.

Therefore, My little one, above all is Love! Love first He who created you that you may love Him. Then love all whom He created to be loved. (Here I looked at His picture.) **You look into My eyes and it is not the physical beauty which draws you into them. Rather, they are pools of My Divine Love, inviting you to drown in them! Please continue to write.**

How little you are, My precious one. Indeed you are more weak than the little bird who sings outside. That little bird sings always in praise of His provider. He worries not regarding shelter or food. Unencumbered, he flies freely. Through the hand of the Mighty One, all his needs are met. There is nothing but for him to sing then. He lives and he dies in the hands of the Creator of all nature. I desire you to learn the way of ascension to the Father Most High, through empowerment of the Most Holy Spirit, in My Name. All the days, rejoice and be glad. I have taken hold of your hand and My Mother takes the other hand. Together, allow us to assist you in ascending the holy mountain, that on the day of your judgment you may be found worthy to enter the gates of paradise. Then, My little lamb, I will show you what is real, that your joy will be complete.

What, therefore, must you do? Love. Only love. Above all, love. The capacity of your heart (to love) is limited. Therefore, purge self-love. Replace it with My own limitless Divine Love. Only My Divine Love in your soul will enable you to love enough to enter the gates of paradise. My peace. Give glory to the Father always and forever. Go forward in discipleship, living the gospel. My peace. I love you.

Jesus

5-18-94 My Home Midnight
Telephone Conversation

Re: Telephone conversation with a friend. Upon hanging up, I was shown immediately the sins I had just committed in that conversation. It was as if my very soul was under the high powered magnification of a microscope. I recall in medical assisting school, putting a drop of blood under the scope to magnify it. It was as if my sin was that drop of blood and it was magnified by the light of the Holy Spirit. I must confess: I was critical and negative of people. I lacked love and charity. I judged people. I divided and spoke against a reputation. Sin is a terrible thing. It wounds the Beloved and darkens a soul. Every transgression is shown to me. My thoughts, my tongue, I must discipline them. My sins cause me much anguish. It is truly painful when revealed to me in such a manner. What a blessing we have in Confession.

5-19-94 Notre Dame, South Bend, Indiana
Notre Dame Conference: Triumph of the Immaculate Heart

My son and I traveled to South Bend, Indiana, for admissions office appointments for the Notre Dame University. As the plane flew over Notre Dame University just prior to landing, I was taken by the beauty of the land. I heard Jesus interiorly:

Indeed I have blessed America abundantly. Her beauty is breathtaking, but the hearts of her people offend My Sacred Heart. Pierced is My Heart by her pride, her greed, her violence, especially her killing of the innocents (abortion). **Pray My little one, for your country as she turns her back on God.** (I beg His mercy!)

Once settled in hotel, I phoned a friend. She advised me that there is a National Medjugorje Peace Conference in Notre Dame! After our appointments, we attended the conference.

Father Luciano, Bishop Hnilica's secretary and interpreter, spoke first regarding the utter priority of the fulfillment of the Fatima message regarding the triumph of the Immaculate Heart of Mary. He speaks of Russia as central to the triumph, of western blindness to the fact that Russia still poses a threat to the world; for if she did not fully convert, if we did not pray for this, there would rise up from her a source of great destruction for the world. She is vital to the triumph as foretold in Fatima, as well as to the secret unknown to us. The theme of the Conference is "Unity for the Mission of the Triumph of the Immaculate Heart of Mary."

We processed to the Lourdes Grotto at Notre Dame. Bishop Hnilica arrived at the altar and led us in prayer as he placed the Blessed Sacrament in exposition for adoration. There was a silent time of prayer. In the silence, under the full moon, I heard the voice of Jesus. He began to dictate the following words: (Second half came on plane home.)

My child, listen carefully to the words of My Apostle of truth (Bishop Hnilica). **The people of the United States are invited to unite under the banner of My Mother, Mary Immaculate. Her Immaculate Heart comes in your midst by heavenly decree. It is her heart's desire to reconcile the children of the world with their God. So it is that I say again to My creation: "Behold your Mother" (John 19:27 child). She comes to prepare her children for a new Pentecost. She is central to the era of Peace, which will come to pass when the triumph of her Immaculate Heart is realized. She is central because her Immaculate Heart is always in perfect union with the Most Holy Trinity. She is central because she serves God by leading souls to Him.**

This is a most critical time in the history of the world. The hour of decision is at hand. Decide for God or you stand against He who is Love. The Most Holy Trinity desires the triumph of the Immaculate Heart of Mary. God has crowned Mary Queen of Heaven and Earth. The world fails to crown her. When she is crowned Co-Redemptrix, Mediatrix of Grace and Advocate, her Immaculate Heart will triumph and Satan will be chained in the abyss. Peace will exist on earth as in heaven for a period of time, as foretold in Fatima. (The "peace" Jesus refers to is spiritual peace – peace of soul which comes when souls are reconciled to God.)

My Peter of today is in union with the Divine Will, working as an Apostle for the Triumph of the Immaculate Heart. The visitations and prophecies of the past century lead toward the fulfillment of the Triumph. This Triumph, which is the will of the Most Holy Trinity, will lead to unity and division at the same time. There will be a profound unity of heart for souls united in and for the Immaculate Heart of Mary. The division

will come as many souls refuse the Will of God by refusing to accept the Triumph of the Immaculate Heart.

Many are called to work toward the Triumph. Prayer groups, apostolates and messengers have been working toward the triumph by answering the call to conversion, prayer, fasting, reparation, repentance. It is this army of little souls who will carry out the Divine Will toward the Triumph of the Immaculate Heart under the leadership of and in union with My Peter of today. The army of little souls will be raised up to witness the triumphant heart as she crushes the head of Satan. Unity within this army is very important. Satan attacks within to cause division and confusion. Strive for unity, My child. The Triumph can be accomplished when unity exists in the hearts of Mary's army. Unity comes only at the cost of much sacrifice, deep humility, profound faith, faithful obedience, constant prayer, cooperation with grace of the Holy Spirit in each soul, perseverance to the cause and your calling - most importantly, love.

Deep is My Love for all souls. Great is My Joy for those who serve to bring about the Triumph. How is it that mortal man cannot see that her Immaculate Heart exists deep within the chambers of My Own Sacred Heart? So united are our two hearts, they cannot be separated. So it is, when her heart triumphs so too shall Mine, to reign over all the heavens and earth. Now My child, please behold your Mother.

My little one,

The path of holiness leading to the gates of paradise is a journey of union to the Divine Will of God. It is the Will of the Most Holy Trinity that the triumph of my Immaculate Heart come in fulfillment of the message of Fatima. The Grace of His Divine Mercy, poured out through my visitations on earth and messages of love, have been for the purpose of leading souls on the path to holiness to form an army of little souls who are called for the fulfillment of my Peace Plan, as given at Fatima and continued in Medjugorje. All modern prophecies lead toward the fulfillment of the Divine Will for the Triumph as spoken at Fatima.

My child, it is no coincidence that you are drawn here on the weekend of the conference dedicated to the Triumph. Let the words you have heard penetrate your heart. Great should be your confidence in Divine Providence. It is He who calls you to serve. Each step you take is ordained by heaven. Though you know not your next step, trust Divine Providence to lead you, teach you and use you as His instrument according to His holy Will. I will assist you always in the carrying out of the Will of the Father. Will you please allow us liberty in you? May your zeal be increased as the words of this conference penetrate your heart, that you may dedicate yourself to work for the Triumph of the Immaculate Heart of your Mother.

Now do whatever my Son, your Savior, tells you to do. My little one, prepare now. There will be much to suffer in the future. However, if my army of little souls will unite, pray, fast, repent, much suffering will be alleviated. Pray always united to my Maternal heart. Unconditional is my love of all souls. Remain little for me, my dear one. Believe. Hope. Praise and glorify the Name of God, most high. I love you,.

Your Mother

Dear Mary, please, please assist me always, that I may do only His perfect Will. Keep me from falling due to vain imaginations or deceptions from Satan. Sometimes, dear Lady, I fear I will falter under my own inspirations or under evil inspirations. Be my confidence, please. May your Heart triumph soon, my beloved Mother. I love you boundlessly!

5-25-94
True Self Knowledge

Waiting for my son who is having a haircut, I hear Jesus and begin to write His words:

Dear child,

Great are the lessons I am teaching you in your soul. Joyfully do I receive the pain you experience as death of self continues within you. Abandonment docs not come easily for you,

My little one. Strong is your human will. Great is your appetite for pleasure. Because of this, great is the difficulty you have in surrendering to your Master. Oh, but how your Master, Lover of your Soul, truly appreciates each and every time you lay your human will down in favor of the Divine Will, especially as you do not understand fully the ways of the Divine Will. Your strong human will is both blessing and cross. It is blessing when you unite it to the Divine Will because strong then is the Union. Yet daily, it is your Cross, because My Divine Light in your soul reveals the sick and weak nature of your human will. Know, My little one, how tender is My Heart for you as I observe you dying daily to your own will. Your nature is rebellious My little one, yet patiently I teach you to overcome your rebellious spirit. I see how deep is your pain. I see how difficult it is to die to your appetite for pleasure. Yet steadily do you learn each day, the way of My tender Sacred Heart. And daily do I reveal yet another treasure of My Heart to you, that I may entice you to live entirely in Me.

Oh, yes, My little one, truth walks side by side with you to keep you on the straight and narrow path. Great is your love for Me and extreme is your poverty, yet I graciously accept you in your wretchedness. Still, you must be patient with yourself as I am patient with you always. Perfection comes at great cost; death of self. Not that you have chosen the path of perfection. Oh, no, child, it is I who have chosen you to come unto Me by way of perfection. Your suffering consists of this. My Divine Light illuminates the particles of your soul. Your weariness comes from the battling of your very self, moment to moment. I see that humility and obedience do not come easily for you. I see the sacrifice required, the turmoil in the deep recesses of your heart. I accept and appreciate your day to day dying of self. Grace illuminates your soul, that each imperfection, sin, appetite, frailty, is exposed clearly, declaring your unworthiness constantly. Yes, My child, I see that from time to time you wish to escape this painful reality. If you would run from it, you would not find rest. But if you choose to stay, with the help of My abundant grace, you will overcome and peace shall be yours. My peace I will give to you.

Dear child, great is My delight in the work I am accomplishing in you. Tenderly I lead you, inch by inch, that you may ascend the holy mountain of the Blessed Trinity. What your soul experiences now will be given unto all souls on earth in the very near future. Better to prepare for the moment of illumination, when truth shines its light into the soul of ever mortal man. Think how unbearable the moment of truth if I had not visited your soul in this hour of great Mercy. My altar, pray for the souls who rejected My Mercy though I came knocking at their door, My Mercy ready to envelop them. Can you hear their cries of agony? Can you see how they will fall to the ground writhing in their misery? What then will be heard over all of the earth? My God, have mercy! Mercy, mercy, mercy! My children, partake of My Mercy now that you may help souls in need at the moment of illumination. My Mercy is an ocean. Come, drink of My Mercy now! Heed My words, My little ones. My altar, let us rest in peace now. I love you.

Jesus

5-27-94 Prayer Group 9 PM
Army of Little Souls

As we prayed from the heart our petitions, I saw our Lady in the following manner: She sat in front of the fireplace on the floor. She wore the most exquisite white gown which draped all around her. Surrounding her head was a crown of twelve stars which sparkled like diamonds in the sun. As we prayed from the heart, she looked at each face, nodding in agreement with our intentions. She radiated Joy! The area of her chest pulsated. It was a beautiful pale pink in color. She was very joyful, as if she was delighted by our prayer from the heart. She listened as each prayed their petition, then she spoke at the Third Joyful mystery.

My dear ones,
Joyfully do I come in your midst to sit in intimacy with you. As you offered your prayers from the heart, I gathered your intentions into my own Maternal Heart. Our very hearts are joined in prayer.

I see how much you are learning as I listen to your heartfelt prayer. Great is the charity of your intentions. Abundant charity toward your brothers and sisters so pleases my Maternal Heart. My heart is touched also by the unity of your hearts. Rare and precious is the gift of unity of the heart. Even in a group of good hearts it is difficult to find unity within. My heart desires only to unify the family of man so as to present all souls to the Most Holy Trinity.

My dear ones, at Fatima I revealed to three shepherd children the utter horror of hell. This would serve to accomplish in them a great zeal to serve God, sacrificing themselves, to avert souls from the pain of hell. Oh how they grew in charity toward poor souls on the path to perdition. I invite you to join in the sacrifice and charity of the message of Fatima, by offering yourselves for the good of souls who are far from God. Many souls will eternally suffer the pain of hell if I do not have holy and charitable souls to offer prayer and sacrifice on their behalf.

You, my little ones, are my consecrated souls. You exist as part of my army of little souls, living in the shelter of my Immaculate Heart. Pray then for my intentions, please. Offer reparation in the form of fasting (self-denial) and prayer, especially the Eucharistic prayer and the rosary. Allow charity to reign in your heart toward poor and lost souls. Carry daily your crosses. Joyfully offer your crosses for souls in most need of God's mercy. In this manner you work toward the salvation of all souls and of the world. You could not possibly offer Me a sacrifice which I would consider too small. Rather, my joy will increase with the smallest of your offerings. Daily, there are so many opportunities for you to offer on behalf of poor and lost souls.

Dear ones, these are trying times in which you live. Do not be anxious as you learn to walk the path of holiness toward your Triune God. I am with you, assisting you always. Thank you for allowing me to be your mother. Many deny me this. Thank you for allowing me to be the center of your prayer cenacle. This night I give to you a very special blessing from the depths of my Maternal Heart. So touched am I by your prayers. I am pleased to be in your midst. I thank the Father always for allowing me to be with you. It is a great grace bestowed upon you by the Father Most High. Live your lives that you may glorify the Father. One day then, together, in

His Kingdom, we will live forever more united in His Joy, Peace and Love. I love you.
 Your Mother

5-29-94 Sunday Noon, my bedroom
Would You Deny Me This?

My little one,
 Please allow me to assist you. I am your Mother. I understand a mother's pain. Deep is the burden you carry for your child. Indeed he has suffered. Yet, heavenly protection covered him. I have said this before, be confident in Divine Providence. He is all knowing, all wisdom, seeing all things clearly, in all time and in all places. Divine Providence seeks only the higher good of all souls. Although the lessons He allows seem difficult at times, they are necessary and precisely pertinent to the soul. Not that God chose this (free will), but that He allowed it so that a child's folly would be brought to light. This is mercy! In embracing you, daughter, I have embraced your family, pressing all of you into the shelter of my Maternal heart. Beware of Satan, who will attempt to destroy you and your family through this. Much prayer will be required of your family in this trial. Grace will joyfully provide for you. Draw your daily requirement through the Eucharist and the Rosary.
 My child, you have abandoned the Rosary for several days now. You tie my hands of many graces I wish to give to you through the Rosary. Please do not underestimate how much I can help you through the Rosary. It is a source of much Maternal Grace. Daughter, when you are hurt, do not avoid me, thinking you should spare me your pain and carry it alone. I am your mother, with many special graces reserved for you. Come ever so close to me in your hour of need. I wish to help you with your burden. I do not wish for you to carry them alone. What mother desires only the joyous times with a child? Is it not in times of tears that a mother's presence is most required? Would you deny me this? Independence proves nothing except that you are not yet little enough! If indeed you truly believe I am your Mother and you are my little child, then come, come, let me dry your tears. I will give you strength in the Name of

*my Son Jesus. In His Sacred Heart there is nothing which you can-
not endure for love of Him. He has chosen you for Himself and He
will provide for you. Now then, turn to me, my daughter, and allow
me to be your mother always and everywhere. I love you.*

Your Mother

Dearest Lady, my Mother,

There is deep in my heart, so sacred a love, words fail to describe. The bond between a mother and a son, I cannot possibly put
into words. Yet I know you understand precisely what I mean. I
only make this entry into my journal to record that on the night of
the accident, in a situation in which I would normally have fallen
apart, it was as if your strength, your quiet dignity, were poured
into me. Instead of crying, I was able to gaze deep into the eyes of
my son and impart into his frightened eyes all my Maternal love
and strength. That evening, and several days after, grace was so
abundant that I knew without a doubt I was functioning on supernatural graces of such quantity that I was amazed and overwhelmed.
My soul was in a state of indescribable peace.

6-1-94 3 PM Rosary with my Spiritual Director
A Great Apostasy Is Underway

Father led the rosary. At the Third Joyful Mystery, the Nativity, I could no longer pray the Rosary aloud. An intense grace overcame me and I witnessed the scenes described below. No language
of this world can capture the sublime reality of the spiritual world.
Yet at Father's request I write my poor description.

Suddenly it is as if I am transported to the Crucifixion of Jesus. I
seem to actually hear the sound of the hammer hitting the nail, driving the nail through the hands and feet of Jesus. The sound is like
thunder. It resounds. It terrifies. I hear it over and over and over. I
long for it to stop but it continues. I am trembling inside and I want
to yell out, "stop it!" The nails are already through His hands and
feet. Still, mankind keeps hammering the nails, causing His wounds
to ooze blood more red than any red of this world. Jesus is silent. He
stares into my eyes, His eyes reflect only profound love. I am made

to watch His nailing on the cross. I understand in my soul that He is crucified again and again due to my sins and the sins of the world. The sins of the world leave no moment free of pain for Him. We drive the nails through His innocent flesh again and again. I begin to feel a little faint. Suddenly as it started, it is stopped. A minute passed. Then I saw devastation of the land, with many people suffering. People were wailing and wailing, many bodies lay on the ground. Many walked around as if in a stupor. I understood they cried because of their pain, their state of being, not because they offended God or desired His Mercy. People simply did not want to suffer anything, so they wailed in self-pity. Suddenly it ended. A minute seemed to pass. I was overcome by waves of grace, of more intense "power" than previously. I heard: **I Am Who Am**. I understood the distinct voice to be the voice of the Father. His power of presence and authority made Himself known to my soul. He spoke again: **A great apostasy is underway.** I sensed a sadness coming from Him. He then showed me the scales of justice. I saw immediately the cup of His justice was just about to overflow. A powerful and steady hand held it so as to balance it preventing it from overflowing. Suddenly it ended.

I resumed the Rosary with Father. Upon completion of the Rosary I could scarcely verbalize to Father what I had witnessed, taking several moments to compose myself.

6-4-94 Vigil Mass for Feast of Corpus Christi
Union in His Passion

Upon returning to my pew following receipt of the Eucharist, Jesus spoke the first paragraph below. He finished the message much later that night.

*Soul, My altar,
My Blood enters your blood and My Body enters your body as My True Presence dissolves in you. Come, little one. I desire to take you deep into My Passion. Allow Me to reveal to you My Holy Wounds, which bleed profusely. Permit Me to take you to Calvary. Enter My suffering with Me. Offer yourself to Me again, asking I teach you everything regarding My Pas-

sion. *Soul, you tremble. I see you desire to grant Me this, yet with some trepidation. My little one, so often I have said to you, "My Grace shall be sufficient always." Surrender, then, unto My Grace. Grant permission that I may share with you My Passion. My Crucifixion continues daily. My executioners increase in number. I am rejected, mocked, blasphemed daily, causing Me to bleed profusely. Will you bear with Me this pain? I know that it is not possible that you comprehend what I ask of you. Nor can you comprehend the mystery of the suffering of which I ask you to share.

3 AM Jesus continued. Had gone to bed and was asked to write. Went downstairs to my Prayer Desk.

You see, little one, the mystery of Divine Love is just that, a mystery. Dear soul, you would understand that I am asking so much more and giving to you so much more. Through My Passion we shall be united. Our union will be your joy and your life. Our union in My Passion will be a hidden mystery between Creator and His creature. Your joy shall be to hear My Sacred Heart beat with love in the midst of agony. I will permit you to hear my sigh of pain, which is My sigh of Love. Through the revelation of the depths of My Passion to your soul, I can teach you more than years of study. You will grow in profound knowledge and union with Me. My embrace of you shall grow, as I press you into the hidden mystery of My Holy Wounds. Submerged in My precious Blood, you shall be made pure by Me and for Me. Your very wretchedness is absorbed inside My Holy Wounds. Deeply rooted in My Passion, you shall bloom and bear good fruit. Many souls then will partake of the harvest I shall bring forth in You. As you enter My passion you shall shed your garments of old, permitting Me to embellish you in new garments of pure white. Great is My offering to you. Though you have nothing to offer Me except your extreme poverty, I accept your sighs of love and your tears as a small sacrifice arising from My altar. I cherish your offering, as few souls permit Me this liberty in them. Fear not, My little one. I will empower you to endure. I am with you always and everywhere. Amen and Amen.

I love you, Jesus

6-5-94 Feast of Corpus Christi
The Deep Chambers of The Sacred Heart

9 AM My bedroom, alone, I contemplate what Jesus spoke to me last night. In the midst of my silent prayer, He spoke: ***Soul, the deep chambers of My Sacred Heart contain the richness of My Passion. For no greater love than this exists! It is written, "Greater Love has no one than this, that one lay down his life for his friends." (John 15:13) I have fulfilled love unto death for you. If then, you will permit, I shall take you into the deep chambers of My Heart, where you may taste of My Passion. This will never interfere with your vocation of mother and wife. At times which have been ordained from the beginning of all ages, I will take you into My Passion, that we may share everything. My flower, your fragrance will consist of the sublimity of My Passion. Oh what joy fills My Heart of Love even as I speak these words to you now. I foretell with much joy, anticipating the transformation of your soul through the tasting of My Passion. Your wretchedness has attracted My pity. Great is My offering to you, revealing the fullness of My Mercy toward your poor soul. Your daily eating of My Body and drinking of My Blood is the foundation upon which I build My Temple. The weakest and poorest of souls cannot help but be transformed by the daily bread of My Body. The consistent eating of My Body creates a docility in the soul, allowing the Holy Spirit to form the soul into a vessel of His desire. The Creator fashions His creature into a holy temple, where He may dwell in freedom and sublimity, which is the full right of the Triune God, who is Love.**

Oh yes, My *Soul, our intimacy will be of a great depth as I share with you My Passion. Your soul will radiate joy as a recipient of my great favor. In moments when you are alone with Me I shall reveal pieces of My agony to you. Then I shall take your suffering and grant mercy to many souls through your charity. It is not possible that I would leave you to suffer alone. If indeed I take you into the depths of My Passion are you not more fully united in your Beloved than ever before? Yes, My altar, greater and deeper shall be our union. Where My Passion is suffered, so too, is My Mother of Consolation,

along with the great protector, Michael. The Saint of My Passion, Francis, will assist you also. Rejoice My little one, My words announce great favor upon you! Love Himself comes to you, His Heart in His hand saying: Come, enter, partake of sublime sweetness. Walk into the deepest chambers of love. Hide yourself within. Become lost in Me. Explore My Heart to the depth of My Passion. Submerge yourself within. Then you shall radiate of My Love for all souls. My Passion will be your passion. My Love, your love. My Joy, your joy.

As always, I await your fiat. I am pleased to be your Teacher and to offer you such favor. My dear one, do not struggle to comprehend. Only love Me and say "yes." Trust in My tenderness. I offer you so much. In return I ask only this: childlike faith and abandonment to the will of the Father through your fiat of love. Our hearts are one. May the steady rhythm of your heartbeat remind you constantly of My Presence within. Do not exclude Me from any area of your life. When you exclude Me, you are vulnerable to many temptations. Satan desires your fall. He will pursue you. I will protect you. You have many Angels of protection. I love you, *Soul, beloved of My heart.

Your Jesus

6-5-94
Fiat

My Lord and Savior, I am but dust and ashes. You are Supreme Omnipotence, Who was, and is and always will be. I belong to You, as I am Your seed. Yet You graciously request my fiat in the offering of Your Passion to me. Rather than take what is Yours, You seek my will to comply with Your Will. If you see fit to offer me union with Your Passion, how could my soul resist its Creator's offer of love? When I belonged to the world, yes, I could resist you. But You have rescued me from the world. Now I desire only to please You. I do not understand the depth of Your words to me, for I cannot take in the fullness of Your eternal Wisdom. I know well my extreme poverty, so that there is nothing but for me to depend entirely upon You. Therefore, I give myself again to You.

You are all goodness, having shown only tenderness and mercy toward my poverty. My Beloved, come and annihilate my will so that Your Will is my life and sustenance. Each minute of my life may I ingest Your Will and may it transform me in You.

Oh my God, is it truly possible that you would visit my soul with the sublimity of Your Passion? You are indeed all mercy! I have prayed that you would teach me everything regarding Your Passion. You have heard and answered my prayer then. Your Passion is my salvation. How then could I hesitate to embrace it? No, I will not hesitate. I will run in my own awkward way into the deepest chambers of Your Sacred Heart, and I will drink of the chalice of Your offering to my soul. Because You will it, so then do I. By Your Grace, then, Your will shall be fulfilled. If then, my soul shall be allowed to become deeply grounded in Your Passion, I shall have before me always the cost of my salvation and the depth of Your Divine Love. It seems then I will be enabled to endure much for the sake of many souls, and it seems that would please you. Is this not the point of my earthly exile? I hunger and thirst for You, Lord, and You come to me offering union in and through Your Holy Wounds. I say yes, my Lord. Come, my Teacher, teach me of every detail of Your suffering for me. Teach me to love as You love. I request only that my Mother be at my side always. I love You in my own poor way. I praise You and thank you, my Lord and my God.

6-14-94 Tabernacle
Satan Toys With You

Dear child,

Satan encamps around you, observing everything about you. He toys with you. He will not hesitate in his attempts to destroy your spiritual life. He dangles the way of the world before you. You have difficulty because you have lacked discipline in your spiritual life. My little one, I am with you even as I permit you to undergo temptations. I permit you to experience the burdens which I experience due to the dark state of the world. This is the Cross I have blessed and bestowed upon you. If you but turn to Me in prayer, I will teach you to endure,

united to Me, that you rise above the Cross. Your soul then attains a higher level of charity for all souls. My little one, you desire joy. Learn, then, the joy of the Cross. Joy is found in abandonment to My Will. There is still resistance in you, My little one. I await the moment when you offer no resistance to your Lord.

Now then, in the midst of your pain you have turned to bury yourself in work. This is the thinking of the world. I have called you out of the world. Recall when you would come directly to Me, and along the way you would enlist the aid of your heavenly helpers, Francis, Faustina, Teresa of Avila. This is the spiritual way. Their works consoled you and taught you much. I am teaching you as I taught them. It is true, My little one, the temptations I allow are much stronger now. Yet the solution is the same; unite yourself to your Lord in prayer. Do not leave Me in the Tabernacle, for you are My living Tabernacle, and I am with you always and everywhere. Though you feel the weight of the Cross, I am carrying most of the weight for you. Do not, then, succumb to the one who desires your return to the world. Offer all the resistance within you to the father of all lies.

My dear one, great is My Love for you. Great is My blessing upon you. The spiritual life is the everlasting reality. Do not settle for mediocrity then. I desire so much more for you. You shall not regret abandonment to My way, My Will. Yes, dear one, the lessons I teach you are painful indeed, because they are the most sublime lessons leading toward the highest of rewards. Come, My altar, offer no resistance. This pains My tender Heart! Allow Me to teach you always. You perceive you are falling backward. But I say unto you, you are growing. The Cross which I bestow upon you causes much growth!

Recall your rose garden. The turning of the soil, the fertilizer, the repellent (insect), the pruning, the dormancy season, all of this is absolutely necessary in order to produce a single beautiful rose in due season. You are My rose garden. I will produce My own exquisite rose in you. Then, I shall behold you, My flower, in My Father's Kingdom. Rejoice. Be glad. Union, beloved union. Please, I ask of you no more resistance, for I am

Your God. Your suffering will not last. Your pain shall end, but the crown of glory shall be everlasting. Your earthly exile is but a few seasons. I desire to make the seasons extremely fruitful in and through you. I give unto you My Peace. I love you.

Jesus

6-20-94 9 PM On vacation with my Family
Could I Be Indifferent to Your Misery?

*Soul, come. I bless you. I desire to teach you. Please write My words.
*Soul, why do you suppose I come to you as I do, My pupil?

Lord, You come to me because You are Mercy. You have pity on my poverty. Your merciful Heart rescued me from death (spiritual). My soul was like a corpse. My soul was cold and hard. Having glanced at my pitiful state, you sent your Mother to me, knowing full well she would bring me directly to You. When you saw how your Mother carried me in her arms, lifting me to You, You did not deny her. You did not deny me. Like a magnet you drew me into the intimacy of your Most Sacred Heart of Love. You revealed Divine Love unto my poor soul. You caused me to be sick with love for you. My soul finds you utterly irresistible. You breathed Your Love in me and my soul awakened to life in You. You revived me, taught me, revealing yourself gently to me so as not to overpower me. You come to teach me to love that I may be a reflection of You. You cause me to desire your will. You draw me deeper into the profound divine mysteries of Your Love. My soul drowns in You, desiring to sink into the depths of Your ocean of Love. You have revealed that You are Love, full and complete. Having the fullness of the circle of love which is the Trinity, I do not understand that You would desire greatly the love of Your creature. Yet, sometimes dear Lord, when You come to me so vividly in my soul, I sense this is why You come - that I may love You as madly as I do. Lord, please teach me Your way.

*Soul, your answer pleases Me. You are learning from My hand. The Most Holy Trinity is complete in and of Himself. God is Love, One Triune God. I am the Son of the Living God. I am to Glorify the Father. In doing so, He glorifies Me, His begotten Son. Love is the way. Love (God) enters the soul that Love (God) may be reflected. In simple terms, I shall teach you. I, the Son of God, lower Myself, condescending into a soul, even to reveal Myself as a beggar, in order to teach a soul that he is to humble himself before God; he is to return love to His God who has loved him. A soul is created to love. Is not the greatest commandment of all to love your Lord, your God with all your heart, your soul, your strength? Only when a soul comes to know the intimate exchange of love between My Sacred Heart and his own heart, can the soul love God, himself and others. So then, I condescend into a soul in order to reveal Love Himself. I make known the Father, the Son, and the Holy Spirit by abiding within to further the work of love. In residency, the Holy Spirit imparts His Truth, His Wisdom, shining His Divine Light into the soul. The soul partakes in the depths and the heights of Divine Love, that the soul give glory to the Most Holy Trinity. I have humbled myself even unto death on a Cross, that I may glorify the Father, that I may save creation from eternal fire. Is it any wonder, then, that I would humble Myself into a soul, reveal Myself as Love, then seek to be loved in return? Is this not My Divine Mercy in a soul?

My child, to many this teaching is unacceptable because creation cannot comprehend the power of humility. Nor can they comprehend a gentle, merciful, loving Son of God. I am perceived as cold as stone, as distant as the heavens, as the most severe judge. Creation cannot perceive My Sacred Heart as tender, merciful, a living flame of love, full of humility and kindness, desiring only to pour My Love upon them. Man has always desired the cloak of supremacy, desiring to adorn himself in royal garments, perceiving himself to be deserving of glory. The self-righteousness of humanity is their ruin. Did I not walk among you in garments of humility, purity, mercy and love? Did I seek to glorify anyone except the Most High King, God the Father? Did I not lower myself to walk among you, to die for you? To this day, do I not condescend to come to you daily in the sacrifice of the Most Holy Mass?

My family, can you not see that I so unite Myself to you that I identify Myself with you in the pain and the joy of your daily life? It is not possible that I would abandon you, even in your wretched state of being. I long only to show you the better way, to feed you the better portion, to remove from you your utter misery. Is it possible you perceive I could stare from the heavens upon the state of the earth, look into your hearts, which know not love, and simply be indifferent to your misery? Do you not know that I run to you now? Awaken, My family, of arid wastelands; the Omnipotent One rains His Mercy upon you. Allow His Grace to penetrate your arid soil. Woe be to those who remain in slumber now. How My Most Tender Heart desires to invade you, My family. Oh blessed are the poor in spirit, blessed are the barefoot, the little ones, for such are the hearts which hear My Voice now, and harden not their hearts. Within the little ones, I shall anchor My Truth and they shall see God. The souls which awaken to see the signs of the times shall be deeply rooted in Me, and the coming tempest shall not shake them from Me. *Soul, tell Me, how many do you think are with Me?

Lord, it seems to me there are many conversions now. I know many who love you. Yet, when you reveal to my soul your lacerated heart, longing to be loved, I can only assume you are not loved as you deserve.

*Soul, My pupil, I love you. Indeed I say unto you, most of creation is not with Me. My Sacred Heart of Love is little loved by souls. There are few fervent souls whose zeal causes Me to be loved. Yet, I can do much within a fervent soul toward the work of the salvation of the world. Yours is such a soul. Burn with love for Me, allowing Me to teach you always. *Soul, go now in My Peace. Be with your family now. I bless you, imparting a fuller portion of My Divine Love into your soul. Do you love Me, *Soul?

Jesus, you know that I love You boundlessly. I am madly in love with You, Lord.

Thank you, My altar. I love you.
Jesus

6-21-94 Vacation with my family, 10:30 PM my room alone
Teachings for Many

My Lord, it seems I seek you constantly. I listen always for Your voice in my soul. I anticipate when You will allow me to be taught by You. Of late, you are so intimate, alive in me. I sense your pleasure in being my Divine Teacher. If I but think of you, if I seek your Divine Counsel, You are there. I am so grateful, Lord. I am hungry for You, Lord. You so generously provide for me. Lord, with my full capacity to love, I love You. Lord, please make my capacity to love You grow. Stretch my heart, Lord, making my soul a reflection of your Divine Heart of infinite Love. My Teacher, thank you for living in me as You are.

My dear *Soul,
Time is short as the hour of purification is soon to come upon earth. There is much I shall teach you. Therefore, often as you come to Me, bowing before Me, seeking My Holy Face, seeking only My Divine Will, I shall teach you. You know well My voice now. Come often to Me and I shall speak to you.

Lord, what would you have me do with these teachings?

***Soul, ingest these teachings from My Divine Heart, even as Ezekiel ate the scrolls of Divine Origin. Live and reflect My teachings in your soul. It is yours to record them. It is Father's to discern them. In due season, I shall give you further instructions. For now, I shall only say to you: what I teach you shall be teachings for many. Wait patiently upon your Lord and Sav-**

ior. Remain My lowly pupil. Give thanks that I am feeding you such heavenly manna.

My God, thank you, beloved of my soul. Search me completely, Lord; see how full of love for You I am. I truly appreciate Your merciful hand, which feeds me of Your Divine Love. (Here I was startled as the presence of Jesus filled me. Suddenly, I knew He was here with me, in my room, sitting on the bed beside me. I saw this clearly in my soul. The power of His Presence caused me to stop writing, to remain perfectly still, hardly able to breathe. He read my heart as He spoke to me.)

*Soul, you may lean close to Me. Rest your head upon My shoulder. Receive My embrace. Never fear to come close to Me. As I have revealed Myself so intimately, it grieves Me that you would hesitate to lean on Me for an embrace of love. I am truly with you. I love you.
Jesus

Accepting His invitation, I leaned upon Him and received His embrace. His Love, His Peace filled me and I fell asleep, my soul filled with Him.

6-22-94 Vacation with family, Morning returning from 8 AM Mass and Holy Hour before the Tabernacle.
Power of Self-Sacrifice

*Soul, what shall you give your Lord today?
Lord, I will give to You whatever You ask of me today.

*Soul, drink only water today. Eat only bread today. When you drink the water, remember Me as having quenched your thirst for true love and life in Me. When you eat the bread, remember Me as having come to feed you with the true bread of life, the everlasting bread of My Body given up for you. Will you do this for Me?

Lord, You know well my extreme weakness in this area. Only by your grace can I offer You this sacrifice. I will do my best for You, Lord.

*Soul, I ask nothing more of you. When you try, I am pleased. I wish to teach you a spirit of sacrifice. My family has lost the concept of self-sacrifice. All is self-indulgence. Little understood is the power of self-sacrifice. Sacrifice is a powerful means of repentance and prayer. The spiritual man knows this to be true. As I have called you out of the world, as I have taken your hand and led you into My Kingdom, I urge you to offer to Me, your Savior, sacrifice, in reparation for your sins and the sins of the world.

When My people decide for Me, I will change their hearts as I have changed yours. I will teach them of the intimate reality of My Love as I have taught you. As I have pity upon you in your wretchedness, I have pity upon My creation in their wretchedness. Tell them they have only to bow before My Majesty, seek Me with all sincerity, and I shall bend from heaven to invade them with My Own Sacred Heart of Love. I shall be their God and they shall be My people. I have never forsaken My people. It is not possible that I could forget My own seed.

For even the least of them, the one most lost, I will search the world to find him, to rescue him from the world who seduced him. I will carry him home in My own arms. Within My arms, the most wretched of souls will find true love, which the world could not give him because the world knows not of love anymore. When a people forsake their God, they forsake the way of love. That is why, in these days which you are living, I am raining My very Self (Love) upon the earth, that once more My family shall know love in God, their Omnipotent and Majestic Triune God. Then the prayer I prayed to the Father, that all may be one as He and I are one, shall come to pass. My altar, sacrifice yourself for souls, sacrifice yourself for your Eternal Savior. I bless you in the name of the Most Holy Trinity. I love you.

Jesus

6-24-94 Feast of St. John the Baptist, Corpus Christi Church, Vacation 9:30 PM
As Mother, I Prepare the Way

My daughter,

Bless you, my child. I am with you. In silence, I observe my son Jesus lead your soul and I am joyful. He has chosen you for Himself. Be His completely. Little one, let us raise our hearts to the Father Most High in gratitude for His infinite Mercy. It is His Mercy which allows my visitations and messages to be heard in every nation under heaven. He permits me to be Mother of all Nations, Mother of all people.

I come to you little ones, as reconciler of all people. Again, I invite you to decide for God. I request of you conversion of heart leading to a complete change of life in God. You have not yet understood the infinite Love and Mercy of the Father. You have not yet understood the Sacred Heart of Jesus is thirsting for love. You have not yet allowed the Holy Spirit of Love to penetrate the core of your heart, leading you into a life of holiness.

God desires intimacy with His creation! So it is that My Sorrowful Heart continually appeals to a world which fails to respond. How blind a generation which fails to see the signs of the times! In God's Mercy He sends little messengers to all the ends of the earth to proclaim what the shepherds hesitate to preach saying, "Awaken, you cannot remain indifferent. God will not permit it! It is time for your decision to live holy, as God intended, or prepare to enter further darkness, which will devour you!" As Mother I come to point the way to my son. Many have not been taught His Traditions, His Truth as God intended His children to be taught, according to His ancient law. I come, then, to feed my children from the Holy Table of God, in my simple way. Before the majestic throne of God, I intercede for you. His infinite goodness then permits I visit you from heaven. Through my tears, I ask of you, once again, return to God now. Only your conversion can dry my tears.

Today, the Feast of beloved John the Baptist, messenger of preparation for the coming of my Son, I say to you, I come to prepare the way for the return of my Son. Soon Jesus shall manifest Himself again, that all nations of the world will look toward heaven and acknowledge Jesus Christ is Lord. All knees shall bend and, together with the Angels and the Saints, all souls will cry out in one voice, Holy, Holy Lord, God of Hosts. The Son of God, Son of man will then draw into His Sacred Heart of Love, His faithful remnant. He will wrap His royal cloak around His flock. Peace shall come upon the earth, where His Holy Will shall be fulfilled as in heaven. This has been prophesied and shall come to pass only after the world undergoes a purification of immense proportion. The conversions taking place now will secure God's faithful remnant to His Grace when the hour of darkness envelops the earth. Even now the presence of evil covers the earth like a dense fog, causing confusion, rebellion, apostasy. Even the Holy Sanctuary of God has been penetrated, causing God's Vicar on earth much agony! Persevere, my faithful children. There will come a time of great glory, when the Victory that is God's will fall like a mist from heaven and all creation will know holiness. I come to prepare the way. Each faithful soul must play their role in God's plan for the salvation of the world in these critical end times.

Daughter, allow yourself to be the lowly vessel of my Son's delight. Trust, my child, that your prayers, your little sacrifices, your tears and sighs of love, indeed mitigate a portion of the purification which has already been written by the hand of God. Intercede in union with my Immaculate Heart. Let us pray, "Maranatha, Maranatha." Dry my tears, my daughter, by offering yourself as a living sacrifice for my Son. I love you.

Your Mother

6-30-94 Tabernacle following 12:15 PM Mass
The Weight of the Ugliness of Sin in the World

My Lord, Your peace fills my soul as I sit in Your Presence before the holy Tabernacle. Each time I am present before Your Holiness in the Tabernacle, I sense a portion of me dying and a portion of You becoming alive in me. If only souls would realize the Fountain of Grace which pours out from the Tabernacle, it seems You'd never have to wait alone again. Even now, in the cathedral, I am alone with You. I never tire of coming before You in the Tabernacle and you never fail to bless me for coming. My God, how I love You! My Beloved Lord, please help me to understand what happened to me as my Spiritual Director prayed the First and Second decade of the Rosary on Wednesday. I felt a terrible pressure or weight placed upon my soul and I could only weep. By the third decade I was myself again. Lord?

*Soul, I placed upon your soul the weight of the ugliness of sin in the world. I pressed upon your soul the pain inflicted upon My Sacred Heart daily. I desired you to bear the pain, in union with Me, for the salvation of souls. The pain you experience in your soul creates an oil within you. It is the oil of love. The tears you shed create a soothing salve, which I apply to the lacerations of My Sacred Heart. I say then to My Father: Look, here is one poor soul who loves Me enough to carry the Cross of man's sins in union with Me, willing to sacrifice her love of comfort to endure My pain, for love in charity. It is My Wisdom and Mercy to grant you the grace to do so. *Soul, you are but clay in My hand. That you and I may be one heart, remain ever so pliable. Will you permit Me this?

Jesus, search me thoroughly and you will find I am madly in love with You and that I will not deny You anything! You have probed me and You know me. The secrets of my heart, You know fully. And though I am full of incapacity, You have permitted me this: to be sick with love for You! It is not the wonder of heaven or the friendship of Saints and Angels which occupy my soul. There is only one target for me and it is Your furnace of Love, Your Sacred Heart. Dear Jesus, I do not understand what You mean when You refer to me as Your altar?

Child, you are My altar of sacrifice. I offer sacrifice to the Father in you and through you. Upon you I will place the Cross of suffering. You have been chosen for union with Me through the sufferings of My Passion. You will taste of the darkness of Gethsemane. You will drink of rejection, betrayal, loneliness. You will be forsaken by friends, spit upon by enemies. Will you bear this for Me, *Soul?

Jesus, you know my incapacity! Only by grace can I bear the sufferings of which You speak.

*Soul, how often have I said to you, My Grace shall be sufficient?

Often, Lord.

I shall ask you again. Will you bear this for Me? (Here, Jesus was very firm with me! He did not want me to qualify my answer! He wanted only a definite "yes" or "no," without any qualifications.)

Yes, Lord.

Then you shall follow Me, walking in My footsteps. You will be taken to Gethsemane, the Scourging, the Crowning of Thorns and the Carrying of the heavy Cross (trials and tribulation of all sorts). **Yes, little one, you will follow Me unto death on the Cross. This is the cup I offer to you. It is My cup of Divine Love. Will you drink of it?**

Yes, Jesus.

Then, *Soul, you shall be completely Mine forever! You are chosen to be My mouthpiece, to proclaim a message contrary to the world. All who are chosen walk the way of Calvary. I have set a path (path to Calvary) **before you. You have only to follow My footsteps. They will lead you to the sanctuary of the Most High God. I, Myself, will open the gates and welcome you. I will remove My cape from My shoulder and wrap it around you. I will stand to the right of you. My Mother will stand to the left of you. Together We will lead you to the Throne of God, the Father. In the company of Angels and Saints, He will deem you acceptable to enter and live forever in His Kingdom because you ingested His Divine Will. Our hearts shall be one forever and ever. Only here will the pain and the tears**

cease. Only here is joy complete. Receive My blessing now. Go in peace as your family awaits you. I love you.

Jesus

7-1-94 7 PM My Home
A Prayer to the Father Given by Jesus

Come, *Soul. I will teach you how to pray to the Father, saying: "My Abba, Eternal God Almighty, I beg of you the grace to know the sufferings of the Sacrificial Lamb, which you sent into the world as ransom for the sin of mankind. Permit me, Father, to enter the agony of Gethsemane, the humiliation of the Scourging, the mockery of the Crown of Thorns, the heavy weight of the Cross of man's sins. Finally, tasting the bitter cup of rejection, let me taste of death on the Cross, all for love of You and love of souls. Permit me this, Holy Father, that I may be one with the Sacrificial Lamb, experiencing a portion of His agony, that I may do as He did, that is, lay down my life for others.

Father, I offer to you the dust that I am. Form me by your heavenly breath into the altar of Your sacrifice. Burn incense upon me, allowing my fragrance to rise to Your heavenly throne. When you breathe in my fragrance, Abba, recognize it as having come from You, through me, as offering for souls. Take my life, Father, and cause me to glorify you. You so loved the world you sent Your only Begotten Son to save us, and we crucified Him. Now, Father, knowing and loving Him as I do, I too desire to walk in His holy footsteps to Calvary. Permit me to gather souls for you. In this way allow me to glorify Your Holy Name, Your Majesty. Make my heart one with the Sacred Heart of Jesus forever and ever. I offer to You my human will. I offer to work all the days of my life for the good of souls, working from within the Immaculate Heart of Mary, my Mother, who surrounds me in her love. I will lay down my life that all may be one in love, giving glory to you, as you intended from the beginning of all time, all ages.

Oh Father, your people will indeed glorify Your name one day in unity and in love! Your Kingdom shall come! Your will shall be done! Father, Your patience is astounding! Your Mercy eternal! Your Love incomprehensible! Your Justice, too, is mercy! Your Majesty reigns even in the midst of the chaos of our day. All the demons combined cannot tear down your holy Temple! Your Truth will stand forever, unchanging and indestructible! You will preserve your faithful children, for your covenant is everlasting! Nothing can separate us from your love! Even the souls who utterly reject you, choosing death eternally, are loved by You! Who then compares to You, God the Father? Nothing created can compare to Him Who was, Who is, and always will be! You are the Alpha and the Omega, Power and Majesty forever and ever.

Abba, we are not orphans, though we walk like orphans, because we have not yet understood your supreme Fatherhood! Gather Your creation into Your holy and Divine Love, healing our misery and making us a holy people. Father, send your Son again. Send Him to harvest the souls He has gained for you. Abba, hear the cry of your family! Transfigure us, Lord! Open up the Heavens, pour down Your reign, purifying Your creation, causing us to respond, once and for all, to Your eternal Power, Wisdom, Truth and Love! Breathe Your Holy Spirit upon us, marking us with the sign of salvation on our foreheads, so that when You send again the Good Shepherd, He will recognize us as His own and pastor us into your gates. Forever we shall adore you, Eternal God and Father Almighty! Amen and Amen."

Will you pray this way to the Father again and again?

Yes, Lord.

Thank you, little one, I love you. Jesus

Thank you, Jesus. I love You endlessly!

7-4-94 12:25 AM
I Am The Hand Feeding You

*Soul, My altar and My flower, you make great strides when you endure a night of suffering. My beloved one, I will never crush you with the weight of the Cross. As you lift it, it lifts you higher in your ascent of the holy mountain. My lamb, have you not yet understood, our union is made more complete when you are bearing the Cross for Me? When you are powerless is when I can rise up in you with My own power. I become your strength, lifting the Cross in union with you. Though the demons surround you and tempt you, they cannot penetrate you, because I am in you and they fear the power of God within your soul. Beloved of My Heart, I desire you to be full of confidence in Me. You are My Temple, My dwelling place. Satan would be satisfied to see you crumble. I shall never permit this to happen. If I permit you to feel powerless, it is because I desire to be the power in you, never to crush you. Because I have chosen you for Myself, I am raising you by My own hand. I am the hand feeding you the most precious bread of the Cross. This bread strengthens the bond of love, imparting the deepest knowledge and understanding of the Son of Man.

*Soul, you have participated in the harvesting of souls. You have presented your God with the greatest of gifts. I bless you little one, for whispering only "Thy Will be done." (In my suffering, I said only this, "Thy Will be done.") **Draw close to the furnace of My Sacred Heart.** The rest and refreshment you seek shall be given to you. *Soul, at the proper time I shall ask you to proclaim to many the intimacy of Divine Love. Tell My people My divine signature is written all over them. Their God desires intimacy. When they turn to Me, I will teach them how to love. Draw close to Me, beloved, for I am truly with you always. I love you.

Your Jesus

7-7-94 Following 12:15 Mass
My Children, Try Harder

Following Mass, I prayed the Chaplet of Divine Mercy. Upon completion, I opened my eyes to look at the crucifix above the altar. I became so drawn into it that I could not stop staring at it. My eyes moved to the beautiful statue of Our Lady. She began to speak: *My daughter, please write for my children.*

My little ones,
You are living in an extraordinary time of grace. God the Father grants this time of mercy as preparation for very difficult days ahead. Now is the time to learn how to live holy lives. I come to call my children to be a holy family of unity and love. I come to remind you of the values of the spiritual life which you have so quickly forgotten. You are created to be holy. You have not yet converted in totality because there are still too many worldly distractions in your daily lives. This is especially true in the land of plenty, America. Too much of your time is spent on earthly possessions and values. Material things replace spiritual values and devotions. I see in your hearts a desire for conversion, but it is only a half-hearted desire. This is because you still value too much the material things of your earthly existence. Your time and energy is spent procuring material things and living the ways of worldly people. You leave little time or energy for living a spiritual life of deep prayer, quiet reflection and solitude with your God. Even those living a sacramental life take little time to prepare, to appreciate and to contemplate the sublime gifts given to them through the sacraments.

My little ones, the Word of God is His letter of instruction. It is alive with love for you. Read the gospels. Strive to live them! His Word is life for you. Ingest it and you will be revived! Too many fail to grasp the seriousness of my call to conversion. I urgently call you to return to God; learn to love and live holy lives! The constancy of my messages and the repetitive nature of them should tell you that you have not yet understood what I am teaching you in the messages. My little ones, strive with earnest hearts to put into practice my messages. Who among you can truly say to God, I am living the gospel of simplicity, striving only for necessities? I am putting much time and effort into loving you and serving you, Oh God, as well as my brothers and sisters. Who among you can sincerely say, "Yes, Lord, indeed I give to you a major portion of my time daily"? Who can say: "Look, my God, You alone are the center of my life now. I put aside my former ways and I am living the new life of holiness"?

My children, try harder to live lives of prayer and repentance! Give to God more of your time, your reverence, your love! Hand to Him your very heart to the deepest core. Reserve nothing for rivals. He desires your heart in totality! Trust your Mother, little ones. Now is the time to prepare. Learn to sacrifice and to do with much less materially because the future will require this of you. My children, through the Mercy of God, you shall become truly rich only when you embrace the call to conversion and live holy lives of simplicity. Live the gospel and you will be liberated from the bondage of your worldly desires. Satan works diligently to rob you of your inheritance. Be alert, rebuking him and his temptations. Put aside, once and for all, the distractions and busyness of your lives. Seek God in the silence of your heart. Abundant life is to be found only in living the gospel message of love. Be pure of heart and live simply. Grow in faith. Trust the Holy Spirit of God within your own heart. Do not resist His promptings just because they are contrary to what the world tells you. He speaks only the truth and what is real.

I warn you, little ones, soon many of your possessions will perish before your very eyes. Store for yourselves that which will never perish. Strive for spiritual treasures, which will await you in your eternal life with God. My children, how very much I love you, each and every one! I implore you to live my messages! I bless you all. Come, enter my Immaculate Heart of Love. Don the virtues contained within. His Grace provided them for me and for you. May the peace of my son, Jesus Christ, be with you always. I love you. I am with you always.

Your Mother, Mary.

7-15-94 My home 3 PM
God's Mercy Extending Out to All the Earth

My child,

It is the desire and pleasure of my Maternal Heart to give freely the grace which is freely given me by God. I am simply a vessel of His Love. He has given unto me, as Mother, the capacity to love to the fullness of His Grace, by creating me without sin. Therefore, there is no hindrance to the grace which God imparts to me. This honor is reserved for me. This has been ordained, in order to provide for all souls the gift of a pure Mother whose being proclaims the greatness of the Lord. Therefore, His Grace flows like a river through me unto you. As Mother I am intimately united to the joys and sufferings of my children. From heaven I look upon my family of children on earth. How great is the need for pure motherly love! Divine Providence permits me, then, to visit my little ones, to intercede on their behalf, to gather and bring them back onto the right path. The right path is Jesus, who is the way!

My child, I have visited many variety of souls in a variety of places. This is God's Mercy extending out to all the earth through a variety of vessels, so that, for every type of need, there is a chosen instrument of God's Grace to provide for the need. God provides for all in this manner having never forsaken His people though they have forsaken Him. There shall be no excuse, then, for having remained indifferent to God's calling, His urgent call to conversion of heart! God is breathing His Holy Spirit upon the earth now to revive the corpses that have fallen asleep in the graveyard of death (spiritual). *He calls the Angels and the Saints, the entire heavenly court, to be active vehicles of His Grace, to cover the earth in its hour of great need, to prepare souls for the victory which is His, but only after the great tribulation and purification.*

The spirit of my son, Francis (of Assisi), *is being conferred upon many to facilitate God's will in the rebuilding, the restoration of the church. Indeed, she shall be restored through the hearts and hands and voices of souls who have embraced the way of St. Francis. That is the little way of humility, obedience and poverty of spirit, with utter acknowledgment, dependence and abandonment into the arms of Christ the King, Christ the Good Shepherd!*

My son Francis, to this day, aids in the rebuilding of the Temple of God, through his assistance of souls chosen to glorify God through their work in and for the church. Francis' love of the Cross, his devotion and unity to the Holy Wounds of Jesus, shall be imparted to many because this is necessary for the challenges (crosses) *of laboring for the good of the beloved Bride of Christ. The haughty and the rebellious shall fall in the great tribulation so that the pure, the simple, humble and obedient can lay their stones upon the foundation of God's Truth and Holy Tradition. Yes, little ones, the Temple of God shall reign victorious to glorify God and she shall not be defiled!*

My little ones, please do not worry about the great tribulation. Be people of faith! There is only one manner of preparation. That is prayer! In prayer you gain peace and security in knowing you are a child of God who is loved infinitely by your Creator. The intimacy and fulfillment of God's love will help you to trust that God alone knows and desires what is best for your soul, in order that your soul participate fully in the banquet prepared for you in your heavenly home, the Everlasting Kingdom, whose gates were opened by the blood of the innocent Lamb!

My children, if you have been revived by the breath of the Holy Spirit, then you are called to pray unceasingly for all the corpses who have yet to respond to God's Grace and Mercy! Only then will more of the family of man be brought to life in God. We are all one, intimate and connected family, my dear ones. Thank you, my little ones, for the sacrifices you offer on behalf of all souls. No matter how small they seem to you, they are not small in the eyes of God, who values greatly a spirit of sacrifice. God shall reward the smallest of sacrifices. The Most Holy Trinity values greatly the tears shed and the deep sighs of love heard only in the silence of hearts, because it is your deepest core crying out to God Most High! Attempt to fast as well, because denial of the flesh raises the spirit!

My little ones, you need not understand God's way, nor should you even try, because your limitations are too great. Rather, have faith and obey like a child. Follow His precepts and decrees, especially the two great commandments in obedience and humility, saying in union with my Son, "Father, into your hands I commend my spirit." Then, my little ones, you shall know joy and peace. You shall gain for yourself abundant and true life in God. You have only to accept my Maternal protection, guidance and love. I am with you always. Praise and glorify God for the grace He permits me (my spirit) to give you. I love you.

Your Mother, Mary

8-6-94 Feast of Transfiguration - 11:20 PM, on airplane to Frankfurt and Rome
The Transfiguration

My creation, Oh My creation, come, come unto Me.

I Am Who Am, the God of Abraham, Isaac and Jacob, He who was and is and always will be, your God. On this, the Feast of My Transfiguration, I say unto you, receive Me through the person of the Holy Spirit. He descends upon the earth in these days, these trying times; like dew He falls upon the heart that is open. If He penetrates you, He will transfigure you. He will transfigure you into My holy reflection, revealing God's glory in your soul, and your heart shall never be the same. Ascend, My creation, ascend above the finite world and encounter your God, even as Peter, James and John encountered Me. I will fortify your faith for the trials ahead, the days of tribulation in which your very faith will be tried. Accept My invitation, My creation, for you know not how great a gift I offer to you in these days of grace, these days of mercy. If you put off until tomorrow what I offer today it shall be too late!* Oh how My Heart, full of love and tenderness, longs to reveal to you My Glory!

You, My creation, fashioned by My own hand — you, whom I breathed My life-giving breath upon, how can you refuse Him who loves you the most? He who offers you everlasting life and beauty beyond your comprehension? You know not, My beloved brothers and sisters, My family of man, what you refuse, because Satan has confused you and twisted you, until I see within you little or no faith at all! But though you have turned from Me, your God, your Savior, I shall not turn from you, but suffer unceasingly, awaiting your conversion! I have purchased

you at a great price and you are Mine, and what is Mine I tend to and care for and provide for.

Look upward, seek a higher ground, a higher existence and permit Me, the God of all ages, to transfigure you in Me, revealing to you My Glory, that you may once again be a people of faith and love. I love you, My creation. I breathe My Holy Spirit upon you, and His wind blows all over the earth. Happy and blessed is the man who receives His breath in his soul! Amen and Amen.

Jesus

Note: My soul is at peace and my heart full of Your love, my God. I love You and thank You! *Our Lord gave me to understand that He is referring to the extraordinary graces which are available now, given in this time of the history of man, to fortify faith, which will be tried in the near future. For souls who receive His Mercy and Grace (Holy Spirit) now will find they are prepared for trials, because His Grace and strengthened faith (through the Holy Spirit) will sustain them through much. Those who do not avail themselves of His extraordinary Graces and Mercy now, through the Holy Spirit, may find they lose their faith when tried. This does not mean God's Mercy, which is infinite, will not be there, but we must accept it, and those who are in turmoil may lose much ground (spiritually), as opposed to those who receive what He offers today.

8-9-94 11:30 AM San Damiano Church, Assisi, Italy
Before the San Damiano Cross

My little one,
Joyfully I receive you on the Holy Ground of Assisi. Gaze upon My Cross (San Damiano cross) and listen as I say unto you, My Church is in need of repair. Tend to her, for she must tend to souls. Yes, My little one, I know that you seek to understand how I would have you go about doing what I have asked. Read 1Cor. 14:4, child. My Word is written, stating he who prophesies builds up the Church. My gift of prophecy I confer upon you that you would build up My church, that you would

ingest My words placed in your soul, that your lips would speak for Me. I shall see to it that the ears who hear shall know that it is My Holy Spirit who speaks and they shall be built up in Me.

I, your Lord and Savior, shall see to it that you grow in love and understanding of the bridegroom, so that you grow in love and understanding of the Bride, who is My beloved mystical Body. She has been penetrated by rebels who disguise themselves as bearers of the truth, but indeed they know not My Truth. As she is the guardian of My Truth and Holy Tradition, the instrument of My Grace for all souls, I shall rescue her from the hands of the rebels. To that end I am raising many messengers of My Truth, voices which will proclaim My way. In these little ones, the poorest in spirit, untrained and snatched from the ways of the world, I will place My holy Wisdom. This, so that all will know that it is My voice who speaks through earthen vessels, calling them home, that My family of man will once and for all abide in the loving heart of their Living God!

Record My words, little one, so that the journey of your soul can glorify Me for the good of many. My love shall be made very evident in you. Allow My hand to guide your every step, so that your mission is accomplished according to My Holy Will. In this manner I shall use you to restore My Church, adorning her in purity, revitalizing her in My Truth, restoring her radiant beauty, for she is to be My home of Truth, a haven of peace and love for all souls, never again to be penetrated by falsehood. So great a work I am accomplishing in her that it shall take many hands, many voices, all abandoning themselves to My holy mission, which unfolds small step by step. What I erect shall never crumble! Fear not, My little one, beloved of My Sacred Heart, for though your incapacity is great, far greater is My Holy Spirit, who shall accomplish My work through you so that all will know indeed, it is I, Lord and Savior of all, who is in you for the good of all.

Pray and receive Me, the Holy One, into your deepest core. I seek only your heart that we may be one. As our hearts are united, so too our will shall be united, glorifying the Most High Father. Abide in Me as I abide in You. I love you, My little ones, I love you with all My Heart!

Your Jesus

8-11-94 7 PM On airplane from Rome to Medjugorje
Greatest of Miracles: Conversion

My dear child,

I who am your Mother welcome you and offer to you my Maternal embrace as you enter the Holy and Chosen Ground of my visitation, Medjugorje. Open your heart to me fully so that I may pour my Maternal love within. Enter my heart, which is an oasis of grace for you and for all pilgrims. You shall witness the greatest of miracles in the village of my visitation, and that is conversion: the changing of a heart from cold or lukewarm to fervent and full of love and faith.

My little one, I come that I may reconcile my children with God, that I may raise them in love and faith. Each and every soul who is present here (Medjugorje) *receives a divine touch, and their heart is never to be the same again. Walk with me then, my little one, bless me with your love as I bless you with my unending embrace of love. My heart is gushing with love unconditional for all souls. Observe my work in the hearts of those around you and rejoice that God the Father has ordained this village as the place of extraordinary grace and love. Permit my mantle to fall around you, draping you with my peace. Open your heart so as to receive all the movements of my spouse, the Holy Spirit of God. Record all that you hear within your soul. Trust that which is given you here, and do not doubt or fear. Receive as a child receives, because the Most Holy Trinity gives to the little ones His greatest gifts.*

I shall bless and fortify my beloved priest who accompanies you. My son, thank you for your love, sacrifice and obedience. Know that I am with you in a most intimate way, granting unto your soul an abundance of grace through my Immaculate Heart. Receive my love, my faithful son! My daughter, I shall touch the heart of my little one, n_____, so that he knows, indeed, I am His Mother, who desires to have a relationship of love.

In the eyes of each pilgrim see the reflection of my Son within them, and praise and glorify the Father for allowing my visitation to be the catalyst for so many conversions. How great the need of my intercession on behalf of the salvation of souls. I desire only to reconcile my children with God, because, at this present time, the world offends God greatly. Pray in union with my heart that many convert now, because the Father has allotted only a certain time for my visitations, which shall one day end, at which time the consolation of my visits will end, but my motherly intercession shall never end! Permit the grace and love of my Son within you to radiate as a sign to others of the joy in your soul which is the fruit of an intimate relationship of love with God. I bless you and I love you.

Your Mother, Mary

8-12-94 3:30 PM Medjugorje, St. James Church
A Strong, Strong Wind Arose

Praying before the Blessed Mother statue in Church, I had prayed a meditation on the Agony of Jesus in Gethsemane and entered contemplation for a long while. Then my mind began to wander and I was distracted by the heat and my fatigue. Here, Our Lady spoke.

My child, my child,

Bow your head before the Tabernacle of the Most High, the Lord of all Creation, my Son, My Beloved Son! Never cease to pray to Him for the salvation of all souls! Adore Him now and say to Him how much He is loved by you; offer to Him, again and again, yourself in totality. Reserve nothing for yourself but give all unto Him. Beg of Him that souls be converted, for truly, my child, the hour is late and many are walking the path to perdition. He has revived you that you would never cease to do all that is possible for the good of souls. Look now, child, how many are at risk.

Immediately I saw the following scene (interiorly): I saw a river of black, muddy water with a treacherous current. Whirlpools sucked people down under the black water. I was shocked to see the great number of souls who were traveling in this river, stuck in its current, unable to get themselves out. The faces of the people looked scared and miserable. There were many and the river seemed endless, the current unrelenting. Then a strong, strong wind arose. So strong was the wind, it reversed the current, retrieving the people one by one from the river's grasp, saving them from certain death. The scene ended and Our Lady spoke again.

The Holy Spirit is the wind which saves those who are on the path to perdition. The Holy Spirit descends now, in this time of grace, to cover the earth, to combat the demons, to retrieve souls from death so as to revive many, so as to build an army of fervent souls whose love and faith will serve for the salvation of many souls. Therefore, child, never, ever cease to intercede on behalf of your brothers and sisters. Believe in deep faith that each prayer is indeed heard and works in the divine plan of salvation to give life in God to those in need. Do this (pray unceasingly) for love of my Son, Jesus, and for love of your Mother. I bless you. I love you.
Your Mother

8-14-94 9 PM On top of Mt. Krizevac, Medjugorje
Jesus' Prayer to the Father

*Soul, you have ascended the mountain, My holy and chosen mountain and you are now removed from the world so that we can be together to pray, as I often went apart from the world so as to be with My Father, to pray to Him for the salvation of souls. My Beloved, My altar, enter now into My Sacred Heart of Love and drink of My Love and My Mercy, for I desire to fill you to overflowing so that, in intimate union, our hearts being one, we can pray to the Father here and now for the world saying:

(Prayer by Jesus)

"Beloved Majesty, Father Almighty, together, Jesus and I pray for all souls, begging of You, Mercy! Reign Your Love and Mercy upon earth, so that you penetrate powerfully all souls, causing them to be full of faith, because we are Your seed, Your very own seed and yet we know not of Your Fatherly Love.

In Your loving Providence you have sent our Mother to this holy place of Grace to be a sign for all the world, that in-

deed, You exist, You are alive, You are Love and full of Mercy, that once and for all, we may be grounded in the reality of Your Fatherly Love and care. Only then will we walk in the security of Your majestic Providence and Fatherly Love. When this becomes our reality, we will have love and faith and hope and charity, but until then we have misery, because we know not faith, hope, and charity, and certainly we know not love. So then, Father, from this holy place of Grace I beg of you to permit Your peace, which permeates this mountain, to descend upon the entire world. You have sent your Mother as our teacher and she has taught us much indeed. Through her intercession many stone hearts have become hearts of flesh, and now thrive in faith and love.

Almighty God, like the stones which form this holy mountain, she has gathered for you many souls, forming for you a holy Army of Love, weaving for you a remnant of humble and obedient souls who will only to do your perfect and Holy Will. Look with favor upon these people, these villages torn apart by war, by the demons of hatred, oppression and persecution. Your Peace, Almighty God, Your Peace. Let it reign here and in all the world. To that end, make my poor soul Your instrument of peace and love. The Sacred Heart of Jesus has inflamed my sinner's heart, so that I am full of charity and desire only to gather for you souls, which I shall present to you as my thanksgiving offering for all the mercy in which you have covered my soul.

Therefore, take me, Father Almighty, and press me close to Your bosom, whispering to me Your Holy Will, that I may understand the path you have chosen just for me. I long to glorify you with the sacrifice of my life. Father, the world has never known such evil and such grace, as you prepare us for the moment of truth. Empower us then to wage the war against evil, so that all souls can share in the victory which is Yours, Almighty and Eternal God. All Honor and glory and Praise be Yours.

Amen and Amen."

8-15-94 Feast of Assumption, 8:45 PM St. James Church, Medjugorje
For the Prayer Groups of America

Mary spoke: *Soul, please write for the prayer groups of America.*

My dear, dear children,
Praised be Jesus! On this day of remembrance of my Assumption into Heaven, I desire to bless you in a most special way, pouring upon you my Maternal graces and love. My little ones, from the holy ground of Medjugorje I thank you for responding to my call to conversion and prayer. Many came to Medjugorje with open hearts and expectant faith. Also, many came of curiosity and disbelief. Yet, as you walked the holy ground here, I planted within your hearts the seeds of conversion and prayer. When you returned home you realized the seed had been planted and you were different, no matter the motive of your heart. As a result, as I requested in my messages again and again, many prayer groups were formed throughout your country.

Your country is in great turmoil. Great is the need of prayer to combat the forces of evil, which permeate every area of your daily lives. Only in eternal life will you be able to understand the power of your prayer. Many are the souls which have converted due to your prayerful intercession and sacrifices. Many of you returned home only to receive the Cross as a means of your sanctification. For this I bless you and tell you that your sacrifice has been found most pleasing to the Most Holy Trinity. The countless decades of the Most Holy Rosary, prayed by prayer groups, have formed a cloud of fragrant incense, which has risen unto the throne of the Most High God. Received in love, He has looked with favor upon your prayer groups, uniting you ever more intimately with His Divine Heart of Love, causing you to be a reflection of His Love for many who know not of His infinite Divine Love and Mercy. You are vessels filled up only to be poured out! Raised by my Maternal love, I place you in the vineyard of Our Lord, that you may participate in the great heavenly harvest, for in this time of visitation the vines are heavily laden with fruit!

Again I must say to you that you are living in the most critical of times. My call is very urgent because Satan has never been more active, releasing his demons all over the world to claim souls for himself. Yet the Mercy of God has responded by opening up the heavens to cover the earth with His Holy Spirit, who spreads His Grace from the four corners of the earth. Without fervent prayer from the heart, without the power of the Rosary, you cannot combat the evil forces which surround your generation. By far the most powerful prayer is the Eucharistic Sacrifice of the Mass. If armed with the power of the Body and Blood of My Son (Eucharist), Satan cannot penetrate you, because the power of the Eucharist is far greater than any power of evil! Continue to pray, pray, pray, my faithful little ones, because prayer will enable you to live the gospel message, and the gospel is the only message which can save souls! Your prayer groups can avert great suffering for your country, as your country will be put to the test. It is important in these difficult, trying times that you do not lose hope. Please live in my Immaculate Heart so that I can give to you my unlimited Maternal hope. Having been assumed into heaven, I know well the glory of your inheritance and the reality of eternal life in the Kingdom of God. Trust in my Motherly heart and trust in your Jesus of Mercy, Fount of Love for you! I love you.

Your Mother, Mary

8-17-94 Medjugorje. Saw Mirjana and Vicka.
Kiss the Cross

In adoration chapel of the Franciscans, I began to pray the Chaplet of Divine Mercy, and almost immediately I was overcome by Jesus' Presence in my soul. We approached a rough wooden Cross - a very large one. He said that together we would kiss the cross, and immediately I saw myself with Jesus kissing the Cross. I was surprised, as I felt only love for the Cross, because Jesus was with me in such an intimate way that fear could not enter.

He began to dictate:

My altar, embrace and kiss the Cross because embracing the Cross requires the greatest love of all. Allow Me, Your Savior, to imprint upon your soul, forever, the love of the Cross, so

that you carry your Cross full of love, inflamed with charity! Your footsteps shall follow the way of My Cross. What appears difficult or even impossible by human standards is made entirely possible by heavenly grace. What the world shuns most is the Cross, but it cannot be this way with you because you have been chosen to embrace the Cross for the Glory of God, for your own sanctification and for the salvation of souls.

*Soul, trust in Divine Providence even as your holy Mother Mary trusted in complete faith, knowing not what the journey would hold. My plan for you unfolds even as the most beautiful rose unfolds, petal by petal. Seek not to discover My Will by reaching for opportunities; rather await what I bring to your doorstep! This is My Will for you. Be patient as your Holy Mother was patient. I have many teachings to give you in between the fulfillment of your vocation as mother and wife. I will, by My own hand, stretch you, raise you and entwine you unto Me so that your branch shall bear much fruit. My beloved one, for thirty years I remained hidden, and in three short years My public ministry was complete. Enjoy your formation and your privacy during these precious, graced times, for one day you will belong to many, hidden no more.

*Soul, I washed you with My Divine Mercy so as to purify you on this Holy Ground. Many are the graces imparted to you here and now. My flower, your fragrance arises and encircles My heavenly throne, and the heavenly court smiles upon you. Embellished by My Love and Mercy, remain in Me and I remain in you! I love you, My altar. With My Cross I bless you in the name of the Most Holy Trinity!

Your Jesus

8-23-94 Tabernacle 9:30 AM
The Whirlwind of the World

*Soul, please write. Beloved one, do not run from Me. Do not venture out on your own. My arms enfold you, but the whirlwind of the world attempts to rip you from My embrace. Do not hide your face from Me! Look at Me, raise your eyes to

Me. Drown in Me, here and now and forever!

Lord, my God, you know the whirlwind of my daily existence, the demands made on my time, the challenges of my duties. You know well that I long for nothing more than to spend hours with you, alone, in silence, in love. Lord, I beg of you to stay close to me in all my undertakings, as you know well how my soul aches and longs for You, how my heart is torn when I cannot spend time with You alone. You have stripped the pleasure of the world from me so that all pales compared to You, my God and Savior. I did not perceive that I had turned my face from You, but rather that You hid Your face from Me! If you do not provide the grace, Lord, even to pray a little prayer, then I am doomed. My poverty is great, my dependence upon You is immeasurable! I know only that I am dust! You alone give me breath and life, even to adore You. So then, do not leave me, a speck of dust, upon the ground! Lift me to You. Do as you please then, but I beg of You, do not let go of Me, my Lord and my God, lest I perish forever.

It is not possible that I would let go of My own seed, that I would leave you dead on the ground for the vultures. You are My dwelling place, My domain. I desire only to embellish my dominion in you. You must not permit your daily duties to rip you from my protective arms, lest you become fully exposed to many spirits which attempt to tear you from My grip. The branch will quickly wither if pulled from the vine!

*Soul, be patient! Indeed I hear your cry, your prayer for My return, for the conversion of all souls, for peace in the world, but you grow impatient, desiring all this to come about quickly. Patience! All this and more shall come about at the precise hour known only to My Father. Do not grow weary of interceding for all creation! The gift of faith brings with it responsibility! Do not delude yourself that perhaps another generation will come to intercede. Prayer is necessary, and interceding your duty! Throughout the day, at all times, think of Me, cry out My Holy Name, tell Me of your love for Me and beg, on behalf of all souls, My Mercy! Never tire of doing this, for such is your role in the salvation of the world.

A rose does not produce its fragrance or beauty until the precise time and season has come. Fruit trees do not bear their fruit until due season. Wine waits until its flavor is perfected in time. A child waits in the womb of his mother, taking the fullness of time within to complete its formation, and the mother awaits in joyful anticipation of the birth. Time and patience. Seasons of waiting and formation. Before you know it, all that you pray for shall come to pass, the hour descending upon you when you least expect. Drink of My cup of Divine Love and refresh your soul in Me. I love you. My Peace I give unto you.

Your Jesus

8-24-94 My Home, 3 PM, Rosary with my Spiritual Director
A Portion of My Sorrowful Heart

During Second Joyful Mystery, I experienced interiorly a tremendous "weight" upon my soul in which I could somehow "feel" the heaviness of the sins of the world, the weight of suffering in the world. I asked Our Lady to help me understand my experience. She replied quickly.

My daughter,

I have given to you a portion of my sorrowful heart. Bear, in union with my Immaculate Heart, my suffering. I see that many suffer because they refuse the love and mercy of my Son. My eyes observe broken hearts and many lost souls. My Maternal love desires to cover all my children like a blanket, to shelter them from the vile ways of the world. I come to you, my child, to give to you a drink, a sip, from the cup of my suffering, asking you to bear with me the piercing of my Maternal heart. I suffer as I witness the way my children continually offend God!

My son is now covered with wounds inflicted by His own creation, yet His Divine and Sacred Heart pours forth only love and mercy! When I come to you from time to time, offering you a portion of my sorrowful heart, please do not deny me. Many souls will be asked to assist me, souls full of charity, souls who will suffer for the good of other souls. My daughter, victim souls avert many from

*eternal death. Great is such an offering in the eyes of the Most
Holy Trinity! I bless you my daughter. I bless my son. Thank you
for your heartfelt prayer. God sees the goodness of your intentions
and He smiles upon you, blessing you, granting unto you His Peace.
Rest in my Immaculate Heart of Love.*

Your Mother

8-26-94 Prayer Group 9 PM during Rosary.
The Father Says: "I am Love; I am Mercy; I am Justice Also!"

As the group began to pray the Rosary, I saw with the eyes of
my soul the crucified Jesus on a Cross, with God the Father to the
left of the Cross, and to the right of the Cross was Mother Mary.
Together, the Father and Mary lowered the Cross into the center of
the room. Lovingly they gazed at Christ crucified, then they looked
at each one present in the room praying the Rosary.

God the Father spoke with much authority, saying:

**Receive My Son! To you I bring Him that you might soothe
His open and bleeding Wounds with the oil of your love; that
you might perfume His Body with the fragrance of your love
and charity; that you might dress His Wounds with your
prayers; that you might take Him from the Cross and hold Him
in your own arms; that you might carry the Cross of man's sin
on your own shoulders, to alleviate for one moment His pain!**

**My children, not much longer will the heavenly court en-
dure the insults of your generation! I am Love; I am Mercy; I
am Justice also! The hour of justice will come when you least
expect. Be prepared, My creation! I am Your Father, He who
was and is and always will be! I give to your generation many
signs, attempting to capture your heart, your soul from the evil
in the world, but many are blind to all the signs around them.**

**My creation, I will not endure much longer to observe the
Crucifixion of My Beloved Son. His blood is spent. Who among
you will endure the Cross? Who among you will be full of zeal
for the house of the Lord? Blessed be those among you who say
to Me: "Father, I offer to you, all that you ask; make Me a**

sacrifice for souls, because I so love Your Son and I can no longer stand to know He suffers." Blessed are you My children, gathered to give Glory to Me through the prayer of the Most Holy Rosary. Now, receive the Most Holy Virgin Mary!

Immediately Mary spoke.

My dear little ones,

Praised be my crucified Son! Behold Him as we present Him to you this night. Little ones, how graced you are this night that the Father would come with me to present His Son to you. Dear ones, receive Him in love and allow me to cause your capacity to love to be increased this very night. By the power of the Holy Rosary, I raise you to be my holy little ones so that you may be a reflection of my Son.

Dear ones, thank my Son, thank the Father and thank the Holy Spirit for the gift of the Cross. Through and in the Cross you are promised eternal life and union with the Most Holy Trinity. Bear in love all your difficulties in humility and without complaint; receive your cross. It is only a portion of God's Love for you. I bless you and I thank you, my dear ones, for your love and for your sacrifice. I am truly with you, and the Holy Spirit dwells in you always, that together we may lead you to your eternal home, the Kingdom of God, reserved for those who respond to the Grace of God, for those who love and walk humbly with God. I love you, my children! (Mary said this with so very much tenderness.)

Long pause. Then she spoke again.

My little ones, when you fall under the weight of your Cross, do not lie there alone. Call on the Angels, who await your command; call on the Saints who intercede and assist you, and call out my name so that evil spirits will leave your side. Then pick up your Cross again and walk upright, like children of the Most High God! You are not broken except when you attempt to walk alone! Avail yourself of all the heavenly grace of this time. Heaven is ready to assist you always! You shall accomplish very much good for the Glory of God. Amen and Amen.

I then saw interiorly: Mary gave us a white cloth and each person shared in the washing of Jesus' wounds until His Body became clean again.

8-31-94 2 PM My home. Rosary with my Spiritual Director
Mary: Anointing and Crown of Thorns

At the Fourth Sorrowful Mystery, I saw Our Blessed Mother, standing next to Father. Facing him, she began to anoint him with the Sign of the Cross in the following manner: First, she laid her hands upon his head and prayed over him. Then she anointed his eyes with the Sign of the Cross. Then she anointed his lips, then his ears. She then anointed his heart and, finally, his hands.

She blessed him saying:

My son, my son,
I bless your eyes that your vision may be clear and far reaching. I bless your lips that you may proclaim the truth of the gospel until the moment of your very last breath, the moment when you enter eternal life in God! I bless your ears that you may hear all that is given you, both within and without, hearing always the whisper of the Holy Spirit in your soul, loving and guiding your every step, leading you to union of heart with my Son, Jesus.

I anoint your heart, that your heart and the Divine and Sacred Heart of Jesus may always be one! Also, that your heart exist within my Maternal heart of love, receiving always the fullness of the graces contained within my heart. I anoint your hands, because they are consecrated instruments of God's work, and through your hands, by the power of the Holy Orders conferred upon your soul, you bring to my people the bread of life, the blood of eternal salvation! Go forward then, my dear son, in the confidence of my love, receiving my full blessing. Be the shepherd for many. I am with you always.

She added:

As I laid my hands upon your head, I drew all your thoughts and your will toward heaven. Through my hands I purify your

thoughts, your will, your intellect, your heart. Contemplate the presence of my Maternal hands upon your head, so that always I will draw you upward toward heaven. I love you. Peace be yours.
Your Mother

At the Third Sorrowful Mystery, I saw the following: I was dressed in a long white gown. Our Lady stood before me. Angels encircled me. Then two Angels carried the crown of thorns to me and they placed it upon my head. Pressing the crown upon me, blood began to run down my face. However, I felt no pain, no fear, only immense love, peace and joy. Our Lady spoke: *Betrothed of my Son, receive your crown. Blessed are you to be chosen by Love Himself to receive the honor of His holy Crown of Thorns! His Crown shall adorn you all the days of your life, until He comes in glory to take you unto the Father's Kingdom, where He will remove the Crown of Thorns and place a wreath of heavenly roses upon your head, receiving you, once and for all, into eternal life. I bless you.*
Your Mother

9-6-94
A Prayer to Jesus: You Take What Is Ugly and Make It Beautiful

Almighty God, Jesus Christ, You command the oceans and the winds; the stars, the moon, the sun, You sustain. You form dust into man, giving dignity to nothingness by breathing your Holy Spirit into a shell. You create and then sustain our lives, that we might experience love and possess eternal life. You possess the ineffable love of the Father who glories in you. You possess the ineffable love of the Holy Spirit who speaks only of You. How then is it that You love wretchedness at all? Is there a creature deserving of even a momentary glance from You? Yet you become the center of a soul. You love the impure, imperfect sinner. So abundant is this love of Yours that you died a hideous death for sinners. Your Majesty, Your Kingship, Your Perfection, willingly condescends, and consents to, the horrendous death of a common criminal, for love of wretchedness - for love of me, that I might one day be one with your perfection and live eternally in You. Who can comprehend this love of Yours? No mortal can take this in! Who can love You as You love? As you deserve? None, except to the degree that You Yourself fill the soul with Your own Divine Love. This love of Yours is the ultimate mystery. Your righteousness, goodness, purity overwhelm me.

All the day and night, my soul languishes for just one glance from You, but then, when You turn my way, I desire only to be annihilated, that You would not be made to look at wretchedness. But You do not annihilate me. Rather You are gentle, kind, forgiving, tender, patient, and loving. Gifts You bring me, and You press me close to You, enfolding me in Your arms. You do not turn away from a sinner - You love instead. You take what is ugly and make it beautiful. No wonder the Father glories in You! No wonder the Holy Spirit speaks only of You! I can think of only one creature who loves You as You deserve to be loved, and that is the Blessed Mother. So it is I will hide in her. Yes, Lord, I will cling to her Immaculate Heart all the days of my life. Jesus, I love You boundlessly.

9-7-94 10 AM following Mass
To Offend God Is a Serious Matter

My child,

To offend God is a serious matter. What man dismisses as trivial, what man easily rationalizes away, is indeed a matter of injustice because God is worthy of only love. There will come a time when all the secrets of a soul will be revealed unto all, but the only eyes to judge will be the all knowing eye of God.

My children, you shall be turned inside out! What is inside of you shall be revealed in the light of truth, and the justice of God shall prevail upon you. So then, children, keep yourselves clean! Avail yourselves of every grace which purifies the soul. Offer reparation for your own sins and stains. Then in charity offer reparation for the sins and offenses of the souls who do not know God as you know Him through grace!

My Son is merciful and takes into account the fallen nature of humanity. Yet, through the fullness of His Blood, His Divine Love and Grace are freely given so as to enable souls to overcome sin and empower them to accomplish much good! The Person of the Holy Spirit is given to your soul for the sanctification of your soul. The Light in your soul grows in proportion to your desire to know and love God, to the degree you are attentive to the movement of the Holy Spirit of Love, making God the priority of your life. God desires to impart Himself to you to the highest degree of union, but you must cooperate with His Grace and give your "fiat." The Bread of Life, the Eucharist, is yours to overcome your human weakness and evil temptations. The Bread of Life, frequent Reconciliation, and the grace which accompanies a prayer life, shall keep clean the Temple of the Holy Spirit (your soul). *What then is there to fear when the hour of revelation comes, and when what is hidden inside of you is fully revealed before the eyes of God? Pray, pray, pray. I love you and I am with you always to assist you to draw close to God, who is Love.*

Your Mother

9-9-94 Tabernacle 9 AM
Lay Laborers

My dear children,

The harvest is great but the laborers are few. The abundant Grace of God has been poured upon you through the love of my Maternal heart, so that you are surrounded by my veil, draping itself around you. In the folds of my gown you are protected and held close. The graces received by you are for the good of the Body of Christ. Grace has been imparted to many lay laborers in the body so as to enable you to be leaven for the Body of Christ (church), *strong, stable pillars of truth during days of purification.*

Many who are shaken, on the verge of losing faith and hope, will come to you to seek the gift of grace which they see in you. Share the graces you have received with great charity of heart! Yet, be prudent always, awaiting the movement of the Holy Spirit. Then, what you give will be whole and truly of God, not of human desires, but of supernatural grace. You shall accomplish much good through supernatural grace. Recall that Peter walked on

*the water, his eyes, his heart, firmly fixed on Jesus. He walked by
supernatural grace. When he reverted to thinking in the natural,
human way, no longer fixed on the Lord but on himself, he sank
into the water.*

*My children, allow your daily lives to be filled with the reality
of God's supernatural grace, so that all the duties of your vocation
are full of supernatural love, becoming a pleasing sacrifice and
prayer. There is so much work to be accomplished toward the salvation of all souls. Pray, my dear children, pray for all souls to be
converted now. The time is short. Each hour that passes is an hour
closer to the hour of purification for mankind. The dawn of the era
of Peace is at hand, for the Triumph of the Immaculate Heart shall
come in this generation, leading to the reign of the Sacred Heart.
Pray in union with me. Thank you for praying the holy Rosary with
great love. I bless you. I love you. Be at peace. Reconcile with all!*
Your Mother

9-11-94 and 9-12-94 5:15 PM Mass
The Three Persons of the Trinity

During Mass, especially at receiving Holy Communion, my
soul was overcome with the presence, the power, the supreme
love of the Most Holy Trinity. Somehow, through much grace,
the Persons of the Trinity presented themselves to my soul, filling me with extreme reverence, overpowering realization and a
fullness of knowledge of the Trinity which I did not previously
possess. I struggle to describe this work in my soul at all, because
words are utterly impotent to describe the reality, which is unspeakable and sublime.

It was as if the Father, the Son, and the Holy Spirit revealed
themselves to the depths of my soul. Being more familiar with
God the Son and God the Holy Spirit, my soul was attentive to
God the Father. Up until now He had remained more hidden, more
mysterious. My soul could only tremble in His Presence, as holy
fear would come over me. Now, however, I found myself, for lack
of a better expression, falling in love instantly and deeply with the
person of the Father. Here and now my soul easily called Him

"Abba" and was filled with great affection for Him. His Majesty presented Himself as a Father who is approachable, and who is utterly lovable. Yet extreme power and authority is in Him. The Father's gaze possessed me to the full, as if a type of umbilical cord had been connected from the Father to my soul. It seemed the ineffable love of God was being poured into every cell of my being. I knew I was His seed. I knew this in a greater way, much more deeply than previously. I thought my heart would explode with Love as He imparted Himself to my soul, filling it! It seemed my soul was united into Him for a moment in time, that I might have knowledge of Him as never before. He who is Love caused my soul to somehow know, to somehow take in, His Fatherly Love, given to all souls in the Person of His Son, the Word Incarnate.

What caused my soul to become inebriated was the grace given to somehow experience a portion (the soul, in this life, cannot take in too much) of His incomprehensible Love for His creation. It was given, in the depths of my soul, to know the longing of His Fatherly Heart to gather His creation unto Himself, that we may be one Holy Body with Him in Love! The tenderness of His Fatherhood is evident even in the midst of His being the Supreme God. In this state, He imparted a profound depth of the realization of His Fatherly Providential Love, together with knowledge of the Trinitarian union and love, especially in the area of the following truths. Here I must explain, though previously known to me through the reading of Scripture, this was a deeper knowledge of Love Himself, not intellectual information. God the Father, whose love for His only Begotten Son is utterly incomprehensible and unspeakable, handed Him over to the world as the living sacrifice to be hung on the Cross for pure love of souls; herein is His Glory. By this act, creation is washed, made holy, fully redeemed by the blood of the Lamb, the Son of God so loved by the Father. His precious Blood covers all souls; herein is His Mercy. Though all are redeemed by the Cross, the blood which washes our soul, the human free will will never be violated by God. Therefore, the soul who chooses death shall indeed receive eternal death. Herein is His justice and herein is His suffering, because the Father wills all souls be saved. With much love and affection for His creation He has prepared a place in heaven for His offspring.

The Father's Love is providential. The Son's Love is sacrificial. The Holy Spirit's Love is the binding force, the breath that gives life to love. The Trinity possesses the fullness of perfect love and unity. The masterpiece of the creative hand of God is the Blessed Mother. In giving birth to the Word Incarnate, she partakes in the full grace of Trinitarian love. This Trinitarian Love possesses her so that she becomes the fullness of Maternal love. Next, I was given to know His Love for my soul, in and through the realization that He Himself had chosen my soul for His Son. Before I could come to the Father I had to know and to love the Son. For it is written, no one can come to the Father except through the Son. The following impression was given my soul. My being lay upon the ground, a corpse, lifeless in the spirit. The Father ordained that Mother Mary attend to me. She came with the Holy Spirit to revive my soul. The Holy Spirit breathed His life in me. He taught me of Jesus. Mary took my hand and led me to her son. His fingerprints were imprinted all over my soul as He revealed to me His Sacred Heart of Love. Falling in love with the Son, I glorified the Father, who had not yet revealed Himself to my soul, except through the Son. Now He presented Himself to my soul and in one tiny second I knew Him as never before. My soul overflowed with love for my Abba.

Oh Master, my God, my all, I desire only Your Will. Yet my soul lingers in thoughts and longings for union, which comes only on the other side. I am filled with thoughts of dying that I might rise to You. My nothingness is lost in Your Majesty. I long only to cease to be, except as a seed hidden in your heart of divine love. Consume me, Father. Yet not mine, but Your will be done. Be glorified. You alone are all good and all beauty. I am nothing. Here, given to me was just a drop of the love that the three persons of the Most Holy Trinity have for one another. (I could not take more.) This love which exists between the Father, the Son, and the Holy Spirit is too perfect, too pure, too full to put into words. It is unspeakable, perfect, silent. I can only record the utter joy of my soul in knowing how perfectly loved each person of the Trinity is by each other person! While I was given to understand, to a very small degree, how they delight in one another, I was given to understand as well that they delight in the Blessed Virgin Mary to such a degree, that, again, I dare not speak it except to say that she is their Masterpiece!

Oh Most Holy Trinity, what a wonder you are! My soul rejoices in you. I am in awe and amazement! You are beauty unspeakable. Perfect silence adorns you, wrapping itself around you. My nothingness is caught up in the veil of silence, and I know as never before that I stand in the presence of perfect and holy Love. There is nothing but to sigh with love, to groan in longing. Your Temple is too holy to approach. Yet you come to me, Father, Son and Holy Spirit, and You create Your heaven in my soul. The void that I am, you fill! Each minute my soul stands on guard, listening for Your voice to call me home in You. Rather, in Your Mercy You come to feed me a foretaste of Your heavenly Banquet of Love. Oh blood that covers me, I am so grateful! I love You boundlessly, to madness it seems, Father, Son and Holy Spirit!

9-14-94 Feast of the Cross - Rosary with Father.
Venerate the Holy Cross

My dear ones,

Venerate the Holy Cross! Allow the love of the Cross to penetrate your very heart. The Cross is eternal and holy Wisdom and Love. If you permit the Cross to pierce your soul, it shall become your intimate friend and teacher. It shall transfigure you into a reflection of love. Holiness is in the Cross. Do not fear the Cross for it is your salvation. It is love poured out. His love gushed from Him for you. I stood at the foot of the Cross utterly pierced with the sufferings of my Son on the Cross. Yet I did not go against the Will of the Father, as I understood that the Father's Love was beyond all my understanding, and I trusted in Him! God is Love. He desires only to embrace us in His Love and make us one with Him. Venerate the Cross. Gaze upon it and adore it. Pour your love upon the Cross. Take joy in it. Give thanks in it. I am always at the foot of the Cross, adoring, loving, and interceding on behalf of all souls. Stand with me at the foot of the Cross and let us adore! I love you, I bless you.

Your Mother, Mary

9-15-94 Feast of Our Lady of Sorrows, Tabernacle, 10:30 AM
Our Lady of Sorrows

Note: Our Lady was so intimate with me that I heard her voice as she dictated these words with such clarity that I had to stop to think if I was hearing them with my proper ear or in my soul, as usual. I believe, to the best of my knowledge, that she spoke interiorly but I can't be absolutely positive. She was so close to me that I knew her disposition to be very somber yet gentle, full of motherly, tender love for us - yet disappointed in us as we continue to offend God. This is her "sorrow" of today. Her words are a plea - to awaken in us - our acknowledgment of God.

My dear children,
My heart is sorrowful and breaking as I observe how you continue to offend God. I have come to you so often to lead you to my Son. Yet many of my little ones are walking dangerous paths which lead away from God. God is Love. Yet I observe today in the world, so very much a lack of love. You reject my Son still! Even some who pray are simply saying words which are empty because they do not have love in their hearts. You need to love one another. You need to be charitable to one another. You cannot walk the path leading to heaven alone. Assist one another in all the needs of the soul. All souls possess great dignity because God is the center core of every soul. Even those who reject Him, He does not reject. God's covenant with His people is everlasting.

Oh my little ones, how very much I love you! I desire to help you to know and to love God. If you only realized the consequences of your decisions which take you away from the path to eternal life! Do not forfeit your inheritance for the trinkets of the finite world. For even one lost soul, my heart breaks. Imagine then my sorrow for the many, many lost souls. I try desperately to reach each one of you, my dear children, to awaken in you the seed in your soul which longs to be united to love. But you do not understand that God is love! Surrender to God and the Holy Spirit will fill you with love!

It is difficult for some of you to love and to hold on to God, who is Spirit. Yet, if you would only be still, silent and enter into solitude every day, you would discover the stirring of His Love in your soul. The reality of God in your soul is the love you cling to. He will make Himself known to you as the true reality. He is the Divine Lover of your soul. So then you will come to know Him, though you cannot see Him. He is the eternal reality. He knows you in ways no one else can know you, and He loves you, delighting in you, having created you for Himself. He loves sinners and He heals them. You must learn to see Him in the eyes of each soul. But you must learn to love Him and know Him in your soul first. You cannot love except in and with Him! You will know Him by the peace He imparts to your soul, for only God brings peace! I am with you always. I do not cease to pray and to intercede for you. Please convert and please do not offend God. I love you and I bless you with the sign of the cross on your forehead. Love one another, but Love God above all!

Your Mother

Dear Lady, thank you. In the midst of your sorrow, you love. Teach us Oh Mother of God, my mother also, to love, to serve, to adore, to hope as you do in Him. Dear Lady of Sorrows, give us the grace through your Immaculate Heart to stop offending Our Lord and Savior.

Note: The Holy Spirit gave me this scripture 1Tim15 - "Christ Jesus came into the world to save sinners, among whom I am foremost of all!" All the day long, this served as my meditation, and when I would stop thinking of it, the Holy Spirit brought it to mind again and again.

9-18-94 My home 10 AM
My Mercy Shall Allow Purification

*Soul, Lift your thoughts to Me now. Do not be concerned that you do not understand all that you wish to understand. I have given to you what I desire to give. You understand precisely what I give you to understand. What do you suppose I

want from you, My pupil? Only your love. You cannot give more. Even the love you give to Me is given by My Grace, initiated by Me. Seek only to love Me. Love is what I seek from you. You are My instrument, a vessel only. I shall put My work before you as I see fit, and you shall accomplish My work by My Grace. Your lack of understanding and weakness is precisely what shall bear witness that what is accomplished through you is indeed only from Me.

I have given understanding to your soul of My Divine Indwelling. You know well My voice, as you exist in My Divine Love. Do you require more understanding than this? You discern well the movement of My Holy Spirit in your soul. All that I shall ever require of you is love. In love you shall be obedient to all that you discern from the Holy Spirit. Your obedience has found great favor with Me. I bless you, My pupil, not for your sake, but for My sake and for the sake of others who will receive through you My blessing and grace. You are a sign professing My Love for sinners. I come for the sake of sinners. All men are sinners. I come for the sake of all who seek truth! What confusion exists today! Rebels have penetrated My Church. My Heart is lacerated. The very instrument (Church) created to shepherd My flock spreads confusion and leaves unattended many who are lost and seeking some knowledge of truth. My flock has need of shepherding. My flock has need of love. The Holy Spirit is being given to many in this era so as to pastor them back into the fold. Many have wandered aimlessly, alone, and misguided. Woe to those who have led My flock astray, into barren wilderness where they starve and die. They shall see the justice of God. I shall come and gather My people. I shall bestow My Divine Love upon the hearts that are longing for love. I shall draw hearts unto the furnace of My Sacred Heart, which burns for love of all souls. My beloved, do you feel the longing in My Heart? I am pleading with My own creation for love. You feel it in your heart now. (Here, I am filled with sorrow that Jesus would plead for love. Such humility and condescension in God. Who can fathom this Lord?)

Yes, My pupil, I am seeking souls to love Me. How many work good works, but without love. Love and works are necessary but above all is love. What is lacking most is love. Not much longer shall rebels lead souls astray. My Mercy shall allow purification. I shall enter My Temple on earth (Church) and once and for all drive out the rebels who defile her. I shall expose them, and under My gaze they shall run from the truth. Those who have suffered much for My sake shall be drawn up to Me. You will suffer as My witness. The world will persecute My witnesses. Suffering is the lot for My chosen ones. History will repeat. The world has rejected the good and persecuted My witnesses. But I shall empower all who stand for My sake. The spirit of the world has already been conquered by Me. Purification is necessary. Purgation will be permitted for the atrocities of this generation, until My creation is pleasing in My sight. Oh what your eyes shall see: suffering brought upon yourselves! Oh what your ears shall hear: falsehood shall abound, causing great confusion and apostasy. Apostasy is underway, yet you shall witness more and more apostasy.

(Jesus, I feel Your heartache as You speak these words. My God, what can be done to avert this apostasy? Lord, have mercy and convert souls to love You. Please.)

My altar, all that I have spoken must come to pass in preparation for the era of Peace. Trust in Me, for I am Mercy and tenderness toward all souls. Fragrance Me with the perfume of sacrifice for My sake and for the sake of souls. I bless you in the name of the Most Holy Trinity. Be at peace. I am with you. I love you.

Jesus

9-18-94 My home, 10 PM
America and Abortion

*Soul, please write My words.

My children,
There is a cloud of black smoke arising from your streets and hovering over your country. It is filled with the stench of death, the atrocity of the killing of innocents. Oh nation so highly

favored, you are turning your back upon the One who favored and blessed you. You are deciding who shall live and who shall die for the sake of your selfishness. Life is no longer as precious as power and money. Your greed is horrendous.

Oh nation founded on principles upholding the value of life, you are traveling the road to destruction. You offend God as you promote your evil ways to all the world. You are not the Supreme Being. It is not for you to decide who lives and who dies. All souls are created for life, eternal life! The souls of the innocent whom you kill shall one day look upon you, and there will be much wailing on your part, as the reality of the death you promoted shall cause you to run from the gaze of the innocent and from the gaze of God. Oh nation that I love, repent! Daily you are killing innocent souls, which I receive into My heavenly Kingdom. The hand of justice shall fall upon you with a mighty force. You are smothering life. In doing so, you choke love and grace. Evil is flowing in your veins. The blood of the innocent line your streets.

Oh nation that I love, where is your love? Where is your goodness? Receive your God and obey My law. Convert and repent. Pray for mercy, which is yours if you keep My commandment: Thou shalt not kill! You violate My law in the name of righteousness. Hypocrites! What is evil cannot be good under any circumstance. Do not rationalize before Me! The truth cannot be denied. How My Heart bleeds for you, Oh nation that I love. Under the banner of freedom, you violate My laws. Death shall beget death. Life begets life. What consequences shall be laid upon you? You must decide. Soul, pray for your country. I love you.

Jesus

9-23-94 My home, 6 PM, For Prayer Group
Listen to Your Mother: You Will Witness Much Suffering

My little ones,
You cannot comprehend the power of the Rosary, especially as it is prayed in union and with much love. Each bead contains the

promise of my Maternal love, the promise of much grace! When you hold the Rosary in your hand, you hold a most precious gift. Let each prayer you pray tonight be love poured out to God. God seeks your love. Indeed, you are created for His delight. He formed you to love Him. What an intimate God we have. Adore Him! Know that you are loved by God, who is with you at every moment. Does He not sustain your very breath? He will never abandon you! What more do you need?

Listen to your mother, my children. There may come a time when you are tempted by Satan to think that perhaps God has abandoned you. You must not fall into Satan's traps. Cling to the truth given you in the Word, which teaches you that God's covenant is eternal. He will never forsake you. You must rely on the truth of His Word. In the near future, you will witness much suffering. You may not understand all that is happening in the world. It may appear that evil is winning, but you must cling to the truth which is stated in the Word; the victory has already been won by Jesus! Do not rely on consolations or feelings. Be grounded in the truth and hold fast to the promises set forth in the Word of God!

Persevere in the spiritual life in spite of any circumstance or hardship. If you persevere, you will not give into the temptation that God has abandoned you. If you are graced with a Cross, carry it with love. God will give you the grace you require. You may find yourselves weeping and in much pain (spiritual). *I, too, weep and feel the pain of all my children. My tears are not a sign of weakness; rather, they are a sign to the world that, as your Mother, I am united with you to such a degree that I weep with you. I am sorrowful for your pain and suffering. So much suffering is brought on by Satan, who toys with you in every way, and at every opportunity he attempts to oppress your soul. God only raises the soul!*

The Father has permitted me to speak so many words of love to you so that you may be encouraged and raised up in the way of sanctity. You will not falter in the time of trial. God is with you. Trust in God. Abandon yourselves into the Father's strong arms. God desires your good only. Be aware of Satan's tactics. He is so active in the world today! Do not give him the power to disturb your peace or interfere with your spiritual journey. Be aware that He works through good people who are unsuspecting. He uses many tactics to achieve his goal of division and turmoil, yet he has no power over you that you do not give him. You easily overcome his temptations if you remain in a state of recollection, a state of grace. The greatest weapon your soul can have? The Eucharist, Reconciliation and the Rosary (prayer). *Persevere in Faith and Hope and Charity, but above all, Love! I am with you always. I love you, my dear little ones. I love you all!*

Your Mother Mary

9-25-94 11:45 PM My home
Our Lady Gives a Prayer About the Divine Will

My child, repeat this prayer, please.

"Oh Most Holy Trinity, Your Divine Will is my desire. Your Divine Will is perfect and holy. Your Will, then, is my life. I beg the grace to surrender unto you at every given moment. I shall ingest your holy Divine Will. It shall be my food, the sustenance of my life. As your seed, I shall never knowingly venture outside your Holy Will. You alone are wisdom. You alone are perfect goodness. I place all my trust in Thee, Oh Most Holy Trinity. I shall rely on Thee only. Oh Most Perfect Will of God, I love Thee! My will shall lead me to folly. Your Divine Will shall lead me to eternal life. Oh my soul, hear the whisper of His holy orders. Follow without hesitation when He whispers, this for the sake of love. Your Will is sweetness in my soul. Nothing less shall satisfy. Oh Holy Will of God, I love Thee! Oh Divine Will of God, caress my soul; cause me to desire Thee fervently above all else! Amen and amen."

10-2-94 Noon My home
Give Unto Me Your Fiat

Jesus spoke:

My altar,
The lessons I teach you in the silence are of such depth that your soul cannot receive them in the way you receive My words

in your soul. In the silence, where you experience absence and suffer longing, here I am imparting to you the purest gift of My Divine Love. It is imparted to the deepest core of your soul so that you cannot perceive it, because you could not take such sublime a gift into your humanness. What you perceive as painful is the suffering of one wounded by Divine Love. Here, your soul is treading the waters of pure love. At once the soul desires to drown in the ocean of pure love, but at the same time it struggles to stay afloat because it cannot take in this much pure love. When your soul surrenders completely, My beloved one, you will not tread on top of My ocean of Love, you will stop all the movement, permitting yourself to drown, completely immersed in My Love.

In the silence I impart pure Divine Love unto your soul, so that your capacity for My Love is being increased moment to moment. Sometimes this produces in you a faintness, fatigue and a sickness of one wounded by Love Himself. So, too, this produces your energy and your joy, enabling growth in all the virtues. Soul, it has pleased Me to observe you receiving my work in your soul with greater peace. I am imparting My strength and courage unto you.

My beloved one, I am preparing you for union, so sublime, that you simply cannot comprehend. It is precisely your inability to comprehend that attracts Me. I, Your God, desire that you receive Me as a child, innocent, pure, and trusting! I am not seeking your understanding of these matters. I am seeking only that you would receive Me in love, pure and simple! Permit Me, Your God, to love you! I will not proceed, My soul, My beloved one, until you give unto Me your "fiat." I am patient. I shall await your "yes" to proceed in My workings in your soul. Receive My peace. I love you.

Your Jesus

Here, I became paralyzed, so to speak. I could not readily give my "yes." I distracted myself with work, putting down my pen and closing the journal. I hesitated to respond to the message, sensing I would be diving into an abyss of unknown territory. Satan targeted me with confusion, doubt, rationalization, and my imagination became carried away with negativity. Realizing I was being targeted by Satan, I renounced him with much authority, in Jesus' name. He fled. Left only with my human weakness, I still felt somewhat paralyzed. This was evident as I tried to write a response, and I was blocked and could not put pen to paper. I called Father and read him the message. He helped me to understand. When we hung up I could respond. The words flowed from my heart onto the paper.

My Fiat: Jesus, my Savior, glance at me, Lord; am I not standing naked before you? You know the secrets of my heart. What is hidden from You? Nothing! You seek my fiat and you see that I tremble as you ask. I tremble before You because I am overwhelmed by Your gentleness and love. You, who are Lord of the universe, seek my fiat and ask that I would permit you to love me? You, who are God, refuse to violate my free will. Is there any greater humility than Yours? Who can fathom Your Love? Oh my God, who will cover my nakedness and cause my trembling to cease? You alone!

Jesus, You have sifted me like sand. I have passed through your fingers. Have your eyes not observed every particle of my being? If then you see a part of me which is being withheld from you, would you please claim that part for yourself? My vision is so limited. I cannot see the particles I am withholding from You. I perceive only that I have been turned inside out, examined by You and claimed by You. Have I failed to commit my nothingness to you from moment to moment? Who else but You occupies my mind, my heart, my soul? Have I not turned my eyes toward You alone? Have you not observed me walking in the desert, in the darkness of faith, crying out to You, searching only for You? Am I not scorned and misjudged because of You? Have I not put You before all others! Have you not taken from me former consolation? Your eyes gaze upon my heart, which is shredded into pieces because I fail to love You as I should. Do I tremble because the cost of loving You is my greatest joy and my greatest suffering? Have pity upon me, my Lord, as I stumble in the darkness. Oh Light, pierce the darkness and illuminate my path. Take away my resistance. Jesus, hold me, so that I am still.

What can I offer the one I love? I hand to You "my will" and I whisper to You my "yes," knowing such an offering can be made only in Your grace. Jesus, proceed! Be my Master, please! Lord, will You permit my "yes" to draw graces for souls? I ache that Your creation would love You and glorify You, and to that end I commit myself for love of You. Oh God of all creation, come and renew the face of the earth!

My altar, I am joyful at your response! I accept your offering, blessing you now as I give unto you My Crucifix. Take the Crucifix to your lips, placing a kiss upon My Holy Wounds; first My feet, then My hands, then My side. Do not doubt. I am with you. (Here it seemed that Jesus was right beside me, holding the Crucifix to my lips.) His Love filled my soul as I did as He asked. My "fiat" was sealed in the kissing of the Crucifix. I am full of His Love, and His Peace permeates every cell of my being. My Beloved Lord and Savior, I am Yours.

10-4-94 Feast of St. Francis of Assisi
A Visit From St. Francis. He Led Me in Prayer

Following 8:30 AM Mass, praying before the tabernacle, my prayer was most graced. I experienced a new sensation of my spirit taking flight. I know only, that upon experiencing a sort of re-entry into my body, I am overcome with joy, peace and the most Divine Love! Throughout the day I walked in much grace. I know this by the most profound Peace in my soul, which stays with me no matter what else I may be experiencing.

Later 10 PM, My home.

I had just prayed the Liturgy of the Hours for the Feast of St. Francis. I heard St. Francis, in my soul, and I knew immediately it was St. Francis' voice saying: "Little one, kneel before the Blessed Mother at your desk please. Pray one Our Father, one Hail Mary, one Glory Be with all your heart. Then I shall assist you in your prayer this night." I knelt before Our Lady, gazing at her (statue), asking her guidance. Could this truly be St. Francis communicating with my soul?

Mother Mary replied:

My daughter,
I beseech you to receive our assistance as a child, with peace
and joy. Do not worry or think it is not possible. All things are
possible with God. You are being aided in your spiritual journey.
Give praise and thanksgiving to the Most Holy Trinity for permit-
ting His Grace to fill your soul. Please receive my beloved son,
Francis now. Trust in me, my little one! I am your Mother. Be my
little child. Peace be with you. Receive the gift of the angelic
Francis.

(Though I was now at peace, just to be prudent, I prayed to St.
Michael three times.)
Then I heard Francis:

"My little flower, receive as a child. I bless you in the name of
the Most Holy Trinity. Little dove, it would benefit your soul to
seek our Beloved Lord in all His creation. You will find Him in
every creature and in all creation. It would benefit your soul to
praise Him always and everywhere. His yoke is light. Praise and
be joyful! Little dove, He is making you pure and white for His
sake. Rejoice as He cleanses you, preparing you for gifts He will
bestow in His perfect time.

Little flower, your fragrance is being made holy in Him. It
would benefit your soul to adore Him in the crucifix. Meditate on
and love His Holy Wounds. Like a dove hiding in the cleft of the
rock, hide your little soul in the depth of His Wounds. Breathe in
His suffering. When He permits you to suffer for His sake, He
gives to you the greatest of gifts. In all trials, adore Him and sing
praise. Embrace the Cross, resting on the wooden beam as a little
bird would rest in his nest. Little flower, be pure, allowing His dew
to cover you. Open yourself up only to the radiance of the Son.
Our Mother, like the moon, will illuminate your path in the darkness of the night. Above all, little one, know the truth of your lowliness! Seek only to serve all of creation for the glory of His Name
only. Atone for your sins through the giving of alms. Let charity
reign in you. It is the outward sign of His Divine Love in your soul.

Simply receive as a little child. You have been given a holy guide (Father) who will discern these matters. The Holy Spirit will guide him as your witness and guide. Many will think you a fool. Praise God and bless them. God has kept hidden from the wise what He has revealed to mere children. The humble and contrite heart shall be one with God. I will assist you in detachment, obedience, penance, and prayer. Whatever the Master ordains to give you shall be recorded for Holy Mother Church. Prepare for her authority to be tried. Her purity shall be restored, overcoming the trial. Humble and obedient souls, the poor in spirit, will rebuild her, in and through the Holy Spirit, who revives in peace and in love."

Let us pray: (Francis dictated this prayer.)

"Oh Most Holy Trinity, be blessed and glorified! I, your little creature, lift my eyes toward You, Almighty God, Father, Son and Holy Spirit. I hope for just a glimpse of Your Majesty, whose hands created all of heaven and earth. Full of poverty, I seek the Wisdom of Your Divine Will. In my nothingness, I bow before You, seeking only to exalt Your Holy Name, that You may be glorified even as the lilies and flowers of the field give you glory as they turn their petals toward the sun and open up to heaven. Fragrance me with Mercy and Love that I may bloom for you, season after season, dying and blooming, dying and blooming. Use my lowliness to adorn your church with humility. Permeate me with Your divine charity so that I may toil in Your vineyard, harvesting souls and beautifying Your Church.

Master, permit me to accompany You on the Cross, becoming one with you, that I may know Your Love. If you find me pleasing in Your sight, when my allotted days have passed, would You pluck Your little flower and carry me to a place reserved for little ones at Your heavenly Banquet? Oh Divine Master, I dare to lift my eyes to the heavens, in the hope that Your all knowing eye will glance and observe me singing Your praises and seeking Your Will. Would You have mercy upon me and draw me unto You, Almighty yet gentle God? Let us close with one Our Father, Hail Mary, and Glory Be. Peace of Jesus Christ be with you always.
His servant (Francis)."

10-4-94 1 AM

As I walked up the stairs to my bedroom after this prayer time, it seemed a little voice whispered to me, "Do not trust Father with this. You cannot trust him." I immediately replied: "You are a liar. Get away from me Satan." He fled immediately, never disturbing my peace, and I rested in the love of my God.

10-6-94 7 PM My home
Persevere in Faith

Please write for my little ones.
My dear children,
I am with you always to bless you, to watch over you, to love you and to lead you to Jesus. Recall how I gathered many of you at Lourdes. I foretold of the many graces which would be yours as you opened your hearts to God in prayer. My little ones, you have been faithful to a life of prayer and docile to the Holy Spirit. Give praise and thanksgiving to our Triune God! His Mercy and Love have showered you like rain from heaven.
As you gather to pray this night, rest assured that I am with you. At each Our Father I raise my voice in union with you. My little ones, it is not possible for you to comprehend how loved you are by God. You are infinitely precious and important to God the Father, Jesus My Son, and the Holy Spirit, who is Love. My Im-maculate Heart surrounds you. In a world that often rejects my Maternal Love, I thank you for accepting me as your Mother. As you pray before your Mother of Medjugorje, contemplate the mes-sage of Medjugorje, that you may inhale the fragrance of my Ma-ternal Love reaching out to all my children to say, "God exists; He loves you and you have great need of His Love, which can and will overcome the present evil situation in the world." God created you for His Glory, His delight. Satan has spread his darkness over the earth. God's Light will pierce the darkness and overcome the evil. God will rescue His creation, and soon.
Little ones, be pure of heart. My Son seeks purity of heart and He delights in blessing such a heart. Humble yourselves before the

Master who created you. Be still, that you may hear the Holy Spirit who is with you always. Your faithfulness has found favor with God. Persevere in Faith. Many of you have walked in the darkness of the desert. Take courage and walk with confidence, because you are blessed and strengthened in ways which you do not perceive at the present moment. Yet when you least expect, you will see and know the value of the darkness of the desert, which is a Cross many are called to carry on their journey to union with God. Do not worry about the future. Trust as a child. Live only in the present moment so that at each moment you are giving glory to God by loving Him as a child clinging to His "Abba." Let us pray in union and in love. I so love each one of you and I bless you.

Your Mother

10-6-94 Following the Rosary and Chaplet with the Prayer Group at my home
Maternal Milk

As we sat in the silence of contemplation for quite some time, I was given the following vision of Our Lady (a full figure of white light; she was sitting) as she breastfed the infant Jesus (a bundle of golden and white rays wrapped in a blanket of white). The tenderness of this vision is beyond description.

I have carried you in my arms to nurture you with my Maternal milk just as I have done for my Son, Jesus. Each one I have raised as a beautiful and unique flower in my garden. Though there is a variety, each is at the precise stage of development to beautify the garden. I bless you this night and present to each one a heavenly white rose. I implore you to place this rose within your heart, permitting it to bloom within you, creating in you a pure heart. God's favor is with such a heart. Each is infinitely precious and important to God. God seeks only to give and receive love from His creation. The bond of love which surrounds you shall not be broken; though tried and tested, it shall remain strong through prayer.

Note: I am humbled as I am used as a vessel to communicate the love of Our Lady and Our Lord. I am privileged and humbled once again to be part of this group. It seems to me that each soul present has greater faith and greater love than I, who am the most skeptical of all. My God, Your ways are so very mysterious and contrary to man's. I will close by saying that the above description does not come close to the reality of the love expressed in the vision of Our Lady breastfeeding Jesus. This was a most special gift for all as we approach the five-year anniversary of praying together.

10-7-94 Feast of Our Lady of the Rosary
Our Lady of the Rosary Blesses Father

I bless you this night, my son and my priest. Bless you, and grace be with you who were chosen from before all ages to exemplify God's Mercy and God's Love for souls. Bless you and grace be with you - chosen to be a sign for many, chosen to be a sign of humility and a sign of strength. Bless you and grace be with you, chosen to protect the everlasting truth. You are God's banner of love. Bless you and grace be with you, formed in secret for many years, to emerge in this time and this place as a pillar of truth, courage and love. Bless you and grace be with you; your sighs and your tears I tuck in my Immaculate Heart. I cherish your offering of love, my son and my priest, because it is pure and selfless. Toil with love in the vineyard of the Lord until your allotted days have passed, and I shall come, together with my Son, to bring you to your everlasting home in heaven. Your presence in the vineyard is vital and I am in the watchtower to assist you, console you, strengthen you and love you. I love you.
    Your Mother

10-11-94 8:30 AM Mass at Communion
St. Francis at Communion

Just prior to walking up the aisle to communion, St. Francis speaks: "Little dove, at the moment when you receive the Master,

pour all the fervor of your heart upon Him. Praise and thank the
Most High God who humbles Himself to be food for His little
wretched creature. You exist to glorify His name." I replied: Dear
Francis, help me to love Him. Thank you for assisting me.

10-15-94 PM Feast of St. Theresa of Avila
There is Little Faith left on Earth

**My beloved, please write. I, Your Lord and Savior, shall
dictate for My creation.**

My creation,
How little you have understood of My divine way of life and
love. Though I knock at the door with gifts of My Divine Love
and Mercy, you are not attentive. Your hearts are hardened.
Your lives are distracted in worldly ambitions. You are drowning in the trinkets of the world. The devil seduces you with the
apples of the world and you fall.
Oh My creation, from the Cross I said, "I thirst," and indeed
you have not yet understood that I thirst for you. I thirst for love.
I thirst that your heart would open to My offering of eternal life,
and that you would accept My Love. The world has captured
your very heart. You are weighted down with anxiety about many
things. You know little of true peace of soul. Rather, you seek
false peace in quiet indifference and irresponsibility, as you lull
yourselves into false security and false happiness. The more
gained of the world, the less satisfied is your soul. You sense occasionally that you are losing a battle, but you know not how to
satisfy the emptiness of your heart. The pain of your life overwhelms you, and pleasure is all that you seek. In this manner you
exist in a state of numbness.
Oh My creation, My Grace I offer to you, that you may grasp
the reality that the God of the universe exists, and I am Love. I
love you intimately. I seek only to teach you of My Love. You refuse
Me again and again. There is so little faith left on earth. My chosen ones, My own seed, you know not how lost you are! Your lack
of faith and lack of love lacerates My Sacred Heart of Love.

Who among you will take the time to open the door of your heart unto Me? I am thirsty to enter into the depths of your soul. With Me all things are possible. I shall transfigure you into a holy people, creating in you a reflection of My own Divine Love. In these times of great mercy, ordained by the most loving and most merciful Father, I knock at the door of each and every heart. I await you. I am thirsting for your love. And when the day of reckoning comes – the time is nearer than you think – do not say to Me: Lord, I did not hear You knocking. I shall say to you then: Oh My wretched creature whom I love, I came to you. I called you by name. I said: Come, follow Me. I am here with you. Let us sup together and I will teach of true life in Me. And when you failed to respond, I sent messenger after messenger, from My holy Mother to the littlest of children. To these I gave My Divine Wisdom and enlightened their souls to truth. But you did not believe, and worse, you persecuted My messengers, sending them away in your arrogance and pride. In their humility they did not curse you and they did not cease to pray for you. Their only desire being the Holy Will of God, they persevered under persecution because they possess the Holy Spirit, who is their courage and teacher. You are blind because your heart is cluttered with the ways of the world, to whom you now belong.

Truly I say unto you, My creation, whom I love unto death: narrow is the path that leads to eternal life and few are the souls who discover the narrow path. Grace shall descend, that, once and for all, the scales can fall from your eyes that you may see with the eyes of truth. Then, only then, shall you live in My Grace as My chosen and holy people. These are times of decision. My creation, I implore you: Do not refuse the Holy Spirit! I thirst still. I thirst more than ever. Do not deny your Lord and Savior! I am the innocent lamb led to the slaughter for pure love of you! I have given My command. Love God with all your heart, your soul, your mind and strength! This is the foremost command. Love is above all! Do not pretend to love me when you offer only empty words for your own selfish motives! Do not profess to love Me if you do not love one another! Do not delude yourself that you can love Me from afar.

You must become intimate with Me. Then you shall know Me as I am. I am Love!

My creation, stand with Me, Your God! Stand against the evil of the world! Dare to love! When I come, will I find any faith left in the world at all? You must pray to understand My messages. In prayer the Light of the Holy Spirit shall enter your darkness. Then you can converse with your God. I shall say to you, My beloved seed, I love you just the way you are. If you permit My entrance, I shall make you beautiful, for you are precious in My sight! Then I will await your words of love. If from your heart, you would simply say, "I love You, Lord," I would be so pleased. I will teach you of divine love. In the quiet and stillness of the night let us converse as lovers. I am thirsty and so are you, my broken creation. I love you. Peace.

Jesus

Immediately Jesus said,

*Soul, please write now for you and Father.
I shall multiply the fruits of your labor, blessing all your endeavors in the days to come, as you undertake to fulfill My Holy and Divine Will. I cannot promise a journey without persecution, but I promise the grace to rise above the trials. The work you produce shall be accepted by many, but rejected by some. You shall be directed every step of the way. The Holy Spirit shall go before you to prepare the way. Yet there will be difficulties and trials that shall test your faith and courage.

My son, you are the chosen witness for the messenger chosen to write My words. Take courage and stand for My work. Discern the truth, which bears witness already, as only a good tree can produce good fruit. Though there may be a time when a door may be closed temporarily, trust My Holy Spirit in your soul. Go forward with My work, seeking only to fulfill the Will of Your Lord and Savior.

My messenger, My *Soul, trust completely in the priest given to guide your soul. He is My choice. It is truly I, Your Lord and Savior, who reveals this to your soul. *Soul, the cup I offer you is filled with suffering. It is the cup from which I drank. It is our wedding cup. Yet I seek that you joyfully partake in order to fulfill the Father's will. He has chosen you to proclaim His Mercy for sinners and His Love for all. Do not fear. Lean on Me. I am Your Lord and Savior. I shall be your strength. I bless you, My beloved priest and My beloved altar, breathing My sigh of love upon you. You bear the seal of Divine Love in your soul, marking you as Mine. My peace be yours. I love you.

Jesus

10-17-94 9:30 AM Tabernacle, Feast of St. Ignatius of Antioch, Martyr
Press the Crucifix to Your Heart

My child,

I, your Mother, request that you gaze upon the Crucifix to your left. (I was positioned right before the tabernacle.) *Press the Crucifix into your heart. Allow the Crucifix to penetrate you. Let it fill your heart. The Cross, being the means of your salvation, is the most profound example of love! The more you permit the reality of the Cross to penetrate your soul, the closer the union with my Son. You are called by the Father to lay down your life for others.*

Little one, you have tasted of the many pleasures of the world. But God has called you out of the world. Now you are to taste of true life and true love, which shall be yours through the tasting of suffering. As your Beloved has suffered to reconcile the whole of creation with God the Father, so too shall you be required to fulfill the Father's Holy Will by serving Him for the good of souls. Your sufferings shall reconcile many souls with God. Oh my soul, I rejoice for you as God has chosen you to co-redeem through the cross. This shall produce the joy and the love which many shall see in you. So then, each day, take the Crucifix to your heart. Press it deep within you. You shall grow in wisdom and knowledge of my Son. By this means you shall be made strong, to endure much suffering and persecution for the good of souls. This you shall learn to accept with great charity and love and joy!

Oh my daughter, please write now for all my children.

The Church Shall Suffer Great Trials

My children,

The Church, the beloved Bride of Christ, and my son, shall suffer great trials. Already my son (the Pope) *suffers more than you can ever imagine. Pray unceasingly for the Church and for my Pope, please. My children, if more souls would convert and pray, if more souls would offer themselves as sacrifices of love, the sufferings of the Church, the Pope and the world could be lessened. However, I have revealed, through many messages, that the mercy of God the Father shall permit a thorough purgation of His Church, so that she may be restored fully in truth and tradition, made pure and holy as one united to the Heart of the Redeemer. So that the Sovereignty and Majesty of God may reign on earth, much must be purged.*

Sacrificial souls will alleviate some of the suffering, and there have been many who are being raised to be of service to God in this manner. My children, truly the Holy Spirit is pouring grace all over the earth now! He who is awake can receive now. Quickly He shall raise souls to be converted children of God. I do not know the exact hour the Father has chosen. I know only that all of heaven is opening up and leaning to earth to gather creation, awaken the sleeping, save the lost souls, because the hour is late indeed. I love you my children. Your Mother is watching over you. Thank you for listening to my messages. Pray that you may live them! Peace of Jesus be yours.

Your Mother

3 PM Feast of St. Ignatius of Antioch
I Was Enjoying All the Pleasures of the World!

Jesus spoke:

My *Soul, when the time arrives, this is what you will say to your brothers and sisters.

I was enjoying all the pleasures of the world, yet I was empty, though I did not know this. Through the intercession of My Mother, Jesus came to cover Me with His mercy. He showed to me the graveyard of dead bones, just as He showed Ezekiel

long ago. I was amongst the bones, all dried up and without life. Jesus said to me, "I shall bring My Spirit into you that you may come to life. I shall make flesh grow over you and put the Holy Spirit in you, so that you may come to life and know that I am the Lord of your life!" Then you shall prophesy and intercede to the Spirit for all the souls slain in the graveyard of death (spiritual) saying: From the Four Winds come, Oh Spirit, and breathe upon these bones that they come to life in God. You shall say to your brothers and sisters, "The whole of creation is like the house of Israel, dried up, hope lost and cut off from the grace of God due to their sins."

Proclaim that I shall restore My people through My Holy Spirit, reviving them from the graveyard that they may know I am God and I am Love. Proclaim that you have eaten of the pleasures of the world and, though you were momentarily satisfied, they did not fulfill you as the holy and perfect Will of God fulfills you! You shall say this and more as I fill your mouth with My words. All this shall come to pass at the designated hour. My *Soul, will you do this for Me?

My Jesus, I cannot refuse You because I love You. Yet I fail to understand your plan for me. I cannot imagine anyone would listen to my words. I will be rejected and ridiculed. Yet, if this is my lot, so be it, if it is your Divine Will. If I have your love, that is all I require. I am in Your hands and at Your mercy. Have pity on my soul. You know how the devil torments me. Jesus, be my stronghold, that I may do the Will of the Father and overcome the temptations of the devil. I love You endlessly.

10-18-94 11 PM My home
Strive for Simplicity of Heart like St. Francis

Our Lady said:

Dear child,
Strive for simplicity of heart; as your brother Francis loved and attained such simplicity of heart, so too shall you strive for

*this. It will be a great help to your soul and to your calling. Also
my little one, simplicity of heart is a good protection against the
temptations of the devil. I love you.*
    Your Mother

    Therefore I turned to the Omnibus of sources on St. Francis, and
found on page 45 his writing entry on "simplicity." For my own reference I shall record his words of wisdom. "We must be convinced
that we have nothing of our own, except our vices and sins. So we
should be glad when we fall into various trials (James 1:2) and when
we suffer anguish of soul or body or affliction of any kind in this
world for the sake of life eternal. We must all be on guard against
pride and empty boasting and beware of worldly or natural wisdom.
The worldly spirit loves to talk a lot but do nothing, striving for exterior signs of holiness that people can see, with no true desire for true
piety and interior holiness of spirit. The spirit of God, on the other
hand, inspires us to mortify and despise our lower nature and regard
it as a source of shame, worthless and of no value. Humility, patience, perfect simplicity and true peace of heart are all its aim, but
above everything else it desires the fear of God, the Divine Wisdom
and the Divine Love of the Father, Son and Holy Spirit.
    Simplicity: A man of holy simplicity is a man who is not affected
by human speculations; he does not calculate nor scheme to realize
his purposes; his heart is not divided between God and the world!
    Pure Heart: With a pure heart, with a pure mind, imply free-
dom from all self seeking and attachment to earthly goods, not
freedom from the guilt of sin. A man is pure if he lives for God
alone, if there is no room in his heart for the desires of the ego or
attachment to the world and worldly goods."

Dear Francis, please help me to live this! Thank you.

10-19-94 Late afternoon, my home
The Feast of Divine Mercy

    As I drove my son to practice, Our Lady spoke: *When you
return home, please pray the penance given you by Father* (the

Chaplet of Divine Mercy) *and I shall instruct you further.* I returned home, and on my knees recited the Chaplet of Divine Mercy.
Our Lady then spoke:

My child,
    You have just immersed yourself in the mercy of the Most Holy Trinity, through the Sacrament of Reconciliation. His Mercy covers you entirely. Reconciliation is a fountain of Divine Mercy, restoring the soul to health. Too few drink of God's Mercy. Proclaim that now is the time of God's Mercy. It is urgent. Souls should avail themselves of His great Mercy now, not that His Mercy will cease. Oh no, His Mercy is eternal and infinite. But His Justice shall be poured upon the earth, finding many souls unprepared. These souls who have not reconciled with God will not withstand His powerful gaze of Truth.
    I request you seek permission to have the Holy Sacrifice of the Mass celebrated to honor the Feast of Divine Mercy on the Sunday following the Feast of Easter. Remember to offer souls the Sacrament of Reconciliation on this Feast Day, if permission is granted you. This shall be a time of much grace for the entire community. Quote Blessed Faustina's diary to the priests and to the people. They will come then to partake of this feast, which is so little venerated (as God requested), but so very necessary for the salvation of souls. Pray the Chaplet daily, please, for the salvation of the world. Blessed Faustina shall intercede on behalf of your endeavors for the good of many souls. My child, it is urgent. Speak first to your spiritual director. Seek his counsel and permission pertaining to my request. Do as he tells you. My child, contemplate the words my Jesus spoke to Blessed Faustina (page 25 of the Diary). I write them: "Distrust on the part of souls is tearing at my insides. The distrust of a chosen soul causes me even greater pain; despite my inexhaustible love for them they do not trust Me. Even my death is not enough for them. Woe to the soul that abuses these gifts."

My child,
    You wound the Sacred Heart of my Son when you fail to trust as a child. Pray for the grace to overcome the temptations to distrust God's work in your soul. Ask Father to pray specifically for

you regarding this matter, which is causing difficulty for you. It is not for you to be concerned of Father's opinion regarding the work being accomplished in and through you. Father is relying on grace and trusting in God. His surrender is received. Now you, little one, must follow his example. Grace shall assist you in this matter. Be at peace. God is with you. Thank you for your obedience to my requests. I am with you to lead you closer to my Son. I love you.

Your Mother

Our Lady led me to the following pages of Blessed Faustina's diary:

Page 26 Child, for your soul.

Page 42 Write this: Before I come as the just Judge, I am coming first as the King of Mercy.

Page 153 And who knows anything about this Feast? No one! Even those who should be proclaiming My Mercy and teaching people about it often do not know about it themselves. That is why I want the image to be solemnly blessed on the first Sunday after Easter and I want it to be venerated publicly so that every soul may know about it.

10-25-94 Tabernacle
A Glass of Water

Following 8:30 AM Mass, I prayed before the Tabernacle for an hour, as usual. After the first half hour, where I seemed to be in deep contemplation with my eyes closed, though I had not prayed with words (only silence), I perceived right before my eyes (though they were shut) a glass of water being held out to me. The clarity of the glass and the purity of the water, I noticed immediately. This was so strong an interior image that I was startled, and I opened my eyes as if I thought upon doing so I would see this beautiful glass of water being offered me. I understood immediately this was being offered by Jesus, though for a long while He did not speak, and I was left on my own to contemplate the meaning of this image (internal). While I was doing this, I heard (with my proper ear) the sound of running water being poured out. Again I opened my eyes and looked all around the church and found nothing or no one that could produce this sound (which was exterior). I finished my holy hour and all through my busy day, the glass of water would come to mind and somehow my soul was consoled.

Midnight (same day) Jesus spoke:

My *Soul, I know you are thirsty. The desert is dry, yet all the while I am with you. I am feeding you the purifying water of Divine Love. Yes, soul, drink, partake of Me. I am making your heart pure as the water, and your soul clean as the glass which contains the water, so pure and so necessary for true life in Me.

Soul, it matters not what you do or do not perceive in the darkness. You have only to cling to Me. I am the Truth. Grow in faith. How I delight in growth, *Soul. Oh the night is beautiful, do not resist, for it is here I take you in My mighty hands, molding you for Myself, into a beautiful creation. In secret this is done. Blessed is the soul who permits the wisdom of the night to enter and conquer.

Long pause and silence here. After approximately ten minutes, Jesus spoke again.

Soul, come. Enter and stay with Me in the Garden (Gethsemane). Oh night of contradiction! Bitter and sweet. Bitter due to man's betrayal and sweet due to perfect fidelity to the Father's Will. Oh night of darkness and light: salvation through bloody sacrifice of innocence. Come, soul. Enter and stay with Me to pray to the Father. You may ask, as I asked: Oh Father permit this trial (cup) to pass (for Me and for all souls) yet, ultimately, you must whisper with Me: Father, not My will, but Thy Will be done! Persevere. The darkness is full of promise. It leads to a new day, new life, a resurrection for you and for all souls. Soul, place all your trust in Me! Give to Me complete trust and allow Me, Your Lord and Savior, to room in My domain as I see fit. You are Mine. I bless you, My beloved one. Trust like a child. I am truly with you. Peace. I love you.

Jesus

10-26-94 8:30 AM Mass
Souls in Purgatory

While the Most Holy Host was not yet dissolved, Jesus spoke.

My altar, there are souls in Purgatory whom I bless through your sacrifices, especially at the moment you receive Me in Communion, but also at the time when you become physically afflicted. These poor souls have no one to offer sacrifice for them. Great are their sufferings, but in My Mercy I draw them close to My Heart through you and other souls who are faithful. My peace. I love you.
Jesus

10-29-94
Tears Are Very Precious

Our Lady spoke:

My child, be not afraid! I am with you. Peace be yours. I am with you. There are evil spirits who are furious with you. They seek to distract you, to cause fear and doubt. They seek mostly to prevent you from accomplishing the Father's Will. But you, my child, must put on the mind of Christ. Do not think in terms of the flesh, the world.

Little one, so much is given you. Therefore, so much shall be asked of you. He has prepared your soul with His grace and indeed He seeks very much from you. God will accomplish His work through the Holy Spirit, who is with you. Be patient. Wait on the inspirations of the Holy Spirit. When you are overwhelmed, it is because you are thinking in human terms. Lift your doubts and fears, depositing them in the Sacred Heart of Jesus. His furnace of Divine Love will annihilate them, and in their place He shall give to you His limitless courage and strength to fulfill the Father's Holy Will. This you shall do in peace and with great charity!

My child, you have prayed to be one with Jesus even unto the Cross. You shall indeed bear much for love of Him. The biggest crosses are reserved for His chosen vessels. Great is the capacity to love in a chosen soul! The Cross teaches growth in faith, hope and charity. The Cross is not crushing you, my child! Oh no, my little one, the Cross is raising you up to greater heights of sanctity! God is increasing your capacity to love, to serve. My child, your tears are so very precious in the eyes of my Son. He, Himself, wipes them from your face. He receives them as pure love, rare and precious! I rejoice when I see what God Almighty has in store for you! Nothing you shall do will be coincidental or in vain! Your every step is protected by many Angels given their command. Many poisonous darts are fired about you, but none shall penetrate.

Yes, child, there are burdens and trials of many sort. Each serves to refine you to a purer image of He who is Love! His perfection seeks to make you perfect in Him. Having created you for Himself, He draws you up unto Himself. Serve Him and serve souls, permitting the Holy Spirit to accomplish His work in and through you. Be full of confidence. He will do it! The Mind of Christ knows this reality, but the human mind struggles to take this in. The Holy Spirit will show you the way, in love, and in peace. I love you.

Your Mother, Mary

11-2-94 Feast of All Souls
Surrender!

Our Lady spoke:

Dear children,

Surrendering to grace and to the Holy Will of God is so very necessary at each moment. Surrender must take place in order that you receive His grace in your soul. You are like a lovely flower opening up into the Son when you surrender. God seeks then to pour His Grace upon you because you have given Him your will to do so. How can God bless you if you are closed? It is so simple, but few understand. You must love and trust like a child. God, your loving Father, can give everything to you.

Pray, my children, that you can surrender continuously. Then His Grace can accompany you continuously. We are truly with you to teach you the way of love, and to lead you to eternal life. Nothing can separate you from the love of God, my little ones. Nothing. He comes to the rescue of the greatest sinners. For sinners He died. So then, what prevents you from giving Him your "fiat," from opening your heart to His Love? Have you not heard? Do you not know God is Love? Has no one loved you?

Oh my little ones, soon He will reveal how much you have been loved by Him. Glance at the Crucifix. He loves you that much! My children, I come to earth to teach you to respond to His Grace in this time of His Mercy. Please children, respond to my call. My messages call you to conversion. It is urgent. I love you. Peace of my Son, Jesus, be yours always.

Your Mother

Then Our Lady spoke for Father saying: *Please tell my son.*

Dear Son,

Abide in my Immaculate Heart. Here is your resting place. Come to me and I will always comfort you in your weariness. My son, you are like a fortress for many souls. This is the Holy Will of God, who is your fortress. But in my Immaculate Heart you will find rest and refreshment for your journey. Oh my son, Jesus shall reveal much to you in the future. You shall understand the piercing of my Heart as you witness the turmoil and rebellion within Holy Mother Church. My son, so few are faithful to her. The Vicar of Christ suffers much on her account. Unite your heart to his as you shepherd souls. The church has great need of you, my son. So few are faithful. Take my hand. I am on the journey with you. Each step of the way you are accompanied by me. I receive your love and sacrifice with much joy. You console my own aching heart. I shall always be present to console you in your need, my son. I am your protector also. Therefore, rest in my arms. I am truly with you. I love you.

Your Mother.

Pause. As Father and I prayed the Chaplet of Divine Mercy, I saw myself on a wooden Cross. The Cross was on the ground. I lay on the Cross. Only my right hand was lifted up to the wooden beam and pierced by the nail. I felt pain and joy at the same time. Jesus was with me. In His eyes I found only love and consolation. I would do anything to be one with Him. He looked with love and approval as my right hand was fastened to the wood. He said only:

Grace above all grace!

Pause. Then Jesus spoke:

My dear son (my spiritual director),
Tell My people of My unfathomable Mercy. Tell them to approach the fountain of My Mercy now. Let no one hesitate and fear. Sinners have first right to My Mercy. See, My son, how fearful My creation has become? Their hearts are like stones. Touch them with My tenderness by speaking of My tender and merciful Heart. I have filled you with a great capacity to love. Let your life be a reflection of My Presence in your soul. My son, I am truly with you and there is much work to be accomplished. I will show you the way. My Grace and Blessings are upon you. Continue to give unto Me your heart in totality! I love you.
Jesus

11-3-94 Tabernacle 9:30 AM Feast of St. Martin de Porres
The Crucifix Is a School of Divine Love

Following Mass, I sat before the tabernacle. My thoughts went to the very graced prayer time I experienced when I said my penance yesterday as Father told me to do, on my knees with a Crucifix before me. I had never done this spiritual exercise. As I prayed, I was drawn into the Crucifix in a very intense way. My little cross dissolved, or melted away, as I gazed upon my beloved nailed to the Cross. All seems bearable in the light of the Cross. He has already borne it all for me. The price He paid for me was too high; how then could I refuse Him anything? As I contemplated, in the quiet stillness, I heard the beautiful voice of my Mother Mary.

My dear child,

The Crucifix is a school of Divine Love. Enter into its teaching as often as possible. Permit your soul to enter into this sign of contradiction, so that you may grow in the wisdom and knowledge of God. Enter into the greatest act of love. See, my child, what Jesus has given unto you is far greater than what He seeks in return. The little crosses He bestows upon you must be seen in the proper perspective, so that you do not lose heart. Do not hesitate to draw close to the passion of my Son, our Savior. Many souls avoid the teaching and beauty of the cross because they do not understand Unconditional Love and Mercy. So many are afraid to think of the passion of Jesus because they have not tasted of His intimate love for them personally. Also, they are afraid of what Jesus may ask of them if they were to follow Him closely.

My child, there is too little faith left. There is too little love left in the world. Souls are full of fear and confusion. Blessed are the souls who draw close to the Cross. They shall be transfigured into the wisdom and love of the Cross, reflecting brightly the face of Jesus. Often my children seek the glory and the consolation of God, giving little thought to the means, the way to glory, which is only through the Cross. Pray my child, pray that God's creation will reverence and love His Holy Cross, His Sacrifice of Love. It is too little appreciated. Will you, my daughter, embrace the Cross for many souls?

I love you, my dear child.

I love you, my Mother.

11-4-94 8:30 AM Mass and Adoration of Blessed Sacrament.
Jesus: Few Spend Time With Me

I sat in adoration of the Blessed Sacrament for two hours. Part of that prayer time was very distracted. Part of the time I entered contemplation, which is so still, so silent that I have only the sense of God. The "I," "me," seems to be annihilated into Him. I do not lose my peace when prayer becomes distracted anymore. We are like two intimate friends; to be in the presence of one another is enough. I have not been blessed with the ability to think lofty thoughts. I am content to simply sit in the presence of my Beloved Lord and Savior. Words do not suffice. My Beloved knows too well my incapacity and wretchedness, yet he loves me with His unfathomable Love. Of this I am confident. All souls should be utterly confident of this. God is Love, and He has mercy on sinners. Why, my Beloved Jesus, must you give us so much grace before we believe and know and trust that we are loved by you and that you are full of mercy? Have you not said that you hold us in the palm of your hand? Have you not said that the hairs on our head you have counted? How then do these words, these truths, penetrate so few souls?

*Soul, it is not possible for you to know or to love someone without spending time with them. My people, this generation spends little or no time with Me, their God and Savior. If souls do not pray, they cannot draw close to My Sacred Heart of Love, to be warmed and enlivened with Divine Love. You cannot know My Love from afar. Souls must permit My entrance into their heart. Only then can My Divine Love penetrate them so they know indeed: God is Love; therefore, God loves His creation. Soon, *Soul, love will walk among you again. Intercede on behalf of the salvation of souls. Many do not hear My footsteps and will be caught unprepared. Pray for conversions, especially for souls in the deepest darkness of sin.

My altar, trust in Me. I love you.
Jesus

11-9-94 Tabernacle following 8:30 AM Mass
God the Father Speaks

In a deep state of contemplation I witnessed the following scene: Jesus entered the Holy Temple of Jerusalem and found the merchants and moneychangers, who did not reverence the Holy Temple, and Jesus became very angry, yelling at them and upsetting their tables, driving them out of His Holy Temple. This is the first time my soul witnessed the wrath of Jesus. Then God the Father spoke:

Daughter, He will come again to drive out the spirit of rebellion in My House! The spirit of rebellion is permeating My Holy Temple, as the rebels take positions of power within My House. Their haughtiness will oppress the little ones who are faithful to my tradition. Their power will attempt to squelch My Truth in the name of progress and modernism. Daughter, only a remnant will carry the banner of truth, until the time when, once and for all, My Son shall enter the Temple and throw out the rebels. These rebels, who defile My House, are calling down the justice of My Mighty Hand. My Hand will put down the proud and raise up the lowly. This is just!

Sensing the Father's stern disposition, I found myself whispering "Mercy, Father, Mercy, please." The Father replied: **Daughter, this is My Mercy! I will restore My House by pouring My Justice upon the rebels, who have exalted themselves and made their authority felt over the poor and little ones, while subjecting themselves to no authority at all! Everywhere in My House there are those serving the spirit of rebellion in My Holy Name. They are their own god. They will not serve! Furthermore, their errors are leading souls, innocent souls, onto the path of perdition, because many are losing their faith. Apostasy is increasing! Daughter, the City of God is in each soul, and when I speak of My new Jerusalem, I speak of the soul of man restored fully by the Holy Spirit. Pray for My cities. Pray for My new Jerusalem. I, Your Father, instruct you. Peace be yours. I love you.**

Your Father

11-9-94 2 PM Rosary with my Spiritual Director
The Sword of Rejection

At the presentation of Jesus in the Temple, when Father spoke of Simeon's prophecy of a sword piercing the heart of Mary, Our Lady spoke:

My dear ones,
My heart is pierced with sorrow. It is not because of my own rejection that I weep. It is because God's creation rejects Him. Little do you know, little ones, how often souls utterly reject my Son and

all the goodness He desires to give unto souls. When you reject my Son, Jesus, you reject eternal life, because no one can come to the Father except in and through my Son Jesus. I who am your Mother weep for you, my little ones, because Jesus desires to lose not a single soul. Yet many are lost indeed! The sword of rejection pierces my motherly heart. What mother could observe her children continually rejecting what is good, and choosing what is evil, and not weep unceasingly? My little ones, allow me to help you, please. If you pray, grace will overcome you and show you the way. Only Jesus is the Way, the Truth and the Life. Peace be yours. I love you.

Your Mother

Pause:

My son and my daughter,

Your faithfulness soothes my heart, pierced of sorrow. When you tell me from your heart that you love me, I am so pleased. Your love dries my tears and eases my sorrow. You know, my faithful ones, that I long to assist all souls so that I may lead them to Jesus. Pray with me then, now and always, for the souls who are on the dangerous path to eternal death. It is for these little ones that I weep. Though the future shall bring much suffering into the path of every soul, those who have converted now will receive very much grace to pass through the trial. Be assured of this. God will be with you soon to restore His Holy House to the order of holiness and to, once and for all, hold truth upright again, so that all His creation will see the light of His truth, and all shall come to know: God exists and God is Love! Thank you for your sacrifice and your love. Remain faithful. Peace of my Son, Jesus, be yours. In all your needs, come to your Mother. I love you.

Your Mother

11-16.94 My home Rosary with my Spiritual Director
I Saw My Soul

Third Joyful Mystery: The Nativity. As Father led the meditation, I saw Our Lady, so very young, so beautiful. She was very simply dressed, as she would have looked on the first eve of Christmas in the stable, a simple and poor Jewish girl, yet glowing with the light of the Holy Spirit, who filled her. She held in her arms an infant. But it was not the infant Jesus, it was me (I was given to understand). She rocked me gently back and forth, never taking her beautiful eyes off of me. Her embrace is comforting and protective, as she is so very full of love. This vision faded away by the end of the decade.

The next decade (The Presentation), I saw the following: Alone, I stood before Our Lord and Our Lady. I was seemingly stripped of my garments. Before God, I was now completely naked. I heard: **Child, I see right through your soul. There are no secrets before Me. There is no hiding before Me. All is revealed.** Here I was given to see my own soul, symbolized by a white host (sphere). This white host or sphere was partly pure white and partly stained with ugly, ugly ulcerations like open oozing sores. I suffered much to see this. I felt I would die. In a way, I wanted to die rather than stand before Our Lord and Our Lady. Our Lord is Perfect and Sovereign. Our Lady is so very pure, unblemished in any way. I did not want their eyes to see me. Must they be made to look upon such ugliness and lowliness? It is shocking to see the state of your soul! Utterly shocking! Sin marks the soul with ugliness. This all took place in an instant. Truth (God) looks right through the soul, and in an instant the soul knows the truth of its state of being. I desired to run to hide myself, desiring to spare the ones I loved so very much from having to behold such a blemished soul. Our Lady then whispered: *Mercy, daughter, beg for His Mercy!*

In an instant, I found myself prostrate before His feet. I whispered, "Mercy on a sinner, Lord, Mercy, please!" Immediately, Jesus spoke: **Child, My Mercy has covered you! Do not look away from Me or you will die. I give unto you My Mercy, now and forever. Already My Mercy has washed away many ugly stains that covered your soul. There are areas which I have washed clean, so My Light shines through them. I, Myself, have washed away some of your wretchedness. Yet wretched you are. But My unfathomable Mercy covers your wretchedness. Do not be afraid. Rather, repent. Offer to Me reparation for your sin and the sin of your generation. I am greatly offended by souls who** do not acknowledge their sin. Attempting to hide guilt, they refuse to acknowledge need of My Mercy.

My altar, much is expected of you because I have blessed you in abundance, giving unto you many good things that you may glorify My Name. Through you, who are nothing, will come much fruit. Do not retreat from the work I put before you. Never cease to pray, to repent, to sacrifice and write My words. Do not ignore My voice. I am speaking to encourage you, to teach you, to prepare you, and through you I will speak to other souls as well. You have not chosen Me. I have chosen you, all for the sake of My Holy House (Church).

Approach My throne for Mercy always and everywhere. Acknowledge all that is yours is from Me so that nothing is yours, all is Mine. Little by little, I will wash away the stains. I shall make you white as snow. Nothing comes to Me except that which is pure! My Mother will assist you. Pray for souls who will not survive when I show them the truth of their soul. Hidden they think they are. Now you can proclaim to souls: the all-knowing eye of God sees right through souls. All that is within the soul shall come to light and be revealed. This shall come to pass soon. Many will perish. Do not fear. Plead for mercy. I offer My Mercy to all, now and forever. Be at peace. I am with you. I love you. You are Mine. You are nothing except that I love you.

Your Jesus

Here I passed these words to Father beside me. I could only weep. Yet Father's presence imparted strength to me. I asked his priestly blessing, and once again I felt strengthened through his intercession. Every day since this grace, I have only to recall it for a moment and I am moved to tears again. These words cannot capture the profound reality of this "grace," this purification sent my soul by the grace of God. A soul's lowliness before God's Majesty is of indescribable disparity. Still, His Majesty's unfathomable Mercy is ours for the asking.

Oh Most Holy Trinity, Perfect Majesty and Sovereignty, how you must suffer to behold this sin of the world! Create in me a pure heart, Oh God, that I might serve you. Make me an offering in reparation for my sins, and the sins of souls who refuse to acknowledge their guilt and thereby do not realize their greatest need - Your Mercy. Lord, more than ever, I trust in Your Mercy because I can only approach You, whom I love above all else, because of Your unfathomable Mercy. Lord, annihilate my ugliness; purify my soul. Let the fire of purification burn away my defilement here on earth, that when you take me home to your Divine Heart, I will stand before You, without the need to hurl myself to the place of detention to suffer the absence of You. But rather that I would run to You, to kiss Your Holy Feet, never again to be separated from You. Oh yes, my Lord, I desire to go straight to heaven to be with You. Please give me the grace. Yes, Lord, I am lowly, needy and nothing. But You love nothingness and You came to save sinners; so in Your Mercy I trust and, in fact, I am confident. Oh how I love You, endless Fount of Mercy. Your Sacred Heart is my refuge. In You I hide and I am safe.

This grace/purification provided the basis of my contemplation this week. Its richness taught me very much! It taught me of His infinite Mercy. It brought to the depths of my being, my lowliness and sinfulness. Here I wish to note that the sins prior to my conversion had been washed away. What I was made to understand is that what greatly offends God is the sin of an enlightened/converted soul. To whom much grace has been given, much responsibility is also given. To such a soul there is much accountability before God. A pure heart is utmost in God's eyes.

Purgatory most certainly exists! Nothing defiled can enter Heaven. There is a place of detention for souls who are not yet able to enter heaven, a place where blemishes must be washed away. Here, the absence of God, whom the soul has had a glimpse of, is the most excruciating pain. The soul's singular desire is to be one with God, whom it has seen for one quick moment, and now must separate itself from its beloved because it is not ready to don the wedding garments of pure white. Suffering here is intense. I must pray more for these poor souls! A pure heart desires only the Will of God.

Lest you become discouraged thinking God seeks from us a level of impossible purity, know that what God seeks is purity of heart and intention. If our intentions are pure (for His Glory only!), He will be pleased. A pure heart simply acknowledges their sinfulness before God and seeks His Mercy. God knows our fallen nature, our human weakness. Therefore, He offers us His Love, Mercy, and Grace to overcome sin. With Him and through His Sacraments of Grace (Eucharist and Reconciliation), we can attain the grace of a pure heart. We must be vigilant not to rationalize away our motives and sins because then, when His Light reveals the truth of our soul, we can run to Him, not from Him. At any rate, never ever think you are beyond His mercy - rather ask and He will grant it.

Another deep lesson imprinted upon my soul as a result of this grace: Mother Mary's assistance is absolutely necessary! It was her motherly love which reminded my soul to cry out for His Mercy. When I was utterly shocked and ready to run, it was my mother who gently reminded me to simply ask for God's Mercy. With her by His side, I knew (after her reminder) I could throw myself at His Holy Feet and He would receive me. Oh how we have need of you, dear Mother Mary! I am sorry, dear Lady, that so many do not know and/or love you as their mother. It is my prayer that souls everywhere be open to you. With you I will pray unceasingly. I love you.

Note: Though I knew previously the truths of the "lessons" provided in the grace of seeing the state of my soul, there are different levels of "knowing." In this experience, it was as if God had plunged a hot iron of these truths to a new depth in my soul so that they are a deeper part of my existence in Him. The other profound lesson in this grace of seeing my soul is to know in a deeper way the need and necessity of reparation for sins! During the past week I found I was more aware of the need to offer reparation. Often I would give up simple things like a cookie or sugar in my coffee, always in relationship to reparation for sin. Yes, simple acts of reparation account for much in God's eyes!

11-17-94 Prayer Group
If I Were to Appear on the Cross in Your Midst

During the Joyful Mysteries, Our Lady was present to bless us. She was very joyful as we prayed together. She spoke: *Dear children, thank you for gathering to pray the Holy Rosary. I am so very pleased with your faithfulness. I love you. Your Mother.*

During the Chaplet of Divine Mercy, I saw Jesus on the Cross, severely beaten and bloodied. He came in the midst of a multitude of people. We were all present in this multitude. As this Cross descended from heaven, most people scattered away from the Cross. The only ones who would readily approach the Cross were the little children and a few adults whose hearts were like a child's heart.

Jesus spoke:

My dear children,

I come this night to teach you of My holy Cross. Do not be afraid of the Cross. I rest on the Cross for pure love of you. Through My holy Cross I draw you up unto My Own Divine Heart, My Own heavenly Kingdom. If I were to appear on the Cross in your midst, would you approach Me and tend then to My Wounds? If you were trusting and open like a little child, you would never hesitate to approach Me. The Cross would not cause you fear. Little children trust readily. They would not hesitate to run unto Me to engage Me into relationship with them. If I would ask of a little child, "Would you help Me to carry this heavy Cross?" a child would surely respond without hesitation: "Yes, Jesus, yes, I will help you!" My little ones, please trust in Me as a little child trusts in His loving Father. I will care for you beyond your expectations, because I know how to give all good things to those who approach Me with a pure heart. I seek pure hearts. In such a heart I am pleased to dwell within.

Dear Ones, come, follow Me. Yes, we will walk the way of Calvary together, leading to a glorious resurrection. I seek from you simplicity, purity, humility, and obedience to the Will of God and to the inspirations of My Holy Spirit. If you persevere to become like a little child, great will be My Grace given unto you. I seek also your sacrifice. Offer sacrifices for the good of the salvation of the world. Offer to Me your sacrifices with much love and much joy. Abandon yourself into My holy service. Allow Me to use you always and everywhere for the good of those who do not believe, those in danger of losing eternal life. See that all souls are your family. I love the family of man

enough to suffer unto death on a Cross for each and every soul. Let us work together, that not a single little one be lost; then together we can present to the Holy Father His own creation in full, unto His Glory.

Little ones, blessed are you that I come to teach you and to bless you. I leave you tonight with the sign of salvation (the Cross) on your forehead. I press your heart to My Own Sacred Heart, that you may be enkindled to love more, to sacrifice more, to pray more. My Peace I give you. I so love you. My Heart is full of tenderness for My own. You are Mine. Let no other come between our hearts. Be one with Me because this is My Father's Will. Peace.

Your Jesus

11-22-94 1:15 AM
The Father Says "My Holy House Is Divided"

Daughter, please write.

My Holy House is divided. Not much longer will I endure to observe division. My Fatherly eyes are made to observe the daily Crucifixion of My Son as His Body is dismembered by division, each member cut off from the head, seeking his own way. Apart from the head, there is only death. Daughter, pray that the body may be one united body again, never again to be separated from the head. My very own Shepherds are rebelling and dismembering the body.

Father, it seems only a miracle of Your hand will unite the body again.

Daughter, I will do it! Heaven will bend to earth to accomplish unity. Pray always, because many are on the path to perdition because they have perpetuated a lie - leading innocent souls astray. Many who call themselves My Shepherds are not of My Holy House! My Justice shall come upon these, the rebels, the betrayers, and the liars. My Omnipotence shall be revealed

soon. Prepare every day! Make ready the way! Daughter, love. Love alone unites. I Am is with you. Peace be yours.
   Your Father

Upon completion of this message, I went up to bed. It was about 1:30 AM now. As I lay in bed, my eyes closed, God the Father seemingly drew this image for me. An arc descended from heaven to earth, symbolizing God's Love and Mercy, which is bending down to us from heaven. Then He drew a straight line from heaven to earth. The straight line symbolized the "truth" - unchanging, constant, never bending. Then He drew an arc from earth to heaven symbolizing the love God seeks from souls on earth. So the image now looks like this: The circle is love, which bends to unite. But the truth is constant and never bends. For the sake of love itself and for the sake of unity, love (the love we possess in our souls) should bend. But the truth remains the same. When there is enough love, there will be unity. Father, I love how patiently and simply You teach, making the most profound realities seem simple. Father, I am getting to know You more intimately, and as a result, I love You more. Thank You.

Note: Jesus remains very hidden to my soul. Now the Father emerges to teach me.

11-27-94
Re-consecration to My Immaculate Heart

Our Lady: *My daughter,*
   You have not yet begun to prepare for your re-consecration to my Immaculate Heart. My child, it is necessary that you begin to prepare for the moment of re-consecration to my Heart, because consecration to my Heart brings forth a wellspring of graces. I desire you to fast on bread and water for at least one meal a day leading up to the Feast of my Immaculate Conception. (I dared to interrupt: Dear Mother, this is very difficult for me.)
   Child, trust in your Mother. I will give you the grace to do as I ask. When you drink of the water, meditate on the cleansing of

your soul which makes you more and more pure for Jesus. When you eat the bread think of the bread of life, my Son, who humbles Himself unto the species of bread to feed your poor soul, to give you life in Him. Your gratitude could never be sufficient for the gift of the Eucharist!

My child, I shall draw you deeper into my Immaculate Heart, through the re-consecration of yourself, so that you will continue to do God's work. As your birthday approaches, pray and fast in preparation of a new birth in your soul. I rejoice on your day of birth because God has chosen you from the beginning of all ages to be the recorder of His words for the present age and thereafter. All shall be for the good of His Holy House, which will be restored. He draws you, as He draws all things, unto Himself. Give thanks. It is so very important that you continue to pray from the depths of your heart, so that you will come to understand God's Holy Will for you. Only in prayer can you begin to understand the messages of this age (the Gospel message through today's prophets), *and only in prayer can you live the messages.*

Oh my child, how near is the hour of trial for all my children. Souls must be raised up to walk in faith. Truly, so little faith remains. Souls must persevere in faith, walking the path of holiness, to which you are called because your Father is holy; then so too are His own. My messages are to awaken love and faith, hope and charity. The messages may end, but faith must never cease. Oh my children, the devil hurls his fiery darts at your souls to extinguish all faith, hope and charity. Pray more and love more. This is your mission. I bless you in the name of the Most Holy Trinity. Persevere. I am with you. I know your difficulties. Together we will overcome them by His Grace. I love you.

Your Mother

11-30-94 Rosary with Father, my home
Mary: I Give You to Drink of the Wellspring of the Heart of Jesus

Second Joyful Mystery: I saw Our Lady, very simply dressed, as a young Jewish girl. She is radiantly beautiful in her simplicity. She is drawing water from a well into a pitcher. The well is the

Sacred Heart of Jesus. She drew water from His heart and approached me and then Father to give us to drink from the pitcher. She held the refreshing water to our lips and we sipped as much as we needed. She was joyful to be the vessel chosen to carry Our Lord to us.

Pause. Then she spoke: *My child,*

Joyfully do I give you to drink of the wellspring of the heart of Jesus. Herein lies refreshment and rest. Partake to the full. I will always draw the water and hold the pitcher to your lips. It is my motherly pleasure to give the drink of life, my Son, to thirsty souls. Fulfill then, my children, the work my Son has brought to your doorstep. There is so much work to be accomplished. Do not cease to offer yourselves completely to the service of God. Souls are at stake.

Here I saw Our Lady walking through a large yard where corpses where laid out. She was carrying the pitcher of water to each person and with her own hand, lovingly opened their mouth and poured the water into each one, trying desperately to revive the body. She glanced up at Father and she glanced at me. She simply asked, "Will you help me? Your 'yes' is necessary to save souls. I carry refreshment to you that you may carry refreshment to others. Give unto God, your fiat. Please do not hesitate. See how many are awaiting. "Then she continued to carry the pitcher to each person. This scene makes it truly evident that Mary intercedes on our behalf, never, ever ceasing to pray for us before God.

Fifth Joyful Mystery: As I completed each "Hail Mary" saying "pray for us sinners, now and at the hour of our death," Mary spoke:

Rest assured that I will be with you at the hour of your death. I will hold your hand as you cross the threshold into eternal life. I am with you now but then you shall see me as I truly am. Then we shall forever more be in the company of our Triune God. Your trials pale in comparison to what God has prepared for you. Go forward in my Maternal love and protection. Peace of my Son Jesus be with you. I love you.

Your Mother

12-5-94
Ask for the Spirit of Prayer

Please write now, for my children.

Dear children,

 In preparing to receive my Son at Christmas, permit Him a birthing place in the depths of your heart. You have not yet understood that you are loved unconditionally by He who is God almighty. You have failed to accept the intimacy of His Love in your soul. Though He calls you each by name unto His Sacred Heart, to feed you His Divine Food, you fail to respond because you are taking too little time to pray. The world convinces you that there is no time or need for prayer. My heart is broken as I observe that many who set out to live a life of prayer are quickly discouraged, and too soon cease to pray. So few persevere. You suffer because there are few teachers to counsel souls in the way of prayer. That is why the Father permits me to come to teach you of the importance of continual prayer. I cry out to you in every message, asking you to pray, pray, pray. If you pray regularly you will grow in wisdom and understanding of prayer. I have asked you to pray the holy Rosary because it is a school of prayer for you. This simple prayer will lead you along the path of committed prayer and growth in holiness. There is nothing more important, my dear children, than prayer. You have not yet understood these words.

 I beg of you to make a decision and commitment to persevere in praying as much as possible. Ask for the spirit of prayer to be given you. If you are sincere and make prayer a priority in your life, God will grace you abundantly. Do not let Satan convince you that prayer is optional or non-productive. These are his lies. Do not be deceived. If you do not pray from your heart, with all sincerity, for pure love of God, your soul becomes dried up and holiness will elude you, so that the sufferings of your human condition will overcome you. Instead of love and hope, you then walk in despair, unable to love God, yourself or others. Joy will elude you. All will become burdensome. Depression and bitterness will cause your heart to become hard like a stone. You will spread neediness, not love. Brokenness will become your lot. When you walk in broken-

ness you are easily penetrated by sin because its immediate grati-
fication soothes your brokenness, at least momentarily. Evil spreads
its errors in this manner. Many good souls become entangled in
nets of darkness and oppression.

My little ones, this is why I weep for you. I observe your bro-
kenness and I desire, with all my heart, to relieve you, so as to lead
you to the most sublime Kingdom of Joy and Holiness, where love
reigns. Even on earth, your very soul can become the domain of
your Lord and Savior, and you can foretaste of the eternal King-
dom. This is yours if you renounce sin, repent, receive Sacraments
(especially Eucharist and Reconciliation). You must pray, dear
children! Live my message. Pray. I offer to you my Maternal assis-
tance, protection and love. Pray in union with my Immaculate Heart,
imploring the Father for the salvation of the world. Please. It is
urgent. I love you my dear little ones.

Your Mother

12-7-94 3:30 PM My Home, Rosary with Father
I Saw the Lord's Banquet

At the beginning of the Rosary, I saw Our Lady descending from
heaven, upon a cloud, bringing with her a torrent of water, which
came from heaven with her. She immersed Father and myself. She
spoke: *These are the abundant graces I bring to you through prayer*
from the heart. Please do not waste them. Use them to glorify our
Triune God. I love you. Your Mother

Fifth Joyful Mystery: I saw Jesus sitting at a long banquet table
with His Apostles. The table was filled to overflowing with all
kinds of delectable delights. I have never observed abundance like
this. Jesus looked upward to heaven, adoring the Father in a mysterious but loving and intimate conversation. At the entrance to the
room where the banquet was, stood Our Lady. There was a long
line of people waiting to enter the banquet. Each carried a wooden
Cross on their shoulder. When a person reached Mother Mary, she
removed the Cross from their shoulder, laying it at the foot of the
table of God. Then she lovingly dressed the soul in garments of
pure white, very beautiful but simple gowns. Then the soul would

join the banquet. All the while Jesus continued to look upward to the Father in adoration and love. After observing this for a while, I noticed that, just opposite this line of people awaiting the Lord's banquet, there were many groups of souls erecting their own temple in which to hold their own banquet. Actually it appeared to me that there were more souls preparing their own banquet than souls patiently awaiting the Banquet of the Lord. Jesus spoke: **Please write for Father.**

My beloved son, My priest,

Be aware that many who call themselves Mine are not of Me at all. There are deceivers and traitors in many corners of My Holy House. Here My Truth is compromised. A great apostasy is underway. My beloved son, My Sacred Heart bleeds for the rebels who have penetrated My Bride. These are the ones leading many souls astray, and great will be My judgment of them.

My son, beloved of My Heart, I am with you, teaching of the intimacy of My Divine Love because I desire, and the Father has ordained, that you and I be one so united so as to shepherd My flock to the absolute truth of My Divine Love. Feed My sheep. I empower you to do so. I, your Lord and Savior, say unto you, lead souls home to My Sacred and Merciful Heart. I have taught you, My Heart is tender and merciful, and I am thirsty for love from My creation.

My priest, My Holiness I give unto you. Be courageous in Me. Be My witness. Pray for My Church, the one you love as I love. She must pass many trials but she shall emerge triumphant! My beloved son, I bless you with the Sign of the Cross on your forehead and in your heart. Let us be one. I love you and I am with you.

Jesus

Later I prayed and asked Our Lady "How do we waste grace?" She spoke: *My child, the grace of the present moment is given unto souls that they may glorify God at any given moment in countless little ways. But often you become too distracted to make use of the grace being given you. If a soul is attentive to the Holy Spirit within, they will make use of the grace of the present moment to affect the environment where they are. Their fragrance is holiness. But if you are not attentive, the grace falls around your feet to be trampled on. Pray, dear child, that you may multiply grace and never waste it. I love you.*

Your Mother

12-12-94 Feast of Our Lady of Guadalupe 10:45 AM
Jesus Speaks of Our Lady of Guadalupe

*Soul, please write My words,

My altar, I bless you for receiving Me into the depths of your heart.

*Soul, your hand is in My hand. I will lead you into My secret sanctuary. My Heart is a Kingdom of Love. Here I will lead you, that I may conquer you completely. My altar, recline upon My Holy Ground, that I may offer sacrifice upon you, forming you into an offering, an offering which will rise to the throne of the Most High. Wretched though you are, I cover your stains, unsightly as they are, with My own garments of purity. Conquering your pride, I form you to be humble. Conquering your willfulness, I form you to be like putty in My hand, forming you to desire My Will over your will. Conquering your selfishness, I annihilate you, that you see Me before you. Conquering your ignorance, I feed you My Wisdom. Reviving you to life in Me, you make up for souls who spurn My Love. I shall make you so desirous of My Holy Will that you make up for many who reject My Will. *Soul, love is with you to conquer entirely the dust that you are.

Now, please write for My creation.

My beloved children,

From age to age, the Grace of the merciful Father has rained from heaven onto earth through the person of My holy Mother, who is your Mother in every sense of the word. On this day of remembrance of her visitation as Our Lady of Guadalupe, it is proper and it is fitting that you honor her, because it is My Divine Will. Sent to be the instrument of conversion of heart, sent to teach souls of love, sent to encourage souls in holiness, she deserves highest honor. As Our Lady of Guadalupe, she brings special graces, much needed graces, to souls who honor her as I ask, and to souls who believe her message of conversion. She is sent as a sign from heaven to usher in a new era. As Our Lady of Guadalupe, she continues to dispense grace upon the Americas. How needy you are, dear ones of the Americas! Still, too few incline toward her as I have asked. How much she can and she does obtain for souls who turn to her and honor her. The most precious jewel of heaven is consistently rejected and belittled. How offensive to God!

Dear children of the Americas, how great is your need of My Mother! How blind you remain. Your sickness grows though I, Your God, have sent the medicine which can cure your sickness. You choose to remain blind and sick. Your infectious errors you spread, when all the while, beside you stands the very cure for your illness. Will you not embrace her? From age to age she has been My instrument of grace for conversion. She is the forerunner of My coming. She prepares the way for Me. Though she invites all, only a remnant will gather under her mantle. Blessed are they who consecrate themselves to her Immaculate Heart! All those within her Immaculate Heart are found pleasing in My sight. A sign of humility, obedience and purity, she is rejected because the Americas are rejecting these virtues of humility, obedience and purity, and in doing so they reject My Holy Spirit.

My beloved children, how long will you fail to receive My Mother? Littlest ones, like Juan Diego, will indeed heed My words, so the radiance of My Holy Spirit, the spouse of the Virgin Mary, will imbue them with the grace of eternal life. Again, I say unto you, receive her, My creation! In her is the Light which will dispel the present darkness. Sit at her knee. Permit her to form you into holy ones, that she can lead you to the throne of the Most High, who will welcome you for an eternity. To reject her is to reject Me! Then, in darkness you shall remain, and suffering will overcome you because you chose to reject My Holy Spirit by rejecting the one who carries the Holy Spirit to you. Again I say unto you, do not continue your rejection. I am knocking at your door through the person of My Mother. Whose house she enters, she will restore, and I will bless this house with My Presence. Where she is, so too am I. Peace be yours, My beloved children. I love you.

Jesus

12-13-94 Feast of St. Lucy 1 AM My home
The Enemy and the Youth

*Soul, please write for Me.

I, your Lord and Savior, say unto you, My beloved children, I seek your trust in My Divine Providence. If you trust you will be at peace, a deep abiding peace which cannot be shaken. Notice, My dear ones, I do not seek your understanding of My way. Even My Apostles, who walked with Me and who talked with Me, did not fully understand My way. If those to whom I spoke and lived with, in the flesh, failed to understand the fullness of my teaching, why do you, this present generation, expect to understand that which is incomprehensible to man? I seek faith, trust, confidence in My Divine Providence. I have given unto you, My beloved children, My Word. I am not a liar or deceiver. He who is the liar and deceiver has indeed captured many of you. My Word is the same yesterday, today, and always. My promises I keep. I have promised to enter the door of the house (soul) that is open to Me.

My children, if your house is open and you have prepared it by repentance and desire, be assured I will enter and make of your soul My domain. I am the guest awaiting the invitation. As long as you invite Me, I remain. But your house cannot be divided. There is no room for Me and for My adversary. Therefore, My beloved ones, you must decide for Me or for him. If you open the door to your house, trusting completely in Me, then you will enter into true life with Me. I will clean your house that I may dwell in the deepest recesses of your soul. Where I dwell I make clean, because I lay My Head to rest upon holiness, which is clean.

My children, this age denies Me more than all previous ages. Even My chosen ones deny Me in ways which are very subtle to them, but very evident to Me. Now then, if you deny Me entry into your house, who will keep the adversary away from you? Will he not deceive you to gain entry and abide in your household? Yes, My dear ones, he will indeed set up his evil way to target your household. But let it be known that his power cannot prevail over one in whom I reside, and one who is accepting of the fullness of My Divine Grace. Only when your house is divided can he wage his war to conquer completely your household. This he does in ways which are very subtle, so that you scarcely notice before he has caused you to lose your peace. When you trust in Me, when you trust in My Word, you do not lose your peace. When you are humble and obedient, he must flee.

Now My beloved ones, I ask you to pray and to sacrifice on behalf of the youth of the world. These are his (Satan's) targets. Your prayers are valuable for the salvation of the youth for whom My Sacred Heart bleeds profusely. These souls I long to help, and I long to make them Mine. To the youth, I say unto you, there is much you do not understand; indeed you know little of love or faith or hope. For you are lonely and you lack proper instruction. I will rescue you from the nets of the adversary very soon, because I cannot much longer stand to observe the torments of your young souls, nor can I stand to observe much longer how many of you are lined up along the path to perdition. Your innocence and your purity the world has taken, but I shall restore you and build of you an army of holy souls.

To My littlest ones, so many adults have failed you. But I, Your Lord, Your God, shall never fail you, for I love you endlessly. I Myself will usher you into an era of Love, unconditional love and profound peace in My Name. I give you My Word and ask you to trust in Me. Have faith and hope. I will not lose you! Listen to My Word of Today through the prophets of your age. These messages are for you. You will rebuild My Holy House. Hear My footsteps and open the door to your house for Me, your Savior. Trust in Me, My dear children. I am for you. I love you.

Jesus

Continue to write for you, My altar.

*Soul, through mortification of your appetites, we will become as one, because mortification raises the soul to peaks of holiness. I find such mortification extremely pleasing. Will you try this for love of Me?

Jesus, help me to do as you ask, please.

*Soul, simply do not give into every desire. Say "no" occasionally. This will please Me and this will become an offering which I can use to distribute graces to souls in serious need of special grace.

12-14-94 Feast of St. John of the Cross 8:30 AM Mass
The Cross

At Holy Communion, Jesus said: **The Spirit of self-denial is the Spirit of wisdom, and she prevails upon chosen souls so the soul may enter into the mystery of the Cross. Love is completely selfless, but this age has forgotten this. When this generation, and all generations to come, look upon all the words I have sent from heaven to call you back to Me, your God, there will be amazement that the world did not convert and follow Me. Then will come a time of enlightenment for all the earth, so she shall know that I, who am God, exist, and I am alive with love for all My creation, with whom I seek an intimate relationship through the Person of My Holy Spirit. My Peace I give unto you.**
Jesus

12-19-94
Never Be Discouraged

*Soul, never be discouraged. You are weak but I am strong. In Me, your weakness is annihilated. You are nothing so that I can be everything. It shall be evident that I have carved My signature all over you, so that man shall know what comes from

Me through nothingness. Again, *Soul, never be discouraged because I can do great things in and through nothingness. Your weakness allows Me to reign in you. In you I am pleased because your intentions are pure and come from love of Me.

Persevere then, My beloved. You know not the work I do in secret. You do not see My hand forming you through all that I permit to touch you. Stone by stone I build a temple in you. This temple exists within the fortress of My Own Sacred Heart. Who then can destroy you? All that I permit is for the good of a soul. And, oh how pleasing is the soul to Me, who permits My hand free reign in them. Remain pliable, that your nothingness receive My holiness. I shall pour My holiness into the deepest corners of your heart and soul. Like a dam which has burst, I shall irrigate your dryness, making fertile the ground within you, so that the garden I have planted in you will grow, bearing much fruit, becoming a rare and beautiful resting place for My Heart, which is today rejected. Never become discouraged, for love is with you always and everywhere. I love you and I have mercy for you. Peace, My *Soul, be at peace. I am here.

Jesus

12-19-94 Prayer Group Rosary
Invoke St. Michael for Families

Our Lady spoke: *My dear children,*

Praised be Jesus. Peace be with you. Dear children, I am with you always. You are like my little garden. Each one is a flower of unique beauty, blooming according to the plan of Our Heavenly Father. It is important that you always face upward toward the Son to receive the rays of grace from heaven, so that the very Light of my Son may penetrate to the deepest recesses of your heart. Then your heart will bloom with love. My dear ones, your heart has many chambers. Jesus will not be satisfied to stay in the upper chambers. Jesus desires to enter the deepest chambers, the very core of your soul, so that He may conquer you completely for Himself.

Again, my children, I must remind you that Satan is raging full war to capture souls. Especially, he targets young children. Again I remind you to invoke the power and protection of the great Archangel Michael. St. Michael awaits your invitation, at which time he comes immediately to your aid with his army of Angels to protect you.

Once again I implore your prayers for the young ones (children). *The breakdown of the family causes young ones to be so vulnerable to the evil spirits. These little ones hunger for unconditional love, after seeking it in wrong people, places, and things. These little ones hunger also for the good things that give them a sense of being loved and protected. Therefore, teach the children the stories, beautiful stories which are woven in the Living Word of God* (Bible). *Teach them the prayer of the Rosary, explaining the mysteries to them. When you embrace my littlest ones, you are embracing my Immaculate Heart. My heart bleeds for these little ones, because their hearts are so empty. I implore you to make your very household a holy household. I shall assist you in this. What I ask from you is necessary and urgent, because Satan targets families to break down societies.*

Prayer is the answer. Soon my Son shall reconcile His creation unto Himself as He separates the sheep from the goats. Blessed are you who believe in these words and blessed are you who strive to live my messages of conversion. Heaven is bending to earth to assist you in the hour of great darkness. Look up, my little flowers. Receive the Divine Light which shines upon your face to make you holy, to make you a reflection of the Son. I love you.

Your Mother

12-23-94 Rosary with my spiritual director 3 PM
A New World

During the Creed, I began to see interiorly the following scene: I was in such a position in the universe that I could see the entire earth and all the sky. Darkness began to fill the sky until all the skies were black. Then the sky began to rain down the blackness or darkness until the earth was enveloped in darkness. This happened quickly. People panicked. There was chaos all over the earth. Then I saw a light. At first it was very small. This light was in the East (Russia, perhaps). The light emanated from the infant Jesus. I saw this as if through a zoom lens which revealed to me the Nativity scene with Jesus, Mary, and Joseph in the stable, and this is where the light came from. I understood this was the sign of a new birth for the earth. This light began to spread. It illuminated one area of the earth after another area, until the light eventually overcame the darkness. The chaos stopped. All peoples noticed the light and pondered the light. The light brought peace upon the earth. All during this scene, there were signs and wonders in the skies, unlike any I have ever witnessed. There were bolts of lightning and long periods of "light shows" in the sky (for lack of a better description). I observed this for quite some time.

Then Our Lady spoke: *Dear Child,*

I am the new Advent. A new birth shall be given the world. This new birth shall be the Era of Peace, which shall come after the great tribulation, when darkness shall be dispelled and the Good Shepherd will have separated the sheep from the goats. In this vision you have witnessed the power and the might of the Almighty Father, who, with one breath, commands the wind and the oceans, the stars, the moon and the sun. When there is mostly darkness, all will search for the Light, which shall indeed be present. And the Light shall lead creation out of the darkness and never more shall the darkness overcome the earth.

Child, this Christmas keep in mind the new birth, the Light which shall dawn to dispel the darkness. Praise be to God, who has ordained a new era of Peace for mankind. *Do not be anxious. Trust in Divine Providence. Pray then for my Peace Plan, for the dawn of a new era, a new earth. The new day shall dawn soon, and, in this day, my tears will be dried and the Heart of Jesus shall no longer be rejected. I bless you now, for your obedience, faithfulness and trust. I am truly with you to bring to you God's Grace. His Majesty finds favor with you. Give thanks. Peace of My Son Jesus be yours. I love you. Your Mother

*Where I have placed the asterisk, I was afraid of the devastation which would cause much suffering.

Our Lady said: *My daughter, do not be afraid of what you have seen. There will be devastation. There will be suffering which will*

give way to new life and lead to peace in the world. Man's heart must be reconciled with God. Trust completely in Divine Providence. Recall what you have been shown. *I am with you always.
Your Mother

12-26-94 Midnight, my home
When the Cross Appears in the Heavens

In praying the Rosary, I saw interiorly, heaven (sky) and earth (globe), and a Cross which reached between the two places.

God the Father spoke: **Dear child,**
It is the Cross which bridges heaven and earth. Blessed be the souls who plant their feet upon the cross and walk from earth into My heavenly Kingdom. When the Sign of the Cross appears in the heavens, know that the hour has come to decide for or against the Cross of Love, and many shall set foot upon the Cross for the first time, and they shall be on their way to My eternal Kingdom. Blessed are they who decided for the Cross of Love before the sign appeared in the sky, because they are aboard the Cross and journeying toward eternal life already. I who am your Father await My creation and with open arms I shall welcome you home. My covenant is everlasting, My Wisdom incomprehensible, My Mercy overflows, My Justice is perfect, My Love infinite. My creation shall cry out "Abba," but only those who cry "Abba" with Love in their hearts shall be counted as Mine. Soul, I bless you with the oil of faith, hope and charity, imparting unto you My own Fatherly Love. I am with you always. Peace be yours.
Your Father

12-28-94 Feast of the Holy Innocents, Tabernacle
Feast of the Holy Innocents

Our Lady speaks: *On this day of remembrance of the Holy Innocents, I bow my head in mourning for a generation which has devalued "life" and chosen death for so many innocent souls. My children, how blind you have become. You have twisted what is evil into something you call "good" and "efficient." To kill is a grave sin. The blood of the innocents overflows your soil and you shall one day wallow in it for a while, until you repent of your errors and seek God's Forgiveness and Mercy. How easily you rationalize away your sin. All of heaven mourns for you. Blessed be the souls of the little ones denied life and woe be to all those who failed to defend them. Bow with me, daughter, in prayer this day, when the pain of the sword pierces my heart. I love you.*

    Your Mother

1-1-95 Feast of Solemnity of Mary
You Are Living In Important Times

My dear child,

    Above the names given unto me, Mother of God is foremost. It is the name for which I am chosen; the name in which my "fiat" is contained in totality. God favored my lowliness by espousing me with His Holy Spirit from the moment of my conception. Thus, He prepared me to be the Mother of His Only Begotten Son. My womb became the sacred dwelling of the Son of God and my being is the dwelling place of the Holy Spirit, according to God's Will. God's Will calls forth my motherhood of all souls.

    My children, as your Mother, I shall never abandon you, for I love each soul unconditionally. My heart embraces all God's creation, but especially I target poor souls who do not believe, attempting to awaken in them a response to God's Love. While I can do much for souls who accept my intercession, I can do little for souls who deny my intercession. Such souls travel the more difficult path, whereas I could assist them in a more direct path by the more gentle route, and along the way obtain for them many blessings.

    My children, you are living in important times. God's Grace falls like rain from heaven for you now. It is all around you; graces of Mercy and Love. You have only to cease your constant motion long enough to grab hold of tremendous grace. Blessed are the souls who are alive and awake in these days of Mercy. The joy of conversion is theirs. There are many seasons ordained by God. This season of Mercy shall become another season, and very soon.

Pray, my dear children, to understand my words; then I can teach you very much. Beside you I remain always. Permit me to give unto you the grace of the Holy Spirit. In Him you shall come to be one with your Savior, who shall lead you to the Father. Paradise awaits you, not in this mortal life, but in the eternal Kingdom of God. Permit me, dear children, to assist you, that you may obtain your inheritance as sons and daughters of Our Triune God. I am honored and blessed by souls who permit me to be their mother. Thank you for blessing me with your love. My dear children, believe and hope. I love you.

Your Mother

1-4-95 My home, Rosary with my Spiritual Director
Our Lady of Guadalupe and Roses

As Father began the rosary meditation, I saw for one brief moment the image of our Lady of Guadalupe. She seemed far in the distance, the image being faint and transparent, yet I knew immediately she was Our Lady of Guadalupe. As soon as I was given to recognize her, she was gone. She was silent during the Rosary except at the very end, the Fifth Joyful Mystery, the Finding of Jesus in the Temple.

She spoke: *My dear children,*

I implore you to seek the most precious gift of Love in my son, Jesus. Many are confused, searching without instead of within. My beloved ones, seek Him within your own heart. He is there. He awaits you. Do not be afraid to look within. Pray, and the Holy Spirit shall give to you true self-knowledge. When you allow the Holy Spirit to "still" your heart, "Love" Himself (Jesus) shall reveal Himself to you in all His wondrous ways, revealing unto you a kingdom of beauty and peace. How little you know of true beauty and true peace. How foreign is His Kingdom to you.

Recall my visitation to Juan Diego and the presentation of the miracle of the roses, born of the frozen ground of winter. I come to

255

you now in the midst of winter to implore you to receive of me, a rose of pure love. Permit me to produce this rose from within your heart, which is not unlike the frozen ground of winter. I desire you bloom into all that God has created you to be. The Holy Spirit shall cultivate you and He shall raise you to be that which God has ordained you to be: His Holy Creation!

My children, you labor for worldly things which pass into dust, but you fail to seek spiritual gifts which are meant to be yours. You do not seek God's ways of holiness because you are convinced by the world that they are burdensome. Believe your mother, my little ones, the world is your burden. God is your Rest, your Peace, your Joy, your Life, your Good, the Way, the Truth, for God is Love and God is all for you! My little ones, why search elsewhere to find that which is inside of you? Your generation exists in a state of falsehood and confusion because you have believed "the liar."

I am your Mother, coming from heaven to bring about the miracle of conversion, to teach you the beauty which exists within your own heart. You have not yet understood that you are created for union with God, destined to live forever with Him. You are created to participate fully in His Kingdom of Love. I come to teach you of His ways. When the time comes that you no longer have my words to encourage you, my lessons to teach you, will you have "faith" to continue to walk the path to heaven? Oh my dear children, I implore you to grow in faith now. Learn to live holy now, so that you shall be prepared for the trials to come. Search your own heart. Is it God's domain? See that within the frozen ground of your heart I have planted a rose. I shall assist you, that it shall bloom eternally. I love you.

Your Mother

1-13-95 Prayer Group Rosary Meeting
Rely Completely Upon Your Father!

God the Father spoke to me for the group. The Father's disposition was most tender and loving, yet His strength is magnificent!

My little children,

I, who am your Father, bless you, breathing My Love upon you. Children of Mine, be alert. Stay awake. Open your eyes. Be sensitive. Open your ears. Open your heart. Your Father is over you, and My Sovereignty is served when you permit Me to be the Lord of your Life. Yes, My children, I am the Provider of many signs, sending My wondrous Graces in these latter times. Persevere. Do not allow the darkness, the confusion, the suffering, to cause you doubt! Have trust in your Father! I am Love, all good and merciful, all knowing and powerful. All which I permit is for your higher good. In due season, this is evident to you.

Remember, My ways are not the ways of the world. You must enter My way of holiness, to see with the eyes of holiness. All is unfolding before you. Do not fall asleep or grow weary. Love, Pray, Sacrifice. Have zeal and charity for My House. Grow in faith and perseverance. I have indeed engraved the sign of salvation upon your forehead. I have set My seal upon your heart. My seal is the Holy Spirit. He is in you and with you always. When you think you are most alone, and doubt begins to creep into your heart, know that you are at that moment, more closely united to Me, because I will not lose you. I have promised this, and I am Truth and cannot lie.

Soon, My little ones, the Good Shepherd I will send to call home His faithful flock. The flock is roaming in many different paths now, as the world has diverted many onto the wrong path. But the Good Shepherd knows how to gather His own lambs. He will search far and wide to carry home in His arms the most lost, most distant lamb. Be comforted then. You need not be anxious about anything. You must rely completely upon your Father, who knows how to care for His own seed, His family. I seek that you trust, like the smallest child trusts his "abba" (daddy). If you love, My Grace can permeate you and I can expand your love, and your faith will grow. Love is the root.

Rejoice, rejoice, My children - I am raising you to be holy and to be among those who shall enter the gates of My heavenly court, singing songs of praise and thanksgiving. It will not be long now. You are being prepared rapidly, and all is unfolding rapidly. You will witness very much in the days to come. Do not be afraid! Walk in faith unshaken! Ingest My words; My promise is within. My covenant stands! Everlasting life is yours. You suffer and toil now, but not for much longer. You shall see the fruits of labor. The little suffering which comes to you strengthens you so that you will stand firm in your faith. The times to come, and even now, your faith will be challenged. Even now your generation is rejecting faith.

My children, Satan is waging his final attempts to cause souls to fall. He releases all his devils to attack you and to entice you into his camp. Know the enemy. Renounce him. Greater is the power within you than his power to cause you to fall. Cling like a child to your Father! In Me you are safe. Do not become discouraged when the Cross is put upon your shoulders. In your darkest hour I am breathing in and out with you and for you. Our hearts become one when you cry out "Abba" and I say, be still - I am with you! I am the God of Abraham, Isaac and Jacob, the Alpha and the Omega, He who was, who is and who will always be, your Father!

If you sacrifice your will for mine, you shall bear much fruit. Rejoice then. Your harvest shall be great. You shall one day see what you have reaped. My blessing is upon you. Rejoice in Me. Lean on Me. Listen for My voice only. Renounce all other voices. My lambs, I love you and My peace I give you.

Your Father

1-18-95 My Home, Rosary with my Spiritual Director
Few Souls Ever Say "I Love You"

First Joyful Mystery, Our Lady spoke.
My daughter, my son,

Joyfully I receive your prayers. Your "I love you" ascends and enters my Immaculate Heart like sweet incense; added is my own fragrance, and together our prayers ascend to the throne of God, where they intermingle with the prayers of the Saints and the hymns of the Angels, deposited in heaven as pure treasure. Few souls ever say "I love you" to their Creator, and fewer still proclaim love for me as mother of all souls. My heart is grateful to receive your love. I know that it is difficult for you to understand that prayer is vital and fruitful, not only for your soul but for other souls who are blessed by your prayer, but I implore you to continue in faith and to pray unceasingly for the conversion of souls and the salvation of the world.

Your prayer resounds before God, entering Him, and He, in turn, enters you and makes of you His true partner in His plan of salvation. His harvest is your harvest and your harvest is His. God is glorified in your prayer and in your partnership. When you have entered into this loving and prayerful partnership with God, He is pleased to grant all that you ask, for your hearts are united, so that which you ask is that which Grace has moved you to ask in His Holy Name. If then it appears your prayers for a particular soul are unanswered, know that perhaps that soul is not yet open to receive God's Grace, and recall that God does not violate human free will, but awaits an opportunity when He will be welcomed.

My daughter, my son, pray unceasingly in union with me, so that souls will cease to offend God and suffer death. Cry out for souls who refuse to cry out to God. God is pleased to receive your love and your prayer. Remain in me so that I may assist you always. God has appointed many angels to surround you. They protect you so that you will not falter on the way to His heavenly Kingdom. Soon God will manifest His Mercy to each soul, shining His Light into their darkness. Pray then, that souls will choose God. I bless you. I love you.

Your Mother

Jesus spoke during the middle of the Rosary for Father.

My beloved priest,

Revealing My Love for you, I have taken you to Mount Tabor. You are standing with Me, that Divine Light illuminate your soul and shine upon you to enkindle your heart, that My Father may be glorified in you, for you also are His son. Glorify the Father by loving Him who called you into intimacy, and by doing His Holy Will. Your path is anointed by the Holy

Spirit. He shall lead you to the union which you so ardently desire. This union is already begun. Partake and be filled!

My Bride is also your Bride (the Church). Protect her, because what is most precious is in her, and that is the Truth. The Truth once permeated every inch of My Holy House, but in these days falsehood has entered. But I have chosen and appointed guardians of the Truth, and you are thus chosen and appointed. Pray, My son. Much will become clear to you in prayer and in the coming days. Trust in Me. I am with you. I bless you, My priest, in the name of the Most Holy Trinity. I love you.

Jesus

1-20-95 Tabernacle, 8:30 AM Mass
The Cross Is Central to Salvation

Praying before the tabernacle, I closed my eyes to contemplate, when I heard Jesus' voice.

*Soul, pray your Rosary meditating on My Sorrowful Mysteries. Then He whispered, "I am with you."

I began to pray the Rosary with noticeably more recollection and love than usual. Each prayer focused on the passion. My soul was inflamed with love for the Cross. It was as if God was pouring love for the Cross inside of me. I was with Jesus, as if inside of Him, as He was in Gethsemane; the Scourging, the Crowning of Thorns, the Carrying of the heavy Cross, and finally His Death on the Cross. At the decade "Carrying the heavy Cross," Jesus whispered again, and, with so much affection for me, He said, **"*Soul, from this day forward I shall call you, *Soul of My Cross."** At these words I sensed myself no longer, only Him in me.

Here followed a vision (deeply interior) - where I saw myself pick up a Crucifix which had been thrown on the ground. I lifted the Crucifix high above my head and I put this Crucifix in front of what appeared to be a multitude of people. I saw this scene again and again. Jesus whispered to me, **"The Cross is central, the Cross is central."** (Here I believe He referred to all of Christianity, to true

life in God, but His words always mean so much more than I understand.) At the end, Jesus spoke: *Soul of My Cross, tell Father
what you have seen and what you have heard. *Soul of My Cross,
there are some who seek to trample the Cross. Within My own
House there are subtle movements to diminish My Cross. Some
are aiming to hide this sign of contradiction, preaching a Gospel which emphasizes salvation, but without the Cross there is
no salvation. Christ crucified is the Gospel. Yet My own household, My own creation is joyful to avoid and diminish the Cross,
which is the very means of salvation for all!

The fiery breath of the devil spreads seeds of deception,
and in their hearts he shouts "put aside the Cross, forget the
Cross." People in darkness welcome these words. Oh how the
Cross has always been a scandal and contradiction to mortal
man, but to push it aside is a scandal to God! Oh prideful generation, you do not see your nakedness, nor do you see that it is
My Blood shed on the Cross which covers you. Your selfishness
makes you stubborn, seeking to find your own way. Your way
seeks self-glorification and self-sufficiency. Therefore, there is
no need of the Cross, no love, no sacrifice.

*Soul, I will make of you a sign of My Cross and you will
hold up this sign before many. Be prepared then, for you too
shall be rejected because your generation seeks to avoid the
Cross. Truly I say to you, the Cross is central to salvation. People
desire words of comfort, words of love, peace and joy, but these
do not exist except in and through the Cross. My creation, you
have not yet understood, My Cross is Love, love for you! Oh
My *Soul of My Cross (as if groaning), comfort Me, for I am
grieved to the depths of My Heart over the waywardness of
My creation, who seek to put aside My Holy Cross. Oh My
children, you have not yet understood the good news: My Gospel, My Tradition, My Love for you - all this you toss aside like
old trinkets. What riches you reject! Indeed, the riches you
cherish are like weights which tie you down, and with them
you will perish if you continue to reject your God.

*Soul, fewer will preach Christ crucified. My passion and
death on the Cross will be questioned and diminished in the
days to come. There will be dancing and celebrating all over

My sanctuary, so that souls are distracted and cannot contemplate the profound richness of My Cross; therefore, they cannot enter into the depths of My Love for them, and away they will go - empty. I will send you to hold before them My Cross! My priest also will hold on high My Cross! Bear witness, My *Soul and My priest, to the Cross of My Love! Open your eyes to see the movement around you, to see how My sanctuary is being made unholy! As the leech drains blood, so too My blood is drained by traitors and rebels who deceive My people, whose roots are shallow because love is the root and love is lacking!

*Soul of My cross, I shall place My Crucifix in your heart and in your hand. They shall melt together as One. Then you shall lift your hand for Me and souls will know the Cross is Love exemplified. How incomprehensible is My Love for all. *Soul, will you do this for Me?

Jesus, I love You. I cannot refuse You - whatever You ask I will do for Love of you!

Prepare then, *Soul of My Cross. I shall embrace your heart until it is a furnace of radiant love for My Cross. Then you will warm many souls. Listen to My priest (Father). He represents Me always. Tell him everything I have said. Go now in My peace. I love you.
Jesus

Note: Daily since this message, I have meditated on the Sorrowful Mysteries of the Rosary and daily it seems God increases my love of the passion of My Jesus.

My Jesus, it seems daily You are increasing my gratitude and understanding of the price You paid for my salvation. As you do this, my Savior, it seems you are taking the essence of who I am, and I am ceasing to be outside of You, but rather I exist as I am meant to exist - inside of You. How quiet and still you make me when you draw me so deeply into You that I cannot perceive me, but only You. It seems we are never separated, nor do I cease to converse with You. Your Holy Spirit, so deep inside of me, cries out in constant prayer to You. The hundreds of times that I say your name in a day - is said only under the power and prompting of Your Holy Spirit of Love. On my own I cannot even whisper Your Holy Name.

I am amazed, dear Jesus, by the way You possess a soul. How utterly irresistible You are! Everyday, all day long, I am like a beggar, approaching You to teach me and fill me. And every day I am in a constant state of waiting and longing. The greater part of me is not present to anything of this earth, for You alone possess me! Though I walk as one wounded, even crawling on the ground, I am somehow partaking of the banquet of Your Divine Love, because I am full of desire and longing to please You. You have said I can do this in one manner only, that is, to do the will of the Father. So I beg of You to give me understanding of His Holy Divine Will for me so that I may live it with all my heart, with as much generosity and charity as possible, from one as incapable as myself. Dear Jesus, have mercy on me and forgive my doubt concerning this writing.

*Soul, My representative, Father, has the ability to discern the spirits; therefore, as long as every word is given unto him for such discernment you shall not be deceived by the devil. In obedience and silence you are also protected. Therefore, rejoice, for I have provided generously for you. Indeed you are in the palm of My hand. There is no time for doubt *Soul. There is too much to be accomplished toward the salvation of souls.

My little one, you know not the significance of the times you are living, but you shall record these times for the good of souls, for the good of My Church, so that she will see that in these days I sent My Holy Spirit upon the littlest ones; so that My Holy Spirit would weave a faithful remnant who will stand against all persecution; so that My Holy Temple will not be trampled upon but emerge stronger than ever, triumphant forever in the united Sacred and Immaculate Hearts. *Soul of My Cross, I am showering you with My riches. Can you not trust in Me? Can the devil quiet your soul or bring you peace that I bring? No, it is not possible - he brings only disturbance. Therefore, soul, revel in My peace. I give you My peace. Give Me your trust, not momentarily, but always.

*Soul, if you knew that your husband or sons were about to perish forever would you work fervently to save them? Of course you would. Truly I say to you, there are many who are in danger of losing eternal life, and I am seeking to save the many who have left the fold. Work with Me, Soul, by My side. Cry out for the lost ones so that our voices resound together, and many can be saved. Take My peace and rest in it, My *Soul. I love you unconditionally. You shall not fail Me. I am with you always.

Jesus

1-25-95 Tabernacle - Feast of Conversion of St. Paul
Every Conversion Is a Great Miracle!

Our Lady: *My child,*

On this occasion when you recall the conversion of St. Paul, I again implore you to pray and to fast for the conversion of souls in this present generation. Daughter, each and every conversion is a great miracle, a miracle which revives and gives abundant life to a soul, an awakening to God and an opening to His Grace. It is so very critical in these days that souls be converted so that faith can grow. Prayer sustains conversion as well as frequent Reconciliation and ingesting of the Holy Eucharist. This is the abundant life of which the scriptures speak!

Daughter, pray with Me, unceasingly. My Immaculate Heart cries out for the grace of conversion for all My children. There is no darkness, no sin which cannot be penetrated and converted through God's Grace. If only souls would heed My words; I have given you a simple formula. Pray the Rosary and I will shower you with grace through this simple but profound prayer.

My children, Oh how I desire you to be holy for God! How lost you are, but if you permit me to be your mother, I will guide you to your one true home in God. Peace of My Son be yours. I love you.

Your Mother Mary

1-26-95 Prayer Group Rosary
Faith, Prayer, and Patience

As we began to pray the Rosary, Our Lady blessed each person by laying her hand upon each head. She was barefoot and dressed in a most simple white gauze type gown. This lasted only a moment; as soon as each had received her touch and blessing, she left us. A couple of decades later, she spoke for the group.

My little ones,

Praised be Jesus. I bless you this night in the name of the Most Holy Trinity, for He is the One who ordains my visitation and my message to you.

Dear children, it is written in the Scriptures that to those who have much, more shall be given. Faith is what is spoken of in these words. You who have responded to my messages with childlike faith and with open hearts, full of expectation; to you who have persevered in prayer and have remained faithful to God, to you, more shall be given. It is God's desire to be generous with souls who are generous with Him. Therefore, dear children, continue to grow in faith and continue to permit me to be your mother so that I can teach you to grow in holiness.

The Holy Spirit is breathing His Breath of Love into your very heart as He binds you together to be one holy remnant of faithful souls, those chosen to give Glory to God. The Holy Spirit is pouring Himself upon the littlest souls because these are the souls who respond with openness and with Love. The little souls permit God to reign in them, and He desires to be Lord of your life, reigning in you in totality. He is not satisfied to be restricted within His Temple. He desires to roam His Temple doing as He pleases, always blessing you, whether you perceive Him or perceive only darkness; He is with you always and everywhere.

Dear children, I desire that you come to realize how very important are your prayers. Your intentions are taken up to heaven, carried in my Immaculate Heart, to the throne of God Almighty. Not one of your prayers is said in vain. Prayer has very much value in the eyes of God. It is in prayer that God can bring about His Peace in your soul. Therefore, little ones, give praise and thanksgiving to God, because He has so blessed you, each and every one! Continue to be faithful. This is what is asked of you, because faithfulness will produce much fruit in due season.

Do not be impatient, my children. God is infinitely patient with His creation. His Divine Providence is over you. Therefore, be patient with yourself. Do not be overwhelmed by what you see happening all around your world. The world will be changed when hearts are converted to love unconditionally. When peace reigns in your heart, then you will be different, and the world will be changed. Many changes must first take place in your very own heart. Do not be anxious about anything. Permit God to be God of the universe. In this way you will have peace in your heart and love will grow.

Dear children, you were chosen from the beginning of all ages to live in this critical time in history. This is the time preceding the Era of Peace. Therefore, you are a vital part of my Peace Plan for the salvation of the world. I implore you to pray and to sacrifice for the salvation of souls and for the conversion of the world. The fruits of your prayer will affect the conversion of those most close to you. From here, even more fruit will be borne. You cannot comprehend how far reaching is pure prayer from the heart. It is this very prayer that unites our hearts. Be joyful. I am with you, dear little children. I will never leave you alone. I love you.

Your Mother

Here followed a silent period. Then at the beginning of the Chaplet of Divine Mercy, it was as if the heavens opened up and rained down Jesus' Blood, and each one of us was enveloped in His Precious Blood. I understood this to be a tremendous blessing upon us.

1-27-95 Following 8:30 AM Mass and Holy Hour before the tabernacle
There Will Be a Great Struggle of Faith

I prayed with Father and a prayer sister at my home. Father suggested we pray one decade and chose it to be "The Descent of the Holy Spirit." Almost immediately, I saw Our Lady present in the middle of us. She placed Father within her Immaculate Heart. He was completely surrounded and protected by her heart. Our Lady held my prayer sister in one arm and me in another. Her embrace surrounded us, to uphold us and to protect us. She requested we pray these decades: 1) The Descent of the Holy Spirit, 2) The Agony in the Garden of Gethsemane, 3) The Resurrection.

Following the three decades, she spoke: *My dear children,*

I bless you and take joy in you. I asked you to pray the mysteries of the holy Rosary which signify your journey. Indeed, the Holy Spirit is filling you and leading you along the path to holiness, to your eternal goal with God. Along the path you shall walk the footsteps of my Son, Jesus. Therefore, you will taste of His Agony in the Garden of Gethsemane. Remember what I have foretold you, because you may be tempted to think that you have been forsaken, but God does not forsake His own. You must turn to the Father with your fiat of love and abandonment, crying out the words of Jesus, "Not mine but Thy will be done"!

When you persevere in this manner of abandonment to His Divine Will, then you progress to your true home in and with God. Thus, you partake in full of the resurrection. You shall witness, even in your earthly pilgrimage, a resurrection of God's creation to holiness and a time of peace. This I foretold in Fatima. Ultimately the Sacred and Immaculate Hearts will Triumph! However, before this shall come to pass, you will witness a great tribulation in the world, and the Church will pass a tremendous trial. In preparation of this difficult time, I am calling you to prepare a place of refuge for my children. This refuge shall be a place of faith and hope and love for my children who desire to remain faithful to the traditions of the Roman Catholic Church. Also, it shall be a refuge of love for all souls, so that not one is left out, but rather that all are welcome in the truth of Jesus.

Teach my children to pray as I have taught you, with gentleness and patience. The graces of prayer which you have tasted so fully should be taught to those whom I send you, so that they too can partake of God's riches. My children, a holy Temple must have a strong foundation to withstand all the storms which will besiege it. You shall be the foundation of such a holy Temple. Therefore, be patient and wait for the wind of the Holy Spirit to go before you, preparing the way. The Holy Spirit will guide you step by step as He opens and closes doors according to His Will. In prayer this will become clear to you. I promise, you will not falter as you seek to do the Holy Will of God. Your intentions are pure, born not of your human will but of the Holy Spirit; therefore, He will do it. Trust in God.

My children, you cannot foresee how critical this place of refuge will be in the future, but I ask your trust. Heed my words because I love you and I love all my children, and I want to prepare a place for them where they can seek refuge, prayer, and peace and instruction from God in the days to come, when much suffering will be upon the world, upon the Church and all souls. There will be a great struggle of faith - a real crisis of faith! Therefore, it is necessary to build a refuge where the faith is kept alive and strong. I love you, my children. I thank you for responding to my call. Pray always and I will always assist you!

Your Mother

1-31-95 Tabernacle
Fear is Useless! Trust!

*Soul please write My words.

My children,

Fear is useless. What is needed is trust! Trust acknowledges God, brings to life the seed of faith, makes you humble because you depend on God, and makes you pure because you are seeking God's Will and living it in trust. In trusting, you

have peace. If you fail to trust, you will not have peace. Instead, you will have fear and anxiety about many things. My creation, you have forgotten I am the Lord of the Universe. I am the Lord of your Life and all things work for the good of those who love Me!

Oh My creation, how you desire to "control," but how unable you are to "control" anything! All things are accomplished in and through Me. My authority is Wisdom! Be under My authority and I will give you My Wisdom, and in My Wisdom, you will be holy for Me. Your very breath comes from Me and I sustain your life because I love you, and I have created you for Love, for holiness, for eternal life. My Heart is tender, just and merciful and I do not want you to be lost forever. You cannot comprehend My Infinite Divine Love for you now, but in eternal life you will be amazed at the depth, the height, the width of My Love for you. You cannot comprehend what My Father has prepared for you in His heavenly Kingdom, but you must desire it to attain it. I will assist you always, leading you to My Father's House, but you must trust in Me! Live each moment under My Wisdom and authority! I love you.

Jesus

2-1-95 8:30 AM Mass
Holy Communion

For weeks Communion has been so very dry, but today it was as if Jesus entered me at Communion, and immediately the temple of my body acknowledged His Most Holy Presence within, and it seemed every cell in my being became alive and rejoiced! Oh what Life the Eucharist brings! What Life! What Love! Oh my Jesus, You are so merciful! I love you.

At communion when I said "I love you, Jesus," He whispered to me: **"Love My Cross then, My *Soul. Embrace My Cross and meditate on My Passion, suffered for love of you and love of all My creation. Draw close to My Cross to love Me."**

2-1-95 My home - Rosary with my Spiritual Director
Our Lady's Maternal Love for Her Priest

As Father prayed for the Pope, at the beginning of the Rosary
I saw the Pope standing while a huge serpent surrounded him and
then began to crawl on the lower part of his legs. I immediately
asked my Spiritual Director to pray the St. Michael prayer and the
vision ended. Following the Rosary, I simply said to Our Lady
"Do you wish for me to write, my Mother?" She replied very joyfully, *"Daughter, please write for my son (Father).*

My beloved son,
You are truly beloved of my Immaculate Heart! My joy and my
consolation is found in your heart. My son, thank you for permit-
ting me to enter your heart so that I can transform you into a fer-
vent instrument of God's Love. Thank you for permitting my Ma-
ternal graces to lead you from mediocrity to fervor and zeal for
God. My son, there is no limit to the graces of the interior life in a
soul surrendered. Grace will lead to union with God. There are
different degrees of union. I am continually leading you to deeper
union with God so that you may partake of Him, and so that He
may delight in you. As you have opened your heart, the fountain of
Grace has poured Himself within you. As His Holy Dwelling Place,
you are an instrument of His divine work of gathering souls. As
His shepherd, you tend to His flock.
My son, you cannot comprehend the many graces He is be-
stowing upon you, because they are beyond all human comprehen-
sion, but indeed I tell you that you are drinking of His divine water
and living in His Divine Will. Thank you for permitting His Grace
to conquer you. Thank you, My beloved son, for your "fiat" of
love. I love you with a Maternal love which never ceases and al-
ways brings you closer to the Heart of Our Redeemer. Prepare, my
son, for temptations and trials, which you shall overcome through
the grace of prayer. Nothing shall come between you and your Lord
and Savior. Trust. In Him you are safe. He is your refuge. May the
Peace of my Son, Jesus, be in your heart at all times. Let nothing of
the world rob you of His Peace in your soul! I love you.
Your Mother

Note: As Father prayed the Fifth sorrowful mystery, he mentioned "taking hold of Mary's hand beneath the Cross as Jesus died." Our Lady was very joyful when he said this.

She said in response: *My children,*

When you hold my hand beneath the Cross you permit me to be your consolation, but also you become my consolation. Hand in hand, we can gather infinite graces from the Cross of Salvation, and the Precious Blood of my Son can fall upon us to make us holy! Thank you for your prayers. I love you.

Your Mother

2-2-95 Tabernacle - Feast of Presentation
I Present Jesus to You, My Children

Our Lady spoke: *My children,*

I carried Jesus to the Temple to offer to the Father His Own Son. Today, I carry Jesus to you, reminding you that you are His Temple and in Him you will be presented to the Father. Simeon's prophecy is fulfilled. The sword of suffering pierces my Maternal heart as I witness and partake in the passion and death of my most holy and innocent Son. My Son underwent horrendous physical torment, but also suffered incomprehensible spiritual torment. His suffering unto death has opened up the gates of eternal life for you. Simeon represents all of you who recognize Jesus as Lord of your life. He sees what others cannot see.

Open your hearts so that I may present Jesus to you. I implore you to receive Him in your heart, permitting Him to be intimate with you. God is calling you to a new intimacy with Him. My heart is pierced today by the sword of rejection as I observe my Son, who still thirsts for love from His own creation. He is today rejected, as many refuse His invitation to love and His call to intimacy.

Dear children, I shall never cease to knock on the door of your heart, to carry Jesus to you. I shall always pray that you and my Son will become as one heart! Pray little ones. All is possible with God. I love you.

Your Mother

2-4-95 My home
Be Open. All is Possible with God

When I sat down to pray before my Fatima statue, I was amazed to see how wide open the rose had become overnight and how it "bent" in the direction of Our Lady. As I gazed in amazement (I can't recall ever seeing a rose that opened so fully), she spoke these words: *Soul, be open. Do not limit God by your lack of understanding. All is possible with God. If you are closed because you do not understand, then you place limits on God's work in your soul. See how the rose opened so fully, presenting her beauty for all to behold? If your heart blooms to the full, opens wide to my Son, Oh what beauty He will produce in due season! Your soul is His garden of delight. His Glory shall fill you, but you must remain open and willing to surrender your human will. Do not be overwhelmed by His power within you, for, though God is incomprehensible power, only in gentleness does He move within you.*

My child, God is truly with you! Walk with Him. He loves obedience and trust. How pleasing is a soul who trusts in Him. It is not possible to fully understand God's infinite Wisdom, nor is it necessary in a life of faith. What is necessary is Love, and Faith that trusts, which leads to surrender and abandonment into the most tender and strong arms of Our Triune God, Father, Son and Holy Spirit.

My daughter, you are His instrument only. Permit Him to play His song in you so that His own beauty resounds from within you for others to hear. Whatever God seeks to accomplish in and through you shall be done by Him alone through His abundant Grace. Rejoice, my daughter, for His favor is upon you and His merciful Heart envelops you. Pray and be at peace. Seek His Mercy always! I love you.

Your Mother

2-7-95 Retreat at Church with Father
Oh Beautiful Lady!

I led the Third decade of the Rosary and immediately Our Lady came and stood so close before me that I was tempted to open my eyes and reach my hand out to touch her and embrace her. She was appearing as Our Lady of Medjugorje, with her short mantle blowing in the wind. My soul filled with joy. Even as I prayed the Hail Mary's, I found myself smiling at her, taking so much delight in her presence. I sensed only her and Me. Even as I led the prayers - I was thinking and praying to her saying: Oh beautiful Lady, you come so close to me, and I want to open my eyes to see you fully and to embrace you. How happy you make me here and now. How radiantly beautiful you are! I wish I could see you!

She smiled and said: *"My daughter, you are seeing me with the eyes of your soul! Your spirit sees me with an interior sight which is deeper than an exterior sight. Oh my child, how pleased I am this night as you gather to pray the Holy Rosary and to adore my Son in the Blessed Sacrament. I bless you and I bless the ministry. Daughter, you cannot comprehend the importance and the need of the ministry.*

The wind of the Holy Spirit is spreading throughout this movement as He gathers women to raise in the way of holiness. This is vital to the future of the world and to the salvation of souls. It is vital because all women are called to a life of prayer, and if they respond to this call, the world will respond as well, because in and through prayer you become a Light of Love and Peace and Hope. And the Light gathers people unto itself. If you pray, my children, you will be different, and the world will change for the good.

In this age, Satan is using women as his instruments of rebellion and division, tempting women to serve their own needs. So it is that God, in His Infinite Mercy, has raised up a movement which holds before women my "fiat" to the Divine Will, which is made possible only through the grace of my Spouse, the Holy Spirit. Thank you, holy ones of God, for having responded to my call. Listen to the Holy Spirit within you so that He can lead you to do the Will of the Father through and in the Name of the Son, Jesus. I love you.
Your Mother

2-8-95 My home, Rosary with my Spiritual Director
Be Like St. Joseph

At the "Presentation," Our Lady spoke: *My dear children,*

Today I present you my earthly spouse and the earthly father of the infant Jesus as an example of faithfulness to God, as an example of a man in union with the Holy Will of the Father. Though St. Joseph understood little of the deep mysteries which were lived out in our humble home, he was always faithful to God's Will. A man of deep faith, he lived out that faith in obedience and humility, never once seeking glory unto himself, but rather seeking to give glory unto his heavenly Father. Chosen from the beginning of time, before all ages, to be the earthly father of the Word Incarnate, our Jesus, he very tenderly attended to Jesus and to me. Now he lives in heaven in the high place reserved for those who faithfully laid down their lives for the sake of the Gospel.

My dear children, when you are faithful, attempting to live out the Gospel message of love, putting God before all else, then you are in union with God and His Will for you. Jesus understands fully your human weakness. Yet He grants you sufficient grace to endure your human condition in a manner befitting one who is striving to be holy for God. Like Joseph, you draw close to my Maternal heart when you are faithful to the movements of the Holy Spirit in you. Like Joseph, you tend to Jesus when you give to Him your heart even in its brokenness and littleness, so that He can abide within and make you well and whole, as He intends for you to be in Him.

My children, I am at your side always. I am holding your hand so that I can lead you to my Son. I seek your prayers because prayer accomplishes the fulfillment of God's words: "I come that you would have abundant life in Me." If you pray, you will come to know the fullness of His Word for you. Be faithful, little children, and God will do the rest. I love you.

Your Mother

Toward the end of the Rosary I had the "sense" Our Lady desired us to pray the Chaplet of Divine Mercy. Father began to lead the Chaplet, and immediately the tone of my interior disposition changed from a lighthearted joy (during Our Lady's message) to a state of profound seriousness. I immediately began to experience Jesus being nailed to the Cross. Every time these words were said, "For the sake of His Sorrowful Passion," I heard Jesus moan in a low deep moan. I saw His head thrust backward in bursts of agony. I heard nails being driven into His hands, and then His feet. My soul was given to know the depth of His sacrifice and love for me and for all sinners. I cried out to Him: Oh my Jesus, so tormented for love of sinners, have mercy upon us! We know not what we do to you even to this day. Oh merciful Heart of Jesus, forgive us and thank you, Savior of the World! I love You.

2-11-95 Feast of Our Lady of Lourdes 5:30 PM Mass
Wear My Crown and Bring Souls to Me

The Sacrament of the Anointing of the Sick was offered to all of us at Mass. I received the Sacrament. At communion, the moment of receiving Jesus, I said, "My Jesus, I love You in and through the Immaculate Heart of Mother Mary"! Then returning to my seat, my mind wandered to something regarding my new home. Catching myself, I looked up at the Crucifix and said, "My Jesus, loving You as I do, how could I be distracted at a moment like this, when You are in me in this humble form? My Lord have mercy on me."

Jesus replied immediately: ***Soul of My Cross, look at Me upon the wooden Cross. Are My arms not opened wide to receive you? They are stretched out fully for love of you. Is My side not gushing out water and blood for your sake? Look at My Heart now. Do you see the rays of love and mercy issuing from its depths? Come, approach Me. Come closer to My Cross. Draw very close, *Soul. I shall lean toward you so that you can remove My Crown of Thorns from My head.** (Here, I had an interior vision of Jesus leaning down to me as I stood at the foot of the Cross so that I could reach up and remove the Crown of Thorns.) Now I held the Crown in my hands. Jesus spoke to me again from the Crucifix saying: ***Soul, will you wear My Crown of Thorns for Me? Will you alleviate My suffering and My thirst for Love?**

Jesus, I find myself unable to refuse You anything, for You are utterly irresistible to me. I do not understand what You ask of me but I say yes to You. I trust myself with You. Please, my Master, teach me to suffer for the sake of love of souls if this gives You Glory. Yes, I say yes.

*Soul of My Cross. I am most delighted when a soul permits Me to conquer. In such a soul I pour Myself, imparting My Infinite Divine Graces. *Soul, few permit My Grace to penetrate, to conquer, to reign in them. Fewer still permit Me to lead them to My Cross of Love. *Soul of My Cross, wear My crown for Me. You will be mocked and ridiculed as I was mocked and ridiculed. This is what the crown signifies, but it is the forerunner to your crown of glory in the next life. (emphasized "life") **In this manner, you shall follow My footprints. Ultimately you will be pierced in the hands and feet and side, and you shall bleed from your heart, as I bleed for souls, for Love. The Father will be glorified in your sacrifice. When you speak to Me say, "Jesus of the Cross," so that we are one, with the Cross uniting us. In this manner, I will teach you to lay down your life by My supreme example of love. In this manner you shall recall always My Love for you. *Soul of My Cross, come close to the wood. Let love pierce you and open you up. Be one with Me, your Redeemer. Do you see how much I love you? I love each soul as I love you, yet I am turned away.**

Oh Sacred Heart of Jesus, how I love our conversations. Your words penetrate my heart as you engrave Yourself and Your teachings all over me. And this You do in the dark and in secret. But always you accomplish your way in me. My Savior, I shall perish if ever you are parted from me. What gratitude fills me, that you have chosen to speak with me in this manner, which is so sublime, but also so natural now. Our conversations are so clear, as if you were truly here, right beside me, in the flesh, as when you walked on this earth, as if You and I were the most intimate of friends and the most faithful of lovers. Oh my Jesus, who compares to You? None. What a lover of souls are You. My Joy, I am fulfilled in You alone and You alone are my true life. How close You are to me at this moment. Must it pass?

*Soul of My Cross, I am beside you, but more importantly I am in you. I surround you, within and without. You are Mine, My handiwork, My creature. From nothingness I called you into being so that I could delight in you. Because you love Me as I loved you first, you can delight in Me as your Lord. Permit Me to reign in you, granting Me full freedom, and I will abide in you all the days of your life, until I come to carry you home to the Father, and you will live forever in Me.

*Soul, few permit Me this. I bleed for love. I bleed profusely as this present age nails Me to the wood again. I suffer rejection again and again. See, *Soul, how I come offering My riches, which are eternal, but this age rejects these eternal riches for the transient ways of the world, making a god of themselves. Few transcend the tangible for the intangible.

*Soul, My Love is like the sun, whose rays shine upon everyone, but whose warmth and light can penetrate only those who expose themselves to the rays, becoming vulnerable, coming out in the open. These receive. But the man who stays in the shadows, who retreats into the darkness, to him, the warmth and the light cannot reach. Though ever present is the Light and fire of Love, some prefer darkness.

In these days, My Light is penetrating certain vessels, whom I shall send into the cold and dark shadows where many are hiding. These little beacons of light will lead many from the shadows of the darkness to the warmth of the Light. My Holy Spirit within these beacons will become evident and attract souls, leading to many conversions of heart. This is how My people will return to Me, one by one, until the moment when My Grace will overcome the world at once.

Hungry for love is My creation. So I shall feed them even as seven loaves fed a multitude; so too, My little beacons (messengers) will feed a multitude. What you perceive as very little, I multiply in Grace. Though you cannot perceive how far reaching is your little prayer, your little love, your little sacrifice and your little faith, I can see and multiply the good. Therefore, what is required is faithfulness and trust, obedience to grace and humility to depend upon the Most Holy Trinity, who lives and reigns over creation.

*Soul of My Cross, thank you for writing My words. (Here Jesus sensed I was tired.) Continue to bring your love for Me to My Cross. Fragrance My Wounds with your love. Anoint Me with the precious oil of sacrifice. As imperfect as it is, I rejoice in it and multiply it.

My Jesus, you inebriate my soul. You heal me from within. I ingest Your words as they inflame my heart into a furnace of burning love for you. So intensely do I love You that I long to die, to fly unto You. What exile is life on earth! Jesus, I am afraid of losing eternal life. I fear I will fall into the abyss. Jesus, please stay with me.

*Soul of My Cross, you must die to fly unto Me, but in your mortal life you can foretaste heaven by uniting your will to mine, your heart to My Heart, and by prayer we can speak to one another at anytime and in any place or situation. You are never alone. Grow in imitation of Me. Draw close, ever so close to Me on the Cross. When you gaze upon Me nailed to the Cross, how can you doubt My Love for you? Rather, it shall become evident that you are incomprehensibly loved by the Father, the Son, and the Holy Spirit. Hear My words whispered from the Cross: "I thirst." Yes, *Soul, I thirst for love. Bring souls to Me, *Soul. Bring souls to Me.

Jesus, how is it I can bring souls to You? What do you mean by these words?

*Soul, when you pray, you bring souls to Me; when you sacrifice your will for Mine, you bring souls to Me; when you serve My people, you bring souls to Me; when you suffer in silence and remain hidden, you bring souls to Me; when you write My words, you bring souls to Me; when you bear witness in My assembly, you bring souls to Me. Do My Will and you shall gather many, many souls for Me.

Jesus, it is difficult sometimes to know your Divine Will for me, though I seek it constantly as the desire of my heart. Lord?

*Soul, it is difficult to discern My will for you if you permit the world to cause you to lose your recollection. You must be peaceful and still interiorly to discern the promptings and movements of My Holy Spirit, who guides, teaches and leads. I know this is challenging. Therefore, I have provided for you a chosen representative of My Church to assist you in the discernment of My Will for you. In obedience to Him I am glorified, and you are led along the proper way of My Will for you, because it is My Holy Spirit within My priest (who represents Me) and who guides you. It is the Holy Spirit who leads you to pray for one another, inclining you toward the Divine Will at each step along the way. In this manner you are protected and blessed, I promise you.

*Soul of My Cross, on this day of remembrance of the Lourdes apparition, I bless you in a very special way, because you have heeded the words of the Blessed Virgin Mary as she spoke to you at the Lourdes Grotto. She asked of you that you be faithful to prayer, and incline yourself toward her so that she may help you along your journey. You have remained faithful to prayer, and open to My Mother's words and requests. In this I have blessed you, imprinting the sign of salvation upon you. This is the Sign of My Cross, in the Name of the Father, Son and Holy Spirit. Peace. Receive now, My Mother, and write her words, please. I love you. Jesus

2-11-95 Feast of Lourdes
The Example of St. Bernadette

Our Lady spoke: *My child,*
   On this day of remembrance of my visitation at Lourdes, I hold before you the example of St. Bernadette. At Lourdes, I spoke to you to teach you of the humility and obedience of little Bernadette. Several years have passed and you have heeded my words. Therefore,

today I impart my Maternal blessing upon you. At Lourdes, the Father sent me to affirm the Church, to heal souls and to lead them to conversion. This was made possible through the humble fiat of a poor peasant girl who trusted in me as her mother. Think and ponder in your heart of the many who have been healed spiritually and physically through a single "fiat" of love. A simple "yes" from a simple soul made possible, through the Holy Spirit, innumerable graces of conversion, issuing forth from the Holy Ground of Lourdes.

Let us rejoice and give thanks to God. What mercy issues forth from His Divine Heart of Infinite Love! He is pleased to do everything to gain a sinner's heart. How He loves to revive the dead, heal the sick and bless His creation! Oh but how little thanks is given Him in return. Therefore, unite your heart to mine, so that as one heart we can offer to God a hymn of praise and thanksgiving. "Oh Most Holy Trinity, all Honor and Glory be yours forever and ever!"

At Lourdes, I came from heaven to reveal my Maternal love to my children through a simple child. Today I am still coming from heaven into the world to bring my Maternal love into hearts and to proclaim that God exists! God is Love, Mercy and Justice. Now is the time for conversion and repentance. Children of mine, let love and peace overcome your own heart so that it can overcome the present evil and darkness, giving birth to a new era of triumph for God; an age of Peace and Love can then be born. First, these must be birthed in your own heart! Pray with me, my children, for many conversions! The mercy of God shall accomplish conversion of the world, but much prayer sacrifice (fasting) is necessary.

The salvation of souls is my deepest intention, because my son and I desire that not one be lost. Evil is strong in the world, and many are drawn into evil because there is no one to pray for them and no one willing to sacrifice for them. Souls who have converted in this Hour of Mercy soon compromise their prayer time, falling back into lukewarmness or even into spiritual death. This happens so often when the Cross enters their path. Souls then revert to old ways. My children, how truly rare is the soul who perseveres through the Cross. Therefore, when God finds a soul who is willing to persevere in the way of the Cross, how much grace is given to such a soul, and how much good is accomplished in and through that soul. Let Bernadette be a light unto you.

*Soul, I called you to come to the Holy Ground of Lourdes years ago, so that I could draw you deep into my Maternal heart, giving unto you a tangible example of a simple and loving "fiat" (Bernadette). Rejoice, dear child. From this Holy Ground, grace drew you to come to know the priest chosen to be your spiritual guide. Thus he would lead you, through the power of the Holy Spirit, onto the path of holiness. God so desired that His priest and His messenger draw ever closer to His Sacred Heart of Love that He drew each of you to come to Lourdes, where your paths would intersect in fulfillment of His Holy Divine Will. Thank you for responding to my call. I love you.

Your Mother

2-14-95 My home, Rosary with my Spiritual Director
Our Lady Carried the Eucharist to Each Patient

As Father led the Rosary, God the Father became present. The Father's disposition was joyful as we prayed each word slowly, with love. He seemed pleased, especially during the Our Fathers. During the Rosary, Our Lady was present as if standing in the center of Father and I, and facing toward us. The Father's presence was above the head of Our Lady. It seemed to my soul that they were present to "collect" our prayers, so to speak. During the Chaplet of Divine Mercy, Mary faded into the far distance while the Father became very dominant.

During the first and second decade (Annunciation and Visitation), I saw the following. Our Lady and I were inside a hospital ward with endless rows of beds, filled with sick patients. Our Lady carried the Eucharist to each patient. I stood at her side with the ciborium (hosts). The sick patients seemed an endless number, but Our Lady was determined to feed the Bread of Life to each one. I was thinking how tired I was (even in the vision), but Our Lady had endless energy to attend to the patients. Then Our Lady spoke.

My dear children, there is much sickness in the world today: sickness of body, mind and soul. The cure is found in The One Source, my Son. I lead you to Jesus because He alone can heal His creation.

My children, many sense their sickness but do not know where to turn. I am here for you. Heaven has sent me to show you the way back to God. One of your greatest needs is the eating of the Bread of Life. Herein is your nourishment. Herein is the grace to be transfigured into my Son, who is Holy. The Eucharist brings incomprehensible grace to your soul. You cannot understand the gift of the Eucharist, but if you ingest it, you will live anew in your soul. A trickle will grow into a running spring.

Dear little children, I implore you to come to the altar to receive Jesus so that you can be healed. Your sickness is grave. It spreads rapidly. If cancer affected your physical being, you would run for medical attention. Your souls are afflicted. You must approach the source of healing. God is the Source. If you do not come, many will perish. I shall always assist you, my children. I am your mother, who loves you unconditionally.

Your Mother

2-14-95 My Home
The Father Speaks - Satan's Time Is Soon to End

After these words, I no longer heard or saw anything until the Second decade of Divine Mercy. Here the Father's presence overcame me once again. My heart was inflamed with love for my Father. His presence is so strong! His omnipotence is so evident to my soul that I tremble before Him, in awe of His Majesty! As the Chaplet continued, a strong interior pain and heaviness overcame my soul. I soon realized that it seemed the Father was sharing a bit of His own grief over the state of the world. He spoke these words then.

My children,

I, who am your Father, impart My Paternal suffering, that you may know My Divine Love for My creation. In these days I am made to observe the Heart of My Son bleed profusely. His

Heart is opened wide, but it is rejected. In these days, I am made to observe the tears cried by Mary Most Holy. Her heart is opened wide, but it is rejected. I so loved you, My creation, I sent into the world My only begotten Son. He was given up as ransom for all souls. I observed you annihilate Him. Now, I observe you deny My Son once again. As well, you deny My Church, My Vicar, My signs, My messengers, My Holy Spirit.

My signs surround you, shouting out My message of conversion (now)! The salvation of the world is in My hands, but also in yours. In these days, the world has forgotten its Creator. I Am created the world to be holy, but instead I observe your unholy ways. My greatest gift I gave up unto you, to suffer on your account. Today He is rejected still. I am grieved to observe what has become of you. The world has seduced you. You trade away pure gold for pure dust! Like orphans you renounce what is good and embrace what is evil. But you are not orphans! I am your Father. I shall gather you up and revive you. Though evil himself entwines himself around you, in one omnipotent breath I shall strip away his power over you. His time is soon to end. My beloved creation, acknowledge and seek Me. I Am is speaking! Listen. Convert (change). I love you.

Your Father

2-15-95 Wednesday PM, Telephone conversation with Father.
Silence

We spoke of the benefits of silence. He advised me to be prudent in my speech, controlling my tongue. Upon hanging up, I went to pray. In order to be drawn into prayer, I asked Blessed Faustina to teach me something pertinent to my soul from her diary. I opened the diary to entry #477, which states: "Silence is the sword in the spiritual struggle. A talkative soul will never attain sanctity. The sword of silence will cut off everything that would like to cling to the soul. We are sensitive to words and quickly want to answer back, without taking any regard as to whether it is God's Will that we should speak. A silent soul is strong; no adversities will harm it if it perseveres in silence. The silent soul is capable of attaining the closest union with God. It lives almost always under the inspiration of the Holy Spirit. God works in a silent soul without hindrance."

2-16-95 Before Tabernacle after 8:30 AM Mass
The Natural Mind Versus the Mind of the Spirit

Before the Tabernacle, I entered contemplation. Approximately twenty minutes later I was awakened out of contemplation. I felt a presence pulling me to leave the tabernacle. I began to feel an aversion to being there. An unnerving voice said, "What a waste of time - a waste of precious time!" I rebuked it. I believe it ceased to bother me. However, the seed was planted. I began to think in a purely human way. The duties of the day played out in my mind, no longer on God. I was anxious to get started on my many duties. I did not want to complete my holy hour. I pleaded with Jesus now:

My Lord, take me into the tabernacle with You! I am here to be with You. Grant me the grace to stay and the grace to pray. I am here in obedience to Your priest. Grant that I may complete this holy hour, please.

Still distracted, I was literally looking all around the church, when my eyes fell upon my bible, which was beside me on the pew. I begged the Holy Spirit to give me a Scripture to help me. Almost immediately I heard 1 Cor. 2:14 which reads: "But a natural (I was thinking in the natural) man does not accept the things of the Spirit of God; for they are foolishness to him, and he cannot understand them, because they are spiritually appraised. (15)But he who is spiritual appraises all things, yet he himself is appraised by no man. (16)For who has known the mind of the Lord, that He should instruct Him? But we have the Mind of Christ."

Then Jesus spoke. **Put on the Mind of Christ, dear child. I am instructing you. Put aside the natural way of thinking. Think as a spiritual being. My Holy Spirit calls you to pray. Your natural mind tempts you to think the time spent in silence is foolishness. You have many duties indeed, but your first is to Me, your God! The Wisdom of God, the food of the Spirit, I** feed you in this time of prayer. What I infuse before the tabernacle you do not perceive, until that moment when My Wisdom prevails over you, causing you to function in My Holy Will. If you think in the natural way, all that is spiritual will seem foolish. My beloved, have I not rescued you from your (former) foolishness, giving unto you My Holy Spirit, so that I can lead you to be holy for Me?

My Jesus, my Teacher, how infinitely patient you are with wretchedness. Forgive me Lord. I love You. Jesus replied: **I love you, *Soul. I am, your Jesus.**

2-22-95 Tabernacle, Feast of Chair of Peter
Pray for My Peter of Today, the Pope

My children,
Peter represents Me on earth. In him I am. He is your pilgrim Father, My voice on earth. Follow him and you follow Me. My holiness abounds in him. Follow his holiness. My Light creates a beacon of him. Follow his Light. In your evil times, the devil spreads his errors, his lies, his death, but I have raised up My Peter to spread My Righteousness, My Truth, My Life, which is eternal.

Pray for My Peter. He suffers on your account. He lays down his life for love of souls. In Me he walks and breathes, so that through him I can gather My faithful flock, My remnant. My Peter of today I have raised as a great sign to you. He is pure gift. Humble yourselves. Listen to him. While evil diverts your path, his holiness, which is My holiness, leads you unto eternal salvation by means of the one straight and narrow path.

My holy Mother protects and guides her son (Pope). She does this for you. Humble yourselves and listen to her. She speaks today for you. She asks for prayers for her son (Peter/Pope) because he is today very persecuted from within and without. The very Church he serves, the Church he loves, persecutes him, but he shall not waiver. I am his strength. I will prevail and so too shall My faithful little remnant. I bless you whose ears are open to hear My words of today, given through My little and poor voices. I bless you because you have permitted Me to be alive today, while others see Me as a dead God of long ago, a God who cannot speak to His people today, when it is so necessary. I live. I speak. Listen, and I shall grant you My Infinite Grace, so that you will know I live now and forever. Pray for My Peter and give thanks for him. I love My Peter, your Shepherd, and I love you, My Sheep.

Jesus

2-22-95 Feast, Chair of Peter
My Spiritual Director Given "Staff of a Shepherd"

Following Rosary and Chaplet with my Spiritual Director, Jesus said: **Daughter, please write for My priest.** Jesus' disposition was very joyful.

My beloved priest,
I come bearing gifts for you. This day I present to you a staff, a sign of your vocation, which is that of a Shepherd. I present to you also a crown covered with jewels. This is the crown of glory which awaits you, My faithful servant. It is in your eternal life. I Myself shall crown you in My Father's Kingdom. As Shepherd, you gather My flock unto Me. Bring them to Me, My priest. Teach them of Me. Walking in My footsteps, tend to them, but remember always to set yourself apart from them, going into the desert, as I went into the desert for long periods of prayer. Bow on your knees and cry out to the Father for His Holy Spirit. It is the Holy Spirit of God who leads you to glorify your Triune God. Never let go of the hand of your Mother; then you shall not falter.

My Shepherd, I pour into you My Own Divine Love. The graces I give to you shall continue. Never will I withdraw from you. I prepare you for many challenges in the days to come. These challenges you shall bring to Me. Again, on your knees, in prayer, My Holy Spirit shall lead you. The Way shall be given unto you. Remain faithful. Remain in Me. Be open and prepared to receive all that I desire to give unto you. This day I bless you. Hold onto the staff. It belongs to Me, but for now I give it unto you. I love you.

Your Jesus

2-24-95 Prayer Group 8:30 PM
Dive Into the Ocean of My Mercy

As we prayed the Chaplet of Divine Mercy, Our Lord spoke. But at the very beginning of the Joyful Mysteries, I saw a vision of a beautiful waterfall issuing forth from the top corner of the room and falling into the middle of the room. The waterfall was powerful, covering us with crystal clear water. It wasn't until our Lord spoke that I understood the vision.

As the Chaplet was prayed, Our Lord said: **My dear children, My Mercy is upon you. My Mercy issued forth from My side, pierced on the Cross. It gushes like a fountain for all My creation. My Mercy is like an infinite fountain. It falls from heaven like a rushing waterfall, emptying itself into the ocean of My Love. Many stand and observe from afar. Few are the souls who trust enough to dive into the ocean of My Love. Many stand on the shore, permitting only a few drops to touch them. They deny themselves the good. They limit Me. My little ones, be willing to come unto Me. Do not fear to dive into My ocean of Divine Love so that I can envelop you. The more you submerge yourself in My living waters of Mercy and Love, the more you shall come to the fulfillment of your True Life in Me. I am your God and you are My people. Do not be afraid to draw closer to Divine Love.**

I purchased you at a great price, not so that you would permit Me to be only a distant reality in your life. Oh no, My little ones. There must be intimacy, so that we can be one. I seek to be first in your life. You are My Temple. I seek to roam My Temple in complete freedom. Many are the riches which await you. Do not limit Me, showing fear or anxiety of any kind. Do not subject Me, your God, to this form of rejection! I seek

your complete trust and abandonment to My Divine Will. I have repeated these words many times because it is necessary! I see that your intentions are good, pure. This is pleasing in My eyes. Still, there is hesitation and doubt in your heart. What are you doubting, My children? Do you doubt that I am communing with you as a most tender God, who loves you with My most tender Heart? Is there doubt that I am a living God, who is with you always and everywhere? Oh My little ones, how weak is your faith, so much smaller than the mustard seed. I Am is speaking to you. Believe because it is true. I am the God of Abraham, Isaac and Jacob, ever living in all ages.

My dear children, prepare for Me by again renewing your vow to do My holy Will in abandonment and trust. Fiat. Give unto Me your Fiat. Dive into the ocean of My Mercy. Do not fight the water that envelops you. Be still. Permit yourself to drown in Me. Oh, how you shall truly live then in Me. What riches I shall give unto you! The world will no longer hold anything for you, because I alone will satisfy your every need. Your heart shall burn with love. Your soul shall drown in peace. I am your Redeemer. I am Love and Mercy. Trust in Me. This night I take your intentions to My Heart, so that the fire of My Divine Love will consume them. Pray always. Seek My Way. Receive My blessing and My Love, incomprehensible and infinite! I love you.

Your Jesus

During the Glorious Mysteries there was silence from Our Lord and Lady until the Coronation of Our Lady, then she spoke.

Dear children,

It is important that you weigh each decision you make, so that you always decide for God as a truly spiritual person. Put aside your human way of thinking. You are my spiritual children. You must decide as spiritual children of God. I shall continue to assist you always, leading you to Jesus. Assist Me, dear ones, by praying always. Have great faithfulness to Our Triune God, whose favor is upon us. I love you.

Your Mother

2-28-95 Midnight, my home
To a Teenage Boy

My teenage son presented to me, seeking my prayer over him. He confided in me that he has felt the presence of evil around him for a couple of days. He was confused, and attempted to pray to God, but God permitted only darkness. No longer able to fight off the evil, he sought my prayer over him. I anointed him with holy oil and I laid hands upon him and began to pray. I prayed aloud for awhile. Then I heard Jesus' voice as He began to dictate the following message. My son prayed the rosary as I wrote the words I was hearing for him.

Dear child named of My Archangel Michael,

My Peace be yours. Son, the spirits of darkness lurk around you. They plot your downfall. They are furious because My hand upholds you on your journey. My graces have carried you through these days. The grace of Peace of Soul is a tremendous blessing. I have provided for you through all your trials.

Son, My Michael, I am calling you. Many more graces of the interior life shall be yours. You are being prepared. Hear My call. Heed My voice. You are about to receive a great outpouring of My grace. The evil spirits lurk around you so that you become distracted and your path diverted. The world desires to entangle you. She entices you. But I have called you. Yours is a higher life of Grace. Therefore, you must pray very much. Pray from your heart, My son. Read My Word. I desire to be your best friend. All that is in your heart is Mine to see and to know. Come unto Me. There can be no secrets. Do not be ashamed of a human heart that is weak. Bring it to Me. I will make it strong and holy. If I hide from you, it is only to test your faithfulness. It is so that you will seek Me with greater fervor. Persevere! Converse with Me. Pray. Do not be afraid to love Me first, as I have loved you.

Michael, named of My great Warrior, you are destined to be My disciple. I am deep within your heart - calling you by name - to be Mine. The choice shall be yours. I shall never violate human free will. But I say unto you, My beloved child,

the Peace you seek shall be found in Me and only in Me. I am your Lord and your Savior. Prepare your heart even as I am preparing it to receive My call. My Holy Spirit shall descend upon you in His power. It shall come to this. You must decide for Me and for My graces of the interior life, or you decide for the world, with its transient ways of delusion. I shall protect you. I shall pour My grace upon you, but be prepared to do great battle. The demons surround you, seeking to pull you away from Me, seeking to divert your walk, seeking to lead you into a life of worldliness, and pulling you into their bottomless darkness. Come, beloved of My Heart. Follow me. Persevere. Be faithful to your God, as I am faithful unto you all the days of your life.

Hold the hand of your Mother, Mary Most Holy. She is the great protectress. Demons flee when they see they cannot penetrate her Maternal Protection around a soul. Seek her intercession often. She comes with a legion of angels to rescue you. She lightens your burdens and makes short the path to holiness.

My child, My path of righteousness is not an easy path to walk. It is a straight and narrow path. It is possible to walk this path only in My Grace. This Grace is yours for the asking, but you must first decide to live holy. In this manner you shall glorify Me, and in turn receive the crown of everlasting glory for yourself in My Father's Kingdom.

Child, let your faith be tested so that it can grow. You are destined to lead souls to Me. I shall transfigure you into My image and likeness. You are in formation now. Is it any wonder you are attacked by the evil spirits? They see My hand upon you. They sense My plans for you, as they observe I have set you apart. You are different and they see this. But I who am your Lord, your God, can, with one breath, annihilate their effect upon you, so that what I have "called" as Mine - remains unharmed by evil.

Child, there is so much you do not understand. It is not for you to understand. If you trust in Me, if you love Me above all else, then you can enjoy the mystery of My ways, which are wondrous indeed! I am the Way, the Truth, the Life. Only in Me shall you find life everlasting. Beloved child, alone you shall falter. **With Me you shall conquer the world and her demons, not of your own strength, for you are weak, but of My limitless strength I give you. I love you beyond all human comprehension. I shall not abandon you. Even in the dark night I am with you because I am in you, breathing life into you. Never cease to seek Me above all else. You shall grow in wisdom and understanding as you grow in faith and in love.**

I am yours. Be Mine in totality. Trust. I love you.

Your Jesus

3-1-95 My home, Rosary with my spiritual director
The Father's Palm Holds the Globe of the Earth

As Father prayed the Sorrowful Mystery of "The Carrying of the heavy Cross," I saw Jesus walking through the street of the Via Dolorosa, with the heavy wooden Cross stretched across His back and shoulders. His eyes met mine and locked. He said: **My physical suffering is inexpressible; My interior suffering is unspeakable! Come, follow Me. I shall lead you to the Resurrection.** Then He continued down the narrow street. Next, I saw Our Lady following behind Him. Her eyes were filled with tears. She remained silent. Her eyes met mine and locked. She remained silent, but her eyes spoke volumes of her suffering. Her Fiat continues. All this ended by the close of this decade.

Following the Sorrowful Mysteries, we prayed the Chaplet of Divine Mercy. As Father finished the chaplet saying "Holy God, Holy Almighty One, Holy Immortal One," I saw God the Father's Almighty Hand holding the globe of the earth in His palm. His hand was much bigger than the tiny globe of the world. He said: **I am sorrowful when I see what has become of you** (My creation). **You who are close to Me, offer reparation!**

My soul was given Light to understand that the evil of this age necessitates sacrificial souls to aid in the redemption of the world. The blood of the Lamb has fully redeemed the world, but it is the Father's plan that souls cooperate with grace to fulfill His economy of salvation of all souls. The more evil, the more good. God raises holy souls in His Grace to complete His work of salvation. This is the Love and the Mercy of Our Majestic Father!

3-5-95 6 PM Mass, First Sunday of Lent
Jesus Exposed His Sacred Heart

(Note: Due to moving, it had been two days since I had received Holy Communion - the longest period since my conversion.) My soul was elated to be able to receive today. Just prior to receiving, my soul was overcome with a deep sense of my wretchedness. I was filled with the awareness of my spiritual poverty. I was filled with sorrow for my sinfulness and lack of virtue. God Himself shined His Light in my soul so that I would see the truth. I began to pray. Jesus, how is it that You who are Perfection could love so imperfect a creature? I know I am unworthy to receive You, but if I were to deny myself the food of Your body I would perish. You reveal my wretchedness to me - it is so evident to me at this graced moment in time, but even more evident to me is Your Love.

Jesus spoke (when I had returned to my pew). *Soul, you ask how is it that I love wretchedness? Am I not Love Himself? I must Love! This Sacred Heart of Mine burns with Love which is Divine, Infinite and Unconditional. I love holy souls and I love sinners. I am Love.** Here I saw the Sacred Heart of Jesus as He exposed it to my soul. The Power which issued forth from His Heart was tremendous. He said, **This is the Power of Love.** I saw a human heart (organ) which was so deep a red it was almost purple. It was beating in a constant rhythm. It was pierced with a sword. He said, **Sin is the sword.** It was crowned with thorns. He said, **This is the Crown of man's rejection. As man crowns himself as king** (God)**, He crowns the Son of God with this crown of mockery.**

I saw rays of many colors issuing out from His heart on all sides, but steady streams of red and white rays poured out as if gushing from a broken dam, forming an endless fountain. He said, **Neither sword which pierces nor crown which mocks can prevent this Sacred Source of Love from loving! Though sin may darken a soul, it cannot prevent this Heart of Mine from Loving! It is written and it is true - God is Love and I am God. Feed upon My body. It is Bread of Life. Feed upon My love. It is food of the soul, spirit. Love this Heart of Mine, which has loved you first. It is so little loved in this age! Permit My Heart** to transfigure you into one who loves as I do. This is My commandment. Oh My creation, I am grieved by your lack of love. The power of Divine Love is incomprehensible. It is the power of God. Nothing can overcome it! Beloved, I give to you My Heart. Give to Me - yours. Please Me. Alleviate the sting of the sword which pierces. Alleviate the puncture of thorns. Your little love can do this for Me. Above all else, I ask that you love. This is how you glorify Me. Wretchedness is made beautiful in and through the rich and Holy Sacred Heart of Love. *Soul, take My peace. I love you.

    Jesus

3-7-95 Tabernacle 8:30 AM Mass
The Lord's Prayer

As I began my holy hour, Our Lady said: *Daughter, pray the Lord's Prayer to the Father with all your heart, with all your soul, with all your strength, with all your love. Say it slowly. Lift each phrase as a song of praise to our Holy Father. I am with you.*

I began to pray the Our Father very slowly, with much fervor. Yet I found myself somehow distracted, sometimes saying the words without thinking of them. I had to repeat the prayer over and over. It took a long time before I could say it in the manner Our Lady asked. When I did this, I sensed the Father's pleasure. I was made to somehow understand how perfect a prayer The Lord's Prayer is.

3-7-95 My home, Rosary with my spiritual director
The Rosary Is the Prayer of the Gospel

Following the prayer of the Rosary, Our Lady spoke.

My dear little ones,
    Through the power of the most Holy Rosary, I can unite many souls for the Glory of the Most Holy Trinity. Thank you for responding to my call to pray the Rosary together. Evil will tempt you to

think that this cannot be important. I, who am your mother, say that there is nothing more important than prayer. The Rosary is the prayer of the Gospel. Only in your eternal life will you see the good of each prayer that you have prayed. Trust me as your Mother when I say to you that it is vitally important that you pray as much as possible. Make your life a prayer, by consecrating your every moment and thought and deed to God as offering and sacrifice.

I am using your prayers. The faithful remnant is growing. In all the corners of the earth the Holy Spirit gathers souls for God. The Holy Spirit leads souls onto the path to holiness, giving unto souls the grace of conversion. Pray then, that souls may be disposed to the outpouring of grace offered today through the Holy Spirit. Though you see evil all around you, and indeed it has spread to its greatest proportion, grace also is all around you, and it is poured out in even greater proportion. Both require your cooperation. You cooperate with evil and you perish, or you cooperate with Grace and you live.

My dear ones, there is much work to be done. Prayer affects so very much. Truly the spirits of darkness are oppressing so many souls. Help these poor souls by Prayer and Sacrifice. Stay awake and alert to all that is happening around you. Do not be blind to the signs of the times. If God brings His work to your doorstep, do whatever He asks of you. Time is running toward the moment when all God's creation will be made to decide for God or against God. My Son and I desire that not one be lost. Toward that end, dedicate yourselves. Be full of charity for souls. This pleases God. Thank you, my little ones, for accepting my words and my love. I protect you always. I am your Mother. I love you all very much. Pray, pray, pray.

Your Mother Mary

3-9-95 Prayer Group
The Holy Spirit Revives

My dear little children,

The Most Holy Trinity permits me to come from heaven to earth because they observe the condition of the world as very grave indeed. Many souls are on the dangerous path to perdition. I come to help revive God's creation. Which one of you could observe your most loved one on the ground as if dead and not run to them, offering to revive them and tend to them? This is the work of the Holy Spirit. In this age He breathes His life-giving Grace into souls who are like corpses. These souls are drunk with the ways of the world. Their spirits are dormant, while they exist as mere flesh and bones. Therefore, the Holy Spirit comes to raise up God's creation.

I come this night to implore you to continue in faithfulness. Persevere toward holiness for God. Holiness consists of this: Do the most Holy Will of God for the sake of Love of God alone! Grace alone can lead you to do this. Therefore, dispose yourselves to all the grace offered to you. Little ones, I have woven you together with a common thread which unites your hearts, even when you go your separate ways. I have woven you into a beautiful garment. The garment I have made of you adorns my Immaculate Heart. When any of you are in particular need, I envelop your soul with the garment consisting of all of you. You are comforted in this manner. My heart has truly received you. I care for you constantly. You cannot comprehend how very close I am to you.

Dear ones, this night my own Immaculate Heart is consoled by your prayers and your love. I take your prayer as one beautiful offering of love to God. I present these to God as reparation for all the offenses made against Him by souls who do not love Him. My dear ones, I remind you this night to learn the way of the Cross so that you may be led to the Glory of the Resurrection, which comes only in and through the Cross. The Cross is supreme Love. Receive it, endure it, for love of our most adorable and lovable God. I am with you always. I love you.

Your Mother

At the Sorrowful Mystery of the Scourging: at the mention of the words "the scourging," it was as if the blood in my body began to "boil." Heat radiated throughout, from head to toe. I seemed to enter a deeper state of contemplation as the prayer group faded only to the background, becoming very vague. I experienced the sense of the whip striking my body along my back and shoulders. All that is inside of me, physically and spiritually, began to quiver and shake. I grew weak. Then I'd experience another strike of the whip. I sensed I was entering a state of shock. Exteriorly, my body "jerked" at each strike of the whip. I attempted to hold myself "still" so that no one would see my movements. Though I somehow experience these bodily effects interiorly, the suffering comes from sharing the interior sufferings of Jesus. The pain consists in knowing what my Savior was made to suffer for me.

My Jesus, You recently said to me, "My interior sufferings are inexpressible." How true! I cannot find the words to describe even the small portion of your pain which you share with me. My heart breaks with love for You. I cannot repay You for what you suffered on my account, and on account of all sinners. Today You are scourged still - each time we reject Your Heart of Love, by failing to love You and one another, again we strike Your perfect and precious Body.

Oh my God, if you were not Love Himself, you would not unite Yourself to our sufferings here on earth, but since You are Love Himself, You cannot separate yourself from our sufferings. When we scourge one another, even with the whip of our words, we scourge You. I shudder to think of You as the whip rips Your flesh and pools of blood collect at Your feet. Yet You love your scourgers. You endure, You forgive, You suffer for the sake of Pure Love of poor souls. King of Kings, You are stripped and lower yourself to become vulnerable to the strikes of mankind. Jesus, teach me to be willing to become vulnerable for the sake of pure love. As quickly as all this began, it ended by the end of this particular decade. Since then, it replays in my mind again and again. It is with me always - the teaching continues. He consumes me.

3-21-95
Blessed Are the Little, the Pure, and the Simple

As I opened my mail, I opened a letter with a picture of Jesus. Someone took a picture of the tabernacle on the altar of the Church where Padre Pio said Mass in San Giovanni Rotondo and Jesus' face appeared. Immediately upon gazing into the picture of Jesus, He spoke. ***Soul, My beloved, bless Me, your Lord and Savior, with the oil of your love and the fragrance of your sacrifice. My altar, come to Me. Your eyes gaze upon My face. My eyes** gaze upon the depths of your soul. Your soul seeks only Me; therefore, I give Myself to you.

*Soul, we are one heart. Love unites us. My Will is your food. My solid food, My Divine Graces, I feed you in the darkness of your soul. I extinguished the Light that you might seek My light with much zeal and pure love, but even in the darkness we commune. Your Creator caresses you in so hidden a manner, you know not you are being caressed, but indeed I surround you as a King encircles His Kingdom. As a King enlists His army to surround and make safe his Kingdom, so too do I, your Savior, call forth My Angels and Saints to surround you. For you are My Kingdom on earth. Your soul is My Kingdom.

*Soul, I lay the foundation of a great work in you, one brick at a time. I am erecting a city of Holiness within you. My city within you shall draw many souls unto My tender and merciful Heart. When I search the world, seeking fertile ground upon which to build My foundation to erect My city, I find few souls willing to forsake the ways of the world for the ways of My Kingdom. Blessed are the little, the pure, the simple ones, for the soil within them is rich, fertile, and I can build in them. These, My chosen ones, gain for the world My Mercy and hold back My Justice upon creation. These voices have much power in their prayer, and these voices raised to heaven as one voice appease My Holy Father, and gain for souls much mercy.

*Soul, you have entered the Garden of Gethsemane with Me, your Creator and Savior. Keep watch with Me; stay and pray with Me. Like the Angel sent from heaven to console Me, console My bleeding Heart. I search the world for faith and love. I find too little. I suffer still for the sake of mankind. Behold your suffering King. I drink of the cup sent by My Father. Sip with Me, My beloved. Recline by Me. Keep watch and pray with Me to the Father, on behalf of all creation.

*Soul, I examine you in love. I find you love Me more than these. I bless you, My bride, My flower. Bloom for Me. Love Himself is conquering you. How little you are in My hand. Remain little for Me. Little one, as physicians examine your physical being, I shall examine your spiritual being in love. Cooperate with both (my physician and Jesus) so that you may be built up in strength to carry out My work. The time is coming when you shall do battle for Me and My Kingdom. I Am is preparing you. Never cease to gaze upon My Face, for My eyes shall never cease to capture you, examine you and penetrate you, so as to make you completely Mine. Soul, take My Peace. I am with you. I love you and bless you in the Name of the Most Holy Trinity.

Jesus

3-22-95 Tabernacle 8:30 AM Mass
Your Resolve to Do Good Is Waning

After 45 minutes of contemplation following Mass, in which there was only darkness, dryness, and silence, Jesus began to speak with great authority and power. His disposition was very firm.

My creation,

I observe your resolve to do good is waning. You are forgetful of your duties to stand up for righteousness and justice. You succumb to your temptations and weaknesses. You fail to stand up for good because you are afraid. Oppression overcomes you. The evil which surrounds you intimidates you. Little do you know that the power within you is far greater than the power of darkness which surrounds you. I observe too few of my followers who are willing to be different - to stand up to be counted as my true disciples. You do not know My Word or My way because you have ingested the ways of the world. My Word lies dormant within you because little do you know of My Holy Spirit, who breathes Life into My Word.

I say unto you, My creation, the hour shall come when all men shall be accountable to God. In that moment of decision man will have to account for his debts. Many will be sent to a place of detention until their debt is reconciled. My heavenly gate shall welcome only a few, because most are unprepared. Many will choose a place of endless torture in a pit of suffering, because they shall refuse My Mercy, deny My Kingship and refuse to serve Me in any way. I do not choose this for you, but man chooses this for himself, for he who is in such darkness hates the Light and loves his evil ways.

The world is being prepared by My sending forth of Mercy, through My Holy Spirit and through My Mother. Souls who respond to the graces of this present age shall form a remnant of radiant Light. These shall stand against all evil. These shall be counted among My disciples, but these shall be persecuted by the world. The world will reject their faith and scorn their faithfulness, but I shall make of them a fortress which cannot be penetrated. They shall not be denied. I Myself shall uphold them in their greatest hour of trial and temptation.

My creation, I am the Way, the Truth, the Life. Come unto Me so that I can transfigure you into a holy people. My covenant is everlasting. He who seeks Me finds Me. You must deny your very self, take up your cross and follow My footsteps. It is not a simple way. You will find opposition all around you, but the treasure I offer to you is Infinite Love and Everlasting Life, in a place where peace reigns, and rest accompanies you all the days of eternal life.

Labor for Me now. Spread the good news. I am calling you to conversion now! Respond. Turn to Me. I will shelter you. My creation, My Blood covers you. Your unworthiness is made worthy by My sacrifice. Because the Father so loved you, He permitted My death that I would overcome death, that all souls would be saved. I so loved you, I shed My Blood, taking on your human form; I condescended to become like you. I ask you to renounce your evil ways, your indifferent ways, your prideful and vain ways, to become like Me.

My creation, you are forgetful of your sins and your need to repent of them! Remember, there will be a full accounting of your ways. Avail yourself of the Sacrament of Reconciliation, the Sacrament of Mercy, and be cleansed and prepared for our meeting. I Am has spoken. I am with you always. I love you.

Your Jesus

3-22-95 10 PM My home
Prayer Difficult

Evening prayer is difficult. I am overcome with a sense of futility. I am in utter darkness. He whom I seek has once again hidden Himself. My soul feels abandoned. I sense only I have lost the battle and I am too weak to go on. But my will clings to my Triune God. If this is my lot, so be it. Not one grace or consolation is deserved. It is God's prerogative to do as He pleases in a soul. The soul must simply love and persevere in the darkness. Father, Son, and Holy Spirit, have mercy upon me, a sinner. Uphold me, for I am very weak at this moment. Still, I love you boundlessly. Be glorified!

3-23-95
Gethsemane

From the moment I awoke, I had a sense of oneness with the Lord. I began to shower for the day, when interiorly I sensed I was in the Garden of Gethsemane. I had a deep sense of being one with Jesus, that perhaps the Father had abandoned me. His cup of suffering, I was to drink. His pain became mine. I was alone in this act of love, betrayed by friends, without consolation. I felt His Agony within as He saw all the souls who would not be converted, even after so supreme an act of love. I sensed my physical torture and death on the Cross. I seemed to cry out to the heavens, to the Father, "If it be possible, let this chalice pass from me." Then, seeing all the souls who would be saved from all ages until the end of time, I cried out in abandonment to the Father, "Not my will but Thine be done." I prayed: "Oh Gethsemane, your soil holds the blood, sweat, and tears of Our Savior. Oh Holy Ground. Master, I share Your cup. I love You.

3-29-95 3:30 PM Rosary with Father at my home
Our Lady Exposed Her Immaculate Heart

Third Sorrowful Mystery – "Crowning of Thorns." Suddenly I saw Our Lady standing before us. She exposed her Immaculate Heart, but not in the usual way. Usually, rays issuing forth from her heart are the prominent feature, but this time it was the Crown of Thorns which became prominent in this vision. She wore a simple white gauze cloth and she was barefoot. She is so simple, pure, and radiant beyond description.

She spoke: *Dear children,*

Approach God like a child, full of simplicity and trust. My Maternal heart shares the Crown of Thorns with Jesus, because we are sorrowful that you have not fully embraced the way of true life in God. Dear children, today my Son suffers more than ever because so many are embracing the ways of the world, which are evil. We observe the little children in darkness. We weep for the next generation. Will there be any faith left in the world? Children who could bear witness to the Light often are not even permitted to be born. Abortion is the greatest atrocity of this age, but there are many atrocities which pierce the Heart of our Redeemer.

Oh my dear children, how grave are the consequences of your ways. So many will be made to suffer. God's Mercy shall enter into the darkness by way of purification. Please prepare yourself. Prayer is the only preparation. Do not worry about physical phenomena. What matters most is the preparation of our soul. Who will prepare the littlest ones? Families are so broken, in your country especially (USA). Join with me please. Intercede before God on behalf of families and the little children. Pray for an end to abortion. This is the sharpest sword which today pierces my Maternal heart. It must stop.

Dear ones, offer sacrifice and fast for this intention. Pray for those involved in this atrocity. Again I invite you to pray unceasingly. It is the only way. In this manner you become my partner in the Peace Plan for the salvation of the world. Time is so short. You will rejoice when someday you see the good of all your prayers.

Right now you do not understand, but what I ask of you is trust. Live your faith. I love you. Always I am with you and lead you to Jesus, our Lord and Savior.

Your Mother, Mary

For Father and myself: (She called us, "my son and my messenger.")

As you are drawn into the life of prayer and you enter a world of sublime beauty, do not forget that the Sacred Heart is pierced today by the abundance of evil in the world - an evil claiming many souls. You cannot comprehend the darkness of the world. It is too much for you. Often as you come to the fountain of life to drink of His abundant graces of the interior life, do not forget to offer sacrifice in reparation for the sin which greatly offends the Most Holy Trinity. Thank you, my son and my messenger, for responding to my call. I protect you and guide you, that you may one day enter into the life for which you were created. My blessing is upon you. Pray, and praise God who is with you. I love you.

Your Mother

3-29-95
Chaplet of Divine Mercy

At the first and second decade of Divine Mercy Chaplet, I saw interiorly - Jesus. He was one open bleeding wound. He had fallen under the weight of the Cross. The crowd ridiculed Him, spitting upon Him and kicking Him. I cannot describe such suffering. Words do not suffice. His eyes turned upward to heaven and then He glanced at me, speaking to me as if from His most beautiful eyes. ***Soul, assist Me to carry the Cross of man's "sin." They weigh heavily upon Me. Peace. I love you.** Then, picking up the heavy Cross, He continued on the way to His crucifixion. This grace came over me like a wave as soon as we began to pray the chaplet. As quickly as it began, it ended.

3-31-95 My home 4 PM
Share My Cup

I was resting on the sofa, when suddenly grace came over me, and interiorly I had a deep sense of the sin in the world, in relationship to the way it wounds the most tender Heart of Jesus. It was overwhelmingly powerful and painful. I cried immediately. I could not contain it. My heart experienced His Heart in the hour of His Passion, as if pressing into me the depth of His suffering. Breathing was difficult. I became a little afraid when Jesus began to speak, as if pleading with me to share His cup. His disposition was very sorrowful.

*Soul, My altar, My beloved one,
Permit Me to fill you with My Passion. I desire to create in you a fire of love for My Passion. Become a furnace for Me. Burn with desire to know and to love My Passion. I desire to transform you into the very fire of My Passion, which is Love. Do not fear. It is I, your Lord and Savior, who burns in you. Share My cup. It is our wedding cup. The fire will not consume you. It will create in you My Image. Radiate My Love - limitless. I choose you for Me, not a part, not a majority, but all of you, for Me. I give to you My Passion, which is My Love. I love you.
Jesus

3-31-95 Prayer Group Rosary
Pope John Paul II

Our Lady became present (interiorly). By the time we prayed the Chaplet, she had already imparted to my soul her desire that we offer the Chaplet for the Holy Father, Pope John Paul. I somehow shared in her love and concern for Pope John Paul and also sensed his suffering. I sensed danger in the light of new opposition rising against him as he just issued The Gospel of Life. Then she began to speak and I wrote.

My dear ones,

Today, again, I invite you to be in union with my Immaculate Heart. Please join me in praying for my beloved son, the Holy Father, Pope John Paul. Great is the burden upon him. Much does he suffer on the account of souls. My heart envelops him completely as I suffer in union with him. He is the voice of God in the world, and he is opposed. He is the echo of the Most Holy Trinity, the guardian of the Truth. He leads you at great cost to himself. The world hears the true Voice of God through him. He is the Light shining brightly into the darkness. Many are disturbed by his voice, and opposition mounts against him. He speaks for life, opposing the ways of death in the world. I invite you, dear children, to support him with your prayers. You can be united to him through prayer. I take these prayers to my heart and I comfort him in his suffering. Little children, love the Voice of God, spoken to the world through your Pope. These words are heavenly words, which must penetrate the world to avert great suffering and loss of souls. You will hear many who will oppose the teachings of this holy man, but you must stand firm in support of him.

My children, I have brought you back to Jesus, that in union with Him you can be His instruments in the world. You are serving toward the salvation of the world when you pray. When you carry your crosses with love, you are loving God and saving souls. You are a vital part of God's work in the world. You were chosen for this particular time on earth. Listen, obey, praise and pray, pray, pray. Much is being fed to you from heaven. Be peaceful in your hearts. The world offers no peace. He alone is your peace. I am with you, dear little children, and I love you - each one of you is precious in my sight. Do not be afraid. God has overcome the world! I bless you tonight on your forehead with the oil of my Maternal love.

Your Mother

Following prayer, Father anointed us with oil on our foreheads. We then prayed over Father and Our Lady spoke.

My son, take my heart as I have taken yours. I have interceded on your behalf for a long time. My Immaculate Heart envelops you. The Father's Divine Providence is over you. The Blood of

Jesus has washed you. The Love of the Holy Spirit is in you. You will stand for my little ones when opposition comes against them. You are their shepherd. You shall not falter because I shall remain with you always. There is nothing that I would not offer you toward accomplishing the work Jesus has called you to do. You are one with Him through my heart, which is one with Him. Son, draw from me. I am yours. You are mine. I love you.

Your Mother

She continued: *My children,*

I am joyful to observe the love you have for one another. This is not unlike the gathering of myself and the Apostles after Pentecost. The Holy Spirit, who is God, descends upon you with His gifts. God is glorified because you accept them for the good of one another. God intends that souls respond to His grace. In this manner He builds you up for your journey. Rejoice as I rejoice with you.

Your Mother

4-2-95
The Furnace of My Heart

I began to reflect on the grace of Saturday night. Light illuminated my mind, and I began to sense what was happening to me in those minutes of difficult crying. It was as if a sledge hammer was pulverizing my being. It was as if I was being ripped apart inside. I was full of "my will" and "my way of human thinking." But God was putting that in its proper place, annihilating it in Him. It was so painful. I thought I had died a little to myself, but still so much of me remains. The point - God alone can be my "focus." Nothing else can distract me, or I will be in turmoil. He alone is my peace.

I began to thank God for the way He works through my Spiritual Director, and almost immediately I had an interior vision consisting of this: I saw flames, roaring flames of fire, radiating much heat, burning with flames of red, yellow and white. In the midst of the flames I began to notice a white disk, a circle of white, reminding me of a host. I was given to know that this white circle represented Father's soul. It was in the midst of the fire and it began to change from white solid to almost clear transparent as the flames surrounded it, actually engulfing it, but not consuming it. It became very transparent.

Jesus spoke: **My son has consented now so as to permit My Divine Love to conquer him completely. Now I create in him My image. The flames exist within the furnace of My Heart, which burns with love for souls. Now My son and priest exists deep within the furnace of My heart. My fire of love consumes only the former man and creates a new being in my image and likeness. In the transparency of his soul, you see Me, the one you love, and not the man who has consented to change for love of Me and love of souls. I can reign now in the temple I have built. I laid a strong foundation in him that I may build to great heights now. I am pleased and glorified to do this. My peace. My love, *Soul. Thank you for writing for Me. I will never leave you. I am your Jesus.**

4-3-95 Tabernacle 8:30 AM Mass
Journal Entry

Following my holy hour, I heard only: ***Soul, fear not. You are about to enter into My sufferings. Peace. I love you, Jesus.**

4-5-95 Tabernacle Holy Hour 8:30 Mass
Journal Entry

Jesus: ***Soul, do not worry about what you do not know. That which I feed you by My own hand is Wisdom itself. Peace.**

4-5-95 3:30 PM My home - Rosary with Father
Divine Love and Divine Mercy

At the Third Sorrowful Mystery (Crowning of Thorns), Father led a meditation in which he asked Our Lady to help us to go forward in spite of mockery and ridicule, as Jesus went forward in spite of such mockery, always toward the Will of the Father. As if to respond to Father's meditation/prayer, Our Lady spoke immediately as he finished his prayer.

She said: *Dear children,*

I will always be with you to help you toward fulfillment of God's Will. Be assured, there will be mockery, ridicule, and persecution of the very work which God will ask of you. But always you must go forward in spite of great hardship. Persevere always toward the fulfillment of the Father's Will. You are journeying toward the highest mountain top. You must not stop until you reach the tent of the Lord. I will assist you along the journey.

My dear ones, the path chosen for you is a challenging one, but His footprints are set before you to show you the Way. You will be made to pass through the fire of persecution by the world. God will test your love and faithfulness. I promise, my son and my daughter, I will be with you through all the trials. No fire will consume you. You will pass the test of love. You will remain faithful. You shall enter the tent of the Most High. With Him you shall partake of the Eternal Banquet of Love. Rejoice. God has chosen you for Himself. I bless you. Pray always.

Your Mother

At the Fifth Mystery (Crucifixion), Jesus said, ***Soul, Love consists not in feeling great things but in great sacrifice. Peace. I love you. Jesus.**

Father's meditation included a petition to Our Lady that she might place souls into the Sacred Heart, out of which streamed forth the red and white rays of His Love and Mercy. Here, Father was seemingly stopped by grace to pause. Here it seemed Our Lord, in a certain way, infused our hearts with these streams of red and white rays. The power of the blessing was very strong. There was silence. I cannot speak for Father, but for this moment in time, all I was aware of was Jesus' Divine Love and Mercy being poured into my soul. It seemed to me Father was aware of this as well. That night, right before falling asleep, Jesus spoke (I believe in reference to the above.)

My *Soul, this day I immersed you and Father in My Mercy and My Love. The red and white rays represent the excess of My Mercy and My Love, which cannot be contained within My Heart. They must be given to souls. As My Love and Mercy are denied by many souls, I give Myself to the souls who will receive Me.

My son and My daughter, I am pleased by your prayer. You pray with your heart. Your intention is pure. I am the center of your life. You have given Me freedom to conquer My domain. You have set no one or no thing of this world above Me. Therefore, My favor is upon you. My Holy Spirit is the fire burning within you. He teaches you and you pray according to the Holy Spirit. Your prayer then is most acceptable to the Father. In the Holy Spirit, your voice and My Voice unite as one voice to praise, to thank, and to petition the Father for all good things. And the Father is pleased to grant all good things to those who love Him. I bless you this day and always. I thirst for love. When I turn to you my thirst is alleviated. The rays of My Love and Mercy penetrate you. I love you.

Jesus

4-7,8,9,10-95
Dryness and Darkness

I experience extreme dryness and darkness. Prayer is difficult. I sense only coldness in my heart. My will alone unites me to God. I am faithful to Mass, holy hour and liturgy of hours but I am not saying my rosary or any other prayers. I find myself watching TV, being distracted and having to drag myself to go and pray. I cannot even say a small prayer without God's grace to move me to do so. In front of tabernacle I enter a type of sleep and stillness which now seems like a void - still I am with God and He with me.

4-11-95 Tabernacle 8:30 Mass
Prayer of Quiet

I entered into a type of sleep state of prayer. While in this state, I was seemingly "taught" by God Himself, through the means of a divine illumination, which is different from the more usual way of His teaching in my soul through the dictation of His words. In this illumination, He does not dictate His words, but somehow imparts His teaching directly upon my soul. Often before the tabernacle I experience this, but I cannot remember the teaching. It is as if it is filed away for recall at a time when it is necessary. But this day I was permitted to remember it. I was shown a parallel between the "sleep" and "darkness" which God has granted my soul for several days, and the work the surgeon did on me in a state of unconsciousness (anesthesia). God revealed in this way that the most profound work accomplished by Him in a soul is done at a level which is unperceivable to the soul, who often senses only darkness or sleep, if you will. As the surgeon operated on my body in this state of unconsciousness, so too Our Lord operates on my soul in the prayer of quiet before the tabernacle. This illumination helped me because I thought perhaps I had offended God in some way. This is very painful for me. God desired I have His peace in the darkness.

4-11-95 My office.
Our Lady Addresses Holy Week

As I was typing invoices at work, Our Lady began to dictate the following message. She waited until my husband took a supplier to lunch and I was alone at the office.

My dear children,
Renew yourselves in the love of God. In this Holy Week, I invite you to immerse yourselves in the love that God has for each one of you. No greater love exists than to lay down your life for

another. This is the love of my Son, who is Lord and Savior. Only with the Light of the Holy Spirit in prayer can you begin to know in your heart the reality of my Son's love for you. In your humanness you will always be in the state of beginning. Conversion is ongoing and new each day. No one can understand the rich mystery of Divine Love that is God. Therefore, do not think in terms of spiritual progress. Rather think in terms of spiritual faithfulness. It is the faithful loving and faithful living of your routine, day to day duties that reveals to you God's calling upon your life.

My dear little children, because your faith is so small, it is difficult for you to believe that God Himself called you into existence for this particular time in history. It is difficult for you to believe that God the Father, Son, and Holy Spirit calls you each by name. It is difficult for you to believe that you are infinitely loved by God Most High. It is difficult for you to believe that you are vitally important to God's plan of salvation for the world. Oh my dear children, how I desire to help you to grow in faith! If you pray as I request, again and again the Holy Spirit will assist you to grow in faith. He will bear witness of God's Infinite Love for you in your soul. You must pray. Still, there is too little time spent in conversation with God. If you do not pray, you will not come to know of God's great love for you. You will fall easily into the temptations of the world. I cannot help you then, because you will not allow me to help you.

My dear ones, when my Son and I observe the world today, our hearts bleed for you. There is too little love in the world. I tell you, that this Holy Week God suffers again, in the same spiritual suffering of almost 2000 years ago, for love of you. Why does He continue to suffer? Because you suffer. He is not separate from you. He is the head and you are the body. He suffers daily, even at every minute, because at every minute souls are lost. These souls He longed to present to the Father. These souls He purchased with His blood. These souls He loves still, but they do not love Him! This is His suffering and mine as well.

Little ones, I am close to you these days because I desire to teach you of His unending personal love for each one of you. My heart aches, that you would love God as I love Him. Let your heart be converted daily. I tell you, that often you are choosing your own will and not God's Will. I want to help you to decide for God's Will;

then He will be glorified in you and you will know true joy and happiness.

This Holy Week, I invite you to spend time with Jesus before the crucifix, that the love He expresses to you from the Cross may penetrate your heart. His Love will set you free from the bondage of the world. Rejoice that you are sons and daughters of so loving and so merciful a God! Pray that one day Jesus will say to you the words he said to the repentant thief on the Cross: "This day you will be with Me in My Father's Kingdom." This is the Love of Jesus. Repent of your sins and acknowledge God, that you too shall be saved. It is never too late. God's Love and Mercy are everlasting. Accept them (Love and Mercy) *now, that my Son's suffering would be alleviated.*

I bless you in the name of the Most Holy Trinity, who permits me to be close to you in these difficult days. I know not how long God will permit me to approach you in this special manner. I implore you to respond. Live the messages now. My Son has suffered much on your account. I love you.

Your Mother

4-12-95 My Home, Rosary with Father
Intercede on Behalf of All the Priesthood

Father's meditation on the Fifth Sorrowful Mystery included the following prayer: "Jesus, You said through Your death on the Cross you would draw all things up toward You. Let the dripping of Your Blood upon the world wash it and purify it. Let the Sacred Heart's rays of red and white (love and mercy) be poured upon the earth to draw us up toward you, Lord. Come, Lord, come. Have mercy on our poor world. Use us Lord, to proclaim Your Love and Mercy to the world - to all mankind - that they would seek and receive Your Love and Mercy."

As Father prayed these words, the presence of God the Father was felt by my soul. As Father prayed these words, it was as if God the Father had come close to us to receive His prayer because He was "touched," so to speak, by the heartfelt prayer of His priest. I was immediately filled with love for the Father, and I was touched that He would unite Himself so closely to the prayer of His priest, as if to be one with His priest, and as if the prayer was precisely what He wanted to hear.

The Father then spoke for Father: **My beloved son and priest, your prayer resounds in My Heart. I have heard your prayer from the heart. Through the sacrifice of My Son, I expressed to the full My Love for all creation. Through the Cross, the Tree of Life, all things shall indeed be drawn to Me. Though the path of My people has taken a wayward turn, I shall set it straight once again through My Son. The foundation is being laid now upon which a new era will stand. My people will live as holy people. Your prayer echoes the prayer of the man** (Pope) **chosen to lead My people in these trying times. It echoes the prayers of faithful priests and holy people, so that I hear as one voice your pang for love, your cry for mercy and your hunger for justice. I hear My people crying in the night.**

My Son will soon manifest Himself again to draw My people back to Me. The sheep and the goats will be separated. Men of darkness will be given the opportunity to come into the Light. Many souls will be converted, but also many will perish. The face of the earth shall be renewed completely. Love must be restored. My people must be united as one faithful remnant.

Pray, My son, for your fellow priests, bishops and cardinals, that they do not fall into temptation in the hour of purification. Pray that more priests, bishops, and cardinals would consecrate themselves to the Blessed Virgin Mary, because she is a great protectress against Satan's assaults targeted for priests. My disciples are today divided and confused. Many are led astray by their disorder. Intercede on behalf of all the priesthood. Pray unceasingly, so that your voice continually resounds in Me, your Father. My Divine Providence is over you. Trust in Me. I am with you always. I love you.

Your Father

4-13-95 Holy Thursday
The Grace of Holy Thursday

In route to 7 PM Mass, I witnessed the most incredible miracle of the sun. The sun itself was of the biggest size I have ever witnessed. Immediately upon my looking at it, it changed from white to red to pink. It spun so fast that it seemingly threw off balls of fire. Rays changed from yellow to pink to red. This was, without a doubt, the most spectacular and dramatic miracle of the sun I have ever witnessed. Not only were my senses touched by God's Majesty and Power, but I took in this exterior phenomenon and somehow internalized it. Correction - I didn't do this, but rather Grace Himself did it. My soul experienced a deep sense of God's Love for me. It seemed God would go to great lengths to reveal His Power and Majesty to me and to bring it into a personal love relationship for me.

I prayed: "Oh my Jesus, You never cease to amaze me. You, who are Master of the Universe, delight to condescend to sinners. You exercise all the power necessary to draw souls unto you. My Lord, You alone, in and of Yourself, should attract us. But, no, we are distracted by the most frivolous things. You literally reach out for us, that we may come to know Your Majesty is alive, and You are Love. How you desire to be intimate with us. God, how incomprehensible is Your Love and Mercy. I love You boundlessly, and I thank You unceasingly for showering me with Your Grace. While I truly appreciate the miracle of the sun because I see Your hand in it, and You have chosen it for me, nothing short of You captures me. You alone are my goal, My God, My All. Amen."

When I arrived at Mass I was distracted. I had run around all day. Shortly, grace filled me and I was overcome with a deep reverence for the priesthood. I carefully observed the three priests concelebrating. Here I was given to know of the infinite love God has for His priests. My own heart became inflamed with love for them. Also, I was given to know that the Blessed Virgin Mary envelops priests in her mantle, whether or not the priest has a devotion to her. She takes it upon herself to be the maternal support of each priest. In a special way, she is the guardian of their vocation.

When the priest spoke of the institution of the Eucharist, my heart was overcome with gratitude that Jesus remains with us in this humble species to give us life in Him. This is the food of my life. I do not have the fullness of my God without the Eucharist. My soul's strength is in the Eucharist. As I observed Father wash the feet of the people, I begged Jesus to give me the grace to serve as He did, with great love, humility and unfathomable mercy. I became saddened at the realization that I so lacked these virtues. But my sadness quickly vanished as Jesus gave me to know that as long as I acknowledged my great poverty (of spirit) that He would grant my soul grace to love, to be humble and merciful. But I must always acknowledge my complete dependence upon Him. Then I must trust completely that He will do in me all good.

4-14-95 Good Friday 12:30 PM
The Darkness of Good Friday

I returned for adoration at the altar of repose. I had much peace in my soul, but I had seemingly entered a place of such darkness that it now seemed a great wall separated me from God. My soul stood paralyzed at the base of this dark wall. I could not penetrate it. I did not struggle. My soul seemed to recognize that God's own hand had permitted the wall between us. I seemed surrounded by a black fog, which I sensed to be from His hand as well. My soul desired to move toward God, but it could not move at all.

In the stillness of this dark night I suffered much. But I was not afraid nor did I lose my peace. In fact, I had profound peace. As the soul seems to recognize what its Creator gives unto it, it somehow accepts it. Even further, it loves it because it is what its Lover has sent it. Here it seemed nothingness penetrated me. It seemed all light, and even life itself, was extinguished in me. It is as if I entered a void - rather I seem to be the void. It is a kind of torture, but I do not lose my peace. I endure because I will to love my Beloved Lord at all cost and in all suffering. I lay prostrate at the wall of darkness until He sees fit to remove the wall. There is now so strong a will to love Him that I am very confident that my faithfulness will draw upon His Tender Heart, moving Him to end the darkness when the good of it has been accomplished. Furthermore, I am confident that His own Sacred Heart surrounds me and the wall of darkness. This reveals that we are not separated at all. But for now I must endure this painful sense of separation, this sense of nothingness. It is a void that tortures.

Good Friday - daytime.

Attend Stations of the Cross at Father's parish. Darkness continues. The only light which enters comes when Father prayed over me. He mentioned "mercy," and I was given to know at that moment that God had completely covered me with His Infinite Mercy. In an instant I was shown that He had diverted me from a dangerous path. He rescued me. I remained in a state of grace and prayer until I arrived home. Then darkness enveloped me again.

4-15-95 Holy Saturday
Holy Saturday's Prayer

Darkness. A void.

"God, You, whom I love above all else, remain hidden. I am alone without fire to warm me. No light is given for me to see. Only my will to love You sustains me. How long, Lord, until you remove this wall of separation? I trust in Your Mercy. Oh Jesus, hear and answer me."

4-16-95 Easter Sunday
To Kiss His Holy Wounds on Easter

All is dark again except for a moment at communion which is indescribably sublime. I prayed with all my heart that Jesus would permit me to kiss His Holy Wounds. As I ingested the Bread of Life, Jesus became so present to me that I could practically sense Him physically right beside me, and He gave me permission to kiss His Holy Wounds. I could practically physically feel my lips press against His wounds, one by one. My heart had melted completely into the furnace that is His Heart. For this quick moment, Jesus gave Himself completely over to me, so it seemed. This is the resurrected Jesus - the One I love boundlessly.

4-18-95 Vacation with family
More Darkness

Again I am in darkness. I find comfort in the words of the psalmist in the Liturgy of the hours. I cry out in union with the psalmist. I rest. I wait. I love. I trust. I pray. I suffer, but I do not lose my peace. This darkness, which is like a great void, is bringing about much good. I have a deep sense of this, a certitude. Jesus, my Jesus, Your Will be done in me. I love you with all my strength.

4-18-95 PM Vacation with family
The Feast of Divine Mercy

Sitting in the kitchen with my family all around me, Jesus began to speak.

Soul, you trusted half-heartedly the words of My Mother, but you obeyed. You have done as she requested. Though I would have been more pleased had you trusted completely, I am pleased that you obeyed. I desire to pour out My Mercy like rain from heaven, to cover My people with fresh living water. The blood of salvation shall wash them, but they must turn to me first and seek My Mercy. To seek My Mercy is to proclaim the need of mercy. I require My people acknowledge the error of their ways, then I shall cover them with the blanket of My Mercy. I shall bring to life what lay in dormancy due to sin.

My Mercy is tied to reconciliation. My Mercy shall flow like a river into the hearts of My people, especially those most burdened by sin. I cannot contain the mercy that is within Me. I desire My people have Trust, to turn to Me without fear. Few are the souls who truly have an attitude of trust in Me. This wounds My Heart, because if the soul knew Me, then they would know I am worthy of Trust. I am the Lover of all souls. I do not

seek to condemn, but to forgive. Only the wicked man who will not turn to seek My forgiveness should fear Me. He who does not turn to My Mercy shall endure My Justice. He who seeks My Mercy shall receive it in proportion to the mercy shown to others. (I dared to interrupt Jesus here - but it seemed so natural to speak to Him.)

Jesus, it is difficult to be merciful at all times. We are human.

Soul, if you come to the Fountain of Mercy and drink often, then I shall give to you the grace to always be merciful. But you must first come to the Fountain of Mercy. Always draw from Me! On this Feast of Mercy I shall pour out My Grace and each shall know they have been touched by My Mercy. I will put My Holy Spirit in the mouths of all who speak of My unfathomable Mercy. This is a message for this age. It shall be proclaimed with the power of My Holy Spirit. In this hour, Satan wants to convince souls that they cannot turn to a merciful God, that they are outside My Mercy, that their sins are too scarlet. I desire to convince souls that there is no sin too scarlet to be covered by My Infinite Mercy, if they but turn to Me in Trust. The fruit of this message of Mercy is setting souls free. It shall be carried out according to My Divine Will. Listen and obey. I give unto you My Peace.

Jesus

Here I put down my pen, thinking Jesus was finished. There was a pause, then Jesus spoke for me. His disposition was extremely gentle and kind.

*Soul, thank you for persevering. You are faithful unto Me. Your love for Me is like fragrant balm, anointing My Holy Wounds.

My altar, do not fear that your love for Me has grown cold. I have simply taken the fire of your love for Me so deep unto My own Sacred Heart of Love that you cannot sense the fire or the passion, because it is in Me.

My altar, I take the fire of your love and use it to ignite souls with hearts of stone. You are My living sacrifice. What I hide from you shall come back to you in greater fullness. You love Me as few souls love Me. You are an ever growing furnace of love for Me. You shall never grow cold. What I have set ablaze I will not extinguish. Trust in Me and do not trust your own sense. I bless you now. You are adorned with the love of the Most Holy Trinity. Peace. I love you.

Jesus

Jesus, You are full of compassion for my poor soul. Only You can know of my longing, my suffering. Make good of it, kind Master. I will endure for love of You. You alone suffice. I belong to You.

4-20-95
Spiritual Reading

On airplane, coming home from vacation, I read the Spiritual Canticle, John of the Cross. I was caught up in Love. It seemed I was aware of only Love Himself. Everything around me seemed to disappear. I was alone with my Lord. The words came alive in my soul as prayer. It did not seem that I was reading the words of someone else. Rather these words seemed to enter through my senses, but go directly to my soul, to be dissolved as love. Here they not only appeared as infilling to my soul, but somehow my soul was praying these words as if they originated in my soul, as love I could give to my Beloved Lord as well. It seemed to be an infilling and outpouring at the same time. I noticed also that these words were easier for me to take in now, compared to the last time that I had read them. When I read such spiritual material, I do not have the ability to retain the material; rather, it is a catalyst only for prayer, or a springboard to an intense exchange of love between God and myself.

4-21-95 12:15 Mass
An Attack Followed by a Blessing

On the way to Mass, while driving, it felt as if little devils were climbing all over me. I heard a voice that I recognize by its ugliness. It said, "You will fail God. You will fall back and we will be friends. God will fail you. His love is not everything. You will never please Him. You will fail, you will fail. Stop this ridiculous writing. Stop wasting this time doing nothing." This I heard as I drove into the driveway of the Church. I rebuked him. I prayed to St. Michael and walked into Mass. I was distracted. I stayed and prayed for about two and one half hours before the tabernacle. Several things happened in these hours of prayer.

At first, still distracted a little after Mass, I knelt down before the Blessed Mother statue. I prayed the Joyful Mysteries with a fair amount of recollection. Then I simply prayed from my heart as I looked up at the face of my Mother. "Dear Lady, my Mother, please help me. I am so empty at this moment. It seems all that is interior in me has been pulled out and I am but a shell. Dear Lady, there is so much that I do not understand. What is happening to me?" Our Lady said: *My child, God is emptying you. God will fill you. You are not alone.*

Dear Lady, I feel like I am about five years old at this moment in time. I have never felt so small, like a helpless child.

My child, God is teaching you of your utter dependence upon Him. He desires you to be like a little child who must come to Him for everything. My Son does not want you to be self-reliant. It is good that you approach us like a child.

Dear Mother Mary, I am so comforted by you. Sometimes the Father, the Son, and the Holy Spirit are so hidden, but you do not hide from me. You are truly my Mother. Mary said:

You are truly my child, my daughter. Do not be afraid. God will never fail you. God will never fail Himself. He has called you for Himself. Think of it, my child. Has there ever been a moment when God did not uphold you? When you feel the emptiness that you have right now, think of it as a state of preparedness. God can fill you in a moment. Rely on God alone. You are His vessel only. A vessel is filled and then emptied - filled and then emptied. Think of a crystal vase. Is it not a thing of beauty even when it is empty, as long as it is kept dusted (reconciled) and clean (pure)? Is it not in a state of readiness? Then, when it is filled with fresh water and beautiful fresh flowers, does it not increase in beauty and usefulness? It is filled only for awhile before the water must be changed and the beauty of the flower fades; then it is once again waiting. But even in waiting, it is beautiful, as long as someone takes care to polish it, and dust it, so that its brilliance is not dulled. You must be like the crystal vase. Will you do this for my Son?

Dear Lady, I desire to do whatever God's Will is for me, but I need your help so very much. Thank you, my Mother. You alone are always "full of grace." Your radiance and beauty is indescribable. Thank you.

4-22-95
A Painful Purification

I forgot to write about a purification I received on Friday night. After a meeting, I talked with my Spiritual Director. In that conversation I said a judgmental thing. As I hung up the phone, an awful feeling overcame me dramatically. I sat to pray and I was given an illumination of divine light. This revealed to me in an instant how judgmental, unloving, and unmerciful I had been - not just to a certain soul but to others as well. It was as if I was made to bear inside of me how I had caused others to feel. I began to feel worthless, like I counted for nothing, unlovable, unjustly judged. This in my soul was like a razor blade that cut it into pieces. I can't describe the horrible pain of this. I could not sleep well. All night long, I wanted it to end but it did not. I didn't fall asleep until about 4 AM - even then, my rest was not deep. I could not wait to confess.

Jesus revealed these things without words, but through Divine Light I was given to know them. I constantly seek His Mercy. My hand is always outstretched to seek His Mercy - like a beggar. I want to take His Mercy for myself, but I do not want to give it to others. To those who are lovable, yes, but to the less lovable, no. He showed me a measuring stick. I could only receive as much mercy as I gave. He would measure it. We are fully accountable for everything! I suffered much on account of causing others to suffer.

Somehow, in the night, as I tossed and turned in torment, unable to rest, I was given to know that if I were to pass to the next life now, I would suffer in purgatory for a long time. I found myself offering to suffer in this life instead. I seemed to know that purgatory's suffering would be far greater. As I offered to suffer, to love more, to be more merciful, to not judge, the purification began to subside. By noon on Saturday, God's Grace began to fill me again with His Love and Mercy. But this was on my heart until I confessed on Saturday night. Then God gave me peace.

4-23-95 Divine Mercy Sunday
Even If You Hate Me, I Love You

When I came home from the celebration at Divine Mercy Sunday, I went up to the Jesus of Mercy picture in my living room. I prayed, thanking Him for the day. I was drawn into His eyes. They seemed very sad.

I prayed: "Dear Jesus, why are you sad in this image? Today is the great feast of Your Mercy. Many came to see You and venerate You in a special way today. You are loved Lord. Why the sadness?" My heart began to feel His sadness as He spoke.

Soul, many are coming to Me, but just as many are being lost. I am sad for the lost ones. I weep tears of blood because I desire all to be saved. Soul, if I were to reveal to you the innumerable souls who are, each day, falling into the abyss of death, you could not bear it. I weep for you, the whole of My creation, because you have not yet understood that I love you. I hear wailing from every corner of the earth. Your cries of desperation resound to the heavens. All the while heaven is opening up to you. The floodgates of Mercy and Love are opened now. The

very air, the atmosphere's charged with My Holy Spirit, but you are an obstinate generation. Dry bones are scattered all over the earth. Oh My creation, if only you would unlock the doors to your hearts, then I would cease to weep for you, but instead My suffering continues. And as long as souls are being lost, I shall suffer, because I love. I am alive, fully alive! I cannot be separated from My own creation. Even if you hate Me - I love you, My beloved people. I will do what must be done to save souls. There is not a Saint in heaven, or an Angel, who is not interceding constantly for you, Oh coldest of generations!

You trust in towers built on shaky ground. Your idols of silver and gold will turn to dust. Already you are crying out as one idol after another fails you. You are sick, and I am the medicine of life. You hide in your shaky towers. One by one these towers will fall all about you. I alone am the Rock who will remain standing. One by one you will come to the Rock whose foundation is everlasting, and My heart of love shall embrace you. I will heal you, Oh stubborn generation. I will teach you to love. My Mercy endures. I would weep for one soul even. I suffer and you suffer over the countless souls on the path to perdition. You have not yet understood: We are One Body. I am the Head and you are My members. Can a body be dismembered and experience no pain? No, the entire body is suffering! The medicine is coming from heaven. Drink of it, or there will be more wailing and more suffering. Love will heal the body, but there is too little love. Pray that love will be restored. Pray unceasingly. My suffering is great because you are suffering. Even if you hate Me, My scattered creation, I love you, and I shall reveal the depths of My Love to you again and again, until you turn to Me once and for all. Then, there will be peace.

Your Jesus

Our Lady speaks: *My child, there are so many souls to save, so much work to be done. Rest only in God. Work unceasingly in the vineyard of the Lord. Make ready for the harvest. Time is short. Pray and labor with me for souls. No greater gift can you give to God. I love you.*

4-26-95
The New Pentecost

At Communion, as the host broke apart in my mouth, Jesus said: **My altar, so too is My Body broken into pieces by division among My people.** Jesus was very sad. I could only weep because Jesus suffers so much and we, His people, suffer so much because we are not one, unified, loving body. Before the tabernacle He began to speak: ***Soul, please write My words.**

My beloved people,
The new Pentecost will be when each heart, each soul, will be open to My Holy Spirit. To be open to My Holy Spirit, to be living in My Holy Spirit, is to be docile at every moment to the Living God within you. It is not living a remembrance of Me, two thousand years ago. I am alive today and always, but you do not see Me that way. You see Me as far away from you.

You are not fully alive in the Spirit until your every breath is taken in union with My breathing in you. You are not fully alive in Me, fully participating in Me, until your heart and My heart are one heart. You must receive My Holy Spirit to be sanctified. He is Life, true Life in God, but you are not docile. You are not pliable. You are not willing to give up control. You are not willing to give up your will or your way of living. But you are living lies. You must abandon yourselves to My Holy Spirit, then you will have the abundant Life of God in you at every moment. I am not a dead God. I am not someone to be remembered. The Eucharist is not a remembrance (of 2000 years ago). **My Word is not dead. I live!**

Until you surrender to the Holy Spirit, you are not alive. As long as you are closed to My Holy Spirit, you will suffer much, because you will suffer on you own. I can help you only if you permit Me to be alive in you. Then you will suffer, but never shall you suffer alone. Do not fear the word "suffer." All men suffer. There is no way to get closer to Me than to suffer. Love is a sacrifice and it suffers. But you, My beloved, do not know this kind of love, and you cannot attain it until you surrender to My Holy Spirit. When you are living in My Spirit,

joy will triumph over the suffering and you can see suffering as an act of love, because you are then My co-worker in the redemption of the world.

All the gifts of My Holy Spirit are intended for you, that you may be fully alive in Me. Let Me live in you, breathe in you. Let your blood and My blood co-mingle. Only in the Holy Spirit can you know Me as the Son of the Living God. I suffer because, for so many, I am a dead God. The resurrection has no meaning to those who will not accept My life in them as ever present and eternal. Oh My beloved creation, I will rejoice when the new Pentecost comes into your heart. Welcome My Holy Spirit into your life now. Be docile. Permit His gifts to bring you to life. I am alive and I await you. The more you delay, the greater My suffering and yours. You must decide for Me, then I will live in you in accordance to My Will. I will bring all the gifts of the Spirit to you, and together we will glorify the Most High God (the Father), who lives and reigns today and always. I love you.

Jesus

4-26-95 My home, Rosary with Father
I Am the Mediatrix of Grace

The moment we began to pray I began to weep, unable to hold back the tears. Jesus' disposition was very sad as He said: **Weep with Me, My beloved. Weep with Me. Souls are being lost.** Father prayed the Assumption of Mary meditation. Our Lady spoke when he finished.

Dear children,

My mission is to lead souls to Jesus. I desire all souls to live forever in paradise with God. Please help me to bring souls to Jesus. The entire world is in need of repentance. That is the reason for this time of visitation. It is the message I bring to the world.

Now Our Lady appeared (interiorly as Our Lady of Grace) with her hands outstretched. Rays of Grace flowed from her hands.

Her disposition was one of joy that she comes offering such gifts from God. She spoke again.

I am full of grace, which God wishes to bestow on souls. Draw from me. Receive God's gifts. I am not the author of grace. I am the Mediatrix of Grace. The author is God. He is an infinite fountain of grace for you. If you seek, you will not be denied. Many of these graces remain unused and unaccepted because many refuse to draw through my Maternal hands. These graces are the remedy for the world. Pray with me that souls will draw from me. I am the Mother of all. I am sorrowful to observe your suffering. I suffer to observe how you offend God daily.

Dear children, I implore you to change your life by deciding for God. His grace will enable you to follow Him. Take my hand. I will lead you. Thank you for your love. Thank you for responding to my call. Use the grace from my hands to give Glory to God. I bless you in the Name of the Father, Son and Holy Spirit. The sign of salvation is imprinted upon your foreheads. Rejoice. God is with you. I love you.

Your Mother

4-28-95 8:30 AM Mass
Wrapped in the Most Holy Trinity

At Communion, it was as if my soul began to chant "Holy, Holy, Holy God," again and again. I sensed many Angels around me, chanting and bowing to God in unison with my soul. This lasted for almost fifteen minutes. Then in prayer before the tabernacle, I prayed only in thanksgiving for all my blessings. God Himself caused me to pray in this manner. The Holy Spirit led me in prayers of thanksgiving, alternating with praises of Holy, Holy, Holy. This was an unusual kind of prayer for me.

After a busy day at work, I rested on the sofa and began to read Poulain's "Graces of Interior Prayer." Immediately, grace overcame me. I read a certain paragraph on prayer of the quiet and the presence of God. Then God Himself seemed to enter my soul in a most powerful way. I stopped reading. I held the book but I could hardly move. I was perfectly still. This lasted about 25 minutes. This was imageless and silent. I have never experienced the intensity of God's Presence and extreme elation of this kind. This prayer of union with God surpassed all previous graces in my soul. I was moved to write of it, but suffer much that I cannot capture even a hint of it in words. Still, this is what I wrote immediately following:

O Most Holy, Most Sovereign, Most Blessed Trinity, Father, Son, and Holy Spirit.

How glorious Your Majesty! You are Infinite and Omnipotent.

O Good and Beautiful God Most High, You inebriate me with Divine Love.

My thrice Holy and Loving God, I taste Your Love now.

Never have I tasted such abundant sweetness.

You pour Yourself into me. I drink of You.

You hold me. I am enclosed in You.

Surrounded by Your Majestic Presence, I am all stilled. You enfold me now.

You permeate my being. You conquer me. I am inebriated with Love.

Father, Your Sovereign power causes me to faint.

Jesus, The Word Incarnate, Your Divine Mercy saturates me.

Holy Spirit, Divine Lover and Resident in my soul, Your sweetness envelops me.

I delight in you.

O Most Holy Trinity, who is like unto You? None!

How tender You are toward me now. Sift me, O Master.

Cast out any rival. Cast out impurity. I am for You only.

Now You are truly inside of me. You are conquering nothingness!

You are like a fortress inside of me! Wretchedness is being annihilated!

You have come to Your domain. You create Your mirror image.

You delight in what is Yours. You adorn Your own household with Beauty, so that You may gaze upon such Beauty - the Beauty of Yourself.

Who could resist You, Father, Son, and Holy Spirit? Not I.

Take what is Yours. Again I whisper my "yes." I sigh with love.

O Father, bless me now that my dust may give You Glory.

O Jesus, cover me that the Father is not made to see wretchedness.

Rather let Him see You all over me.

O Spirit of the Living God, teach me how to love with all my heart and strength.

Permit my wretchedness to die in You, Most Holy Trinity.

Permit Your Majesty to reign in me.

I can scarcely move now. I can't perceive my breathing.

You are the object of my everything. Right now, it is as if I have expired!

You alone are present. I am full of joy. Supernatural joy!

Your love is ineffable. I am suspended in Your Presence.

Hold me, my God. I am enfolded in Your mighty arm. O that I could rest here always.

O that this Love would never cease.

How long, my God, will You hold me captive? An eternity, I pray.

You are filling me with honey, Sweet Love and Unspeakable Beauty.

O Most Holy Trinity, delight in Your work.

Be glorified in Your triumph, Father, Son, and Holy Spirit.

It is as if we are passing in and out of one another. I am transparent, it seems.

O God, must this moment end?

Lord, do not leave me for I will be wounded and sick with love.

Now, elation fills me. For now I am with my Triune God. We are one.

(Never have I been more confident He is over me. I am His. Love suffers. Love triumphs.)

5-2-95 Writing regarding above grace four days later.
Regarding Above Grace Four Days Later

The above grace has stayed with me four days now. My soul remains in the state of elation. Each day I am more and more convinced, I should say without doubt, that I have been with the Lord. I have been with the Most Holy Trinity! There is no joy on earth which equals this supernatural joy. There is no greater pleasure, no deeper love.

The grace has continued in two ways:
(1.) I can remember it. It stays very fresh. No matter what my exterior duties, my interior is recalling this prayer of union.
(2.) Since that time, I have experienced the same grace two times.

Once on 5-1-94, while alone, I began to read again Poulain's book, the chapter on "The Presence of God," and almost immediately the grace came again. This time, my entire body began to tingle. The tingling intensified in my hands and my feet. Impelled by the profound Presence of God, I lay prostrate on the floor. I recall praying only "My God, My All," perhaps twice and then silence. The delight of it is indescribable because the delight is God Himself. The peace is profound. This incident seemed more "violent" than the first one on 4-28-95. I am overcome with love of such Power and Might that it seems violent to my soul. Fire is inside of me. This grace lasted probably fifteen minutes. (Not as long as first one. Though more physically violent, it was not as sublime as the first time.) Still, it is more sublime than words can express.

Again on 5-2-95, I was reading Poulain's Book (chapter on Sentiments of Love), when God's Presence overcame me. I stopped reading, closed my eyes; waves of grace caused tingling and warmth all over. Then these ceased. They are like a foretasting of the grace. Then I am stilled. I cry out "My God, My God." I am filled with joy, peace, love. This lasted about twenty minutes. I cannot cause it to stay, though I would love to do so. In between such graced prayer I am in longing for God. My soul, for now, is in a state of elation, but my mind seems to be thinking of how painful it will be when this grace ends, though it seems the memory of this Trinitarian Grace could last a lifetime. My soul already suffers to be possessed by the Trinity again. My God, have mercy on me.

This grace leaves a profound impression upon my soul and many are the effects. Also there are temptations.

Effects:

Elation!

Increased knowledge of love for my Triune God.

Increased certainty of His Love for me.

Increased desire for solitude and prayer.

Increased recollection in all duties - greater attention all day long to God - almost constant conversation or silent longing and loving.

Increased patience and charity.

Increased detachment from created things.

All things seem new - everything seems renewed to me.

Ability to see God in everything increased.

New appreciation for those closest to me - my family and my spiritual director.

Increased devotion, appreciation and love for the Eucharist, Reconciliation, and the Church.

Desire for mortification of self.

Strong inclination for much less talking.

Temptations:

I want to stop all ministry, to contemplate God always.

This is wrong because God calls me to charity - to serve.

Temptation to tell closest friends of the grace.

This is wrong because God desires I tell confessor only.

While I am experiencing sublime elation in this prayer, the devil is tempting me that this will only precede great trial and severe suffering. Although I sense this is true in part, the devil would like to emphasize and enlarge this aspect to cause fear. (I must rebuke this fear.)

The devil tempts me to pride that God is granting me great favors. I rebuke this immediately. The grace of this union with God leaves no doubt in my soul that it is pure gift. My nothingness is more illuminated during this union with God. I am convinced that God takes possession of me only that He could delight in Himself within me. Even my "yes," that permits this grace to overcome me and then proceed, is His Grace in my soul. The devil is a liar, always present to distort and pervert God's work in my soul. But the power of this grace leaves my soul too strong to permit the devil to toy with me. Still, he continually attempts to cause me to fall to pride.

Note: Regarding effects.

It seems to me, by far the greatest effect is knowledge and love of God, for who He is, utterly lovable, worthy of all Honor, Glory, and Praise.

Note: Regarding suffering.

Some of the suffering which results from this graced prayer arises when my prayer time is not particularly graced. For example, today at the Tabernacle, my prayer was very distracted compared to the recollection that comes in this prayer. I persevere, but it is dark and dry. There is temptation that it is not worthwhile because it is not as sublime, but I rebuke this temptation. Still, I suffer.

4-28-95 Prayer Group Meeting
Adore Our Triune God

At the beginning of the Rosary, I saw a house with Our Lady standing over it. I heard Our Lady say only, "A House of Prayer." Graces poured out from her hands and heart and covered the house. As we prayed, I saw a very large Cross. I saw the Most Holy Trinity, in the symbol of a triangle with a circle around it, above the Cross. Then I saw Our Lady kneeling before the Cross. She prayed fervently. She never took her eyes off the Holy Trinity. She looked beyond and above the Cross and upward to the Holy Trinity.

She spoke: *My dear children,*

You are beloved of God. I implore you to pray unceasingly with me. I kneel before the Most Holy Trinity, adoring God in repa-

ration for all souls who do not love Him. Prayer is the way to change the world. The world offends God at every moment. In prayer you offer a pleasing sacrifice of love, in reparation for the sins of the world.

Again, my dear children, I seek your assistance. Adore Our Triune God! Turn your eyes to the Cross, but see beyond it to the Risen and Triumphant Jesus. He reigns with God the Father and the Holy Spirit. He lives! Speak of your love to God. Be simple and pure like a child. Allow God to love you. He seeks your heart for Himself. He does not require great deeds, only great love - love that sacrifices. Remember, dear children, it is almost harvest time. Work now in the vineyard of the Lord. Work while there is time. You shall bear much fruit for the glory of God. Seek to do His Holy Will at all times. Prayer will lead you to find His Will for you. In His perfect and Holy Will you will find joy and peace. I love you.

Your Mother

5-2-95 Feast of St. Joseph, 8:30 AM Mass
Ponder the Life of Beloved St. Joseph

Our Lady speaks: *Daughter,*

On this great feast of the beloved St. Joseph, give honor and gratitude to this humble man of God. Always obedient and humble before God, Joseph provided and protected our Holy Family. Now he continues to be a humble servant of God who intercedes on behalf of all families. In a special way, he intercedes for the Church, who is God's family. Now Joseph is raised to a high place in heaven. Here, Jesus inclines His Heart to the petitions and intercessions Joseph makes on behalf of souls. Joseph continues to provide and protect. Let him be a light for the world. In him you find an example of a life in submission to God. In him you find an example that work can be sanctifying. Work can serve to raise a soul for the glory of God. Ponder the life of beloved Joseph, and you will learn much about serving and loving God. God is glorified in Joseph. Blessed be this man of God now and forever. I love you.

Your Mother

5-3-95 Rosary with my Spiritual Director, my home
Satan's Net

At end of Chaplet of Divine Mercy, I saw Jesus observing the following scene, from a cloud above the scene. Jesus asked me to write "for Father" (my spiritual director). There were people entangled in nets which the devil had caught them in. Satan's nets were huge. Many people were caught in them and trapped. The people were sick, confused, and some were dying. The people were crying and full of misery. Jesus wept for them. Then I saw that Jesus sent Father to them. Father was vested in white. He was radiating light. Father approached the nets, looked up to Jesus and Jesus spoke to Father, **"Please assist Me to set them free."**

To Father's right stood Our Lady. Father began to untangle the people from the net. Wherever Father placed his hand, the net opened up. People were freed one by one. Our Lady received the people as they were freed. Jesus observed this scene for a while. Then He spoke to Father saying:

My beloved son and priest,

I am in you and with you always. You are My hands. You are My voice. My Heart and your heart are One Heart. Your hands are consecrated instruments of My Divine Love for My people. Allow Me to use you to set My people free from the nets of evil. Satan's darkness permeates My people. You are My Light, piercing the darkness. Bring souls to Me. Your labor is not in vain. Your harvest will be great. I do not withhold Myself from you, My son. Rather, I come to you that you may foretaste of My Father's Banquet. Give unto Me your heart; then I shall give you My Heart. Give unto Me your will in exchange for My Will; then I will be glorified in you. I bless you now in the Name of the Most Holy Trinity. I love you.

Jesus

5-4-95
The Flow and Ebb of Grace

The elation from the Trinitarian Prayer of Union on 4/28 is now subsiding. It is rolling away from me like a wave rolling back to the ocean. Another wave is overcoming my soul like a wave rolling onto the seashore. A sense of loss and emptiness overcome my soul. I now feel pains of longing and suffering. I am sick with love. God is now hiding. I sense only the longing for Him, and the memory of the Trinity occupies my mind almost constantly. All created things are tasteless after tasting God. Love suffers. Love endures.

5-4-95 Tabernacle 8:30 AM Mass
The Bread of Life

Dear children,
I am the Bread of Life. The bread which I give is My flesh for the life of the world. I spoke these words and many turned away. These words proved too much for many. Today also, many are turning from the Bread of Life. Too many do not believe in My True Presence. The Eucharist is not a symbol, not a representation. It is My perpetual sacrifice. My flesh is given unto you to eat, that you may have life in Me. I remain with you as bread for the life of the world. Many are rejecting this truth. Faith is dying among you. You want knowledge and understanding of My great mysteries.

Beloved creation, you are dying and suffering needlessly. My bread is remedy for you. I assist you, but you do not come to Me. Day by day, My Truth means less and less to you. How weak is your faith. Quickly it evaporates. You compromise again and again. If you do not turn to Me as a little child, I cannot help you. You are choosing death then. Then you are creating your own suffering, a suffering which is without good. Turn back to Me, your Lord and Savior, now!

Come, follow Me. When will you cease to tempt your God? When will you cease offending Me? Eat of My flesh now while it is available to you. It is life for the world. Eat of Me and live with Me forever. But do not eat of Me unworthily. Repent. Cleanse yourself and then come. I will give you all that you need. How long must I wait? I love you.

Jesus

5-8-95 8:30 AM Mass
Love Suffers. Love Saves.

Before the tabernacle, I prayed some of the Liturgy of the Hours. Then I put it down and entered a silent, sleep – like state for approximately twenty minutes. Upon coming out of this I had a strong temptation that I had not prayed at all, only slept. I became frustrated. I became keenly aware of my spiritual poverty. Like a little child, I find myself literally begging God Almighty to take hold of me – to put His arms around me securely so that all this motion in me can stop. I am very troubled and literally beg for His Mercy. As soon as I prayed from the depths of my heart, He answered my prayer. I felt for a moment that indeed Jesus' arms were wrapped around me. Peace came. I was still.

Jesus spoke: **Soul, take My Peace I give unto you. Your poverty is indeed great. My Mercy I give to you. *Soul, do not harden your ears to My words. Return to a state of constant listening. Heed My voice in you. Yes, you suffer; I see everything. Great is the wound in your heart. You think you cannot bear it, but truly you can. I shall increase your capacity to suffer for Me. I shall increase your capacity to love. You hear Me whispering "*Soul of My Cross." You carry this Cross of suffering for love of Me. The eyes of mortal men cannot see the suffering that is for My eyes only. I alone see the Cross you carry. Can you see now that love is the Cross?**

Soul, carry out your duties in My Peace. You know not the hour I will come again to you, uniting you with Divine Love. Trust in Me, *Soul. You know that I do not leave you. You know

when I am hidden I am working in a mysterious way which you cannot perceive. *Soul, truly few souls love Me as you love Me. You are nothingness, yet I delight in you. Your love of Me draws great favor upon your soul. Your prayer is most pleasing unto Me. Your longing and waiting for Me will not be in vain. Your suffering makes you beautiful in My eyes. I desire souls see My Own Beauty reflected in you.

*Soul, do not be afraid to "feel" the Cross inside of you. It is I, Your Redeemer, who marks you with the Cross and wounds you with My Love. Rejoice that you are so marked and so wounded. Pour out your love for Me always. I never tire to hear how you love Me. Rare is the soul who loves Me for My sake. I will be your strength. I uphold what is Mine. You are Mine. Your love of Me draws My Mercy upon many souls. *Soul, I suffer when you hesitate even momentarily to entertain Satan's temptations. Do not turn away in your suffering. Run to me. Love suffers. Love saves souls. My beloved, share My cup and I will share My Kingdom. You gain everything when you lose everything for love of Me. Sacrifice for Me. Wait for Me. Be faithful unto Me. In the Name of the Father, the Son, and the Holy Spirit, I bless you always and everywhere. I love you.

Your Jesus of Mercy
Take My Peace.

5-9-95 Father Jozo's Mass
The Father Speaks About America

Only after communion did I enter into truly deep prayer. Then God the Father spoke interiorly, saying: **Daughter, My Divine Providence brings My priest and My prophet to the soil of your country, as one who comes to fertilize the seeds planted by the hand of the Blessed Virgin Mary. Her hands, her Immaculate Heart, her entire being, is full of Grace. The Grace of her visitation and Maternal intercession is in the heart of many, but these graces must be cultivated or they do not bear fruit. Once again I send a prophet to this country. The soil of this country is stained with the blood of innocents. The air all around you is** polluted with falsehood and darkness. The very fiber of your culture is being stretched and torn apart. The forces of evil are waging full warfare upon this country. Its goal is the removal of God, the separation of God from the country, the separation of God from family, and the breakdown of My Church.

My prophets repeat the warning and the remedy. Turn back to Me. Remain united as Church under My Peter (Pope John Paul II). As one faithful remnant of little souls, unite in prayer. Fortify yourselves with the Bread of Life. Repent, and Mercy shall be yours. Gather under the mantle of the Blessed Virgin Mary. She is protectress for all. Satan despises her because she protects souls from his lies. Her virtues of humility and obedience drive him away; he cannot bear such virtues!

Daughter, America will be tried and put to the test. Difficult times are in store for this country. The greatness of this country lies in My Fatherly blessing upon it. I will bless this country when it turns back to receive My blessing. Until that time, there will be much to suffer. Pray then, My faithful ones, that your suffering will be short, that your country will be reconciled with Me, that I, Your Father will bless you again saying, "This ground is once again holy ground; these are My holy people. Let their suffering cease." I bless you with the reminder that the death which is permeating your culture, I have already overcome, and so, too, shall you, but only in Me. I love you.

Your Father

5-11-95 Prayer Group Rosary
Be Patient With Your Families

The Descent of the Holy Spirit Decade, Our Lady spoke: *My dear children,*

I am joyful to be in your midst. We pray together to the Father. We pray for the conversion of the world, for the Glory of God. My children, tonight I observe in your hearts many burdens. Dear little ones, do not worry. Do not be anxious about things. I see that many of you are very worried about your families. You are praying for your children, your parents, your brothers and sisters and spouses.

God sees your longing, your desire for their conversion. God is with you and He desires conversion of all souls.

You who have received the grace of conversion must be an example for your loved ones. Your families should observe that you are different: more loving, more peaceful. You aid their conversion through constant trusting prayer of the heart. Empty the burdens of your heart to the One who can take these burdens and convert them to love. Radiate Love. Love unconditionally, because God has loved you unconditionally. Radiate Joy. If you are with God, He is with you and He is your joy. Permit your loved ones to see your joy. Radiate Peace. Let nothing rob you of the Peace of my Son. Even in the midst of trial and suffering, God grants you His own Peace. Be patient with your families. See how patient God has been with His family of man! If you radiate God's love, joy, and peace, if you are patient and prayerful, souls will see that you possess a great Good. That Good is God Himself.

This night I impart to you the virtues of my Maternal Heart. But only through prayer can you radiate these virtues which I desire to give to you. Therefore, dear little children, pray always from the depths of your heart. You must grow in Love, in Peace, in Joy and in Faith. Rejoice that you have received the grace of conversion. Trust exceedingly in the Mercy of God. God grants the grace for the conversion of the whole world, but few accept the grace. Rejoice that Jesus came to save sinners. Rejoice that Jesus would leave the ninety-nine to go after the one lost soul. He will not forsake your families. All belong to Him. Please trust me. I am your mother, and always I am leading you to the most loving Heart of Jesus. Peace of my Son, Jesus, be yours. Pray and Persevere. I love you.

Your Mother

5-12-95
Journal Entry

God grants me the grace of His Presence in my soul almost continually this day. He is very, very tangible to me. I accomplish many duties this day (home and office) in an almost automatic way. My will and my mind are constantly with God. What I do in the world is done on a very superficial level, none of which "absorbs" me. God alone "absorbs" me!

5-15-95 8:30 Mass and Tabernacle
Praises to His Glory

I prayed before the Tabernacle and then came home to complete my prayer. I felt very weak and full of God's Presence, so I lay down on the sofa to continue to pray. I began to enter a prayer state very much like the prayer of union on 4-28, but not quite as intense.

It seemed I was observing choirs of Angels singing, "Glory, Glory, Glory to God." I seemed to go in and out of a sleep, but in this prayer time it seemed that the "Glory" of God was being revealed to my soul. Somehow I observed the Throne of God in heaven, surrounded by His Majestic heavenly court. This heavenly court consisted of Angels of many kinds, holy men, Patriarchs, and Saints – many, many of them. All paid reverence and homage to God Most High. There were continuous praises to His Glory. Somehow I was in the midst of this heavenly court, observing and singing the praises of "Glory to God." Such Majesty is indescribable. This grace lasted perhaps fifteen minutes. I was in a very peaceful and joyful state.

5-16-95
How Much Do You Love Me?

My eyes were drawn to the crucifix on the wall above the phone. I took the crucifix off the wall and held it, looking at it, loving Jesus on the Cross. I embraced the crucifix in my arms, when Jesus spoke: ***Soul, *Soul of My Cross. This is love. This is real. I love you this much. How much do you love Me, *Soul? Do you love Me enough to open up your arms and embrace My Cross? Rest upon My Cross. Put your own "will" upon the Cross and let it be crucified. Then My Divine Will can live and reign in you.**

*Soul, look at My nakedness, My vulnerability. Look at My obedience to the Father. What man has crowned with mockery and rejection, the Father has crowned with glory and acceptance. If the Father has thus crowned Me in glory and accepted Me as ransom for all, will He not do the same for those who are with Me and in Me? This is your inheritance. Paradise and Eternal Life are His promises.

*Soul, *Soul of My Cross, the Cross is the Way. The Cross is Love. Love is real. Your tears are a prayer because they are pure love for Me. We suffer together the pangs of love. My thirst for love is far from satisfied, yet your love for Me alleviates My pain. You accept what others reject.

*Soul, give Me to drink of your love continuously. Do not run from suffering. Did I not comfort you from the Cross this night? Look at your Beloved, stretched out on the Cross for you. Who could love you this much? None! Then press My Crucifix to your heart and embrace My Cross. Lay down your life for Me. Be My lamb. Sacrifice for Me. Your sacrifice and your love draws grace upon many souls. Do not be afraid to suffer. You will never suffer alone. I am with you always. I bless you, My beloved one, in the Name of the Most Holy Trinity. Take My Peace. You are Mine. I love you.

Jesus

5-19-95
Jesus Said: "These Are the Latter Days of Decision."

My Lord and my Savior,

I observe your teachers in the Church and Schools teaching falsehoods, leading mere children into darkness. Lord, I cry out to you. I observe my own son led astray by teachers who have deviated from Your Truth. Darkness has crept into Your household, Lord. In Your Mercy, how long will you endure such apostasy? How grave is the situation. Jesus, souls are dying. Faith is evaporating. Your Church resembles you upon the Cross, bleeding and wounded. Satan is claiming Your young ones. Jesus, come, stop this apostasy, please. There is chaos in the hearts of Your people.

Your law is no longer observed. The Truth is twisted every which way. We call evil good and good, evil. Lord, how is it that you hold back the hand of justice? Send Your Holy Spirit down upon Your creation. Claim what is Yours, my Lord. Your people are wayward. Faith is dying.

Those who speak Your Truth according to Your Law and Tradition are persecuted. Ears quickly turn deaf to them. Lord, in Your Mercy, pour out Your Spirit of Truth. Revive Your Church, restoring her to full orthodoxy; revive her credibility. Turn hearts of men toward her. O my Lord and Savior, how is one to come to you and to the Father, without the graces given through Your Mystical Body? Jesus, You are the Lamb who takes away the sin of the world; take away our sin, Lord. Cause Your creation to give You Glory. Lord, forgive my incapacity, but You have said that You are for all. How is it then, that so few truly know You, love You and follow You? All things are possible for You; open the hearts of Your creation! Pour Your Holy Spirit upon us that all may turn back to You. Teach us to love. Grant us Faith. O Eternal Life, who will enjoy You if this present darkness steals what belongs to You? Look with pity upon our sickness. Heal Your Body, Lord. Forgive my impatience, Jesus, but souls are sick and dying. Satan is taking what belongs to you. It appears he is claiming a whole generation of youth for himself. How will the Father be thus glorified?

My heart, which is so small, suffers, but Your Heart, which encompasses all, must suffer all the more. How long will we be permitted to grieve You and the Father and the Holy Spirit? How long must the tender heart of the Blessed Virgin Mary observe her children grieving and offending the Most Holy Trinity? Come, Lord, come.

Jesus said: ***Soul, please write.**

Only a short time ago, you walked in darkness toward perdition. Who revived you? Only a short time ago, you grieved the Most Holy Trinity. Who restored you? Answer, *Soul.

Lord, the Blessed Virgin Mary came to me through one of her messages and she taught me to pray the Rosary from the heart again. Then she led me to You, Jesus, to Your Heart. And through her

Maternal heart, the Holy Spirit descended upon me. Then the Holy Spirit and You, Jesus, led me to the Father, who is Love. That is how I was revived, as You know well, Jesus.

Yes, *Soul. I am sending My Mother to all. Blessed are they who receive her. My Holy Spirit is sent to revive the world. My Spirit is Love, which brings Peace, but also My Spirit is fire that purifies (justice). **My creation shall be restored by fire that tries and fire that restores. I shall reveal Myself to all because I am for all. All shall recognize My Light piercing the darkness, which shall descend for a time. The sheep and the goats will be separated as the heavens reveal My Face to all. All creation shall know then that I exist. I Am Who Am lives! Then each will decide for Me or against Me. Such is the Mercy of the Most Holy Trinity.**

Before this comes to pass, there will be much to suffer, for, indeed, there is sickness, bleeding, brokenness, which is spreading now. This is the work of men who have turned from God, rejected the Truth and accepted lies. These men are communing with spirits of darkness and leading others along the path to perdition. Men of the flesh cannot judge things of the spirit. Therefore, My Holy Spirit knocks, but ears do not hear, eyes do not see, hearts do not open, because this generation is lost in the flesh. But My Mercy endures from age to age. My Mystical Body shall be triumphant. She bleeds now as I bled on the Cross, but she shall rise again as I rose from the dead. Resurrection is victory and the victory is hers, and victory is for all. You share My cup of sorrow because you share My rejection. You are persecuted because of your love for Me. Blessed are you. I have taught you that I am in You and you are in Me. When you are persecuted, I am persecuted. The cup of My suffering overflows, because the sin of the world is like fire, consuming soul after soul. But the fire I send, which is from the Holy Spirit, shall purify and restore all of creation. Then those who are for Me will follow My Way and My traditions shall be revived. Those who are against Me will choose death over life. They shall perish, never to lead others astray. These are the latter days of decision. What Satan appears to be gaining in My own

household, he will lose in the end. Woe to the ministers who, proclaiming to be Mine, shun My Holy Truth, My Holy Spirit, My Holy Mother; compromising My Body, they shall be fully accountable on the great and terrible day of the Lord.

*Soul, your prayer from the heart resounds in the heavens. Pray that My house be restored to a House of Prayer. Pray for conversion. Each converted heart is My Holy City, restored in My Holy Spirit, becoming My new Jerusalem. When My Holy Spirit converts this generation, all My creation shall be My Holy City, and My new Jerusalem shall reign victorious. The Father will be glorified then, because all shall be One Heart, just as He and I and the Holy Spirit are One Heart. The Father's justice will purify and prevail at the appointed time, known to Him; then the earth shall be restored. *Soul, let your heart be My house of prayer. Prayer saves souls. It is not for you to ask when and how. It is for you to trust and pray in faith. Do not be discouraged when I share My Cross with you. It is My gift of love for you. Offer to Me your love and your suffering. All of you belongs to Me. Know that I am with you always. Do not lose your peace, because then the flesh takes over the spirit. Live by My Spirit who breathes in you. Bear fruit for Me. The fruit you bear shall be presented to the Father. These are the souls you will bring to Him by your prayer and by the Cross. Harvest time is close at hand. Work while the climate permits. Make ready the crop, for soon the sickle will strike. The good wheat shall be gathered for the restoration of the world, and the good grapes will be pressed into new wine for the restoration of the world. *Soul, until the appointed time has come to pass, you shall share My cup of suffering. I have revived many souls in your generation, that they would carry My Cross for love of Me and love of souls. Exist for Me, *Soul. Love the Cross. The Cross is love and the Cross saves souls. Peace I give unto you. I love you.

Jesus

5-23-95 Tabernacle, 8:30 Mass
"Lay Down Your Life for Others"

I prayed saying to Him: "Jesus, my Savior, I love You with all my heart and strength. He said: **Then love souls for Me. Lay down your life for Me. Learn to endure the Cross and suffering. Now I am not speaking of suffering which is useless, but I am speaking of suffering which comes from laying your life down for others. I am speaking of the suffering which comes as you permit your human will to be crucified - put your will on the cross and receive My Will from the Cross.**

Soul, do not love comfort. Do not confuse peace and comfort. My peace is not lack of turmoil. My Peace is Faith, unshakable in the face of turmoil. Now if you have faith, you have trust. The greater the faith, the greater the trust. If you trust in faith, that is My Peace. Now you say that you love Me, and I know that truly you do love Me, but I shall increase your capacity to love Me more and more. *Soul, there is a certain way that I shall accomplish this, and it is through the Cross. Know that I love you infinitely. Having chosen you for Myself, I will lead you into the depths of My Merciful Heart, creating in you, who are nothingness, My Living Flame of Love. Therefore, carry the Cross as one set on fire in and for Love. I bless you and I love you.

Jesus

5-24-95 Rosary with my spiritual director, my home
You Shall Witness the Battle

Fifth Glorious Mystery, Our Lady began to speak after Father's meditation.

My son and my daughter,

My Son has overcome the world and the victory is His, but there is a battle being waged at this present time. There is a battle for souls. God, the Father, pours graces from Heaven to combat the present darkness. You shall witness the battle, both the good from Heaven and the evil perpetuating the darkness. I come from heaven as the Reconciler of all peoples. My Maternal Love encompasses all of God's creation. I never cease to intercede, especially for those souls closest to being lost forever. You who are with me must fight the great battle by my side. Pray with me constantly. When the Holy Spirit calls you into prayer, obey His call, for, perhaps at that very moment, you are to intercede on behalf of a soul in grave danger. In this manner, you are my prayer partner. When our hearts are united, our Triune God is glorified. I have called you by name into my Immaculate Heart. As you have consecrated yourselves unto my Heart, you are instruments through whom I work. As instruments of grace, you unite with me to fulfill the Holy Divine Will of God.

My son and my daughter, stay alert. I will share much with you. Draw from me and do not be afraid. Though you shall witness suffering and confusion all around you, in my heart you shall find comfort. I will take you to the Heart of Jesus. He is your Peace, your Hope, your Love. Persevere in the battle. Remain steadfast in Faith. Heaven is with you. You shall not falter. Responding to my call, your harvest shall be great. In prayer you shall come closer to the Heart of Love. The Most Holy Trinity desires to give to you everything that is Good. Your loving and longing for God is a response to His loving and longing for you. Exist for Him by responding always to His call for Love and Sacrifice. Rejoice. At every moment He upholds you, blesses you and loves you, seeking only your "fiat." How glorious a mystery, how great His Mercy. The Redeemer seeks our continuous "yes," in order to bless us as He desires. He is the King, offering us His riches. Truly, the Lord has prepared a place for you in His Father's House.

Thank you, my son and daughter, for praying the Most Holy Rosary from your heart. Thank you for telling Jesus that He is loved by you. I love you, dear ones, and I am with you always. Peace.

Your Mother

5-26-95
This Flower Shall Be Called "Charity"

I heard Jesus interiorly: **"*Soul, the power of your prayer, your intercession, and your blessing comes from the Eucharist!"** (I had overslept and thought about missing Mass.) Following Mass, I knelt before the statue of our Blessed Mother. There was a period of silence. Then, interiorly, I heard her voice. Her voice is so beautiful, so gentle, yet full of strength. Even her voice radiates Light. She is radiant beauty and ever so loving. Her voice fills my soul with joy.

My little child,

I anoint you with the oil of my maternal love. I anoint you with grace from my Immaculate Heart. I give unto you my own heart. It is crowned with thorns and pierced by a sword. The Crown of Thorns is my union with the Passion of my Son. The sword that pierces is the continuous sufferings, due to the rejection of God and the sins of the world. Embracing my heart, share my joy and my suffering. Love as I love, being for others what I have been for you, a vessel of the Holy Spirit. I bless you in this graced moment. You are being fashioned into a new creation, into the image of your Creator.

My Son has chosen you to be His little flower. When He glances to observe you, let Him observe His own reflection; let Him observe His own Light radiating from within. Let your fragrance be the fragrance of Divine Love in your soul. Let Him observe His own joy radiating within you. Let Him say, "This flower shall be called 'Charity'; she is pleasing and pure in My sight." Let Him observe the fire within you to be His own Divine Fire, the fire that enkindles souls. Daughter, be the delight of the Father; be the wedding flower of my Son; be the pure vessel of the Holy Spirit. Daughter, for me, be my intercessor, prayer partner, and echo. My heart surrounds you. Thank you for writing my words. I love you.

Your Mother

5-28-95 and 5-29-95
My Soul Is Anemic Without the Eucharist

I missed Mass these two days. I must note the tremendous difference in the strength of my soul to do good, practice virtues, and avoid temptation, when I miss the Eucharist. Eucharist is my daily life - my strength, the central point of my spiritual life. When I do not receive, I am not full of fervor for God. My soul without the Eucharist is anemic. My prayer life suffers. My recollection and peace are more readily disturbed when the Eucharist has not entered my soul on a daily basis. Of all the graces I receive in my soul, the Eucharist is the greatest! On these two days I suffer as one abandoned by God. I am in darkness. My will alone unites me to God.

5-30-95
There Will be Signs and Wonders in the Sky

I received a message following 8:30 AM Mass, in prayer before the tabernacle, in an unusual way. I entered a sleep-like state of prayer, a state of profound silence, profound stillness and profound light. Somehow I sensed I was with God, as if before Him, communing, adoring, loving. I remained in such a state for about twenty minutes. Then I began to hear the voice of Our Lady, as if whispering, more faint than usual. Usually I receive messages as if I am on earth and Our Lady has come to earth to dictate the message, as if she is standing before me. Then, I am in a state of listening, and her words are the focus. But today, this is not the case. It is as if I have been taken to heaven and my soul is attentive to God. My focus is not listening, but rather "being with God," a sense of being in an elevated place of prayer, not on earth. Our Lady speaks, but almost as if in the background; yet the message seems more "impressed" upon my soul.

After the Holy Hour before the Tabernacle, I enter my car to write. I believe I am only given a portion to remember. This is what I recall. Now the Holy Spirit is giving this memory to me. It is not Our lady "re-dictating" the message. It is like prayer continued.

Dear one,

It shall come to pass that the Lord Himself shall descend as the Light. The Lord Himself shall call each by name, one by one, into His Light. The darkness of this age will be eclipsed by the Light Himself. Soul after soul will be called out of darkness. The Light will overshadow each soul. Darkness shall lay no claim to God's creation. Souls have been created for the Light. Illumination shall come upon the earth. Souls will walk into the Light. Mercy shall enter the darkness and make of it Light. Every soul shall enter the Light, but some will pass through the Light only to return to the darkness, because their preference is for darkness, and God shall not come against man's free will; weeping, He will endure ultimate rejection. Rejecting the Light who is God, and God who is Love, souls will perish in the darkness.

Dear one, the Light called you, and the Light is in you and you are in the Light. Love and Sacrifice for souls who have yet to come into the Light. The Light shall descend suddenly, passing as if in a moment. The illumination shall come from the heavens and descend upon earth, upon all souls. There will be signs and wonders in the sky. There will be changes in the weather. There will be tragedy and calumny. There will be weeping and depression. Faith, Hope, and Love will be waning. When all these converge, the Light Himself will come from Heaven, and He will call each by name into the Light.

Dear one, happy the souls who walk in the Light now. Great is the responsibility of a child of the Light. Before God, they shall be fully accountable for the grace bestowed upon them. In this meeting with God, He will say, "Soul, I removed the scales from your eyes, restoring your sight that you would enter the Light, walk in the Light, forsake all darkness and serve the Light. What glory did you give to the One who rescued you from the darkness?"

Dear one, this is what you must do to give Glory to God. Lay down your life for God. Surrender your will to God. Take up your Cross, day in and day out; walk the way of Jesus to Calvary. Die to self, rising to God. Forsake the darkness, repenting, and embrace the Light that embraces you. Trust in my words. Trust in God, who is the Light for the world. I bless you.

Your Mother

5-31-95 Feast of Visitation
The Mission of Every Christian

Following 8:30 AM Mass and Holy Hour, while driving in my car, Our Lady spoke these words:

Dear child,

The visitation is remembered from age to age because it contains the mission of every Christian, the mission to love and to serve; the call to carry the Holy Spirit to one another; the call to rejoice in God, who is merciful to His creation. The visitation contains and bears witness to the love and the Mystery of the Most Holy Trinity. Follow the Holy Spirit, who is with you wherever He may lead you. For where He leads is Holy. I love you.

Your Mother

6-1-95 3 AM, my home (Holy Spirit guide my words.)
An Earthquake?

I awoke out of a dream or a vision. I'm not sure which of these I had experienced. I saw the scenes as if dreaming, but the imagery was stronger than any dream. I must note that I rarely recall dreaming. If this was a dream, it was more vivid than any I have ever experienced. I could see things as if watching them on TV. But I was included in the scene, as if watching myself. At the same time, I was experiencing the scene itself, feeling the fright, with physical manifestations of my heart racing and my body shaking. When I awoke out of this, I tried with all my strength to put it off, to stop thinking of it, to discount it as a dream which was unimportant. Yet the strength of it is still with me, though to a slightly lesser degree. I thought it so unimportant that I had decided to not even mention it to Father or anyone else. Yet, it would not leave my memory. I decided that perhaps I would advise Father. I told him the following and I record it out of obedience to him.

I was in a building of small to medium size that appeared to be a church or a chapel. There was an altar in the usual place and

Father was saying Mass at the altar. With me toward the back of the Church was the rest of the prayer group. We were all in prayer. Suddenly the earth shook and the building began to buckle and sway. I was utterly astonished to see how the floor was buckling under my feet. It had a movement upward of about two or three feet. I watched as the floor all around my feet continuously moved, thinking the floor would certainly open up and swallow me alive. Then I noticed the entire building was buckling and swaying with such a stress that I was literally shocked that it did not crumble to pieces. It protected us. For some time, I observed this. Then, after it stopped, we opened the door to the outside. It was shocking to observe that nothing was left. Everything, as far as we could see, was leveled, almost pulverized. We saw no sign of life. It was here that my heart began to race, my body to shake. It was as if I was in the state of shock in the dream. Even in this state (in the dream), I recall thinking that God had spared us and protected us so that we would rebuild on His Holy Foundation.

I was awakened at this point. Shaking, I moved into the arms of my husband. He asked me what had happened. I shared only a very little (saying, I had a very realistic dream of a devastating earthquake). I tried to return to sleep and forget it, but could not. Then, after a long while fighting the memory of this, I fell back to sleep. When I awoke in the morning, my mind was full of this dream, though I continued to try to put it aside.

Note: I believe that if this was a sort of "message" from God, that in this experience He took me to the point of my greatest endurance to date. In the dream or vision, when I got to the point that I could not have endured more, He stopped it.

Note: There are many ways to interpret this, but it is not for me to do so. However, I was left with the sense that this was not very far away. On the other hand, this sense of urgency could have simply been God's way of increasing my urgency to pray, pray, pray. God has indeed caused this to come about as a result of what I experienced. All Praise, Honor, and Glory be to the Most Holy Trinity.

6-2-95 Prayer Group Rosary
Prepare to be Persecuted

At the beginning of the Rosary, I saw Our Lady presenting Jesus to us. Jesus was wounded as if from the scourging. Also present (on His Body) were the five wounds from the Crucifixion. Light illuminated the upper portion of His Body. From the wounds I saw a sort of umbilical cord issuing forth from the wound and extending into the heart of each person present. The umbilical cord (for lack of better description) was both red and white. I observed this for some time, then it disappeared. After a long pause Our Lady spoke.

My dear children,

Receive my Son, Jesus. The Holy Wounds of Jesus are Love and Mercy for you. Tonight I observe you to be full of love for God. I am joyful for this. Also, I observe that there are some among you who are doubting their gifts from the Holy Spirit. Dear ones, grow in faith to a spiritual maturity. God has said, "I will give you My Holy Spirit." Trust in the Holy Spirit and His gifts. These are given for your own sanctification and also for the sanctification of people put in your path.

Tonight, your hostess placed fragrant flowers (gardenias) around the room to perfume the air with beauty. Each called by name, God has raised you to pray so that He can fragrance you in holiness. When you walk your daily journey you are the fragrant and holy perfume which transforms your environment.

Dear children, some among you think you are walking in circles in your spiritual journey. You are not walking fruitless journeys. You are growing indeed. Waiting on the Lord is growth. Abandonment requires patience. Please persevere. Do not seek consolation; rather, seek God's Holy Will. Offer yourself to God each and every day. Learn to be silent before God. Exist in a state of listening (recollection). Do not be troubled by the flow and ebb of the Spirit and His gifts.

Dear children, grow in faith and courage, for much is about to unfold before your very eyes. Your faith must be strong. Little ones, be willing to suffer for the sake of souls. Be prepared to be persecuted for the Holy Name of Jesus. Be prepared for turmoil in the

Church. The Church will resemble Jesus' passion and crucifixion for a period of time. This will pass, and she (the church) *will resurrect! Victory is yours. Be strengthened by the Holy Spirit at Pentecost. My children, receive all that the Holy Spirit brings to you. Little ones, I bless this night. Thank you for your prayers. I love you.*

Your Mother

6-5-95 Church
Always Invite the Holy Spirit

Soul, the Holy Spirit is Love. He is My breath in You. He is My Life in you. Love teaches and brings forth love. His Breath is Life, which brings forth life in God. The Holy Spirit is your Sanctifier. Listen and obey the Holy Spirit. The Holy Spirit always waits for your "fiat." Child, breathe in love and breathe out love. Always, above all, Love. Always invite the Holy Spirit so that He is your constant guest. I love you.

Jesus

6-6-95 Tabernacle 8:30 AM Mass
Jesus Said, "Pray in This Manner."

At communion, filled with the Presence of my Beloved Savior, I was silent and then prayed, "O Jesus, how I love You, what could I give You? How should I pray?" I said this with all the love in my heart. Jesus, full of love, said: **Offer to Me your human will.** I said, "again"? He said: **Again. Pray in this manner.**

"Lord, take from me what you have given me, that is, my own human will and give to me Your Divine Will. Lord, cause my human will to die at every moment, because at every moment you permit me freedom to choose my will or your will. When I choose Your Holy Will, permit the death of my will to be a pleasing sacrifice to you. The Father has created me for His Divine Will. Father, Son, and Holy Spirit, let it be done to me according to Your Holy Divine Will. Use me as you please, my Triune God. In the night, hide me and permit me to suffer

351

the death of self. Teach me the way of the Cross, that I may learn the Way of Love. In the morning, let me rise to the sunlight as one transfigured. Transfigure me, Jesus, so that I no longer live, but you live in me on earth.

Lord, my offering is so little, yet it is all you seek from me. You have given me freedom. In freedom I say, Yes, Lord. Jesus, hide me in prayer; permit me to be with you, to love you and to suffer with you. Let all be done according to Your Holy Will. Lord, if you call me to emerge from the hiddenness, I will emerge a person of prayer, still willing, still suffering, still dying to self, but always obedient to Your Holy Will. Lord, I give you permission to reign in me, to conquer me and to love me again and forever. Amen and amen."

Then Jesus said, **Peace, *Soul,** and I prayed the prayer he taught me.

6-11-95 Feast of the Trinity
I Say "Yes," Father, Son, and Holy Spirit

From the moment I awoke I was covered in the Grace of God. Peace filled me. All day my soul is still and quiet; the presence of God permeates me. I am in loving conversation with the Most Holy Trinity all the day long. He pours His love upon Me. I am made to feel His love for me, and gratitude fills my soul. The more I pour out my Thanksgiving for all His grace and blessings, the more He shows me that, indeed, every moment is graced by Him. He is the architect of my life; at every moment He is there. All that is permitted is for my good and for His Glory. A grateful heart is loved by God and rare indeed. The more we give thanks the more He gives the grateful soul.

I prayed:
"O Most Holy Trinity, my thrice Holy God, how glorious a mystery You are,
Lover of my soul and guest within.
O Abba, my Father, I love You, I praise You, and thank You.

I say yes, Father! I am a grain of sand, but Your Majesty is over me.

You cover me with Fatherly Love and feed me Your Wisdom.

Your Authority is Perfect, Holy and Loving.

O Jesus, my Savior, my Redeemer, the Word Incarnate, I love You, I praise You, and thank You.

I say yes, Jesus! You are my Savior; You lift me up as You lifted all things up to heaven when You were lifted on the Cross.

The Father accepts me, because through You I am made acceptable.

O Spirit, O Life, O Love itself, Gift of the Father and the Son to one another and to all creation. I love You, I praise You and thank You.

I say yes, Holy Spirit! You are the Breath of God and Breath of my soul. You breathe in me and fill me with Your gifts.

You seduce me with Love so divine my soul cannot resist Your Beauty, Your Majesty, Your Fire within!

O Sweet Surrender into the Almighty and Sovereign Arms of the Father, the Son, the Holy Spirit.

O Eternal, O Immortal, O Sovereign Majesty, Creator and Lord of All.

O Love, O Love, O Love, this grain of sand is in Your vast ocean.

Take me to Your deepest center. Give me Life in You. Let me love You Most Holy Trinity. Let me adore You forever.

O my Triune God, I desire to love you enough for all the souls who fail to love You.

Let all be done according to Your Most Holy Will.

All Honor and Glory, and Praise be Yours."

6-12-95
A Variety of Temptations and Suffering

Temptations of every sort bombard my soul today. I suffer that all is in vain, as the devil tempts me to give up prayer. I suffer the absence of God. I spend time pondering and discerning the movements within my soul. It is as if God has vanished. I have a deep sense of loneliness. Only God can fill this void. I ache for God. At one level all these temptations assail my soul, but deep within I notice strength that cannot be penetrated by temptation. I see great value to the darkness. Faith grows in darkness. My level of "knowing" and "willing" to love God is deeper now. I can suffer more now. There is no temptation to "run," only to "endure." There is no doubt that God is with me, in me, even though I ache and I suffer only absence. Patience is growing. Faith is growing. Love is terribly painful, yet God commands me to Love above all else. Interior suffering is the greatest of sufferings. It is an offering only God can see. Love suffers and endures.

O my God, how much I love Thee! When I pray, and truly, it is as if my soul prays always, it is as if I haven't prayed at all. It is as if I have not loved God, but indeed, I have loved Him. I am loving Him. No one can console me. I find I go out of my way to seek solitude. In solitude, I am made to experience a storm within, but I do not want to run or be distracted. I want only to experience that which is inside of my soul.

In this tempest, these are my temptations:
Be more active.
Abandon prayer.
Prayer and Sacrifice and Suffering are futile.
I am damned and so is the world.
All grace has been imagined.
Work such as ministry is futile.
God has abandoned me.
I am full of sin and God finds me offensive.
I am too dependent on spiritual direction.

Try to be more independent.
Messages are false, of no value.
I am a fool.

If I were to illustrate this, I would describe my soul as an ocean, and these temptations are the winds which come to "stir up" the surface. They would like to penetrate deeper but they can only touch the surface. These are the little devils that cause little ripples, but the soul must take care not to allow them to go very deep, where they can cause bigger waves.

There is another kind of suffering that is at a deeper level. It gives Him glory because it tests and strengthens the soul and it produces courage and fortitude, patience and humility. Still, it is exhausting, and painful to suffer. This suffering includes: Longing, yearning for God that is indescribable. The stronger the desire for union, the greater the abyss between my soul and God seems to be. Suffering is in union with Jesus, as He suffered in the Garden of Gethsemane. "Father, have you abandoned me? If it is possible, may I pass up the cup? Not my will but Yours be done." No Angel is sent to console Me. There is only suffering to know what tribulation and trial is at hand, not only for my soul, but for the world - for all souls. I suffer that God is not loved by all souls. I cannot convert the world, so I long to love God enough for all souls. I long to serve for all the souls who will not serve. I long to adore for all the souls who refuse to adore. God is so worthy! Further suffering is this - all that I long to do I cannot do, because God's Light in my soul reveals only neediness and incapacity. The greater the darkness in the love between God and I, the greater the illumination in my soul as to my utter dependence on God, and my nothingness, my unworthiness.

All of the above is beneficial to my soul. Recollection and solitude are necessary to come to this conclusion. When I was in more "public" or active ministry, there was always someone to call attention to the "gifts" they saw in me. Though I always referred such compliments back to God, still some of that praise "sticks" to the soul and the soul is comforted by the esteem of others. It is only when I go apart from the rest, in solitude, where no one can uphold me, no human can esteem me, that God and I can face one another. I am made to acknowledge my true poverty and beg for His Mercy (which He gives immediately!). Before God I am always dressed in rags, with hands outstretched like a beggar! The miracle is that God loves me with an incomprehensible Love. He clothes me with Himself and permits me to become one with Him. How glorious is God, who is Love!

6-13-95 My Home 8 PM
Discern the Spirits!

Our Lady spoke: *My dear children,*
I have warned you of Satan's ploys, his lies, his divisions. He is causing much confusion in prayer groups, in families, in the Church, in individual souls. More devils surround the souls of priests and religious. Pray for them. Devils surround the converted souls to tempt them to fall backward into a lukewarm state. Satan is mimicking the messages. He causes confusion by sending false messengers. Be at peace. Be in prayer. Discern. A good tree produces good fruit. Do not worry or judge. God will take care of such falsehood. Pray, because many prayer groups are being diverted by following false messengers. This is causing divisions, as some say, "I follow this message and this messenger," and others say, "I follow a different messenger and their message." Truly God is speaking to many in this age, but the message that is important is the Gospel message. The messenger is not important. The Gospel is important. Live the Gospel and you will be living the messages. I am coming from heaven to enliven faith and hope and love in and through the same Gospel message.
O my dear children, my heart aches for you to focus only on God. God desires to pour His Love in you, but you are not permitting Him to do so because you are always running. You are full of talk and activity that serves to keep you distracted from God. I offer to you my heart. If you enter my heart, I will teach you to be quiet and still before God, and we can pray together for the salvation of the world. I warn you again that Satan will continue to cause confusion and division through false messages and messen-

gers. Pray and discern. Obey the authority of the Church. Live the message of the Gospel. My words are not idle words. They are meant to enter your heart and cause you to think of God again. Let God do as He wills with you, but always pray. Then you will have Peace. I am with you to protect you and guide you. I love you.
    Your Mother

6-14-95 Rosary with Father, my home
Our Lady Helps the People of Jerusalem

First decade: Interiorly I saw Our Lady walking around the streets of Jerusalem. I recognized the Via Dolorosa and the Holy Sepulcher area of the city. Father walked on her right and I on her left. We were dressed in white gowns/robes. Much of the city of Jerusalem was in ruins. We were there to assist Our Lady as she swiftly walked from one person to the next to help them up off the ground. People were lying all over the ground, but Our Lady was reviving them, nursing them back to life.

Second decade: At the part of the "Hail Mary" where we say "pray for us now and at the hour of our death," Our Lady spoke with much love, affection and tenderness toward us, as if whispering: *My son and my daughter, I, myself will be with you at that most precious hour when Jesus calls for you to "come." Do not be afraid. I look forward with love and joy to that moment when you have fulfilled the will of the Father on earth, so that I can take you by the hand and lead you to your true home with God. Each time you pray "I love you," these words enter my heart as treasure amassed within. Dear ones, desire only God and long for heaven. You are no longer of the world. My Son has called you out of the world. Live in my heart. Thank you for responding to my love.*

Third decade (Nativity): Our Lady said, *Thank you, my son and my daughter, for allowing me to give you a new birth to life in God!*

Fifth decade: Here I experienced tremendous pain for loving God so much. I began to cry. Our Lady said: *Do not be afraid to love Jesus with all your heart and strength. It is a kind of suffering, but also it is a great joy. Love always. Above all love God. Your love for God brings me joy. Your longing is love. This love and sacrifice shall accompany you always. Great is the reward in heaven for your tears, your prayer, your sacrifice, and love. All that you offer to God now is for the good of many souls. Many unbelievers shall come to believe because of your love. Peace be yours. Persevere child. I love you.*

Your Mother

6-21-95 Tabernacle after Holy Hour
All Should Prepare to Meet My Son

Upon walking to my car, Our Lady spoke to me.

My dear child,

Thank you for your obedience to God. Obedience is very pleasing to the Most Holy Trinity. An obedient soul is blessed with many graces from heaven. God loves humility and obedience. Continue to walk in such obedience so that the hand of God, which is upon you, can raise you up to Him. Know that your obedience is a great protection for your soul. The devil cannot enter a soul who is walking in obedience to God and His authority on earth. (The Church, i.e., Father)

Pause. Then I saw Our Lady of Grace standing over the Globe of the earth. Tremendous rays of grace issued forth from her hands and poured upon the world much light. This was over in an instant. And she spoke: *I am present in the world today to prepare each soul for God's Presence to come. The soul who is open to me shall receive much grace now. Any who dispose their heart to me shall know me, because I shall present myself to them as their Mother and intercessor. I give my Maternal assistance to any soul that is open to receive. This is why I am present in the world today. These are critical times. I am preparing the way for Jesus. All should prepare to meet my Son. Blessed are they who "awaken now" and "prepare now," for the hour is almost at hand. Pray and sacrifice for the salvation of the world. I love you.*

Your Mother

6-21-95 Rosary with my spiritual director, my home
Prayer Has Incomprehensible Power

At the third or fourth Joyful Mystery, Father prayed that Our Lady please give "power" to our prayer so that our prayers would intercede for many. Our Lady became present and exposed her Immaculate Heart. She was very joyful at his prayer because that is precisely her desire. Filled with joy, she turned to Father and drew very close to him to bless him. She never ceased to smile upon him. Then I could not see her, but I heard her speak these words.

Thank you for your prayer. It is the same prayer of my heart. When you permit your prayer to come to me so that I can join in union with you, I can add much power to your prayer, because the Holy Spirit, who is my spouse, grants me the Grace to do so. Know that I protect you, my son and my daughter, from evil temptations which may tempt you to give up your prayer life. I have surrounded you with Angels and much protection which comes from my Maternal Heart. This I have done because I desire your prayer life to be a continuous offering and movement of love to God.

For years now, God has permitted me to come to earth. I have asked again and again for one thing in particular, and it is prayer, prayer from the heart. Only through prayer from the heart can the salvation of the world come about. Creation must cooperate with God to bring about its salvation. Prayer which is united to my Immaculate Heart has power which is incomprehensible. I am close to you now so that you can pray with me for all souls. I protect you so the devil does not tempt you to stop praying. Thank you for responding to my messages. Please trust in the Sacred and Immaculate Hearts. We are one Heart of Love. The peace of my Son, Jesus, be with you. Do not lose your peace because of things of the world. Through prayer you can always have peace. I love you and bless you today and always.

Your Mother

During the Chaplet of Divine Mercy, I saw Jesus carrying the Cross through the Via Dolorosa. His suffering is incomprehensible. He spoke, saying, ***Soul, meditate upon My Passion again, so that through My Passion we may be one. Peace.** Here I had a sense of great suffering to come (for myself and for the world). His passion puts suffering in its proper place. The Cross is Love. There is no easy way. Suffering is part of our journey. Our inheritance is so sublime, it requires it!

6-23-95 Feast of Sacred Heart of Jesus, Prayer Group Rosary
Behold the Heart That Loves You

The Most Sacred, Most Tender, Most Loving Heart of Jesus presented Himself and said: **My beloved ones,**

Receive My Heart. Behold the Heart that loves you. From this Heart issues forth My Love and Mercy for each of you. What more can be done to reveal My Love for you? Poured out completely for you, I did not withhold Myself from you. Yet, how many truly love this Heart, which burns with Love for all souls? My suffering is this: Those who profess they love Me but truly, they do not. Neither is their love pure or holy. Rather, it is self-centered, and it grieves Me.

Your love for Me, this night, is a consolation to My tender Heart. Tonight, from the shoreless ocean of My Heart, I bless you with a drop of My Blood upon your forehead. Making the Sign of the Cross, I mark you as Mine. You are My seed. My beloved ones, receive My Sacred Heart. Love Me with all your heart, your soul, your mind and with all your strength! Put none before Me. Permit Me to reign in your heart. Offer to Me continued reparation for the many offenses against My Sacred Heart of Love. Glorify the Father by loving this Heart of Mine, because in this way His Will is fulfilled.

Tonight My Joy is that you honor My Mother as I desire her to be honored. My Sacred Heart is one Heart with the Immaculate Heart. Each heart exists within the other heart. Therefore, when you listen to My Mother and you honor her through the Holy Rosary, My Heart is glorified and pleased. Show your

love for My Sacred Heart by loving one another as I have loved you. Care for one another as I have cared for you. Rejoice in Me as I rejoice in you, because each one of you has disposed your heart to Me. Thus, I have blessed you. I love you with Infinite Love from My Sacred Heart.

Your Jesus

After the Prayer Group meeting, at home I was drawn to enter into solitude and to be with Him alone. I was filled by His Majesty. His Love overpowered my soul. He began to speak: *Soul, My soul, Let Me ravish your heart for My own Heart. My domain, let Me take you to My Heart of Love. Lean on Me and come. Come to the Fire of My Love. (Here, I did not want to write anymore. His love was too intimate, but He said here: *Soul, do not be afraid to write My words of love for you. By recording My intimate love for you, souls shall see that indeed, I am an intimate Lover of souls. As I love you, I love each soul.) (So I continued to write.)

*Soul, you are My delight. I would not permit this glorious Feast Day of My Love to pass without taking you to the Heart that so loves you. See now, My beloved, all that I have is yours. In My Heart, I give you everything. My treasures are for you. My riches I bestow upon you. Beloved of My Sacred Heart, sup with Me now. Let Me feed you My fruit, which is Divine Love. Let us drink of heavenly wine. See, I have adorned your nakedness with My white cloak of holiness. I have perfumed you with heavenly roses. Your fragrance fills the heavenly courts. Our love is the sweetness filling the house of the Lord. *Soul, see the banquet I have provided for you.

O My beloved one, your heart is all aflame now. You are enkindled in your soul's Lover. Do not be afraid, My lamb. Your weakness is supported by My own arm. My arm presses you to My Heart. You are so little, My lamb, but Oh, how you love me! Your little heart is so pure, and it is all aflame with love for Me. Your heart exists now to sing the praises of your Triune God. *Soul, observe the Father at the head of the table. He smiles upon you. You are His little flower. Oh, how well the Holy Spirit has prepared you for this heavenly banquet. *Soul, you are consuming the love of the Most Holy Trinity, and the Most Holy Trinity is consuming you.

Here, I begged Jesus to permit me to stop writing His words. He said: **Prostrate yourself before Me and let us continue to love one another.** The Sacred Heart of Jesus is unutterable Love! The banquet is one of inexpressible Love and Joy. Jesus' own hand fed me understanding, that I may understand the Most Holy Trinity is Love, Love so powerful nothing can take it from us unless we so will. He feeds me understanding to know Him. And the more I know Him the more I love Him.

6-28-95 Rosary, my home with Father
A Cry from the Cross

At the Fifth Sorrowful Mystery, I saw Jesus hanging on the Cross at Calvary. From the Cross, He seemed to cry out from the depths of His Sacred Heart, addressing all His creation, from the beginning unto the end saying, **Look upon the One who loves you, hanging on a tree. Let Me love you. Oh My creation. Open your hearts to Me. I died for your salvation.** Here, I was overcome with sadness and I said, "My Lord and my God, You shouldn't have to beg us to love You!

Jesus said, ***Soul** (whispering my name), **I humble Myself that man would come to know Me, that man would love Me as I love all humanity. Creation is made for the delight and the glory of the Most Holy Trinity, who is Love. Love loves and desires love in return. Only through Love is the Father Glorified. I humble Myself again and again that man would follow My example of humility and obedience to the Father.**

Indeed, today I am shouting from the heavens to awaken My creation. Today I am giving mankind many signs of the times. My "shouts" are unlike the devils shouting. Satan is shouting loudly, and in the noise and the chaos he brings, man is confused and running nonstop in directions which lead to death ultimately. My shouts are a cry that comes within the soul, and in the silence of the soul is where I speak. It is from "within" that a corpse is "awakened" to "life" again.

At the foot of the Cross, I gave to all creation My Mother. Again, today, I give her to you. She is a sign of the times. She prepares the Way. She is the door to the new dawn. Blessed is the man who takes My Mother now, for she will prepare him for what is to come: The Day of the Lord. Pray for the salvation of mankind. Thank you, My son and My daughter, for praying together faithfully. I have thus spoken and blessed you with the oil of My Divine Love. Peace I give to you.

Your Jesus

P. S. Jesus said, "Peace I give to you" with such an abundance of love straight from His Heart, that I understood the fullness of this "gift" He gives our souls to be an extraordinary "gift" from Him. Prayer is absolutely necessary to dispose our souls for this gift of His Peace in our soul. It is foretaste of our inheritance.

6-30-95 Prayer Group Meeting
Jesus Is The Divine Bellwether

My dear ones,

It is the time of the unveiling of Bellwether. My Son, Jesus, is the Divine Bellwether. Now is the time that He be "held up" for all mankind to "behold." For man has forgotten the Lamb of God; He who intercedes to the Father for all souls; He who is ransom for all sin. He alone is the salvation of the world. I come from heaven to present, once again, the Lamb who takes away the sin of the world.

My little ones, thank you for responding to my call to prayer. I have called you each by name, into intercession, together with my Immaculate Heart, for the salvation of the world. As you have come to knowledge and love of my Son, I desire all souls come to knowledge and love of Jesus. There is a great battle for souls today. Please join in my army of little souls to bring souls back to God. Do not be afraid of what I ask of you, little ones. Have I not been your guide every step of the way? Am I not with you always and everywhere? There is nothing to fear, even amidst the confusion and sufferings of this age. God upholds His own and Love casts out fear.

Dear children, you cannot fathom the tribulation which is to come upon the world. My Son's Mystical Bride (the church) *shall pass a difficult trial. Both the good and the bad will suffer much. Build for me a holy place of refuge where souls can be sheltered in love. Carry the fullness of the love of the Lamb to many souls. Assist me in the gathering of souls for God. Unfathomable Mercy is being poured out from heaven. Teach souls to listen to the Holy Spirit within them. There can be Peace on Earth only when each soul has Peace within. There can be Love on Earth only when each soul has love within. God is glorified when you live the Gospel in ardent love of Him and one another. "Light" is given to the soul who turns to God in prayer.*

Embrace all my children as I have embraced you in my Immaculate Heart. Be little, my children. Unveil the Lamb so that all may behold and glorify the Savior of the world. I shall bring souls to your doorstep, and the scales will fall from their eyes. Please do not be afraid to say "yes" once again to God's Will for you. Trust that God Himself shall accomplish many conversions, and you need only to be His willing vessels. I shall guide you always. I bless you this night in the Name of the Most Holy Trinity. I have wrapped my mantle around you. I am joyful that you have responded to my Maternal love and guidance. Pray for the salvation of the world. Persevere, walking step by step with me. I, your Mother, love you very much.

7-1-95 Prayer Group
I, The Lamb, Bless You

My beloved ones,

My Heart is an abyss of Love for you. Longingly I await your "openness." I desire to be the living and tender Lover of your soul. The world has forsaken Me, but you have been faithful. Permit Me to go deeper inside of you. Give to Me your entirety and I shall hold nothing back from you. Rather, I shall feed My Love to you. My hand shall examine you, and every void shall be filled by My loving and living Presence. Oh My

little ones, do not deny Me the freedom to cover you in My Love. The world denies Me but you do not deny Me. Do not be afraid of what I seek from you. Give to Me your "yes" and I shall do the rest. Do not think that so small a group cannot save many souls through intercession. The Church began with twelve, and she exists two thousand years later and she will continue to exist. But she shall suffer a terrible apostasy; she will suffer a purification from within which shall affect the entire body. There are many who will seek shelter and direction.

I have prepared a remnant that shall withstand all persecution and chaos. These are people of prayer, of faith, and they shall remain My faithful Church. Like a fortress they will stand. These people are full of zeal for My House. The Truth is with them and in them. You are My people of prayer and faith. My Love shall fortify you to endure much for Me. Do not worry. Let Me love you and guide you, but be attentive to My Holy Spirit at every moment. Satan will tempt you in many subtle ways. In Me, in intimacy, you shall not be deceived. Be humble and obedient to My shepherd. In the midst of great darkness in the world, there shall be cenacles of great Light. And the Light shall overcome the darkness. Prepare your hearts to love as never before. First, I shall teach you of My intimate love for you. Then you shall teach others as I have taught you. Love will conquer and triumph. I, the Lamb who takes away the sin of the world, bless you with My Love and My Mercy. Prepare the Way.

Your Jesus

7-3-95 On Vacation with Family
Journal Entry

On vacation, I was being "tempted" by the devil that I had "made it" and could "relax," so to speak, "lighten up" and "enjoy life a little." This lasted a little while. Then His Majesty moved me to open St. Teresa's book (Interior Castle) to the part where she states that a soul who thinks she's "made it" has truly "not made it." I rebuked the temptation and prayed, and it was over.

7-6-95 10 PM, My room, on vacation
Teach Souls the Secret of Prayer

My beloved son and priest,

Having removed the scales from your eyes, I have given unto you My own vision, that you may see clearly My Grace and My Love in your soul, drawing you into the intimate chambers of My tender and Merciful Heart. Our hearts are together , beating as one united heart, crying out to the Father the priestly prayer, crying "Abba." Let all hearts be one union of love in the image of the Most Holy Trinity.

Beloved priest of My Sacred Heart, let us continue to intercede to the Father on behalf of the conversion of the world and the restoration of the Church. Within you is a holy city, which is my dwelling place, and I find refuge within. Your heart is My home, where I can open the floodgates of My Divine Love and pour Myself into your open and responsive heart. Keep your eyes open to observe the interior movements of the Spirit in your soul and in the souls of those who surround you. Keep your eyes open to observe the exterior signs and graces given unto this age in preparation for the conversion of the world.

Beloved priest, I have brought to your doorstep a mission to prepare the way for the day of My coming. Your own prayer from the heart, together with your sacrifice for My Church, is a great intercession on behalf of all souls. However, there is more I seek from you. Teach souls to pray, so their hearts can be prepared for My coming. Teach souls the Secret of Prayer, so this heart of Mine can pour itself into one holy city after another. Only when I can exist inside each heart will the priestly prayer for unity and love be fulfilled. The restoration of My Church, the Bride whom we love, shall come to pass, in the manner of one heart after another, being transfigured into My image.

You are an interior man and a holy temple. Assist me to form more interior men and more holy temples. Transformation must take place within the hearts of people. Observe and ponder all that is unfolding around you. It should then become evident to you that I am raising an army of prayer warriors, to combat evil, to restore My Church, to bring hope to the world through zeal and love for God. Your assistance now alleviates the sorrow of the United Sacred and Immaculate Hearts, made to observe the absence of love and peace in the hearts of mankind. The Father is grieved by the state of souls, and offended at every moment by the atrocities of man's way of power, greed, and hatred. Yet, through the intercession of the Blessed Virgin Mary, there is an army of prayerful, humble and obedient souls who are alleviating the Father's grief, interceding for souls and preparing the way for the day when the Father will no longer grieve for His people, but rather rejoice in them, for they shall become a holy people to the Honor and Glory of the Most Holy Trinity.

My Sacred Heart of Love loves you and abides in you. The Light of the Holy Spirit shines upon you and within you. The Hand of the Father upholds you and blesses you. The Immaculate Heart of the Blessed Virgin Mary comforts and protects you in her love. My Peace I give to you. Rest in Me.

Your Jesus

7-7-95 On Vacation
A Litany of Trust

Many temptations regarding the cost of discipleship. As I tried to sleep, it was as if the weight of many crosses in my life was being pressed down physically upon my chest. Interiorly as well, I felt very "oppressed." I can discern the devil's presence because my soul senses him trying to "crush" it to pieces. Jesus never crushes a soul, but the devil delights in crushing souls.

For a long while I experienced the devil trying to oppress me and crush my soul. The suffering was indescribable. It seemed my soul had been torn to pieces under the weight of the Cross. I was in such agony that I began to think that I could not carry these crosses. Then Jesus' Presence came, as if He was standing right in front of Me. He didn't speak. He only gazed into my eyes. We only had to look at one another, and the love was so powerful that it penetrated my soul. It fortified my soul with such power that I knew that I would carry these crosses, and many more, with the very power given to me from His Heart of Love.

I was given to know that Jesus would indeed permit the devil to test me but that he would never permit the devil to crush my soul. All during the night I suffered the "tests" by the devil who constantly tried to oppress my soul. As each trial began, I had to say these words with all the courage and love that I could muster, "Jesus, I trust in You." I repeated these words as if I was praying a litany of "trust" to my beloved Jesus. After approximately four hours of this testing and praying, I was permitted to rest and fell asleep.

7-11-95
True Presence

At Communion, Jesus said: **My True Presence in the Eucharist is little appreciated in this age. I am grieved that few believe in My True Presence in the bread and the wine, which is My Flesh and My Blood, given unto you for life in Me. I am revealing many miracles of the Eucharist in this age to confirm again My True Presence in the Eucharist. Oh how little faith is left among you. Oh generation of doubt and unbelief! I am grieved when you approach My altar in disbelief, in lukewarm states, in sinful states, without preparation or reverence. Awaken, O generation of little faith and cease to offend your God. My Flesh and My Blood are Sacred gifts for you. Approach My altar and receive Me in the state of Grace, or you are once again crucifying My Body!**

7-11-95 Vacation 8:30 AM Mass
A Birthing Again

In contemplation before the tabernacle, I was given the following "vision" (intellectually). I saw the Nativity scene. However, inside the manger was the globe of the earth. Mary and St. Joseph knelt right beside the manger (crib), bending down as close to the "earth" as possible. The infant Jesus was in the crib and held the earth which rested on His abdomen. The light from Jesus was concentrated upon the earth/globe. Mary and St. Joseph were filled with light. Their light was also concentrated upon the earth. I observed but did not understand, until Mary said: *My child, I am once again giving birth to Jesus in the hearts of men.* Throughout the day I was given "light" or illumination regarding this vision as I pondered it in my heart. I knew it contained a rich message and I contemplated to discover the message within the vision. The following are the "lights" given me in contemplation throughout the day and including the next day.

1.) Mary is once again "birthing" Jesus in the hearts of His people. Just as she was the instrument of His birth two thousand years ago, she is again today the vessel bringing Jesus to the world again. She births Him in the intimacy of the heart and soul of each man through conversion, one by one, through her visitations around the world, her messages, and the grace she is obtaining from heaven. Consecration to her Immaculate Heart is very vital now. Souls consecrated to her become her "army" of prayer warriors. These souls obtain many graces through her Immaculate Heart, and they are very powerful intercessors for the salvation of the world. Consecration is very important.

2.) St. Joseph is a very vital intercessor for the Church and for all the world. St. Joseph is extremely important for this age and for the preparation of the hearts of men for "the day of the Lord." Joseph is the great Patriarch of the Church. He obtains many graces for the Church and souls devoted to him. He is very much involved in assisting Mary and Jesus.

3.) In the vision, Jesus is the "infant" Jesus, signifying His humility, obedience, and humanity. He approaches us in this "little" way - as an infant desiring to be held inside the hearts of His people. His "infancy" signifies that He does not want us to be afraid of Him, nor does He want us to fear being small and vulnerable, as He has permitted Himself to be for love of us.

4.) The Light in the vision, concentrated upon the earth, signifies the Holy Spirit who is being poured upon the earth to illuminate soul after soul. The Holy Spirit will bring about the illumination of the entire earth and drive out the darkness.

5.) The earth in the crib or manger signifies the "birth" of the earth into a new era. Just as the birth of Jesus two thousand years ago caused a new era, we will also experience a passage into another era, and enter a covenant of peace on earth - a reconciliation of man with God.

7-14-95 Regarding trial of 7-7-95
St. Michael!

During the night of "trial" when God permitted the devil to "try" my soul, when I reached the point of feeling "crushed" by the weight of the Cross, before I began the litany of Trust (Jesus, I trust in You), I prayed to St. Michael the Archangel. I prayed to St. Michael as I have never prayed to him before. My need of him was great. As I prayed the prayer of St. Michael, I experienced such a presence of Michael in the room with me that I became very aware of with his presence. His presence is distinctive. He has a warrior's presence of authority. There is a "power" that accompanies him which is like a warrior's power. It is evident He comes prepared to battle. There is nothing timid about St. Michael. He is an "enforcer" with God's authority to "enforce." The evil spirits that tried my soul dared not remain in the presence of St. Michael. He is our protector indeed. He is swift. He comes quickly when it is required of him. His presence accomplishes the task and swiftly he flees, when his mission has been accomplished. Praise be to God for St. Michael.

7-12-95 Rosary with Father, my home
My Maternal Heart Is Pierced by the Atrocities of Sin

At the onset of the Rosary, I began to see myself being nailed to the Cross. Then suddenly, once I was raised up on the cross, a sword was plunged into my heart. Repeatedly the sword pierced my heart. My physical heart began to hurt. It felt engorged like a muscle that is enlarged from over-use. I was given an illumination to know that the heart that was pierced was Our Lady's Maternal Heart of Love. I was given to experience her pain. She did not speak at the time, but, twenty four hours later, she spoke the following words as I prayed before the Tabernacle at Church.

My beloved child and daughter,

Your consecration to my Immaculate Heart means that you have been drawn into existence (life) *within my Maternal heart, which is today pierced again by the atrocities of sin which continually wound Jesus, offend the Father, and grieve the Holy Spirit. Having given to me your heart, I have given to you my heart. Each sword plunged into your heart represents my pain and my suffering due to abortion; immorality and impurity; hatred and violence; pride, arrogance, greed; the demise of the family; the perversion of society; apostasy and division; the infiltration of rebels in the Church, the Mystical Body of Jesus. The swords which pierced your heart are all of these, assailing my Maternal Heart now.*

Dear soul consecrated to my heart, suffer with me now and offer with me, yourself, in totality. Be a living sacrifice upon the altar for the conversion of sinners; for the restoration of the Church; for the Triumph of my Maternal Heart which shall bring forth the birth of a new era of Peace; the reign of God on earth. My little child, my tears are watering the earth now. They fall like dew, bringing forth springs of living water (Holy Spirit) upon parched wasteland. Everywhere there are little signs of life breaking through the death, signs of light breaking through the darkness. Mercy is like a fountain overflowing upon the earth, yet also the cup of Justice is overflowing, and already coming upon the earth in this time.

Little child, my tears do not cease to flow for all the suffering and pain I observe in the hearts of God's children. Because so many have forsaken God, the stench of decaying corpses fills the atmosphere. This is the offering arising to heaven now, instead of the sweet fragrance of pure love for God. My little ones, I long to help you but many will not permit me to help. Your self-sufficiency, then, shall lead you along the dark and dangerous path. Little ones, now is the time to yield to God and give to God what is His. You belong to God.

Little one, because you exist inside my heart, through consecration to my heart, I grant to you many blessings and graces, which God ordains for His Eternal Glory. Therefore, be prepared always to answer the call to be a living sacrifice, whose fragrance is pure love of God, with willingness to hand over your life for the good of souls. I have said that my tears do not cease now, but I have joy in my heart through those who have consecrated them-

selves to my heart. These avail themselves to me and permit me to guide them to the heart of Our Redeemer, who then presents them to the Father. These souls are simple, poor and humble. Yet in their extreme poverty they have given me the freedom to guide them, protect them, and love them. These are a holy army whose very power is the power of God's Love in their soul. Child, pray with me always so that my army of little souls will gather more souls for God through the power of prayer. Thank you, my daughter, for your faithfulness and service to my Immaculate Heart.

Pause. *Now please continue to write my words.*

Please tell my son and my priest that he, too, exists in my Maternal heart, for I have plucked him from the many, from the world, and taken him to the abode of my Maternal heart, where I have nurtured him with the food of heavenly grace from the storehouse of grace, because The Father chose him from the beginning to be rich with Divine Love; full of His Wisdom; one with the Word; illuminated with the Holy Spirit, to prepare the way for the reign of God, which is at hand.

Please tell him, because he opened his heart to me, because he is my advocate, I have given to him "vision" which is my own, so that he recognize the signs of the times, so that his lamp will be full of oil for the day of the Lord, so he can prepare the flock, that their lamps are found to be full of oil. For the day is soon to arrive when all will be tried in darkness which purifies, bringing forth the Light which will illumine the world again. Preparations are underway so that I shall again present to the world the Word, my Son, Christ the King and He shall be born into each and every heart who lives. The Kingdom of the Divine will shall descend upon the earth!

Listen to your Mother, my son and my daughter. Be still and listen. I am with you and I bless you in the Name of the Most Holy Trinity. You bring me joy because you permit me to help you and you strive to live my messages. I know your struggles and temptations. Heaven's way is very contrary to the ways of the world, but God's way is eternal and you are to exist in the Way and the Life of God, who has revived you and chosen you for His Eternal Glory, in the fulfillment of His Divine Will in your soul. You are no longer of the world, my little son and daughter, you are living a new life.

Trust completely the One who gives you new life in Him. He is Love. Peace of my Son, Jesus, be yours. I love you.
   Your Mother

7-19-95 Rosary, my home
Our Lady Takes Us Through the Joyful Mysteries

   As Father led the meditations of the five Joyful Mysteries, Our Lady began to "present" the following scenes. All this takes place in a very "deep" place in my soul and does not involve my senses. Again, I see or hear nothing. It is a "knowledge imprinted deep within my soul, that gives me to know and receive the "communication" from Our Lady or Lord, whoever it may be. This "knowledge" or "scenes" given me are much different from knowledge I would receive from reading or being taught by an exterior teacher. It seems to be a completely different place of knowledge that is superior, deeper, instant, embedding itself in my soul, sometimes at such a deep level, that I think I am not given to recall all of it, at least until the time comes when it is necessary to recall the information/knowledge. Peace accompanies it, and increased love and knowledge of God accompanies it. Understanding of the scene may or may not be given to me at that particular time. Lately I see the scene and in the next twenty four hours or so I am given an understanding of it.

1.) At the "Annunciation,"
   Our Lady presented a rushing river, practically overflowing the banks. Father and I were standing on the bank with Our Lady. She offered us to drink of the water, to drink to the full. The river represented the Holy Spirit and the graces available to us if we but drink of them. The river was endless; it is flowing all over the world. Those who are "awake" will drink of it and live!

2.) The Visitation:
   Our Lady presented a human heart with chains all around it. The heart was closed. The chains bound it. Our Lady appeared to

be present to assist the heart to open and to undo the chains, but the human heart was hard and would not permit her to assist it. Our Mother was very sorrowful.

3.) The Nativity:

I saw a human heart again. Inside was baby Jesus. This human heart had allowed her to birth Jesus inside of the heart and now Jesus lived in that heart. Our Mother was joyful.

4.) The Presentation:

Our Lady presented the Sacred Heart of Jesus. My soul felt faint to observe the Heart of my Redeemer. Our Lady took hold of Father's hand, and then mine, and she led us to a ladder leading down into the deepest chambers of this Sacred Heart of Love. She was very joyfully guiding us. She moved swiftly. There was no end to the ladder. The depth of His Sacred Heart is infinite.

5.) Finding Jesus in the Temple:

Our Lady again presented a human heart bound by chains, and suffering very much, because it was closed to Divine Love and to Our Lady. Then she showed me two hearts - mine and Father's. They were surrounded by the Rosary. They were soft and supple and docile, receptive to Divine Love and to Our Lady. She said with much love and joy: *Thank you, my little son and daughter for your heart and for your prayers. I love you.*
Your Mother

7-21-95 My home, Sorrowful Mysteries
Suffering the Sorrowful Mysteries

For two hours (1-3 PM Friday) I began to experience the interior sufferings of the passion of Jesus. As soon as I began the meditation of the Agony in the Garden, I experienced a sense of my "insides" boiling. My body shook interiorly, as if each individual cell was brought to the boiling point. The Holy Spirit gave me to pray the most fluent and sublime prayers to my Savior in the Garden. I am writing after the fact, so I cannot recall all the sublime prayers my soul uttered in union, because I believe I had slipped into another state of being as I became absorbed more and more into each scene of the passion. What I can recall I shall record for my Spiritual Director so he can discern what is happening in my soul. I found myself praying like this (without a doubt, the Holy Spirit led me in prayer to glorify Jesus) even as I somehow experienced a portion of each of the Sorrowful Mysteries:

1.) The Garden of Gethsemane: The Agony

My Sacred Heart, my Holy Savior, now I am in the garden with You. O night of nights! Inside of me is fire and agony. Loneliness besets me. I see now all that is about to take place. The hour of darkness has descended. The hour of man's betrayal has arrived. I feel your agony, Jesus. Your body and mine are as one now. I am shaking. I am sweating. I am writhing in pain both spiritual and physical. My days are up now. It is time that my body be given over as ransom for all souls, in fulfillment of the Scripture, for the salvation of the world. The blood vessels beneath my skin are bursting from the pressure within, and blood is seeping from my pores. My hearing fades in and out. My vision is blurred; my eyes ache with pressure and pain. My heart beats so fast it resounds throughout my body. The night grows darker. My agony progresses. I cry out to the Father. My breathing is labored. My mouth dry. Father, take this cup from me - still not my will but Yours be done! The sin of the world is upon me.

I prayed:
"Yes, Lord, always the Father's Will. Beloved Jesus in my soul, Your agony is incomprehensible! I taste of its bitterness now. Love and gratitude fill me for what You suffered on my account. O Sweet and Innocent Victim for my sins!

O tender Lover of my soul, You give to me a taste of Your hours in the Garden in the Mount of Olives, O Holy Ground!

You press me deep into Your heart and reveal to me Your Agony. I suffer with You, yet union with You is my joy. My heart breaks for love of You, that You are made to suffer for me and for all.

My beloved Savior, cause me to endure this moment, then, because Your Love in my soul is my only strength. Pure love casts out fear.

Love triumphs over all suffering. Suffering with you saves souls.

You, the innocent Lamb led to the slaughter in silence, in humility, in obedience, in purity, in submission to the Father's Will, in love, are the eternal Victor and King forever and ever. Amen"

2.) The Scourging:

I began to shake again both interiorly and externally. The whip strikes. The metal carves rivers into my flesh. I am paralyzed with pain. The whip strikes again and again. I am barely conscious now. I cannot focus my eyes. My hearing fades in and out. I stand in a pool of my own blood. My mouth is parched. I taste only my own sweat. The whips strike again.

I prayed:

"O my Beloved Savior, what a dark moment for man, imparting man's "justice" upon our God! What contradiction! We give You a scourging and You give us Your Love.

What humility! What compassion! I cannot fathom the breadth of Your Love, Your Majesty, Your dignity, Your sacrifice.

Purest Lamb of God, in silence, You endure.

We, Your creatures cannot comprehend You. We cannot take in such love as You.

You are lofty, too sublime. We are base, lowly.

Jesus, come into Your creation again and live in our hearts, causing us to love You, to honor You and glorify You. In loving You we shall then be able to love one another.

Thank you for being vulnerable to show us that we are little son and daughters of the Glorious Father, whose providence shall cover and care for us if only we permit it, becoming vulnerable as You did."

3.) The Crowning of Thorns.

I am mocked and ridiculed. My head is pierced by one sharp point after another. My eyes are blinded by my own blood. My tongue tastes blood and sweat. Each wound pierces deep into my head. The pain is inestimable. Once again, I am barely conscious.

I prayed:

"O my Beloved King, Your crown now is a mockery. It pierces Your most perfect head. Your precious blood flows from each puncture. Jesus, I love You.

Thank you, Savior. Your crown will soon be transformed into the Eternal Crown of Glory, but for now You wear the crown of our disordered actions toward our King Eternal. Thank you, my Beloved Redeemer, for permitting me a portion of Your Crown of Thorns. Your gift to my soul is too sublime for expression."

4.) Carrying the Cross:

Weakness possesses me. All my senses are failing me. My breathing is labored. My muscles are in knots, hardened with fatigue and pain. Profuse sweat overcomes me. My eyes are blurred by the sweat. I fall. I get up. I fall again. I get up again. Assistance is given me, and I progress toward my death, amidst a crowd of angry, mocking and cheering people.

I prayed:

"Abba, I turn to You now. You so loved us, Your lowly creatures, You gave to us Your only begotten Son, that through Him we would know You and love You as You have loved us. Now You observe this atrocity of crucifixion carried out. Because You are in Him, You too, suffer this passion.

O my Triune and Holy God - what Love! He was with us and we knew Him not.

Father, today also we have Your Holy Spirit with us, yet we fail to know You and we fail to love You. Father, open up the heavens and send down the reign of God. Send us again the Lamb in all His Glory. Grant us the grace now to "know" and to "love" He who is with us. Father, Thy Kingdom come on earth as in heaven; Your Will be done."

5.) Death on the Cross:

Nails pierce my hands and feet. I am now affixed to the wood. I am raised up and hang between heaven and earth. I am the bridge connecting them now. My being (physical) is spent. I look one last time with my eyes, at the crowd gathered around me. My eyes fix on my beloved Mother. She, too, is dying with me. I look to John, my beloved apostle. He suffers with me. I beseech the Father's forgiveness upon my executioners. I am full of love and mercy for each one. These last few minutes of my earthly life are most excruciating. I am one open bleeding wound. My body writhes in pain as each internal organ ceases to function. My lungs cannot expand. My breath is gone. My heartbeat ceases. I expire into the hands of my loving Father. Love has conquered everything from the beginning to the end. It is finished.

I prayed:

"Jesus, I am dying with You now. I must die so that You live in me - glorified. Beloved Savior of my soul, I am with You in death and in life. I suffer with You, all for You, my King. My will is Yours completely. Search me, try me. You'll find no resistance. I am "dying" for pure love of You! Have mercy on me, a sinner who crucified You. Yet, You have taught me to accept and trust in Your unfathomable mercy. I am all burned up in Your Divine Love now. I am a sacrifice for You, a lowly offering indeed. I love You boundlessly, my beloved Savior and God Eternal."

Note: It took two hours to complete the Five Sorrowful Mysteries going through this passion. The first three decades had a greater intensity of my actually experiencing what Jesus experienced. The Garden of Gethsemane was the most intense, then the Scourging and the Crowning of Thorns. Each decade seemed a little less intense, perhaps because the first decade, the Agony, took so much out of me, both physically and spiritually. Also, I am weak from surgery four days ago. I am not on any pain medication. My expression of this experience is so lacking that I have a strong distaste of it. The words are so far from the reality of it. I cannot express the fluent and sublime prayers that the Holy Spirit led me to say to Jesus and the Father, but they flowed like a dam that burst with power, full of light and love. I was acted upon by the Father who willed it; Jesus then transfigured me into Him; then the Holy Spirit led my soul to exalt and glorify the Most Holy Trinity. It is like comparing a picture of the sun to the actual sun. The picture is flat, lifeless, and it cannot capture the life, the radiance, the brilliance, the dazzling color of the actual sun. I suffer to express such grace in my soul, but out of obedience and for the discernment of my spiritual director I continue to write. Upon completion of this grace, I resumed my normal state of being. Peace, Joy, and Love filled my soul. I am weak from surgery but my heart is strong with love for my Most Holy and Loving Triune God. My Abba, my Jesus, my Holy Spirit, together with Our Lady, my soul exalts You. I love You boundlessly, and gratitude overcomes me for what You have done for me, a sinner.

Note: Our Lady often remains in the background but she never ceases to prepare and enable my soul to receive the graces of the interior life which God has ordained for me.

Fruit of such prayer:
Love increases. Faith increases. Knowledge increases. Peace, Joy, Hope, and Courage fill the soul. The soul "knows" it is loved! Gratitude increases! There is little doubt in this particular case because clearly I am "acted upon" by God. It is very interior, though I believe there are physical manifestations as well, because I seemed to go through physical shaking, sweating, labored breathing, my heart rate would increase or decrease at different times. These seem violent interiorly, but exteriorly they are subtle. There is pain involved, indeed, yet at the same time it is as if the soul is being caressed by God to compensate for the pain or suffering. All honor and glory and praise be to my Triune God for His mercy and love in my soul.

7-25-95 My home, 12:30 AM
Gospa

While trying to sleep, I heard both interiorly and exteriorly the name "Gospa, Gospa, Gospa." Interiorly I sensed Our Lady calling me. Exteriorly, I sensed Angels saying Gospa, Gospa, Gospa, reverently, almost singing the name. This took place for almost ten minutes. To be honest, I was touched, but also I wanted to sleep so I turned over in bed, almost dismissing the call. The more resistant I was, the stronger the call became. I got up and went to my prayer chair. Mary's presence was electrifying! After sitting in her presence for probably fifteen minutes, feeling electrified, she began to speak and I began to write.

Dear children,
As you prepare the distribution of "Gospa," my Maternal hand is guiding you and blessing your efforts. I go before you to open hearts and open doors according to the Will of God. Be assured then, you are walking in God's Divine Will. It is the Father who ordained my visitation to the little village of Medjugorje. It is the Father who ordained this project to spread further the message of Medjugorje, which is a universal call to conversion. Man must be reconciled with God, turning from his self-sufficient pride to acknowledgment and dependence upon the Father, whose Divine Providence is over all people.
As Gospa, I am reconciler of all God's children. The graces of Medjugorje are universal graces, transcending man's ways and calling forth a response from the hearts of God's children, to love, once and for all. These graces have reached the far ends of the earth. This project is carried by the wind of the Holy Spirit. The Holy Spirit inspired it and the Holy Spirit has carried it thus far. It shall continually be graced by the Holy Spirit. By means of this movie, the message of Medjugorje shall enter many hearts. These hearts shall receive the graces of conversion, reconciliation and healing. Many beloved priests shall be "awakened" to the call for repentance, conversion, and prayer.
My beloved priest, Father Jozo, continues to be God's instrument of love and mercy for the world. Know, dear little ones, as

you labor toward the distribution of this blessed project that I, who am your Mother, truly bless you and your loved ones for your sacrifice and obedience. All who have labored in this project from the onset to the completion have responded to my call. Therefore, abundant graces from my maternal Heart are yours. The task at hand is extremely important for your country. America will benefit greatly as it beholds the heroism of a holy priest and the example of true faith in God set forth by the people of the village who responded to "the call," in spite of great hardship.

I, who am the Gospa, Mother of All, Reconciler of all people, call forth a continuous plea from heaven, imploring that mankind today turn from its present disordered course, heading away from God, towards God's intended course, back to Him by means of Peace and Love in the hearts of all people. The Holy Spirit is actively calling people back to God. One of the many ways He is doing this is through the project to which you find yourselves dedicated. Your efforts shall be fruitful because they are born of God's Will, not yours. Persevere, carrying out your task diligently. Much is at stake! Do not worry! Trust! I am your Mother and I am truly with you always! I bless you in the name of the Father, the Son, and the Holy Spirit. I love you.

Your Mother "Gospa"

7-26-95 My home, Rosary with Father
Be Vigilant Always and Everywhere

My little son and daughter,

As you have gathered again today to pray with me, I have blessed you as you offer to me your prayers and your love. I who am your Mother have called you together, that you would fulfill a mission together which has been ordained by the Father. All is unfolding according to God's Will. Remain faithful to the call, faithful to prayer, awake to the movement of grace in your soul.

I surround you, my little son and daughter, with much heavenly protection. You have many Angels and Saints who are protecting and interceding for you now. The devil encamps around you. At any given moment he would delight in causing you to be distracted from God's Will. Be vigilant always and everywhere. If he cannot distract you directly, he will attempt to do so through those around you. I warn you of this because he is furious with your obedience and your faithfulness. He observes the Peace and Grace that is with you. I shall always provide protection, but you must always be aware that the spirits of darkness are constantly attempting to thwart my Peace Plan and divert a soul from God's Will. You shall observe the escalation of both good and evil now. All shall unfold rapidly now. You cannot comprehend the importance of the time you are living. Remain close to me. Cling to Jesus as you observe more pain and suffering in the world. In contrast to the pain and suffering, you shall also observe the great Light of the Holy Spirit diffusing the darkness. This is a special grace given to you by God. Many of His faithful will undergo a purification, in which they will not see the Light diffusing the darkness.

My dear little son and daughter, I have knit you together for God's greater glory, for the fulfillment of a mission which is unfolding now, for the good of souls, including your own. Always uphold one another in prayer because then you protect and aid one another to remain faithful in your response to God's call. You are living in close union with the Most Holy Trinity in your soul. Continually, you are being drawn into deeper union with Our Triune God. This is a very special grace, in preparation for all that is to come. Rejoice, my little ones! You have been chosen by God today, tomorrow and from the beginning, to live in union with Him, to fulfill His Divine Will in your soul in and through your response to His call on your lives, a call for the good of many souls.

Trust. Your prayers are powerful. Live in my Maternal Heart. Draw everything from within my Heart of Love. Through your consecration and fiat to my Maternal Heart, I am able to intercede on behalf of all your needs and petitions. Though you have responded, do not be deceived to think many souls have responded. The truth is that many souls have refused to respond to God's Grace and my Maternal intercession. These souls are in grave danger! This is the time of great spiritual warfare! Truly, many souls are tormented, with no peace of soul, and no love within. The Grace in your soul is God's abundant gift to you. Therefore, to Him offer unceasing gratitude; unselfish sacrifice; continuous abandonment and all your capacity to Love! He alone is your Peace. I who am your Mother remain close to you to enable you to do God's Will. I am joyful to assist you. I love you.

Your Mother

Note: Our Lady's disposition was very strong, especially when warning us about the devil. He truly seeks to thwart her Peace Plan.

7-28-95 Prayer Group Rosary
Cenacles Are Satan's Special Targets

My dear little children,

As you have gathered together this night to give to God your love and prayers, I who am your Mother, join in union with you. Dear little children, you have been so very blessed by the Most Holy Trinity, who bestows His abundant Graces among you. Rejoice together that God has chosen you for Himself and thus raised you to be His holy little ones. Tonight I remind you not only of His Grace in your midst, but also of the importance of your remaining very "little." Spiritual poverty is not only pleasing, but necessary before God. You are like little beggars with hands outstretched to God. Acknowledge your extreme poverty before God because without Him you can do nothing.

I come to inform you tonight, you shall witness much, unfolding rapidly. Darkness is widespread, but also the Light is widespread to combat the darkness. Now is the time of great spiritual warfare on earth. Satan encamps around you constantly. If he cannot disturb you personally, he will do so through people around you, causing you to lose your peace. Pray often to St. Michael. Be on guard if someone or something is causing you to lose your Peace of Soul. I surround you with much protection from heaven. Saints and Angels are interceding for each one of you. As a prayer group, you should continue to uphold one another in prayer and support always. Daily commit yourself to prayer on behalf of your cenacle. Cenacles are Satan's special targets.

Much has been given to you, my little ones. Much shall be asked of you. Each shall continue to be tried in fire that purifies, transforms, and beautifies. Each of you is suffering in your own special way. Be means of this suffering, you are formed by the hand of God into His image. Give to God your complete abandonment. Live each day in a true spirit of sacrifice. Your sacrifice and prayers are very powerful toward the salvation of souls. Do not worry, my little children. Worry is useless. Pray and trust; then you will find yourselves passing through great trials in much peace; with much patience and endurance. Only in these virtues will you be able to fulfill the tasks God has set before you. Offer yourselves to His service daily, thus, He can use you daily as His instruments of love and charity.

My little ones, these are critical times and much shall be required of God's faithful. As you observe the great darkness and pass through much suffering on earth, know that the Holy Spirit is with you. He is bringing forth the Will of God to purify the earth, preparing the way for Peace on Earth. Love shall enter the hearts of God's people and they shall be knit into one holy, united remnant of faithful souls, to His Honor and Glory forever. Peace of my Son, Jesus, be with you tonight and always. Thank you for responding to my call. I love you!

Your Mother

8-2-95 Rosary with Father, my home
Purification and Transformation are Underway

Joyful Mysteries

1.) Annunciation:
The Holy Spirit overshadows Mary and she utters "Fiat." I saw myself, Father and a few other people (I did not recognize) hidden in the cleft of a huge rock. The Holy Spirit, in the form of a most strikingly beautiful dove, descended upon the cleft in the rock and gathered us under His wing. He wing sheltered us completely. He carried us up, up into the heights of the sky. He soared and we were with Him. Only when we give our "fiat" can the Holy Spirit cause us to soar.

2.) Visitation:

Our Lady held a bottle of perfume before me. She took the cap off the bottle and a cloud of fragrant smoke or incense rose above the bottle and up toward heaven. She said, *"When you pray the rosary, each and every time you pray the holy rosary with much love in your heart, you are like the bottle of perfume. I open you up to permit the beautiful fragrance that is within you to be offered up to God as an offering of Love, pure incense, pure precious Love!*

3.) Nativity:

If we permit, Mary will "birth" Jesus in our hearts daily and always.

Our Lady said: (as if teaching me with great Maternal concern, patience, joy and love.)

Your heart is the pulsating center of life for your body. When you sense your heart "full" in prayer, know that Grace has acted upon you, in your vital, life-giving center. Your heart is expanding, your capacity to love is growing; then I am depositing into your heart my Maternal love and the Graces of the Holy Spirit. It may be physically painful at times because I desire to deposit so much, to expand your heart to the full, that you grow and grow. In this manner, you permit me to "birth" Jesus within you.

4.) Presentation: (Mary is always presenting Jesus)

Father prayed regarding Mary presenting Jesus in the Temple. Our Lady responded:

Just as I presented Jesus in the Temple, giving unto the world my Son, so it has been given to me to present the world back to God. When I hold the world in my arms and present God's creation back to Him, I must present a transformed creation, a worthy creation. I cannot give to God the world as it is now. It is too offensive to behold. It is not a fitting offering. I am in the world now to prepare the way for the complete transformation of creation. The entire world shall be made worthy, beautiful, holy and good. Creation will reflect its Almighty and Perfect Creator. This purification and transformation is underway now. Through your love, your sacrifice, your obedience, your humility, you can assist in this transformation. Then, united in my heart, you can present with me, all of God's creation, rightfully His, completely restored by Love into the beauty and Majesty that it is meant to be.

5.) Finding Jesus in the Temple:
(The work of The Father should always be our priority!)
Our Lady awaited Father's meditation (she really listens!) and then she responded.

I found Jesus in the temple after much searching. Jesus is, to-day, searching in His temples (people, souls). *He finds only a great void, an emptiness within. He searches the souls of His people. He is met with rejection. He is denied. His temples are empty. He knocks, but He is not admitted. He is no longer recognized. His people have forgotten His voice. He is present, but not recognized. Hearts are hardened. Sin is alive in His temples. He cannot enter because sin holds His people captive. Some are so content in the dark they see no need of the Light. Some are struggling and confused, and these do not recognize "The God" who knocks at their door.*

Soon the Hand of the Father shall again send the Son in all His Glory to open wide the temples, to lay bare all that is within. Then, once and for all, sin will vanish from the hearts of His people. Love will enter. New life shall begin upon earth. The reign of God shall come after the consequences of man's choices are experienced by all of creation. Man's rejection of God has brought about his (man's) *immense suffering. My children, God is greatly offended today! Pray with me that man will cease to offend His Creator. When God searches you, His temple, let Him find "Love." I love you.*

Your Mother

8-3-95 11:30 PM My Home
Prepare America!

Jesus said: **Dear child, please write.**

America, you are wounded and bleeding because you are like a harlot, selling your heart and soul for the sake of pride,

power, and greed. In the name of freedom and progress, in pretense, you spread your errors, offering poison to be exported throughout the world.

Prepare, America. The very poison you seek to propound to the world shall return to your soil. You shall continue to bleed. Your wounds will heal only when you return to a nation under God, willing to keep My law and acknowledge My authority over this once great nation. That which you take most pride in will be taken from you. What then, My beloved country, when one idol after another fails you and you stand empty-handed, having sold your heart and soul to godless passions of self-interest? What then, land of plenty, when you find what is plentiful to be violence, hatred and poverty? The harlot finds no peace, no love, only false comfort, fleeting in a moment's time. In the din of her existence, there is only restlessness, perversion, sickness. Repent. Convert. Pray. Love.

The prayers of your poor, your forgotten and little ones, together with the prayers and sacrifice of your forefathers, have purchased for you My patience and mercy for today. Repent. Convert. Pray. Love.

Your Jesus

7-17-96 Rosary with Spiritual Director, my home, 5 PM
The Empty House

The first image I saw was a house. The house looked beautiful from the outside. Seemingly then, Jesus took me inside the house. The inside of the house had been pillaged. I observe with Jesus a "nothingness," a profound "emptiness." That was all that was left inside the house. I experienced a "chill," a "coldness" remaining in the emptiness. Jesus' heart was pierced with pain, even agony, over the way this house has been ravaged. He suffers this. I suffered this. I asked Jesus, "Is this Your house, Your Church?" He said: **Dear child, this is My creation. This is the state of many men.** I understood that each human being is his house. Then Jesus spoke.

My creation,

The love of the Most Holy Trinity created you for love, for beauty, goodness and life abundant. But the spirit of the world has ravaged you, leaving behind empty shells, houses that have been gutted. You know not the dignity of your being. You are My creation, each a house created for Me, to be a reflection of My own Beauty, Goodness and Life, full of every virtue, adorned in Love and Holiness. Instead, the spirit of the world has entered in the night, caught you unprepared and asleep, and took from you the beautiful and good things I had placed within you, robbing you of true life and true love. And in the night, because you slept without Light, without awareness, you gave up so easily all that was rich and everlasting. You awakened, hardly noticing that your everlasting riches had been replaced with trinkets, trinkets that you readily accepted instead of true riches. Now even the very trinkets that you settled for are being taken from you. I observe you as empty houses. I receive from your emptiness only cold indifference, because you have little or no love inside you. Yet from the outside, you look as you always looked and the world perceives that you are alive as always. But truly you are like walking dead men. Asleep to the truth, emptied of Godliness. The void that you are walks the days and sleeps the nights of one orphaned, lost and without meaning. Some of you are awakening now to begin to see what has happened to you. You will begin a search for new life. Some will begin to fill the house with trinkets of a different variety. Some will begin to fill the house with true and meaningful things because your search, your desire, has led you to Me, the Lord and Savior of your life. If you but seek Me, you will find. If you desire Me, you will have Me.

Oh My Creation, you fail to understand that the God of the Universe loves you, individually and collectively! The Love of the Most Holy Trinity is the creative master architect of each living house. You are living temples. I am within you by the powerful unifying love of the Holy Spirit. If you are an empty house, a pillaged temple, I am with you still. I do not leave you. If you are a full and beautiful temple, I am with you, filling you all the more with every good and holy thing of God. Oh My

Creation, you fail to believe that I, your Lord and God, never leave you. I do not abandon My own. And each belongs to Me. Each one of you is My own house, My temple. Fitting or unfitting temples that you are, I am in your midst! Do I, the Lord of the Universe, suffer because you suffer? Yes, I choose to be united to your every suffering, your every joy, your every thing! Why? Because I, your Lord and Savior love you with an everlasting, unconditionally merciful Love. Open your eyes that you may see Me with you! Do not be afraid! Take My hand. Allow Me to fill your house with My Love. Permit me to restore your house to Goodness. My Blood washes you clean and makes you acceptable to the Father if you but desire it! How long will you turn from Me! Embrace the world and you embrace death. Your very life is at stake. You consider not that you are but dust. You gamble that time is on your side. You are walking a dangerous path. All the while you add to your suffering and to the demise of many. The enemy gives you moments of pleasure, false peace and security. You while away time on these. But when you try to rest at night, you sense an emptiness. Perhaps there is more than this? I say to you, Come. Follow Me. I am in your house already. Awaken. Let Me teach you to live as I intended for you to live. All that I have is yours. I alone can fill the void. One by one I call you each by name. My temples, let Me restore you to love!

Your Jesus

8-28-96 Feast of St. Augustine in Doctor's waiting room
How Little You Understand of Suffering

Reading a secular magazine, I heard Jesus say, **My little one, please write.**

My beloved creation,
It grieves My Heart to observe how little you understand of suffering. Suffering is touching your lives, and throughout the world it increases daily. Suffering in and of itself is an evil that touches humanity, and is permitted because of origi-

nal sin. Yet through Grace, suffering is transformed into good. First, let it be known that much of the current suffering you endure is precisely because you have turned from My commandment to Love. For I have said, Love God with all your heart, your soul, your mind, your strength. Love one another as yourself. If you fail to make Love Himself the center of your existence, then you become the center of your existence, living a life that is not in balance. This brings forth suffering. It is the interior sufferings of the heart that manifest themselves in many various exterior sufferings. For example, today the demise of the family is causing untold pain for many souls. Often men or women make a decision to pursue life outside of the family, satisfying their selfish and worldly desires at the cost of a family that becomes divided. Then there is untold suffering for many. It begins a chain reaction of pain. Only the greatest love and sacrifice can heal those deep wounds of rejection and division. Let it be known that I, your God, have not ordained such suffering for you, but rather I permit you to walk in the freedom of your own will, never ceasing to offer you the grace to live My law of Love. My Law of Love preserves unity and forsakes self for the good of others. Your very sins are perpetuating great suffering in the world. Sin always causes suffering. Suffering is a consequence of sin. You cannot escape the consequence of your decisions and actions. In this age, many fail to even acknowledge sin. Therefore, all the more rampant and serious are the consequences of the sin of the world. All the more suffering exists today because of such blatant and rampant sin. One human heart that is out of balance touches another human heart and perpetuates that which is within them, so that the entire world becomes out of balance, one man at a time, because one affects the whole. Does not an infection in one part of the human body affect the entire body with fever? Indeed, this is the case in the world today. My creation, you are diseased due to selfish sinfulness!

Let it be known, My beloved creation, that I, your Savior, your Redeemer, enter into all your suffering, your disease, and with the help of My Grace, pure gift of My Love for you, I turn your suffering into merit after merit, bringing great good out of it. Indeed the more you continue to walk in the darkness of sin the greater your suffering, but in My endless Mercy, I pour more grace upon earth so that never is there more evil than Good! You cannot perceive this truth if you do not have Me, your Lord and Savior, in the center of your existence, because evil darkens your ability to see the Truth, perpetuating the lie that Good is waning. Only in the Holy Spirit, in My good Grace, can you see and know the Truth that I, who am all powerful and all Good, shall prevail. Remember, My little ones, the enemy wants you to despair, to feel abandoned, to be deceived again and again so that you continue to lose hope, to despair in your suffering, and finally to come to the point of not believing in God at all!

Your suffering is in vain only if it is not offered up or endured in the spirit of faith, hope, and charity. If you wrap love around each and every one of your sufferings, you gain for yourself and the world, more grace, more merit, and indeed, you are perpetuating the Kingdom of God on earth. I who created you, I who took on your humanity, embracing your very lowliness, know all too well the pain that exists in your heart, your body, in your world. And still, I unite Myself to your pain and suffering today. Indeed, I suffer with you, but not in vain, not for the sake of death, but for the sake of Life - only Life - Life that is eternal, unlike you can even imagine.

Therefore, My little ones, do not be fooled by the suffering that exists in the world. Nor should you accept the lie that suffering is punishment from God, or that it is useless! Without My Good Grace that would be the case, but I, who am all Love and all Mercy, permit suffering to touch the world in order to bring great good out of it. Those who accept My Grace have the wisdom that comes from Wisdom Himself to know that often it is in and through your human suffering, often at moments of your greatest pain, that My Grace can reach deepest into your heart and cause your very soul to draw closer to Me, your Lord and Savior. This awakening, these moments of conversion are worth far more than any suffering that leads to it. Therefore, My little ones, be hopeful and confident in the security of My Divine Love. Your suffering will end in triumph when My Grace leads you to a place that exists without evil or pain, but only Love Eternal. To those little ones who wrap love around every pain and suffering, who refuse to sin and try wholeheartedly to live My Law of Love, to you I say, you are the remedy for the world! Your sacrifice draws healing grace for the world, because you are in Me and I am in you as offering for all. I so love you, My creation! Repent of your sin and cease to follow your selfish ways, so that the entire body can begin to heal in My Great Grace. Your suffering shall not be in vain! Be at Peace. Abhor sin, that your suffering may be lessened. My Goodness shall be made manifest in the world if you but turn from sin and walk in Love.

Your Jesus

1-15-97 Rosary with my Spiritual Director, my home
Light To Illumine Souls

After Father heard my confession, we began to pray the Chaplet of Divine Mercy for a certain soul close to me. Then Father began the Joyful Mysteries of the Rosary. Immediately, I was absorbed in prayer of union at the onset of the Chaplet. I did not hear Father's meditations on the Mysteries of the Rosary until the fifth decade, the Finding of Jesus in the Temple.

Toward the beginning of this prayer time, I saw the following scene:

I saw myriads of angelic beings poised at attention, gathered as a vast army. I understood through "light" in my soul that they were in heaven. I saw the word, "sentinels." These angels formed countless lines. Leaders stood facing the vast army assembled before them. Every angel held a torch-like candle. The leaders of the army held torch-like candles that were already lit on fire. They proceeded to light the first row of candles. Then the first row proceeded to light the second row. I watched this process and saw that most of them had candles that were lit now. On either side of this vast army were angels with trumpets. The trumpets were ready to be sounded. I sensed a true readiness. This was a magnificent sight to behold. Then I watched one angel travel from heaven to earth in an instant. The angel proceeded to place the candle of light into one human heart to illumine it. I only saw one angel do this to one human heart. But I understood that each one of these angels would transport their candle of light into a human heart so the human heart is illumined in a new light, the Light of Truth. It seemed every soul on earth would be given the opportunity to view itself as it is seen before God, in bare truth.

After the Rosary, I told Father about the above and asked him to pray for confirmation of it. We prayed together and The Holy Spirit gave him a confirmation which included that while this Grace would be granted to every soul, not every one would accept it. That is, some will rationalize it away, but multitudes of souls will accept this Grace and there will be many conversions of heart.

I became absorbed in prayer of union again until the end of the Rosary, that is, the decade of Finding Jesus in the Temple. Father offered prayers that Our Lady would assist us and another certain soul to find Jesus always and everywhere. I received an image of Our Lady and St. Joseph finding Jesus in the Temple. Jesus was busy teaching in the Temple.

Then, Our Lady said: *My children,*
You are busy about many things in the world. Some of you seek my Son, Jesus, but many do not. A light shall illumine your heart so that you will see without obscurity or deception, the state of your soul before God. This Grace will cause you to realize that you are the Temple in whom God dwells. You will see clearly the Temple's state of being. Is it fit for God? Every human heart will receive the Light of Truth. In an instant, this heavenly Light will penetrate your being and reveal true self-knowledge along with true knowledge of God's existence. God will cause you to look at your guilt so that He can grant you His Mercy and reconcile you to Himself. This is a great gift for the world. All of heaven is prepared for it. It will bring many souls back to God. I will be with you to strengthen you. I love you.
Your Mother

Here, I began to have doubts about the illumination. I was tempted to push aside what I saw and heard. I thought I was being influenced by other prophecies, so I prayed to Jesus to help me discern the Truth. I asked that He would point me to Scripture to confirm the illumination of souls. He said (patiently): **Soul, this Grace has never been granted to all the world.** (Pause.) **My lamb, think of My public Ministry on earth. I healed people. I reconciled people. I entered the world's darkness as The Light to illumine the human heart, mind, and soul.** Here, I had an image of Scripture. It was St. John's Gospel Prologue about "Light."

Jesus continued: **A ray of Light shall pierce the heart of every man to illumine My Temples with Truth. My priestly Ministry was about reconciliation. The Grace of the Light of Truth in every soul will provide an opportunity for man to be reconciled to God again.**

Jesus

Notes

(from Introduction)

1. The definition given in the New Catholic Encyclopedia: "Interior illuminations by means of words or statements, sometimes accompanied by a vision and seeming to proceed from the object represented." Art. *"Mystical Phenomena,"* New Catholic Encyclopedia, McGraw Hill.

The classic book on all mystical phenomena is A. Poulain, S.J., *The Graces of Interior Prayer,* (Celtic Cross Books, Westminster, Vermont 1978) Part IV "Revelations and Vision" pp. 299-397 deal with our subject matter. Originally printed in 1901 entitled *"Des Graces D'Oraison."* The first English translation was 1910.

2. *The Collected Works of St. John of the Cross,* (ICS Publications, Institute of Carmelite Studies, Washington, D.C. 1979 Second Edition)

3. *The Collected Works of St. Teresa of Avila* (ICS Publications, Institute of Carmelite Studies, Washington, D.C.

4. St. Catherine of Siena, *The Dialogue,* English translation by Suzanne Noffke, (Paulist Press, New York 1980)

5. Garrigou Lagrange, *The Three Ages of the Interior Life* (Tan Books and Publishers, 1989) Original edition 1947 and Fr. John G. Arintero, O.P., *The Mystical Evolution, Volumes I and II,* also from Tan, are examples of texts that treat of the various stages of the spiritual life. All references to this book are from Volume II.

6. It is only by this process that one becomes familiar with the mystical experiences of the Saints. All of this is very alien to the post-Christian culture in which we live. Science fiction fantasy has replaced the reality of the experiences of holy men and women.

7. Fr. John G. Arintero, O.P., *The Mystical Evolution, Volumes I and II* (Tan Books and Publishers, Inc., Rockford, Ill. 1978) p.309

8. Locutions are of a personal nature, i.e., they are for the sanctification of the individual. They can also be in the form of teachings that are meant for the good of the Church.

9. This theology is rather unique in that it treats of the development of the life of the grace in the soul as seen through the lived experiences of the Church's mystics. It strives to understand the mutual dance of love between God and the soul in its progression to total union, described by St. John of the Cross as "Spiritual Marriage."

10. *Catechism of the Catholic Church,* The English translation for the United States of America, copyright 1994, United States Catholic Conference, Inc., Libreria Editrice Vaticana. Pgh 65.

11. Collected Works, p.179

12. Fr. John G. Arintero, O.P., *The Mystical Evolution, Volume II* (Tan Books and Publishers, Inc., Rockford, Ill. 1978) p.306

13. idem.

14. idem.

15. idem.

16. Arintero, Volume II, p.310

17. Thomas Dubay, *Fire Within* (Ignatius Press, San Francisco 1989) pp. 252-254

In Poulain's book there are various extracts from the lives of the Saints that illustrate these points after each chapter.

18. Dubay, p. 249

19. Dubay, p. 267

20. The present Pope John Paul II has characterized our modern world as a culture of death. The practical and philosophical denial of God in the West is eroding and destroying our sense of the "human."

21. At no time in the history of the Church has the Vatican received so much information and material from purported visionaries, locutionists, and apparitions of Mary throughout the world. Either our faith is suffering a mass delusion, or it behooves us all to listen to the modern prophets who call for us to "repent and believe," for the ax will soon be laid to the roots. It will be done not from revenge but rather from Love, the love of a Father who sees His children on the path of self-destruction.

List of Recommended Books

1. The Mystical Evolution, Volumes I and II. Fr. John G. Arintero, O.P. (Tan Books and Publishers, Inc., Rockford, Ill. 1978)

2. Fire Within, Thomas Dubay, S.M. (Ignatius Press, San Francisco 1989)

3. The Graces of Interior Prayer, A. Poulain, S.J. (Celtic Cross Books, Westminster, VT 1978) This is a translation of the sixth edition.

I WILL RESTORE YOU

Visit your local bookstore for other great titles from:
QUEENSHIP PUBLISHING

Do Whatever Love Requires - *Carol Ameche & Harriet Hammons*
ISBN# 1-882972-61-1 $2.95

Prpare for the Great Tribulation and the Era of Peace - *John Leary*
Vol I - ISBN# 1-882972-69-4 $7.95
Vol II - ISBN# 1-882972-72-4 $8.95
Vol III - ISBN# 1-882972-77-5 $8.95
Vol IV - ISBN# 1-882972-91-0 $2.95
Vol V - ISBN# 1-882972-97-X $2.95

For the Soul of the Family - *Thomas W. Petrisko*
The story of the apparitions of the Virgin Mary to Estela Ruiz
and how one family came back to God.
ISBN# 1-882972-90-2 $9.95

Call of the Ages - *Thomas W. Petrisko*
The Apparitions and Revelations of the Virgin Mary
Fortell the Coming Fall of Evil and an Era of Peace
ISBN# 1-882972-59-7 $11.95

Trial, Tribulation and Triumph - *Desmond A. Birch*
Before, During and After Antichrist
ISBN #1-882972-73-2 $19.50

Mary: God s Supreme Masterpiece - *Fr. Bartholomew Gottemoller*
ISBN# 1-882972-48-1 $5.95

Jesus, Peter and the Keys - *Scott Butler, Norman Dahlgren, David Hess*
A Scriptural Handbook on the Papacy
ISBN# 1-882972-54-6 $14.95

The Coming Chastisement - *Br. Craig Driscoll*
ISBN #1-882972-41-X $1.95

The Light of Love - *Patricia Devlin*
My Angel Shall Go Before Me
ISBN #1-882972-53-8 $8.75

Marian Apparitions Today - *Fr. Edward D. O'Connor*
Why So Many?
ISBN #1-882972-71-6 $7.95